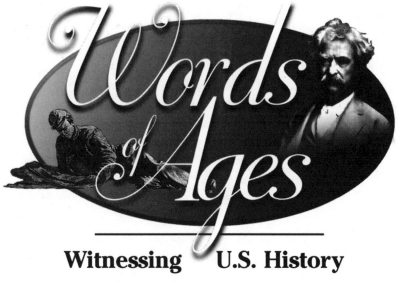

Words of Ages

Witnessing U.S. History
Through Literature

CLOSE UP
FOUNDATION

Close Up Publishing

Close Up Publishing

Director, Publications
George W. Dieter

*Managing Editor,
Academic Publications*
Amy E. Tarasovic

*Senior Editor, Academic
Publications*
Charles R. Sass

Copyeditor and Proofreader
Lucy Keshishian

*Manager, Art, Production,
and Scheduling*
Tisha L. Finniff

Graphic Designer
Deborah A. Stalford

Photo Researchers
Susan Ballinger
Renée Bouchard

Photo Research Intern
Matt Payne

Cover Design and Layout
C. Stephen Allen

Close Up Foundation
Stephen A. Janger, President

*The Close Up Foundation, a nonprofit, nonpartisan, civic
education organization, informs, inspires, and empowers
people to exercise the rights and accept the responsibilities
of citizens in a democracy. Close Up connects individuals
of all ages to their communities and institutions through
challenging educational programs and products. By building partnerships with the education community, the private
and philanthropic sectors, and all branches and levels of
government, Close Up makes civic participation a dynamic
and meaningful experience.*

*Close Up Publishing, a branch of the Close Up Foundation,
develops books, teachers' guides, video documentaries, and
other materials that encourage critical thinking and interest
in current issues, government, international relations, history,
and economics. To find out more about Close Up's original
and timely resources, call 800-765-3131.*

*Close Up Foundation
44 Canal Center Plaza
Alexandria, VA 22314-1592
www.closeup.org*

Library of Congress Cataloging-in-Publication Data

Words of ages: witnessing U.S. history through literature / [edited by Tiffany Farrell Larbalestier].
    p. cm.
Includes bibliographical references.
ISBN 0-932765-84-X
  1. United States–History–Literary collections. 2. American literature. I. Larbalestier,
Tiffany Farrell.

PS509.U52 W67 2000
810.8'0358–dc21

00-024

*"The same truth that guides
the pen of the historian should
govern the pencil of the artist."*

—Benjamin West

Preface

The poet Walt Whitman inspired the title of this book. In "Song of Myself," he catalogs the great diversity of the nation, claiming to act as poet-spokesperson for all Americans. Whitman exclaims, "Endless unfolding of words of ages! And mine a word of the modern ... a word en masse." Such a phrase captures this anthology's broad scope and intent.

Words of Ages: Witnessing U.S. History Through Literature brings together enduring American works—novels, short stories, poems, speeches, letters, biographies, plays, and journalistic reports—to illuminate events and trends of the past. Featuring the immediacy of great storytelling, *Words of Ages* allows readers to "witness" events—from the European exploration of Virginia to the Vietnam War.

Excerpts were chosen for their historical connections, literary merit, and the varied views they represent. Diverse voices—such as those belonging to immigrants, minorities, and women—reveal the richness and complexity of U.S. history. Much to the editor's vexation, however, any anthology is necessarily limited. The hope is that *Words of Ages* will encourage its readers to explore the works that breadth and page-limit excluded.

Personal history—perhaps most history—is biased. In *Words of Ages*, biases are made explicit in author biographies and historical introductions. Far from a drawback, such biases charge these readings with intimacy and realism. In this framework, personal viewpoints, accompanied by contextual information, provide a fuller understanding of historic events and provoke thoughtful analysis beyond the facts.

In addition to great literature, *Words of Ages* culls history from visual art, architecture, and music. These elements illustrate the important role of the arts and remind readers that all of these disciplines are tightly intertwined in the complex and fascinating story that is America's past.

TIFFANY FARRELL LARBALESTIER

About the Editor

Tiffany Farrell Larbalestier developed the concept for *Words of Ages* and served as the book's primary author and editor. In almost seven years at the Close Up Foundation—most recently as managing editor—Larbalestier authored and edited dozens of educational texts and teachers' guides, including *Current Issues, International Relations, Looking Toward the Pacific Century*, and *Perspectives*. Tiffany Larbalestier, a graduate of St. Mary's College of Maryland and an M.Ed. candidate at the University of Virginia, currently edits publications at the Smithsonian Institution in Washington, D.C.

Acknowledgments

In addition to Close Up Publishing's editorial and design staff, many people dedicated their time and expertise to the production of this book. Amy Tarasovic and Tim Walker wrote introductions and edited readings for several chapters. Garland Baum provided research and draft manuscripts in early stages of the project's development. Michael Glaser, Ph.D.; Candyce Griswold; Linda Monk, J.D.; Bettye Yates, Ph.D.; David Zack; and John Zaphyr thoughtfully reviewed outlines and manuscripts. Karen Chong and John Norris assisted with photo research. C. Stephen Allen gave our words and images final form in his book and cover design.

Table of Contents

Theme 3 **The Search for a National Identity** *60*

UNIT 4 • DEMOCRACY AND ADVERSITY *1919–1945* 218

*W*hat was "new" about the "New World"? To the Europeans who began to settle in North and South America after Columbus's voyages, the lands on the other side of the Atlantic were new, but to the natives who were living on these continents in 1492, this was not a new world. From the Arctic Circle in the north to Tierra del Fuego in the south and from Atlantic to Pacific, Native American tribes occupied the lands that their ancestors had come to thousands of years before. The Mayas, Incas, and Aztecs developed advanced cultures marked by complex architecture, mathematics, astronomy, and in some cases hieroglyphics of a written language. But with the coming of European settlers, around 1600, Native American culture was soon to be overwhelmed, and in many cases swept away.

The first colonists to cross the Atlantic came from all over Europe: Spanish and Portuguese adventurers staked claims in the southern regions; French fur trappers plied the rivers of Canada and the Mississippi valley; Dutch settlers occupied both banks of the Hudson River from Long Island to Albany. But it was the English who made the most important and far-reaching European effort to settle in North America. It was their culture, particularly the English language, that had a great effect on the new nation. The uniformity of communication gave the colonists a great advantage in trade, government, and culture. Some historians believe it was English that enabled the colonies to evolve into a new nation—with a unique identity and sovereign government—in just two hundred years.

The influence of the written word is present in every major event of this period. Farmers read almanacs to learn about weather patterns for their crops. Bibles and sermons advised pioneers how to live upright, moral lives. With the emergence of the plantation system, slavery was both criticized and defended in print.

The words of European philosophers of the Enlightenment—particularly John Locke—were a major influence on the "Founding Fathers." Locke and other

1607
Virginia Company settlers found the Virginia Colony.

1620
Separatist Puritans sail to America and found Plymouth Colony.

1630
Massachusetts Bay Colony is founded by John Winthrop.

1675
Chief Metacomet launches attacks on white settlements, starting King Philip's War.

1754
The French and Indian War begins.

1776
Thomas Paine publishes his pamphlet *Common Sense,* urging independence from Great Britain.

The Second Continental Congress issues the Declaration of Independence.

thinkers highlighted the ideal of democratic self-government that undermined the rule of monarchy. The influence of Locke's philosophies is found in Thomas Paine's famous pamphlet *Common Sense* and the Declaration of Independence. Later, supporters of a strong national government wrote essays, known as *The Federalist Papers,* to help win ratification of the U.S. Constitution in 1788.

The seeds of American national identity and culture were sown during this period of immense change in the "New World." Miraculously, a single nation, with a unique national literature, emerged from varied peoples, geographies, languages, religions, and ideals.

1783
The Treaty of Paris ends the Revolutionary War.

1787
The Federalist Papers urge New Yorkers to ratify the U.S. Constitution.

1789
George Washington begins his first term as president.

1791
Virginia ratifies the Bill of Rights.

1803
France sells the Louisiana Territories to the United States.

1804
Lewis and Clark set off to explore Louisiana.

1812
The United States goes to war against Great Britain.

Explorers and Early Settlers

Captain John Smith and the English settlers who followed did not shed their attachments to Great Britain when they landed on North American shores. Most colonists still had relatives, and sometimes property, in England. Literate settlers still read books printed in Britain. Therefore, when colonists chose to write, they used English writing conventions. In addition, if they planned to publish, their works were usually meant for readers in the Mother Country. During the 1600s and early 1700s, Europeans wanted to learn about the natural wonders, Indians, and rigors of colonial life in North America. Therefore, nonfiction was the dominant literary form. Americans published their journals and local histories in London to document their surroundings, important events, institutions, and beliefs.

However, colonial personalities differed dramatically between Virginia, which was founded by businessmen, and New England, which was founded by religious refugees. Their geography as much as their immigration purposes and patterns influenced their writings. In the South, the immigrants were often young men—usually non-first-born sons who could not inherit family property in England. The average Chesapeake settler traveled alone as an indentured servant and worked on a farm for about seven years before he was free to obtain his own land. Virginia settlers generally lived far apart, on large farms that were situated along waterways which could carry their staple crop, tobacco, to Europe. There was a shortage of women in the Chesapeake colonies; therefore, much of the writings from the South came from men, usually the wealthier ones who had education and leisure time. Besides recording history, some writers from the South poked fun at their predicaments.

On the other hand, New Englanders immigrated to escape religious persecution, so the tone of their writings is more serious and devout. Unlike the Chesapeake settlers, most traveled in families. Children in Massachusetts commonly knew their grandparents. In addition, each settlement was organized around its meetinghouse, or church, which all residents attended daily. Early New England colonists were closely knit by family, physical proximity, and faith. Moreover, Puritans believed in being able to read and interpret the Bible oneself. High literacy rates in New England meant that many Puritans could keep journals to record town events and scrutinize their consciences, looking for signs of good and evil. Not surprisingly, these religious colonists often wrote sermons and proverbs too.

While the English settlers were not the only people living in North America at the time, these writers reveal what early colonial life was like, how they met and dealt with Native Americans, and how the settlers began to impose their values and lifestyles on the land.

Featured Authors

John Smith
Robert Beverley
William Bradford
John Winthrop
Anne Bradstreet
Nathaniel Hawthorne

JOHN SMITH (1580–1631)

John Smith left his family in Lincolnshire, England, at the age of 19 to begin an adventurous life on the high seas. In December 1606, he sailed with about 140 other passengers to establish what would become the first permanent English settlement in North America—Jamestown. Although Smith was accused of mutiny during the journey, he later became a leader of the colony. As a writer, he is famous for composing the first English book in the Americas, A True Relation of …Virginia, *published in London in 1608. His 1616 book,* A Description of New England, *contained maps that William Bradford and the first English colonists used to settle that region. In general, John Smith's works had two purposes: to satisfy English curiosity about North America and to recruit settlers. Describing the "New World" relied on elements of truth, but convincing people to become colonists required some fiction as well.*

Unlike the earlier, lost colony of Roanoke that was privately funded, Jamestown was supported by a joint stock company—the London Trading Company. This arrangement pooled the money of several financial backers who expected to make a profit on the venture. The people who accompanied Smith were all young men who hoped to find gold and prosperity in the "New World." Though they came with organized backing and practical goals, the adventurers were unprepared for the harsh conditions that awaited them. Thirty-nine perished on the journey, and half of the remaining 100 died of malaria within the first year.

The following excerpt comes from Captain John Smith's General History of Virginia, New England and the Summer Isles, *which was published in 1624. Written several years after the events took place, this volume probably contains elaboration and fictional interpretations. In particular, Smith defends his own character, which had suffered numerous attacks, and in effect, creates his own heroic myth. Referring to himself in the third person, Smith portrays an upright, honest citizen; a brave explorer and settler; and of course, a man women admire. This selection includes his first written account of the Pocahontas tale. While Chief Powhatan and his daughter Pocahontas are true historical figures, no one is certain that Pocahontas actually saved Smith's life. Nevertheless, the kind Indian princess caught the imagination of readers and has remained a powerful figure in American history and literature.*

"Round about him those fiends danced a pretty while"

The General History of Virginia, New England, and the Summer Isles

The Third Book, Chapter I

On the 19th of December, 1606, we set sail from Blackwall, but by unprosperous winds, were kept six weeks in the sight of England; all which time, Mr. Hunt, our Preacher, was so weak and sick, that few expected his recovery. . . .

We watered at the Canaries; we traded with the savages at Dominica; three weeks we spent in refreshing ourselves amongst these West India Isles; in Guadaloupe we found a bath so hot as in it we boiled pork as well as over the fire. And at a little isle called Monito, we took from the bushes with our hands, near two hogsheads [large barrels] full of birds in three or four hours. . . . We daily feasted.

Gone from thence in search of Virginia, the company was not a little discomforted, seeing the mariners had three days passed their reckoning and found no land, so that Captain Ratliffe [captain of the pinnace (a small sailing ship)] rather desired to bear up the helm to return for England than make further search. But God the guider of all good actions, forcing them by an extreme storm to hull [travel with sails furled] all night, did drive them by His providence to their desired port, beyond all their expectations, for never any of them had seen that coast.

The first land they made they called Cape Henry, where thirty of them recreating [relaxing] themselves on shore were assaulted by five savages, who hurt two of the English very dangerously. . . .

Many were the mischiefs that daily spring from [the settlers'] ignorant (yet ambitious) spirits, but the good doctrine and exhortation of our Preacher, Master Hunt, reconciled them and caused Captain Smith to be admitted of the Council.

The next day all received the Communion; the day following, the savages voluntarily desired peace, and Captain Newport returned for England with news, leaving in Virginia one hundred [men], the 15th of June 1607.

The Third Book, Chapter II

Being thus left to our fortunes, it fortuned [happened] that within ten days scarce ten amongst us could either go or well stand, such extreme weakness and sickness oppressed us. And thereat none need marvel if they consider the cause and reason which was this: While the ships stayed, our allowance was somewhat bettered by a daily proportion of biscuit which the sailors would pilfer to sell, give, or exchange with us for money, sassafras, furs, or love. But when they departed, there remained neither tavern, beer house, nor place of relief, but the common kettle. . . . [T]hat indeed he [the President] allowed equally to be distributed, and that was half a pint of wheat and as much barley boiled with water for a man a day, and this, having fried some twenty-six weeks in the ship's hold, contained as many worms as grains so that we might truly call it rather so much bran than corn; our drink was water, our lodgings castles in the air.

With this lodging and diet, our extreme toil in bearing and planting palisades so strained and bruised us and our continual labor in the extremity of the heat had so weakened us, as were cause sufficient to have made us as miserable in our native country or any other place in the world.

From May to September, those that escaped lived upon sturgeon and sea crabs. Fifty in this time we buried....

And now the winter approaching, the rivers became so covered with swans, geese, ducks, and cranes, that we daily feasted with good bread, Virginia peas, pumpkins, and putchamins [persimmons], fish, fowl, and diverse sorts of wild beasts as far as we could eat them.... But our comedies never endured long without a tragedy, some idle exceptions being muttered against Captain Smith for not discovering the head of Chickahominy river and [being] taxed by the Council to be too slow in so worthy an attempt. The next voyage he proceeded so far that with much labor by cutting of trees in sunder he made his passage, but when his barge could pass no farther, he left her in a broad bay out of danger of shot, commanding none should go ashore till his return; himself with two English and two savages went up higher in a canoe, but he was not long absent but his men went ashore, whose want of government [discipline] gave both occasion and opportunity to the savages to surprise one George Cassen whom they slew....

Smith little dreaming of that accident, being got to the marshes at the river's head ... was beset with two hundred savages, two of them he slew, still defending himself with the aid of a savage his guide, whom he bound to his arm with his garters and used him as a buckle [shield], yet he was shot in his thigh a little, and had many arrows that stuck in his clothes but no great hurt, till at last they took him prisoner....

Six or seven weeks those barbarians kept him prisoner, many strange triumphs and conjurations they made of him, yet he so demeaned himself amongst them, as he not only diverted them from surprising the fort, but procured his own liberty....

When King James I granted the patent for the colony of Virginia in 1606, it included land along most of the eastern seaboard. Shown here is John Smith's 1607 map of the Chesapeake Bay area of the Virginia Colony.

The manner how they used and delivered him, is as followeth....

Not long after, early in a morning a great fire was made in a long-house, and a mat spread on the one side as on the other; on the one they caused him to sit, and all the guard went out of the house, and presently came skipping in a great grim fellow, all painted over with coal mingled with oil, and many snakes' and weasels' skins stuffed with moss, and all their tails tied together, so as they met on the crown of his head in a tassel, and round about the tassel was as a coronet of feathers, the skins hanging round about his head, back, and shoulders, and in a manner covered his face, with a hellish voice, and a rattle in his hand. With most strange gestures and passions he began his invocation and environed the fire with a circle of meal; which done, three more such like devils came rushing in with the like antic tricks, painted half black, half red, but all their eyes were painted white, and some red strokes like mustaches along their cheeks. Round about him those fiends danced a pretty while, and then came in three more as ugly as the rest, with red eyes and white strokes over their black faces. At last they all sat down right against him, three of them on the one hand of the chief priest and three on the other. Then all with their rattles began a song; which ended, the chief priest laid down five wheat corns; then straining his arms and hands with such violence that he sweat and his veins swelled, he began a short oration [prayer]; at the conclusion they all gave a short groan and then laid down three grains more.... Three days they used this ceremony; the meaning whereof they told him, was to know if he intended them well or no....

At last they brought him to Werowocomoco, where was Powhatan, their Emperor. Here more than two hundred of those grim courtiers stood wondering at him, as [if] he had been a monster, till Powhatan and his train had put themselves in their greatest braveries [costumes]. Before a fire upon a seat like a bedstead, he sat covered with a great robe made of raccoon skins and all the tails hanging by....

At his entrance before the King, all the people gave a great shout. The Queen of Appamatoc was appointed to bring him water to wash his hands, and another brought him a bunch of feathers, instead of a towel, to dry them; having feasted him after their best barbarous manner they could, a long consultation was held, but the conclusion was, two great stones were brought before Powhatan; then as many as could, laid hands on him, dragged him to them, and thereon laid his head and being ready with their clubs to beat out his brains, Pocahontas, the King's dearest daughter, when no entreaty could

Pocahontas married Englishman John Rolfe to cement an agreement between Powhatan and the early Virginia settlers. She visited England, where she sat, dressed in the height of fashion, for this 1616 portrait.

Ætatis suæ 21. A. 1616.

prevail, got his head in her arms and laid her own upon his to save him from death. . . .

Two days [later], Powhatan having disguised himself in the most fearful manner he could, caused Captain Smith to be brought forth to a great house in the woods and there upon a mat by the fire to be left alone. Not long after . . . Powhatan more like a devil than a man, with some two hundred more as black as himself, came unto him and told him now they were friends, and presently he should go to Jamestown to send him two great guns and a grindstone, for which he would give him the country of Capahowoasic and forever esteem him as his son Nantaquond.

ROBERT BEVERLEY (1673–1722)

Born on a Virginia plantation, Robert Beverley was the son of a wealthy landowner. Like many landed colonists of the period, Beverley's family sent him to England for his education. He returned to Virginia in 1687, inheriting a plantation and another large tract of land. After serving as a clerk in the colonial government, Beverley was elected to represent Jamestown in Virginia's colonial legislature, the House of Burgesses, in the late 1690s.

Robert Beverley is best known for writing what has been called the first truly American book. Published in 1705, The History and Present State of Virginia *aimed to tell the historical truth in a straightforward, simple style. Beverley wrote from his experiences as a Virginia planter, documenting the region's history, institutions, natural surroundings, agriculture, and Native Americans. Consequently, Beverley's book marks the beginning of colonial identification with the land and the first hints of an "American" identity.*

At the time of his writing, Virginia's plantation system had already evolved from the individual speculators who settled Jamestown into a complex economic system. By the mid-seventeenth century, the Chesapeake region had begun to cultivate its cash crop, tobacco, on a large scale. However, tobacco depletes the soil, so most successful businessmen needed large tracts of land to alternate their crops. In addition, prices for tobacco changed, and farmers had to grow other crops when tobacco did not earn them enough money.

Initially, these plantations were run with the help of indentured servants from both Europe and Africa. Under this system, a planter paid for the servant's ocean crossing in exchange for a fixed period of labor. Thereafter, the workers were free to obtain their own land and start businesses. However, laws crafted in the 1660s and 1670s relegated

"They are called slaves . . . [because their servitude] is for life."

African laborers to lifelong, hereditary servitude. Thus, by the late-seventeenth century, Virginia farmers, even those with smaller properties, began relying more heavily on slaves than on indentured servants.

In this selection, Beverley points out the rights of slaves and servants in Virginia to defend the colony's reputation in England. However, in 1705, the same year Beverley's book was published, the Virginia legislature passed a law that entrenched the already inferior condition of African laborers in the colony. This law defined those of African origin and those born to African mothers as the personal property of their masters, conferring a new legal status to the institution of slavery.

The History and Present State of Virginia
Book IV, Part I
Chapter X: Of the Servants and Slaves in Virginia

Their servants, they distinguish by the names of slaves for life, and servants for a time.

Slaves are the Negroes, and their posterity, following the condition of the mother. . . . They are called slaves, in respect of the time of their servitude, because it is for life.

Servants are those which serve only for a few years, according to the time of their indenture, or the custom of the country. The custom of the country takes place upon such as have no indentures. The law in this case is, that if such servants be under nineteen years of age, they must be brought into court, to have their age adjudged; and from the age they are judged to be of, they must serve until they reach four and twenty: But if they be adjudged upwards of nineteen, they are then only to be servants for the term of five years.

The male-servants and slaves of both sexes are employed together in tilling and manuring the ground, in sowing and planting tobacco, corn, etc. Some distinction indeed is made between them in their clothes and food; but the work of both is no other than what the overseers, the freemen, and the planters themselves do.

Sufficient distinction is also made between the female-servants and slaves; for a white woman is rarely or never put to work in the ground if she be good for anything else. And to discourage all planters from using any women so, their law imposes the heaviest taxes upon female-servants working in the ground. . . . Whereas on the other hand, it is a common thing to work a woman slave out of doors. . . .

Because I have heard how strangely cruel and severe the service of this country is represented in some parts of England; I can't forbear affirming, that the work of their servants and slaves is no other than what every common freeman does. Neither is any servant required to do

Indians and Southern Colonists Interact
"very often [the Indians] laugh at the English"

William Byrd of Westover, the wealthy brother-in-law of Robert Beverley, was a Virginia planter and prolific writer. Byrd is known for his humorous accounts of colonial life, a style and subject that were typical of southern writers in the colonial age. In late 1728, he wrote this description of Native Americans, while also noting their perceptions of the white man.

The Indians, who have no way of traveling but on the hoof, make nothing of going twenty-five miles a day and carrying their little necessaries at their backs, and sometimes a stout pack of skins into the bargain. And very often they laugh at the English, who can't stir to a next neighbor without a horse, and say that two legs are too much for such lazy people, who can't visit their next neighbor without six. For their parts, they were utter strangers to all our beasts of burden or carriage before the slothful Europeans came amongst them. They had on no part of the American continent, or in any of the islands, either horses or asses, camels, dromedaries, or elephants to ease the legs of the original inhabitants or to lighten their labor.

Besides their strength, Native Americans became known for their accomplishments in farming. Indians introduced the Europeans to corn, which became the most widely grown of all crops in the colonies. It provided food for the poor and livestock feed for wealthy planters. Moreover, Native Americans grew corn and beans together, which was a major contribution to agriculture. Robert Beverley wrote, "All these sorts [of Indian corn] are planted alike, in rows, three, four, or five grains in a hill. The Indians . . . plant a bean in the same hill with the corn, upon whose stalk it sustains itself." Beans fixed nitrogen in the soil and conserved moisture while increasing the crop yield from the same plot of land.

more in a day, than his overseer. And I can assure you with a great deal of truth, that generally their slaves are not worked near so hard, nor so many hours in a day, as the husbandmen and day-laborers in England. . . .

But to complete this account of servants, I shall give you a short relation of the care their laws take, that they be used as tenderly as possible.

By the Laws of their Country.
1. All servants whatsoever have their complaints heard without fee or reward; but if the master be found faulty, the charge of the complaint is cast upon him. . . .
2. Any Justice of Peace may receive the complaint of a servant. . . .

3. All masters are under the correction and censure of the County-Courts to provide for their servants good and wholesome diet, clothing, and lodging....

10. The property of all money and goods sent over thither to servants or carried in with them is reserved to themselves, and remain entirely at their disposal.

11. Each servant at his freedom receives of his master fifteen bushels of corn, (which is sufficient for a whole year) and two new suits of clothes, both linen and woolen, and then becomes as free in all respects, and as much entitled to the liberties and privileges of the country as any other of the inhabitants or natives are.

12. Each servant has then also a right to take up fifty acres of land, where he can find any unpatented....

This is what the laws prescribe in favor of servants, by which you may find that the cruelties and severities imputed to that country are an unjust reflection. For no people more abhor the thoughts of such usage than the Virginians, nor take more precaution to prevent it.

"what could they see but a hideous and desolate wilderness"

WILLIAM BRADFORD (1590–1657)

Unlike their business-minded counterparts to the south, the first New England settlers came to the "New World" to escape religious persecution. William Bradford sailed aboard the Mayflower in 1620 to help found the first English colony in New England. Bradford served as governor of Plymouth Plantation for about thirty years, and his strong administrative skills helped ensure the colony's success. He wrote his famous account of that settlement, Of Plymouth Plantation, *between 1630 and 1650. This work is regarded as one of the finest literary achievements of the period, largely because Bradford had a unique voice. In his introduction, he stated that he deliberately wrote "in a plain style" to reflect his beliefs in simplicity and truth. These convictions—and variations on his style—later became the hallmarks of a distinctly American literature.*

However, the story of Bradford and his fellow Pilgrims begins before their settlement in Massachusetts. When King James I took the English throne in 1603, many were dissatisfied with the Church of England. Puritans wanted to work within the Church to "purify" it of all elements of Roman Catholicism. For example, they did not believe that there should be human intermediaries, such as bishops and popes, between believers and their God. Bradford was a member of a radical sect of Puritans called Separatists, who wanted total separation from what they saw as the cor-

ruption of the Church of England. Under King James, Puritans became the object of frequent persecution. Bradford and his group went to Holland in 1608, where they stayed for twelve years. There they enjoyed religious freedom but lacked economic success. After reading John Smith's accounts of Virginia and New England, Bradford's group decided to get financial backing in London and then emigrate to North America.

In Of Plymouth Plantation, *William Bradford frames the Pilgrims' quest in grand, biblical terms. He portrayed the Pilgrims as God's chosen people, and their settlement, Plymouth, as the promised land. This concept is not merely literary allusion and metaphor. The Puritans believed that the Lord literally guided them, and they often likened events in their lives to biblical teachings. Bradford and others kept detailed journals because they believed they could see God's—and even the devil's—influence in their daily experiences. Therefore, their religious beliefs shaped their actions, their interpretations of events, their civic institutions, and ultimately the success of the colony. For example, Puritans believed in hard work, sobriety, and good deeds in order to win the favor of God. These overarching values sustained their society through the harsh realities of carving towns out of wilderness. Such ideals also created strong senses of cooperation and community that helped their colony grow.*

Of Plymouth Plantation
Book I, Chapter 9

Sept. 6 [1620]. These troubles being blown over, and now all being compact together in one ship, they put to sea again with a prosperous wind, which continued divers days together, which was some encouragement unto them; yet, according to the usual manner, many were afflicted with seasickness. And I may not omit here a special work of God's providence. There was a proud and very profane young man, one of the seamen, of a lusty [strong], able body, which made him the more haughty; he would always be condemning the poor people in their sickness and cursing them daily with grievous execrations [curses]; and did not let [hesitate] to tell them that he hoped to help cast half of them overboard before they came to their journey's end, and to make merry with what they had; and if he were by any gently reproved, he would curse and swear most bitterly. But it pleased God before they came half seas over, to smite this young man with a grievous disease, of which he died in a desperate manner, and so was himself the first that was thrown overboard. Thus his curses light on his own head, and it was an astonishment to all his fellows for they noted it to be the just hand of God upon him....

But after they had sailed that course about half the day, they fell amongst dangerous shoals and roaring breakers, and they were so far entangled therewith as they conceived themselves in great danger; and the wind shrinking upon them withal, they resolved to bear up again for the Cape and thought themselves happy to get out of those dangers before night overtook them, as by God's providence they did. And the next day they got into the Cape Harbor where they rid in safety. . . .

Being thus arrived in a good harbor and brought safe to land, they fell upon their knees and blessed the God of Heaven who had brought them over the vast and furious ocean, and delivered them from all the perils and miseries thereof, again to set their feet on the firm and stable earth, their proper element. . . .

But here I cannot but stay and make a pause, and stand half amazed at this poor people's present condition; and so I think will the reader, too, when he well considers the same. Being thus passed the vast ocean, and a sea of troubles before in their preparation . . . they had now no friends to welcome them, nor inns to entertain or refresh their weather-beaten bodies; no houses or much less towns to repair to, to seek for succor. It is recorded in Scripture as a mercy to the Apostle and his ship-wrecked company, that the barbarians showed them no small kindness in refreshing them, but these savage barbarians, when they met with them (as after will appear) were readier to fill their sides full of arrows than otherwise. And for the season it was winter, and they that know the winters of that country know them to be sharp and violent, and subject to cruel and fierce storms, dangerous to travel to known places, much more to search an unknown coast. Besides, what could they see but a hideous and desolate wilderness, full of wild beasts and wild men—and what multitudes there might be of them they knew not. . . .

What could now sustain them but the spirit of God and His grace? May not and ought not the children of these fathers rightly say, "Our fathers were Englishmen which came over this great ocean, and were ready to perish in this wilderness; but they cried unto the Lord, and He heard their voice and looked on their adversity."

While in the Netherlands, Bradford and his cohorts might have seen paintings similar to this one. Puritanism strongly influenced Dutch painting, famous for its realism and moral symbolism. The Dancing Couple (shown below) shows a festive occasion, but art critics believe that some details warn viewers that life is short and enjoyment is transitory.

JOHN WINTHROP (1588–1749)

we shall be as a city upon a hill

Raised on his father's estate in Suffolk, England, John Winthrop led a privileged life. He attended Cambridge University and later became a lawyer. Nevertheless, his Puritan beliefs threatened the security of his family's manor under King Charles I, so he decided to emigrate to Massachusetts. In 1632, with a charter from the king, Winthrop joined several hundred settlers aboard six ships to help found the Massachusetts Bay Colony—an area including Boston Harbor and its vicinity, north of the Plymouth settlement. John Winthrop became the colony's first governor, and his steady leadership helped guide Massachusetts Bay for about twenty years.

Most of Winthrop's followers did not have the extreme bent of the Plymouth colonists a decade earlier. Many Massachusetts Bay settlers were mainstream Puritans who hoped to reform the Church of England from within. However, like the Separatists, these newcomers saw the world in starkly religious themes. John Winthrop kept a journal, but his best-known literary contribution is the sermon entitled "A Model of Christian Charity." Delivered during the ocean-crossing aboard a ship called The Arabella, *the sermon outlined the ideal Christian community. Winthrop impressed upon his listeners that others would judge them and their faith according to the success or failure of their colony. Therefore, he called upon them to band together, and through their unity, industriousness, and quiet piety, to act as a beacon to all who would live a Christian life. In his later journal entries, Winthrop realized that his concept of the perfect Christian community was unattainable. However, historians have quoted his instructions to create "a city upon a hill" for more than 350 years because they eloquently convey the fervent hopes that characterized the founding of the nation.*

A Model of Christian Charity

Now the only way to avoid this shipwreck, and to provide for our posterity, is to follow the counsel of Micah, and do justly, to love mercy, to walk humbly with our God. For this end, we must be knit together in this work as one man. We must entertain each other in brotherly affection, we must be willing to abridge ourselves of our superfluities, for the supply of other's necessities. We must uphold a familiar commerce together in all meekness, gentleness, patience and liberality. We must delight in each other, make other's conditions our own, rejoice together, mourn together, labor and suffer together, always having before our eyes our commission and community in the work, our community as members of the same body. So shall we keep the unity of the spirit and the bond of peace. The Lord will be our God, and delight to dwell among us as His own people, and will command a blessing upon us in all our ways, so that we shall see much more of His wisdom, power, goodness and truth, than formerly we have been acquainted with. We shall find that the God of Israel is among us, when ten of us shall be able to resist a thousand of our enemies; when He shall make us a praise and glory that men shall say of succeeding plantations, "the lord make it like that of NEW ENGLAND." For we must consider that we shall be as a city upon a hill. The eyes of all people are upon us, so that if we shall deal falsely with our God in this work we have undertaken, and so cause Him to withdraw His present help from us, we shall be made a story and a by-word through the world. We shall open the mouths of enemies to speak evil of the ways of God, and all professors for God's sake. We shall shame the faces of many of God's worthy servants, and cause their prayers to be turned into curses upon us 'til we be consumed out of the good land whither we are going.

"she was but as a withering flower"

ANNE BRADSTREET (1612–1672)

At the age of 18, Anne Bradstreet sailed to Massachusetts Bay aboard The Arabella *with her husband, her parents, and other Puritan settlers, including John Winthrop. Her family probably took Winthrop's shipboard sermon to heart, because they became prominent members of the community. Anne Bradstreet's father became the second governor of Massachusetts, and later her husband held the same office. While the men in her life pursued public service, Anne Bradstreet spent her time raising eight children and writing poetry. In 1650, her brother-in-law secretly took copies of her poems to London, thus helping her to become the first English writer in North America to have published a volume of verse. Bradstreet's collection,* The Tenth Muse, *was listed among the "most vendible," or most marketable, books in England. Today her writing remains popular not only because it reflects the Puritan preoccupation with God and morality, but also because her later poems are intensely personal and engaging. Unlike most poets of the period, Anne Bradstreet wrote about her love for her husband, family illnesses, the deaths of grandchildren, and the fire that destroyed her house—all with a probing mind that searched for lessons from God.*

Religious Tolerance in the Early Colonies
"the better to preserve mutual love and unity"

Though the Puritans suffered religious persecution in England, they were not models of religious toleration once they settled in North America. Rather, they believed that their own religious purity would suffer if other factions gained followers in their midst. In Massachusetts Bay, two famous cases of religious intolerance involved Roger Williams and Anne Hutchinson, both of whom were banished from Massachusetts between 1635 and 1638. In a short story attributed to John Winthrop, the Puritans interpret the spreading of Anne Hutchinson's contrary opinions as the work of the devil.

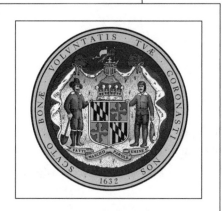

The seal of the Maryland Colony incorporated the coat of arms of its proprietor, Lord Baltimore. Translated from Latin, the motto means "Manly Deeds; Womanly Words."

Mistress Hutchi[n]son, being banished and confined, . . . she thought it now needless to conceal herself any longer, neither would Satan lose the opportunity of making choice of so fit an instrument, so long as any hope remained to attain his mischievous end in darkening the saving truth of the Lord Jesus. . . . Therefore, . . . her opinions came abroad and began to take place among her old disciples. . . .

On the other hand, the Maryland Colony was founded in 1634 by a Catholic proprietor, Cecil Calvert (the Second Lord Baltimore), and was named for the Catholic wife of King Charles I. Members of a religious minority, Lord Baltimore and his heirs protected a certain measure of religious freedom from the colony's inception. In 1649, the colony's general assembly passed the "Act Concerning Religion"—the first law establishing religious toleration in America.

And whereas the enforcing of the conscience in matters of religion hath frequently fallen out to be of dangerous consequence in those commonwealths where it hath been practiced, and for the more quiet and peaceable government of this province, and the better to preserve mutual love and unity amongst the inhabitants here, Be it, therefore, . . . ordained and enacted, . . . that no person or persons whatsoever within this province . . . professing to believe in Jesus Christ, shall from henceforth be in any ways troubled . . . for or in respect of his or her religion, nor in any way compelled to the belief or exercise of any other religion. . . .

While New England settlers lived on average about twenty years longer than those in the Chesapeake, both regions suffered from disease, illness, and premature deaths. Women often died during childbirth, and children were especially prone to disease. Smallpox was particularly devastating, especially to the Native American tribes. In the following poem, Anne Bradstreet affirms her faith in God despite tragic events.

Puritans rejected all forms of sculpture except tombstones because they represented the gateway to the afterlife. The famous John Foster headstone, shown here, was made by an unknown but skilled stonecutter in 1681.

In Memory of My Dear Grandchild Anne Bradstreet Who Deceased June 20, 1669, Being Three Years And Seven Months Old

With troubled heart and trembling hand I write,
The heavens have changed to sorrow my delight.
How oft with disappointment have I met,
When I on fading things my hopes have set.
Experience might 'fore this have made me wise,
To value things according to their price.
Was ever stable joy yet found below?
Or perfect bliss without mixture of woe?
I knew she was but as a withering flower,
That's here today, perhaps gone in an hour;
Like as a bubble, or the brittle glass,
Or like a shadow turning as it was.
More fool then I to look on that was lent
As if mine own, when thus impermanent.
Farewell dear child, thou ne'er shall come to me,
But yet a while, and I shall go to thee;
Meantime my throbbing heart's cheered up with this:
Thou with thy Saviour art in endless bliss.

"Our parson has gone mad!"

NATHANIEL HAWTHORNE (1804–1864)

While Nathaniel Hawthorne lived in the early- to mid-nineteenth century, he is most famous for his historical fiction about Puritan New England. The descendant of Puritan immigrants, Hawthorne went to Bowdoin College and then returned to his home in Salem, Massachusetts. Thereafter, Hawthorne spent twelve years researching New England history and focusing on his writing. After his marriage in 1842, he accepted political appointments, first as the surveyor of the Port of Salem, and then as American consul at Liverpool, England. Between these two jobs, however, his writing flourished. The fruit of this period, The Scarlet Letter, was published in 1850 and brought him literary fame on both sides of the Atlantic. In his best works, Hawthorne expresses keen psychological insight into his characters. In keeping with his religious and historical subject matter, his most common themes revolve around morality,

King Philip's War

"the dolefulest day that ever mine eyes saw"

Tribal confederacies were commemorated by wampum belts (shown here). Native Americans often demonstrated sophisticated weaving arts.

At the start of both the Virginia and New England colonies, settlers developed friendly relations with the local Native American tribes. However, as thousands of new colonists arrived and fanned out across the frontier, territorial wars with Indians ensued. Between 1642 and 1660 alone, about 75,000 English immigrants arrived on American shores.

Shortly after their arrival, the Pilgrims of Plymouth made an alliance with Massasoit, the chief of the Wampanoags. However, fifty years later, Puritan towns had surrounded ancestral Indian lands, and Christianity and European lifestyles were diluting native culture. Between 1675 and 1676, Massasoit's son, Chief Metacomet (called King Philip by whites) led three tribes in a series of attacks on more than fifty white settlements.

At the time, Mary White Rowlandson and her family lived in the frontier town of Lancaster, Massachusetts. In the winter of 1675, Indians attacked Lancaster and took her prisoner. Her work, *A Narrative of the Captivity and Restoration of Mrs. Mary Rowlandson,* described the attack and her three-month ordeal in explicit detail. Tales of captivity at the hands of Indians fascinated Europeans and became a popular genre of literature. Rowlandson's account is considered among the best examples.

On the tenth of February 1675 came the Indians with great numbers upon Lancaster. Their first coming was about sunrising; hearing the noise of some guns, we looked out; several houses were burning, and the smoke ascending to Heaven. . . . Another [white man] there was who, [when] running along, was shot and wounded and fell down; he begged of [the Indians] his life . . . but they would not hearken to him but knocked him in [the] head, and stripped him naked, and split open his bowels. . . .

At length they came and beset our own house, and quickly it was the dolefulest day that ever mine eyes saw. . . . But now, the next morning, I must turn my back upon the town and travel with [the Indians] into the vast and desolate wilderness, I knew not whither. It is not my tongue or pen can express the sorrows of my heart, and bitterness of my spirit, that I had at this departure: but God was with me, . . . carrying me along, and bearing up my spirit, that it did not quite fail.

Despite these unflattering accounts of Indians, a few white settlers did speak up for Native American land rights. One was Roger Williams, who argued that natives—not the king of England—owned the land in Massachusetts. This view undermined the legitimacy of the colony's charter, and Williams was banished. In 1636, Williams founded the colony of Rhode Island. However, Williams's efforts to befriend the Indians could not overcome the clash of cultures in the late 1600s. Local tribes attacked settlements in Warwick and Providence during King Philip's War.

conflicts between the individual and the society, and the influence of the past upon the present.

The following excerpt from Hawthorne's short story "The Minister's Black Veil" was written in 1836. Subtitled "A Parable," the story is meant to be read like biblical parables—as a guide to moral or religious principles. Parables are usually interpreted by members of the clergy in a homily or sermon. However, Hawthorne does not explain the mystery of the black veil. Why is Parson Hooper wearing it? Is he testing the faith of his parishioners, or has he come under the influence of the devil?

Such questions are particularly relevant in light of the Puritan principle of congregationalism. Under this system, each meetinghouse was independent from other churches, and no bishops or other authority figures presided over it. Most important, church members were able to reject ministers and their teachings if they did not approve of them. In Hawthorne's story, would the Milford congregation remain loyal to the parson?

Using the form of a parable, Hawthorne poses to readers the very moral questions with which Puritans wrestled. How can one fairly judge the heart of another? Is a particular event the work of God or the devil? At the same time, by focusing on the minister and church members, this story illustrates the centrality of meetinghouses and religious leaders in Puritan society.

The Minister's Black Veil
A Parable

The sexton stood in the porch of Milford meeting-house, pulling lustily at the bell-rope. The old people of the village came stooping along the street. Children, with bright faces, tript merrily beside their parents, or mimicked a graver gait, in the conscious dignity of their Sunday clothes. Spruce bachelors looked sidelong at the pretty maidens, and fancied that the sabbath sunshine made them prettier than on week-days. When the throng had mostly streamed into the porch, the sexton began to toll the bell, keeping his eye on the Reverend Mr. Hooper's door. The first glimpse of the clergyman's figure was the signal for the bell to cease its summons.

"But what has good Parson Hooper got upon his face?" cried the sexton in astonishment.

All within hearing immediately turned about, and beheld the semblance of Mr. Hooper, pacing slowly his meditative way towards the meeting-house. With one accord they started, expressing more wonder than if some strange minister were coming to dust the cushions of Mr. Hooper's pulpit.

"Are you sure it is our parson?" inquired Goodman Gray of the sexton.

"Of a certainty it is good Mr. Hooper," replied the sexton. "He was to have exchanged pulpits with Parson Shute of Westbury; but Parson Shute sent to excuse himself yesterday, being to preach a funeral sermon."

The cause of so much amazement may appear sufficiently slight. Mr. Hooper, a gentlemanly person of about thirty, though still a bachelor, was dressed with due clerical neatness, as if a careful wife had starched his band, and brushed the weekly dust from his Sunday's garb. There was but one thing remarkable in his appearance. Swathed about his forehead, and hanging down over his face, so low as to be shaken by his breath, Mr. Hooper had on a black veil. On a nearer view, it seemed to consist of two folds of crape, which entirely concealed his features, except the mouth and chin, but probably did not intercept his sight, farther than to give a darkened aspect to all living and inanimate things. With this gloomy shade before him, good Mr. Hooper walked onward, at a slow and quiet pace, stooping somewhat and looking on the ground, as is customary with abstracted men, yet nodding kindly to those of his parishioners who still waited on the meeting-house steps. But so wonder-struck were they, that his greeting hardly met with a return.

"I can't really feel as if good Mr. Hooper's face was behind that piece of crape," said the sexton.

"I don't like it," muttered an old woman, as she hobbled into the meeting-house. "He has changed himself into something awful, only by hiding his face."

"Our parson has gone mad!" cried Goodman Gray, following him across the threshhold.

A rumor of some unaccountable phenomenon had preceded Mr. Hooper into the meeting-house, and set all the congregation astir. Few could refrain from twisting their heads towards the door; many stood upright, and turned directly about; while several little boys clambered upon the seats, and came down again with a terrible racket. There was a general bustle, a rustling of the women's gowns and shuffling of the men's feet, greatly at variance with that hushed repose which should attend the entrance of the minister. But Mr. Hooper appeared not to notice the perturbation of his people. He entered with an almost noiseless step,

Meetinghouses were central features of Puritan life. Villages were organized around these buildings so that all residents could walk to the site and worship daily. Shown here is the Old Ship Meetinghouse in Hingham, Massachusetts, which was built in 1681.

bent his head mildly to the pews on each side, and bowed as he passed his oldest parishioner, a white-haired great-grandsire, who occupied an arm-chair in the centre of the aisle. It was strange to observe, how slowly this venerable man became conscious of something singular in the appearance of his pastor. He seemed not fully to partake of the prevailing wonder, till Mr. Hooper had ascended the stairs, and showed himself in the pulpit, face to face with his congregation, except for the black veil. That mysterious emblem was never once withdrawn. It shook with his measured breath as he gave out the psalm; it threw its obscurity between him and the holy page, as he read the Scriptures; and while he prayed, the veil lay heavily on his uplifted countenance. Did he seek to hide it from the dread Being whom he was addressing?

Such was the effect of this simple piece of crape, that more than one woman of delicate nerves was forced to leave the meeting-house. Yet perhaps the pale-faced congregation was almost as fearful a sight to the minister, as his black veil to them.

Mr. Hooper had the reputation of a good preacher, but not an energetic one: he strove to win his people heavenward, by mild persuasive influences, rather than to drive them thither, by the thunders of the Word. The sermon which he now delivered, was marked by the same characteristics of style and manner, as the general series of his pulpit oratory. But there was something, either in sentiment of the discourse itself, or in the imagination of the auditors, which made it greatly the most powerful effort that they had ever heard from their pastor's lips. It was tinged, rather more darkly than usual, with the gentle gloom of Mr. Hooper's temperament. The subject had reference to secret sin, and those sad mysteries which we hide from our nearest and dearest, and would fain conceal from our own consciousness, even forgetting that the Omniscient can detect them. A subtle power was breathed into his words. Each member of the congregation, the most innocent girl, and the man of hardened breast, felt as if the preacher had crept upon them, behind his awful veil, and discovered their hoarded iniquity of deed or thought. Many spread their clasped hands on their bosoms. There was nothing terrible in what Mr. Hooper said; at least, no violence, and yet, with every tremor of his melancholy voice, the hearers quaked. An unsought pathos came hand in hand with awe. So sensible were the audience of some unwonted attribute in their minister, that they longed for a breath of wind to blow aside the veil, almost believing that a stranger's visage would be discovered, though the form, gesture, and voice were those of Mr. Hooper.

At the close of the services, the people hurried out with indecorous confusion, eager to communicate their pent-up amazement, and conscious of lighter spirits, the moment they lost sight of the black veil. Some gathered in little circles, huddled closely together, with their mouths all whispering in the centre; some went homeward alone, wrapt in silent meditation; some talked loudly and profaned the Sabbath-day with ostentatious laughter. A few shook their sagacious heads, intimating that they could penetrate the mystery; while one or two affirmed that there was no mystery at all, but only that Mr. Hooper's eyes were so weakened by the midnight lamp, as to require a shade. After a brief interval, forth came good Mr. Hooper also, in the rear of his flock. Turning his veiled face from one group to another, he paid due reverence to the hoary heads, saluted the middle-aged with kind dignity, as their friend and spiritual guide, greeted the young with mingled authority and love, and laid his hands on the little children's heads to bless them. Such was always his custom on the Sabbath-day. Strange and bewildered looks repaid him for his courtesy. None, as on former occasions, aspired to the honor of walking by their pastor's side. Old Squire Saunders, doubtless by an accidental lapse of memory, neglected to invite Mr. Hooper to his table, where the good clergyman had been wont to bless the food, almost every Sunday since his settlement. He returned, therefore, to the parsonage, and, at the moment of closing the door, was observed to look back upon the people, all of whom had their eyes fixed upon the minister. A sad smile gleamed faintly from beneath the black veil, and flickered about his mouth, glimmering as he disappeared.

Voices of a Revolution

The ideas behind the American Revolution—like many of the colonial era—trace back to Europe. Enlightenment thinkers there such as Isaac Newton and John Locke advocated viewing the world in scientific, rational terms, rather than religious ones. Consequently, their followers no longer believed that God gave power to kings and queens. Instead, Locke argued that groups of people could make agreements and govern themselves. Enlightenment ideas prompted some colonists to question the authority of the British king. Others tried to right injustices and win Christian converts.

In the 1740s, a religious movement called the Great Awakening began. After reading Enlightenment philosophers who argued that people learn through experience, revivalists devised a new way to convert people to Christianity. In addition, Enlightenment thinkers believed that people could improve society. Consequently, many Quakers helped build hospitals and questioned cruel social institutions such as slavery.

As settlers continued to flood the colonies in the early 1700s, the frontier expanded westward. Soon pioneers came into conflict with Native Americans over land ownership. This situation worsened when the French settled the North American interior along the St. Lawrence, Ohio, and Mississippi Rivers. Indians were caught between two land-greedy empires. Thus, from 1754 to 1763 many colonists fought in the French and Indian War (sometimes called the Seven Years' War).

That conflict directly led to the American Revolution. In order to pay its large war debts, Great Britain heavily taxed the colonies, causing friction between King George and his American subjects. In addition, after the French were defeated, the colonies no longer needed British military protection, and independence from the empire became more plausible. The French defeat spelled disaster for Native Americans because they could no longer play their European rivals off of one another. Thus, they became caught in an ongoing fight for rights to their lands.

Throughout this period, literacy in the colonies continued to improve. However, the scarcity and poor quality of paper meant that printers produced very few books. Instead, American publishers printed newspapers, pamphlets, broadsides, almanacs, and government documents. Books were imported from Europe.

Moreover, pioneers and patriots did not have time to create poetry or fiction. As readers, they valued pieces that were quick to skim and immediately useful. In fact, many colonists thought that reading novels was a waste of productive time. Consequently, literature of this period takes the form of letters, sermons, autobiographies, essays, and political pamphlets.

Featured Authors

Jonathan Edwards
Benjamin Franklin
John Woolman
James Fenimore Cooper
Thomas Paine
Thomas Jefferson
John Adams
Abigail Adams

JONATHAN EDWARDS (1703–1758)

Jonathan Edwards is commonly regarded as colonial America's greatest philosopher and theologian. Raised in a family of devout Puritan ministers in Connecticut, Edwards decided early to become a clergyman. He studied for thirteen hours a day, reading the works of John Locke and other philosophers of the Enlightenment. After the death of his grandfather in 1729, Edwards assumed leadership of his church in Northampton, Massachusetts. He enjoyed widespread popularity until his parishioners tired of his over-zealous methods and expelled him in 1750. After having served as a missionary to Native Americans and as the president of a college, Jonathan Edwards died in 1758 from a smallpox vaccine.

Edwards was pastor at Northampton during the Great Awakening. The following sermon, "Sinners in the Hands of an Angry God," was written in 1741 at the height of this religious fervor. Edwards based his teachings on the Puritan tradition. He believed that man's nature was essentially immoral and that sinners relied only on the grace of God for their salvation. However, Edwards updated his sermons with emotional appeal. Many revivalist ministers spoke passionately, raising their voices at important junctures and gesturing dramatically. Edwards is particularly well known for his vivid imagery, as in the following excerpt where he compares sinners to a spider being held over a fiery pit. Frequently, listeners were moved to tears, remorse, and fainting spells. Evangelicals believed the force of these emotions would convert people to Christianity and encourage them to live upright lives.

Although science had begun to filter into colonial society, religion remained the center of everyday life. During the Revolutionary period, people were still deeply religious and worshipped regularly. The works of Jonathan Edwards prove that Christianity dominated American culture well beyond the Puritan heyday.

> *"The God that holds you over the pit of hell . . . abhors you"*

Sinners in the Hands of an Angry God
[DOCTRINE]

There is nothing that keeps wicked men, at any one moment, out of hell, but the mere pleasure of God.

By the mere pleasure of God, I mean his sovereign pleasure, his arbitrary will, restrained by no obligation, hindered by no manner of difficulty, any

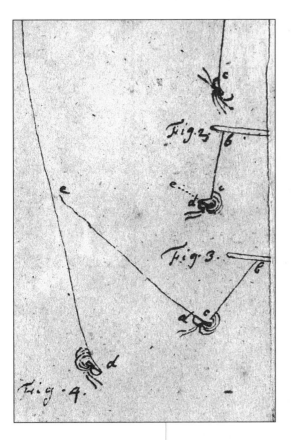

Shown here is a drawing by Jonathan Edwards to accompany his observations on spiders spinning their webs. Scholars think he planned to publish an article on the subject.

more than if nothing else but God's mere will had in the last degree, or in any respect whatsoever, any hand in the preservation of wicked men one moment.

The truth of this observation may appear by the following considerations.

I. There is no want of power in God to cast wicked men into hell at any moment. Men's hands can't be strong when God rises up: the strongest have no power to resist him, nor can any deliver out of his hands....

II. They deserve to be cast into hell; so that divine justice never stands in the way, it makes no objection against God's using his power at any moment to destroy them....

III. They are already under a sentence of condemnation to hell. They don't only justly deserve to be cast down thither; but the sentence of the law of God, that eternal and immutable rule of righteousness that God has fixed between him and mankind, is gone out against them, and stands against them; so that they are bound over already to hell....

So that it is not because God is unmindful of their wickedness, and [doesn't] resent it, that he [doesn't] let loose his hand and cut them off. God is not altogether such a one as themselves, though they might imagine him to be so. The wrath of God burns against them, their damnation doesn't slumber, the pit is prepared, the fire is made ready, the furnace is now hot, ready to receive them, the flames do now rage and glow. The glittering sword is whet, and held over them, and the pit hath opened her mouth under them....

So that thus it is, that natural men are held in the hand of God over the pit of hell; they have deserved the fiery pit, and are already sentenced to it; and God is dreadfully provoked, his anger is as great towards them as to those that are actually suffering the executions of the fierceness of his wrath in hell, and they have done nothing in the least to appease or abate that anger, neither is God in the least bound by any promise to hold 'em up one moment; the devil is waiting for them, hell is gaping for them, the flames gather and flash about them, and would fain lay hold on them, and swallow them up; the fire pent up in their own hearts is struggling to break out; and they have no interest in any mediator, there are no means within reach that can be any security to them. In short, they have no refuge, nothing to take hold of, all that preserves them every moment is the mere arbitrary will, and uncovenanted unobliged forbearance of an incensed God....

The God that holds you over the pit of hell, much as one holds a spider, or some loathsome insect, over the fire, abhors you, and is dreadfully provoked; his wrath towards you burns like fire; he looks upon you as worthy of nothing else, but to be cast into the fire; he is of purer eyes than to bear to have you in his sight; you are ten thousand times so abominable in his eyes as the most hateful venomous serpent is in ours. You have offended him infinitely more than ever a stubborn rebel did his prince: and yet 'tis nothing but his hand that holds you from falling into the fire every moment: 'tis to be ascribed to nothing else, that you did not go to hell the last night; that you [were] suffered to awake again in this world, after you closed your eyes to sleep: and there is no other reason to be given why you have not dropped into hell since you arose in the morning, but that God's hand has held you up: there is no other reason to be given why you haven't gone to hell since you have sat here in the house of God, provoking his pure eyes by your sinful wicked manner of attending his solemn worship: yea, there is nothing else that is to be given as a reason why you don't this very moment drop down into hell.

BENJAMIN FRANKLIN (1706–1790)

A "Founding Father" of mythic proportions, Benjamin Franklin hardly needs introduction. He was raised in Boston and, at the age of 12, apprenticed to his brother, a printer. Five years later Franklin went to London and soon thereafter settled in Philadelphia, where he founded his own printing shop. Benjamin Franklin's long career spanned from witty editor to earnest social reformer, from curious inventor to worldly diplomat, and finally, to a revered elder statesman at the time of the American Revolution. His early independence and diverse accomplishments made him an icon of the "self-made man," an ideal that many Americans share today.

In 1681, King Charles II granted the charter for the Pennsylvania colony to William Penn, who created the colony as a haven for Quakers and others who suffered religious persecution. The Society of Friends, as Quakers call themselves, held beliefs that were fundamentally different from the Puritans, particularly the idea that "every man is enlightened by the divine Light of Christ." Unlike their neighbors to the north, Quakers believed in the equality of all men and were tolerant of other religions. William Penn actively promoted his colony as a refuge for other European religious minorities. Thus, from the 1730s onward, tens of thousands of

"The people heard it . . . and immediately practiced the contrary, just as if it had been a common sermon"

Lutherans and Presbyterians from Europe arrived in Philadelphia harbor. Quakers then became a minority in the colony and by the 1750s ceded governmental power to moderate politicians such as Franklin.

Compared with his contemporary, Jonathan Edwards, Benjamin Franklin marks the beginning of a new force in colonial New England— the practicality and ingenuity of Yankee merchants. In 1732, when Pennsylvania was welcoming its waves of immigrants, Franklin printed the first edition of Poor Richard's Almanac. *The great success of this work spread his humorous opinions among tens of thousands of homes in Pennsylvania. At that time, almost every family had two books—a Bible and an almanac. An almanac forecasted the weather and noted tides, moon quarters, court sessions, and schedules for coaches and post riders. Richard Saunders was the fictitious editor of the first volume. Under that guise, Franklin advised colonial Americans to work hard and spend their money and time wisely. His maxims, or rules of conduct, became known as "the Sayings of Poor Richard."*

Franklin wrote his famous essay, "The Way to Wealth," as a supplement to the twenty-fifth anniversary edition of Poor Richard's Almanac. *Taking the form of a letter to readers, "The Way to Wealth" quotes many of Poor Richard's most famous adages, or proverbs. Several in the following excerpt derive from Puritan religious beliefs, particularly the emphasis on hard work. However, Franklin promotes these values in a secular, or nonreligious, context. Perhaps Franklin should have listened to his own advice on thrift because, after a life of great success, he died with very little money.*

The Way to Wealth

Courteous Reader,

I have heard that nothing gives an author so great pleasure as to find his works respectfully quoted by other learned authors. This pleasure I have seldom enjoyed; for though I have been, if I may say it without vanity, an eminent author of almanacs annually now a full quarter of a century, my brother authors in the same way, for what reason I know not, have ever been sparing in their applauses, and no other author has taken the least notice of me, so that did not my writings produce me some solid pudding, the great deficiency of praise would have quite discouraged me.

I concluded at length, that the people were the best judges of my merit; for they buy my works; and besides, in my rambles, where I am not personally known, I have frequently heard one or other of my adages repeated with "as Poor Richard says" at the end on 't; this gave me some satisfaction, as it showed not only that my instructions were regarded, but discovered likewise some respect for my authority; and I own, that to encourage the practice of remembering and repeating those wise sentences, I have sometimes quoted myself with great gravity.

Judge then, how much I must have been gratified by an incident I am going to relate to you. I stopped my horse lately where a great number of people were collected at a vendue [auction] of merchant goods. The hour of sale not being come, they were conversing on the badness of the times and one of the company called to a plain clean old man, with white locks, "Pray, Father Abraham, what think you of the times? Won't these heavy taxes quite ruin the country? How shall we be ever able to pay them? What would you advise us to?" Father Abraham stood up, and replied, "If you'd have my advice, I'll give it you in short, *for a word to the wise is enough, and many words won't fill a bushel,* as Poor Richard says." They joined in desiring him to speak his mind, and gathering round him, he proceeded as follows:

"Friends," says he, "and neighbors, the taxes are indeed very heavy, and if those laid on by the government were the only ones we had to pay, we might more easily discharge them; but we have many others, and much more grievous to some of us. We are taxed twice as much by our idleness, three times as much by our pride, and four times as much by our folly.... However, let us hearken to good advice, and something may be done for us; *God helps them that help themselves,* as Poor Richard says, in his Almanac of 1733.

"It would be thought a hard government that should tax its people one-tenth part of their time, to be employed in its service. But idleness taxes many of us much more, if we reckon all that is spent in absolute sloth, or doing of nothing.... Sloth, by bringing on diseases, absolutely shortens life. *Sloth, like rust, consumes faster than labor wears; while the used key is always bright,* as Poor Richard says. How much more than is necessary do we spend in sleep, forgetting that *the sleeping fox catches no poultry* and that *there will be sleeping enough in the grave,* as Poor Richard says.

"*If time be of all things the most precious, wasting time must be,* as Poor Richard says, *the greatest prodigality;* since, as he elsewhere tells us, *lost time is never found again;* and *what we call time enough, always proves little enough:* let us then up and be doing, and doing to the purpose; so by diligence shall we do more with less perplexity. *Sloth makes all things difficult, but industry all easy,* as Poor Richard says; and *he that riseth late must trot all day, and shall scarce overtake his business at night;*

Shown here is a page from Poor Richard's Almanac. Each was crowded with tables, woodblock images, advice, and lighthearted poetry.

while *laziness travels so slowly, that poverty soon overtakes him,* as we read in Poor Richard, who adds, *drive thy business, let not that drive thee,* and *early to bed, and early to rise, makes a man healthy, wealthy, and wise.*

"So what signifies wishing and hoping for better times. We may make these times better, if we bestir ourselves. *Industry need not wish,* as Poor Richard says, and *he that lives upon hope will die fasting. . . . There are no gains without pains. . . .*

"And now to conclude, *experience keeps a dear* [expensive] *school, but fools will learn in no other, and scarce in that;* for it is true, *we may give advice, but we cannot give conduct,* as Poor Richard says. . . ."

Thus the old gentleman ended his harangue. The people heard it, and approved the doctrine, and immediately practiced the contrary, just as if it had been a common sermon; for the vendue opened, and they began to buy extravagantly, notwithstanding his cautions and their own fears about taxes. I found the good man had thoroughly studied my almanacs, and digested all I had dropped on these topics during the course of five and twenty years. The frequent mention he made of me must have tired any one else, but my vanity was wonderfully delighted with it, though I was conscious that not a tenth part of the wisdom was my own, which he ascribed to me, but rather the gleanings I had made of the sense of all ages and nations. However, I resolved to be the better for the echo of it; and though I had at first determined to buy stuff for a new coat, I went away resolved to wear my old one a little longer. Reader, if thou wilt do the same, thy profit will be as great as mine. I am, as ever, thine to serve thee,

Richard Saunders
July 7, 1757

"innocent men . . . were not intended to be slaves"

JOHN WOOLMAN (1720–1772)

Born in New Jersey among a tightly knit community of Quakers, John Woolman became a spokesman for injustice in colonial America. His work spanned several fields, including owning a store, surveying, teaching, farming, and on a limited scale, practicing law. In his journal entries and essays, he wrestled with conflicts between his Christian beliefs and accepted social norms, particularly slavery.

If Quakers have a central identifying feature, it is their pacifism. Thus, Woolman opposed military conscription (the draft) and paying taxes to support wars. Woolman warned of the dangers of a materialist society and the exploitation of workers—issues that did not come to prominence until the twentieth century. In addition to sharing these concerns in local Quaker meetings, he set out on several missions and, on his final trip, died of smallpox in York, England. Woolman's new ideas were part of a bigger trend that changed the way colonists thought about society, government, and the rights of individuals. Later, this mindset paved the way for colonial leaders to challenge Great Britain's rule.

The year John Woolman penned his 1754 essay, "Some Considerations on the Keeping of Negroes," marked the beginning of the French and Indian War. Within two years, Quakers lost power in the Pennsylvania Assembly because they did not support taking up arms against Native Americans on the frontier. Nevertheless, their conscience continued to influence the colony through their avid social reforms. They built hospitals and sought to improve conditions in prisons and insane asylums. In addition, many Quakers were strong abolitionists.

Following is a selection from Woolman's 1762 essay on slavery, "Considerations on Keeping Negroes." It addresses two abuses in the forced labor system—the cruel punishment of people regarded as "property" and the separation of African-American families. Although most abolitionists of the period emphasized slavery's moral degradation of whites, Woolman bases his argument on sympathy for fellow human beings.

Considerations on Keeping Negroes

[T]o take [Africans] from their own land, with views of profit to ourselves, by means inconsistent with pure justice, is foreign to that principle which seeks the happiness of the whole creation. Forced subjection, on innocent persons of full age, is inconsistent with right reason. On one side, the human mind is not naturally fortified with that firmness in wisdom and goodness, necessary to an independent ruler. On the other side, to be subject to the uncontrollable will of a man, liable to err, is most painful and afflicting to a conscientious creature....

Placing on men the ignominious title SLAVE, dressing them in uncomely garments, keeping them to servile labor, in which they are often dirty, tends gradually to fix a notion in the mind, that they are a sort of people below us in nature, and leads us to consider them as such in all our conclusions about them. And, moreover, a person which in our esteem is mean and contemptible, if their language or behavior toward us is unseemly or disrespectful, it excites wrath more powerfully than the like conduct in one we accounted our equal or superior; and where this happens to be the case, it disqualifies for candid judgment; for it is unfit for a person to sit as judge in a case where his own personal

Phillis Wheatley on Slavery
"Some view our sable race with scornful eye."

The African-American poet Phillis Wheatley took a surprising view of slavery. Despite being kidnapped and sold into bondage as a child, Wheatley was thankful because the experience introduced her to Christianity. To dispel racism's "scornful eye," this poem referred to her African heritage and reminded readers that blacks can be educated and "refined."

Wheatley herself proved this assertion. Unlike most slaves of the period, she read English and Latin and studied the Bible and English poetry. In 1773, at the age of 19, Wheatley became the first black writer in America to have a volume of her work published.

On Being Brought from Africa to America

'Twas mercy brought me from my pagan land,
Taught my benighted soul to understand
That there's a God, that there's a Savior too:
Once I redemption neither sought nor knew.
Some view our sable race with scornful eye.
"Their color is a diabolic dye."
Remember, Christians, Negroes, black as Cain,
May be refined, and join the angelic train.

resentments are stirred up; and, as members of society in a well framed government, we are mutually dependent....

Seed sown with the tears of a confined oppressed people, harvest cut down by an overborne discontented reaper, makes bread less sweet to the taste of an honest man, than that which is the produce, or just reward of such voluntary action, which is one proper part of the business of human creatures....

In our species the mutual ties of affection are more rational and durable than in others below us; the care and labor of raising our off-spring much greater. The satisfaction arising to us in their innocent company, and in their advances from one rational improvement to another, is considerable, when two are thus joined, and their affections sincere; it however happens among slaves, that they are often situate[d] in different places; and their seeing each other depends on the will of men, liable to human passions, and a bias in judgment; who, with views of self-interest, may keep them apart more than is right. Being absent from each other, and often with other company, there is a danger of their affections being alienated, jealousies arising, the happiness otherwise resulting from their offspring frustrated, and the comforts of marriage destroyed. These things being considered closely, as happening to a near friend, will appear to be hard and painful.

He who reverently observes that goodness manifested by our gracious Creator toward the various species of beings in this world, will see, that in our frame and constitution is clearly shown that innocent men, capable to manage for themselves, were not intended to be slaves.

JAMES FENIMORE COOPER (1789–1851)

Best known for his novels about a rugged scout and hunter, James Fenimore Cooper himself led the comfortable life of a wealthy aristocrat. Cooper was raised in upstate New York in a town bearing his family name—Cooperstown, which his father cleared, settled, and founded. In his Leather Stocking Tales—*a collection of five novels featuring woodsman Natty Bumppo—James Fenimore Cooper sketched the first American frontier hero, a character type that would later dominate U.S. literature. Producing more than thirty popular novels during his lifetime, Cooper blazed the trail for others to make a living by writing fiction. Although some readers note Cooper's romantic slant on historical events, they also point out strong elements of social criticism in many of his works.*

Perhaps the most popular Leather Stocking Tale *is* The Last of the Mohicans, *written in 1826 as a reflection on the French and Indian War (1754–63). Because this novel was written after the American Revolution, it was a product of emerging nationalism in U.S. literature. At that time, writers focused on their own history and local subjects rather than on European topics. In this novel, Cooper documented the elimination of Native Americans in the state of New York during the 1750s. Although the policy of removing American Indians cleared the way for settlers like his father to expand westward, Cooper's novel criticizes the treatment of native peoples.*

The Last of the Mohicans *is set in 1757, the third year of fighting in the French and Indian War. Colonial militias and English troops had joined forces to fight the French, who had colonized the North American interior from the St. Lawrence River to the Mississippi. Westward expansion of English settlements along the eastern seaboard trapped Native*

"My tribe is the grandfather of nations"

American peoples between two great European powers, both vying for increased territory and trade rights.

In The Last of the Mohicans, *Cooper's friendly Indians are of the Mohican, or Delaware, tribe which was the first to lose land with the arrival of European settlers. Chief Chingachgook and his son Uncas ally themselves with Natty Bumppo, called "Hawkeye" in this story. Together they try to rescue two English women who were captured by Iroquois (here called "Maquas," part of the Five Nation Confederacy). In this tale, a British fort is overtaken by the Iroquois on behalf of French general Montcalm. Today this story is read not only for its heroic battle scenes, but also for Cooper's foreshadowing of the tragic removal of virtually all Native Americans from the eastern half of the country.*

In the following excerpt, Chingachgook recounts his tribal lore about coming to their ancestral lands on North America's east coast, their first encounters with whites, and the constant relocation that decimated his people.

The Last of the Mohicans: A Narrative of 1757
Chapter III

> "Before these fields were shorn and till'd,
>   Full to the brim our rivers flow'd;
> The Melody of waters fill'd
>   The fresh and boundless wood;
> And torrents dash'd, and rivulets play'd,
>   And fountains spouted in the shade."
> —Bryant

On that day, two men were lingering on the banks of a small but rapid stream, within an hour's journey of the encampment of [British general] Webb, like those who awaited the appearance of an absent person, or the approach of some expected event. The vast canopy of woods spread itself to the margin of the river, overhanging the water, and shadowing its dark current with a deeper hue. The rays of the sun were beginning to grow less fierce, and the intense heat of the day was lessened, as the cooler vapors of the springs and fountains rose above their leafy beds, and rested in the atmosphere. Still that breathing silence, which marks the drowsy sultriness of an American landscape in July, pervaded the secluded spot, interrupted only by the low voices of the men, the occasional and lazy tap of a woodpecker, the discordant cry of some gaudy jay, or a swelling on the ear, from the dull roar of a distant waterfall. These feeble and broken sounds were, however, too familiar to the foresters to draw their attention from the more interesting matter of their dialogue.

While one of the loiterers showed the red skin and wild accouterments of a native of the woods, the other exhibited, through the mask of his rude and nearly savage equipments, the brighter, though sun-burned and long-faced complexion of one who might claim descent from a European parentage....

"Even your traditions make the case in my favor, Chingachgook," he said, speaking in the tongue which was known to all the natives who formerly inhabited the country between the Hudson and the Potomac.... "Your fathers came from the setting sun, crossed the big river, fought the people of the country, and took the land; and mine came from the red sky of the morning, over the salt lake, and did their work much after the fashion that had been set them by yours; then let God judge the matter between us, and friends spare their words!"

"My fathers fought with the naked red man!" returned the Indian, sternly, in the same language. "Is there no difference, Hawkeye, between the stone-headed arrow of the warrior, and the leaden bullet with which you kill?"

"There is reason in an Indian, though nature has made him with a red skin!" said the white man, shaking his head like one on whom such an appeal to his justice was not thrown away. For a moment he appeared to be conscious of having the worst of the argument, then rallying again, he answered ..."I am no scholar ... but, judging from what I have seen at deer chases and squirrel hunts ... I should think a rifle in the hands of their grandfathers was not so dangerous as a hickory bow and a good flint-head might be, if drawn with Indian judgment, and sent by an Indian eye."

"You have the story told by your fathers," returned the other, coldly, waving his hand. "What say your old men? Do they tell the young warriors that the pale faces met the red men, painted for war and armed with the stone hatchet and wooden gun?"

"I am not a prejudiced man, nor one who vaunts himself on his natural privileges ..." the scout replied, surveying, with secret satisfaction, the faded color of his bony and sinewy hand, "and I am willing to own that my people have many ways, of which, as an honest man, I can't approve.... For myself, I conclude the Bumppos could shoot, for I have a natural turn with a rifle, which must have been handed down from generation to generation.... But every story has its two sides; so I ask you, Chingachgook, what

During the 1830s, artist George Catlin packed his paints and trekked westward in search of his beloved Native American subjects. He lived among dozens of tribes, observing and documenting their customs. Catlin painted more than 500 canvases, including this portrait of Sioux chief One Horn.

passed, according to the traditions of the red men, when our fathers first met?"

A silence of a minute succeeded, during which the Indian sat mute; then, full of the dignity of his office, he commenced his brief tale, with a solemnity that served to heighten its appearance of truth.

"Listen, Hawkeye, and your ear shall drink no lie. 'Tis what my fathers have said, and what the Mohicans have done." He hesitated a single instant, and bending a cautious glance toward his companion, he continued . . .

"We came from the place where the sun is hid at night, over great plains where the buffaloes live, until we reached the big river [Mississippi River]. There we fought the Alligewi, till the ground was red with their blood. From the banks of the big river to the shores of the salt lake, there was none to meet us. The Maquas followed at a distance. We said the country should be ours from the place where the water runs up no longer on this stream, to a river twenty sun's journey toward the summer. The land we had taken like warriors we kept like men. We drove the Maquas into the woods with the bears. They only tasted salt at the licks; they drew no fish from the great lake; we threw them the bones."

"All this I have heard and believe," said the white man, observing that the Indian paused; "but it was long before the English came into the country."

"A pine grew then where this chestnut now stands. The first pale faces who came among us spoke no English. They came in a large canoe, when my fathers had buried the tomahawk with the red men around them. Then, Hawkeye," he continued, betraying his deep emotion, only by permitting his voice to fall to those low, guttural tones, which render his language, as spoken at times, so very musical; "then, Hawkeye, we were one people, and we were happy. The salt lake gave us its fish, the wood its deer, and the air its birds. We took wives who bore us children; we worshipped the Great Spirit; and we kept the Maquas beyond the sound of our songs of triumph."

"Know you anything of your own family at that time?" demanded the white. "But you are a just man, for an Indian; and as I suppose you hold their gifts, your fathers must have been brave warriors, and wise men at the council-fire."

"My tribe is the grandfather of nations, but I am an unmixed man. The blood of chiefs is in my veins, where it must stay forever. The Dutch landed, and gave my people the fire-water; they drank until the heavens and the earth seemed to meet, and they foolishly thought they had found the Great Spirit. Then they parted with their land. Foot by foot, they were driven back from the shores, until I, that am a chief and a Sagamore, have never seen the sun shine but through the trees, and have never visited the graves of my fathers."

"Graves bring solemn feelings over the mind," returned the scout, a good deal touched at the calm suffering of his companion. . . . "But where are to be found those of your race who came to their kin in the Delaware country, so many summers since?"

"Where are the blossoms of those summers!—fallen, one by one; so all of my family departed, each in his turn, to the land of spirits. I am on the hilltop and must go down into the valley; and when Uncas follows in my footsteps there will no longer be any of the blood of the Sagamore, for my boy is the last of the Mohicans."

Benjamin West's Historical Paintings

"It [is] thought very ridiculous to exhibit heroes in coats, breeches, and cock'd hats."

Benjamin West was one of the first great American-born artists; however, West's aspiration to paint historical scenes—the most noble subject of his day—led him to Europe in 1759. He settled in London and produced several historical paintings for King George III. In this 1770 work, West depicts the death of British major general James Wolfe during the Battle of Quebec in September 1759. There English troops defeated the French, effectively winning the French and Indian War in North America.

The Death of General Wolfe *by Benjamin West was a controversial painting in 1770. Today it is regarded as a masterpiece.*

This painting glorified the battle, its participants, and the expanding British empire.

However, King George warned West against displaying historical figures, even those from recent events, in contemporary uniforms with modern weapons—instead of the conventional way, with classical togas and javelins. He wrote, "It [is] thought very ridiculous to exhibit heroes in coats, breeches, and cock'd hats." West replied:

The event to be commemorated took place on the thirteenth of September 1759, in a region of the world unknown to the Greeks and Romans, and at a period of time when no such nations, nor heroes in their costumes, any longer existed. . . . The same truth that guides the pen of the historian should govern the pencil of the artist.

The artist, however, could not instill patriotism without some fiction. For example, not all of the people in this painting witnessed Wolfe's death, and no Native Americans served the British forces in this battle.

"there is some-thing very absurd in supposing a continent to be perpetually governed by an island"

THOMAS PAINE (1737–1809)

Thomas Paine—America's most fiery advocate for independence—lived in England until the age of 37, when he emigrated to Philadelphia. Paine quickly became embroiled in political debates of the day, and although he had resided in North America only a year, his revolutionary work, Common Sense, *appeared in January 1776. The first pamphlet to urge immediate independence from Great Britain,* Common Sense *was by far the best-selling political publication of its time. It sold as many as 500,000 copies.*

Paine, like William Bradford, used a plain, accessible writing style. His everyday language made references to the Bible and almanacs, the two best-read books in the colonies. Paine's arguments were based on straightforward logic that appealed to "common sense." Paine adopted an adamant, raging tone that helped whip up support for his cause. Common Sense *and his later essays became models for political propaganda in the United States for centuries to come.*

By the time Common Sense *was published, the battles at Lexington and Concord had already been waged in April 1775. Paine likened plans made before that bloodshed to an old almanac—proper for its time, but now useless. Since then, the Second Continental Congress had met in May 1775 and created the Continental Army. The British army in Boston and the patriots that encircled the city fought little during the first year, and loyalists were still arguing for reconciliation. However, Paine rebuts many of their points, asserting that, during the French and Indian War, Britain had exploited the colonies for its own interests rather than protecting them for the colonies' own benefit. Within a few months of the release of* Common Sense, *the move toward independence became inevitable. In June 1776, the Second Continental Congress introduced a resolution to sever ties with Great Britain.*

Common Sense
Thoughts on the Present State of American Affairs

In the following pages I offer nothing more than simple facts, plain arguments, and common sense; and have no other preliminaries to settle with the reader than that he will divest himself of prejudice and prepossession, and suffer his reason and his feelings to determine for themselves; that he will put on, or rather that he will not put off, the true character of a man, and generously enlarge his views beyond the present day.

Volumes have been written on the subject of the struggle between England and America. Men of all ranks have embarked in the controversy, from different motives and with various designs; but all have been ineffectual, and the period of debate is closed. Arms as the last resource decide the contest; the appeal was the choice of the king, and the continent has accepted the challenge....

The sun never shined on a cause of greater worth. 'Tis not the affair of a city, a county, a province, or a kingdom, but of a continent—of at least one-eighth part of the habitable globe. 'Tis not the concern of a day, a year, or an age; posterity are virtually involved in the contest, and will be more or less affected even to the end of time by proceedings now. Now is the seedtime of continental union, faith, and honor. The least fracture now will be like a name engraved with the point of a pin on the tender rind of a young oak; the wound would enlarge with the tree, and posterity read it in full-grown characters.

By referring the matter from argument to arms, a new era for politics is struck—a new method of thinking has arisen. All plans, proposals, etc., prior to the nineteenth of April [1775], i.e., to the commencement of hostilities [the battles of Lexington and Concord], are like the almanacs of the last year, which, though proper then, are superseded and useless now....

As much has been said of the advantages of reconciliation, which, like an agreeable dream, has passed away and left us as we were, it is but right that we should examine the contrary side of the argument and inquire into some of the many material injuries which these colonies sustain, and always will sustain, by being connected with and dependent on Great Britain. To examine that connection and dependence on the principles of nature and common sense; to see what we have to trust to, if separated, and what we are to expect, if dependent.

I have heard it asserted by some that, as America has flourished under her former connection with Great Britain, the same connection is necessary toward her future happiness and will always have the same effect. Nothing can be more fallacious than this kind of argument. We may as well assert that because a child has thrived upon milk that it is never to have meat, or that the first twenty years of our lives is to become a precedent for the next twenty....

But she has protected us, say some. That she has engrossed us is true, and defended the continent at our expense as well as her own is admitted; and she would

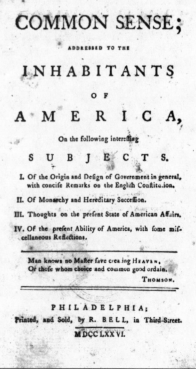

One popular art form before the Revolution was the journalistic print, which appeared in newspapers or broadsides to document some important event. Like Common Sense, *Paul Revere's 1770 engraving of the Boston Massacre is a propaganda piece. Although the "massacre" was a minor scuffle incited by colonists, Revere portrays the British firing on a peaceful, unresisting crowd.*

have defended Turkey from the same motive, viz., for the sake of trade and dominion.

Alas! We have been long led away by ancient prejudices and made large sacrifices to superstition. We have boasted the protection of Great Britain without considering that her motive was interest, not attachment; and that she did not protect us from our enemies on our account but from her enemies on her own account, from those who had no quarrel with us on any other account and who will always be our enemies on the same account....

But Britain is the parent country, say some. Then the more shame upon her conduct. Even brutes do not devour their young nor savages make war upon their families; wherefore the assertion, if true, turns to her reproach....

Not one third of the inhabitants, even of this province [Pennsylvania], are of English descent. Wherefore I reprobate the phrase of parent or mother country applied to England only as being false, selfish, narrow, and ungenerous.

But admitting that we were all of English descent, what does it amount to? Nothing. Britain, being now an open enemy, extinguishes every other name and title; and to say that reconciliation is our duty is truly farcical. The first king of England of the present line (William the Conqueror) was a Frenchman, and half the peers of England are descendants from the same country; therefore, by the same method of reasoning, England ought to be governed by France....

Europe is too thickly planted with kingdoms to be long at peace; and whenever a war breaks out between England and any foreign power, the trade of America goes to ruin because of her connection with Britain. The next war may not turn out like the last; and should it not, the advocates for reconciliation now will be wishing for separation then, because neutrality in that case would be a safer convoy than a man-of-war. Everything that is right or natural pleads for separation. The blood of the slain, the weeping voice of nature cries, "'Tis time to part." Even the distance at which the Almighty has placed England and America is a strong and natural proof that the authority of the one over the other was never the design of heaven....

As to government matters, it is not in the power of Britain to do this continent justice. The business of it will soon be too weighty and intricate to be managed with any tolerable degree of convenience by a power so distant from us and so very ignorant of us; for if they cannot conquer us, they cannot govern us. To be always running three or four thousand miles with a tale or a petition, waiting four or five months for an answer, which, when obtained, requires five or six more to explain it in, will in a few years be looked upon as folly and childishness. There was a time when it was proper, and there is a proper time for it to cease.

Small islands not capable of protecting themselves are the proper objects for kingdoms to take under their care, but there is something very absurd in supposing a continent to be perpetually governed by an island. In no instance has nature made the satellite larger than its primary planet; and as England and America, with respect to each other, reverse the common order of nature, it is evident they belong to different systems—England to Europe, America to itself.

I am not induced by motives of pride, party, or resentment to espouse the doctrine of separation and independence; I am clearly, positively, and conscientiously persuaded that it is the true interest of this continent to be so; that everything short of that is mere patchwork, that it can afford no lasting felicity—that it is leaving the sword to our children, and shrinking back at a time when a little more, a little further, would have rendered this continent the glory of the earth.

THOMAS JEFFERSON (1743–1826)

Like Benjamin Franklin, Thomas Jefferson was a "Renaissance man" of many interests and achievements. His luminous political career included terms as a Virginia legislator, a delegate to the Second Continental Congress, Virginia governor, American minister to France, the first secretary of state, vice president, and finally, third president of the United States. Nevertheless, he once said that he wished to be remembered for only three things: drafting the Declaration of Independence, writing the Virginia Statute for Religious Freedom, and founding the University of Virginia.

Through his clear and eloquent prose, Jefferson breathed life into what we now regard as the most basic American ideals: liberty and equality. The collected writings of Thomas Jefferson fill about fifty volumes, largely due to his prolific correspondence. However, the only books he published during his lifetime were Notes on the State of Virginia, *which appeared in 1784 and 1785.*

The following excerpt is one of Jefferson's original paragraphs that the Second Continental Congress deleted from the final Declaration of Independence in 1776. Adding to the list of King George's offenses, it

"Determined to keep open a market where men should be bought and sold"

notes his roles in instituting slavery in the colonies, banning local legislatures from restricting the slave trade, and encouraging slaves to take up arms against the colonists in order to win their freedom.

This paragraph was omitted from the Declaration of Independence because delegates from the Carolinas and Georgia opposed it. Nevertheless, between the 1770s and 1790s, a debate about slavery swelled. Many white patriots who fought Britain for their own freedom realized that the fundamental right to liberty belonged to blacks as well. However, some wealthy planters saw slavery as a "necessary evil" to maintain their large farms and customary lifestyles.

Although Jefferson wrote stirring criticism of slavery, he appears to have held conflicting views. In condemning slavery in Notes on the State of Virginia, *he wrote, "Indeed, I tremble for my country when I reflect that God is just; and that his justice cannot sleep forever." At the same time, Jefferson did not free his own slaves, even though many of his contemporaries were doing so under Virginia's Manumission Act of 1782. Despite his ambivalence about slavery, Jefferson believed that the country could grow large and wealthy through agriculture. Ironically, Jefferson's fundamental ideals of liberty and equality were the very concepts that sparked the Civil War and, in the long term, overturned his idyllic vision of a nation composed of rural plantations.*

The missing paragraph from the Declaration of Independence

He [King George III] has waged cruel war against human nature itself, violating its most sacred rights of life and liberty in the persons of a distant people who never offended him, captivating and carrying them into slavery in another hemisphere, or to incur miserable death in their transportation thither. This piratical warfare, the opprobrium of INFIDEL powers, is the warfare of the CHRISTIAN king of Great Britain. Determined to keep open a market where MEN should be bought and sold, he has prostituted his negative for suppressing every legislative attempt to prohibit or to restrain this execrable commerce. And that this assemblage of horrors might want no fact of distinguished die, he is now exciting those very people to rise in arms among us, and to purchase that liberty of which he has deprived them . . . thus paying off former crimes committed against the LIBERTIES of one people, with crimes which he urges them to commit against the LIVES of another.

JOHN ADAMS (1735–1826) & ABIGAIL ADAMS (1744–1818)

"and the cry . . . was 'God save our American states'"

Abigail Smith, the daughter of a Massachusetts minister, and John Adams, the son of a farmer, embarked on their remarkably happy marriage in 1764. Soul mates and best friends, the two built a partnership that endured until Abigail's death fifty-four years later. As a lawyer, John Adams frequently traveled, so Abigail managed the children, the house, the family farm, and business affairs. Her management skills were a great asset when John Adams went to Philadelphia in August 1774 as a delegate to the First Continental Congress. By all accounts, Abigail ran the family and its business well, sparing them the financial losses many other "Founding Families" suffered. John Adams's lengthy absences were prolonged by serving in the Second Continental Congress, two vice-presidential terms, a term as president, and finally, as U.S. minister to France. Between 1774 and 1783, the couple exchanged some three hundred letters that document the Revolution, nation building, and their effects on this devoted family.

In July 1776, John Adams writes in patriotic language that Congress has unanimously declared independence from Great Britain. He also mentions their developing a "Plan of Confederation," the Articles of Confederation that ultimately proved too weak to govern the new nation. Abigail's responses do not use standard spelling because women did not attend formal schooling. Nevertheless, her letters convey her heartfelt support for independence as well as her grief in being separated from her husband. These candid expressions hint at the extraordinary sacrifices the "Founding Families" made in the name of public service. In addition, the letters include references to religious beliefs, scripture, and sermons, indicating that religious faith remained a central feature of this New England family.

John to Abigail
Philadelphia, July 3, 1776

Your favour of June 17, dated at Plymouth, was handed me, by yesterday's post. I was much pleased to find that you had taken a journey to Plymouth, to see your friends in the long absence of one whom you may wish to see....

One of the most impressive public buildings in colonial America was Pennsylvania's Old State House in Philadelphia, built between 1731 and 1753. The meeting place for the Continental Congress, this building became known as Independence Hall.

Yesterday the greatest question was decided, which ever was debated in America, and a greater perhaps, never was or will be decided among men. A resolution was passed without one dissenting colony "that these united colonies, are, and of right ought to be free and independent states, and as such, they have, and of right ought to have full power to make war, conclude peace, establish commerce, and to do all the other acts and things, which other states may rightfully do." You will see in a few days a declaration setting forth the causes, which have impell'd us to this mighty revolution, and the reasons which will justify it, in the sight of God and man. A Plan of Confederation will be taken up in a few days.

When I look back to the year 1761, and recollect the argument concerning Writs of Assistance, in the superior court, which I have hitherto considered as the commencement of the controversy, between Great Britain and America, and run through the whole period from that time to this, . . . I am surprized at the suddenness, as well as greatness of this revolution. Britain has been fill'd with folly, and America with wisdom, at least this is my judgment—time must determine. It is the will of Heaven that the two countries should be sundered forever. It may be the will of Heaven that America shall suffer calamities still more wasting and distresses yet more dreadfull. . . . The furnace of affliction produces refinement, in states as well as individuals. And the new governments we are assuming, in every part, will require a purification from our vices, and an augmentation of our virtues or they will be no blessings. The people will have unbounded power. And the people are extreamly addicted to corruption and venality, as well as the great. I am not without apprehensions from this quarter. But I must submit all my hopes and fears, to an overruling providence, in which, unfashionable as the faith may be, I firmly believe.

Abigail to John
Sunday July 14, 1776

By yesterday's post I received two Letters dated 3 and 4 of July and tho your letters never fail to give me pleasure, be the subject what it will, yet it was greatly heightned by the prospect of the future happiness and glory of our country; nor am I a little gratified when I reflect that a person so nearly connected with me has had the honour of being a principal actor, in laying a foundation for its future greatness. May the foundation of our new constitution, be justice, truth, and righteousness. Like the wise man's house may it be founded upon those rocks and then neither storms or tempests will overthrow it.

Abigail to John
Boston, July 21, 1776

I have no doubt but that my dearest friend is anxious to know how his Portia [Abigail's pen name] does, and his little flock of children....

I received a Letter from you by Wednesday['s] post 7 of July and tho I think it a choise one in the litterary way, containing many usefull hints and judicious observations that will greatly assist me in the future instruction of our little ones, yet it lacked some essential engrediants to make it compleat. Not one word respecting yourself, your health or your present situation. My anxiety for your welfare will never leave me but with my parting breath, tis of more importance to me than all this world contains besides. The cruel seperation to which I am necessatated cuts of[f] half the enjoyments of life, the other half are comprised in the hope I have that what I do and what I suffer may be serviceable to you, to our little ones and our country; I must beseach you therefore for the future never to omit what is so essential to my happiness.

Last Thursday after hearing a very good sermon I went with the multitude into Kings Street to hear the proclamation for independance read and proclamed. Some field peices with the train were brought there, the troops appeard under arms and all the inhabitants assembled there [the small pox parevented (prevented) many thousand from the country]. When Col. Crafts read from the belcona [balcony] of the State House the proclamation, great attention was given to every word. As soon as he ended the cry from the belcona, was "God save our American states" and then 3 cheers which rended the air, the bells rang, the privateers fired, the forts and batteries, the cannon were discharged, the platoons followed and every face appeard joyfull. Mr. Bowdoin then gave a sentiment, stability and perpetuity to American independance. After dinner the kings arms were taken down from the State House and every vestage of him from every place in which it appeard and burnt in Kings Street. Thus ends royall authority in this state, and all the people shall say "Amen."

In town squares throughout the colonies, the Declaration of Independence was read aloud, as Abigail Adams describes in her letter.

The Search for a National Identity

Between the signing of the Treaty of Paris in 1783 and the Battle of New Orleans in 1815, the United States of America began to forge a national identity. A heated swirl of international and domestic events prompted American leaders to discuss, write, and publish their ideals of government and nationhood. From these sometimes bitter debates, a governmental experiment emerged. A unique national literature was not far behind.

In this thirty-two-year period, the U.S. government was tested many times over. So fierce were political differences that at several points, the union itself was in doubt. In 1787 the Constitutional Convention proposed a new government. Despite heated debate, the Constitution was ratified in 1788 and a new form of national government was instituted.

George Washington became the first president the following year, but political differences soon grew. Wars in Europe threatened U.S. trade rights, causing arguments over whether the United States should ally itself with England or France. These debates helped formulate the first political parties. In the election of 1800, Thomas Jefferson, a Democratic Republican, defeated Federalist president John Adams. With the peaceful transfer of power between the two parties, the nation passed another test in forming a stable democracy. Later, continued trade disagreements with Great Britain led to the War of 1812. After routing the British at New Orleans in 1815, the United States had finally proven itself a unified nation, as respected as any in Europe.

As the United States defined its political landscape, the geographic landscape of the new nation changed as well. Through the Treaty of Paris and the Louisiana Purchase, the territories of the original thirteen states expanded fourfold. In 1804, President Thomas Jefferson sent Meriwether Lewis and William Clark to explore and document the land west of the Mississippi River.

The spirit of exploration spilled over into new literary subjects and forms. Noah Webster published the first American English dictionary in 1783 and declared that "America must be as independent in literature as she is in politics." In the 1790s, the first public schools were instituted in New England. As U.S. audiences became more literate, authors started to identify American subjects—including local settings, Native Americans, history, and tales. By the 1800s, white writers began to chronicle the expansive nation in short stories and novels. Moreover, Olaudah Equiano, a former slave, published a detailed autobiography, while Tecumseh, a great American Indian chief, made speeches to rally tribes against U.S. expansionism. Altogether these authors—like political leaders—helped mold a distinct identity for the new country.

Featured Authors

Philip Freneau
John Jay
Olaudah Equiano
Meriwether Lewis
William Clark
Washington Irving
Tecumseh
John Dos Passos

PHILIP FRENEAU (1752–1832)

*Known as the "Poet of the American Revolution," Philip Freneau made
his living as a seafarer and newspaper editor. In addition, he published
poems that scolded the British and sang the praises of the new nation.
After the Revolution, he became intensely involved in politics. In the
early 1790s, Freneau published his newspaper,* The National Gazette, *which criticized Alexander Hamilton and other Federalists who wanted
a strong national government.*

*By the time Freneau wrote "On the Emigration to America" in 1785,
the United States had signed the Treaty of Paris ending the war with
Great Britain two years earlier. In the treaty, Britain agreed to cede the
new nation a vast territory that extended west to the Mississippi River.
Unfortunately, in giving so much land to the United States, the British
overlooked the territorial rights of their Native American allies.*

*In 1785 and 1787, the U.S. government enacted Land Ordinances—
systems for settling western lands, organizing formal governments, and
admitting new states to the union. However, trouble ensued when pioneers ventured into the then-called "northwest territories," now in the
Midwest. In the 1790s, U.S. forces fought about eight Indian tribes
(called the Miami Confederacy) over rights to that land.*

*Freneau's poem, written in the postwar optimism of 1785, did not
anticipate these clashes. Instead, it follows a traveler from Europe to
America. Assuming the retreat of the Native tribes, Freneau hails the
new, expansive country and its bright future. The traveler motif allows
Freneau to juxtapose corrupt European monarchy with America's rational laws and freedom. However, he admits the embarrassment of slavery and predicts the rise of a better system.*

On the Emigration to America and
Peopling the Western Country

To western woods, and lonely plains,
Palemon [a name for a traveler] from the crowd departs,
Where Nature's wildest genius reigns,
To tame the soil, and plant the arts—
What wonders there shall freedom show,
What mighty states successive grow!

From Europe's proud, despotic shores
Hither the stranger takes his way,

*"No realm so
free, so blessed
as this"*

And in our new found world explores
A happier soil, a milder sway,
Where no proud despot holds him down,
No slaves insult him with a crown.

What charming scenes attract the eye,
On wild Ohio's savage stream!
There Nature reigns, whose works outvie
The boldest pattern art can frame;
There ages past have rolled away,
And forests bloomed but to decay.

From these fair plains, these rural seats,
So long concealed, so lately known,
The unsocial Indian far retreats,
To make some other clime his own,
Where other streams, less pleasing flow,
And darker forests round him grow.

Great sire of floods [Mississippi River]! whose varied wave
Through climes and countries takes its way,
To whom creating Nature gave
Ten thousand streams to swell thy sway!
No longer shall *they* useless prove,
Nor idly through the forests rove;

Nor longer shall your princely flood
From distant lakes be swelled in vain,
Nor longer through a darksome wood
Advance, unnoticed, to the main [ocean],
Far other ends, the heavens decree—
And commerce plans new freights for thee.

While virtue warms the generous breast,
There heaven-born freedom shall reside,
Nor shall the voice of war molest,
Nor Europe's all-aspiring pride—
There Reason shall new laws devise,
And order from confusion rise.

Forsaking kings and regal state,
With all their pomp and fancied bliss,
The traveler owns [admits], convinced though late,
No realm so free, so blessed as this—

The east is half to slaves consigned,
Where kings and priests enchain the mind.

O come the time, and haste the day,
When man shall man no longer crush,
When Reason shall enforce her sway,
Nor these fair regions raise our blush,
Where still the *African* complains,
And mourns his yet unbroken chains.

Far brighter scenes a future age,
The muse predicts, these states will hail,
Whose genius may the world engage,
Whose deeds may over death prevail,
And happier systems bring to view,
Than all the eastern sages knew.

JOHN JAY (1745–1829)

A "Founding Father" and diplomat of great influence, John Jay's contributions extended far beyond his native state of New York. He served in both the First and Second Continental Congresses and helped write the New York State Constitution. After the British defeat at Yorktown in 1782, Benjamin Franklin called on John Jay to help negotiate the Treaty of Paris. Thereafter, he was the first chief justice of the U.S. Supreme Court. His treaty with Britain in 1794, the Jay Treaty, was criticized by Democratic Republicans as too "soft on England."

Because John Jay supported a strong national government, the governor of New York, a political opponent, prevented him from attending the Constitutional Convention in Philadelphia in the summer of 1787. Even without Jay, most of the delegates decided that the Articles of Confederation were beyond repair and that a new federal government was needed.

However, the convention required nine of the states to ratify, or approve, the Constitution before it could be enacted. Two factions formed when the document was presented to the public: Federalists, who supported the Constitution's more powerful national government; and Antifederalists, who mistrusted centralized governmental authority.

At that time, New York was an influential state with a well-organized Antifederalist group. Most Federalists knew that even if they got nine

"this plan is only recommended, not imposed"

smaller states to approve the Constitution, they still needed the support of large states such as New York and Virginia for a legitimate government. Between October 1787 and mid-1788, three Federalists—Alexander Hamilton, John Jay, and James Madison—published essays under the pen name "Publius" to convince New Yorkers to ratify the Constitution. Collectively, these eighty-five articles are now called The Federalist Papers.

Over the years, Americans have read The Federalist Papers *to learn about the hopes, fears, and values that motivated the framers of the Constitution. In the following article, John Jay bases his argument for unity on the geography of the states, the common heritage of the people, revolutionary patriotism, and faith in the great statesmen who formed both the First Continental Congress and the Constitutional Convention.*

Although historians are uncertain whether The Federalist Papers *helped win the ratification of the Constitution, for 200 years politicians around the world have read these essays to gain insight into the arguments for and development of new republican governments.*

Federalist No. 2
Concerning Dangers from Foreign Force and Influence

To the People of the State of New York:

Nothing is more certain than the indispensable necessity of government, and it is equally undeniable, that whenever and however it is instituted, the people must cede to it some of their natural rights, in order to vest it with requisite powers. It is well worthy of consideration therefore, whether it would conduce more to the interest of the people of America that they should ... be one nation, under one federal government, or that they should divide themselves into separate confederacies....

It has often given me pleasure to observe, that independent America was not composed of detached and distant territories, but that one connected, fertile, wide-spreading country was the portion of our western sons of liberty....A succession of navigable waters forms a kind of chain round its borders, as if to bind it together; while the most noble rivers in the world, running at convenient distances, present them with highways for the easy communication of friendly aids, and the mutual transportation and exchange of their various commodities.

With equal pleasure I have as often taken notice, that Providence has been pleased to give this one connected country to one united people—a people descended from the same ancestors, speaking the same language, professing the same religion, attached to the same principles of government, very similar in their manners and customs, and who, by their joint counsels, arms, and efforts, fighting side by side throughout a long and bloody war, have nobly established general liberty and independence....

A strong sense of the value and blessings of union induced the people, at a very early period, to institute a federal government to preserve and perpetuate it. They formed it [the Confederation gov-

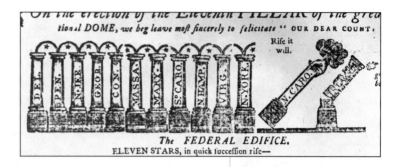

The FEDERAL EDIFICE.
ELEVEN STARS, in quick succession rise—

In July 1788, New York became the eleventh state to ratify the Constitution. The "Federal Edifice" above illustrates the order (from left to right) in which the first eleven states ratified the Constitution.

ernment] almost as soon as they had a political existence; nay, at a time when their habitations were in flames, when many of their citizens were bleeding, and when the progress of hostility and desolation left little room for those calm and mature inquiries and reflections which must ever precede the formation of a wise and well-balanced government for a free people. It is not to be wondered at, that a government instituted in times so inauspicious, should on experiment be found greatly deficient and inadequate to the purpose it was intended to answer.

This intelligent people perceived and regretted....Still ... being persuaded that ample security for both [union and liberty] could only be found in a national government more wisely framed, [the delegates] ... convened ... to take that important subject under consideration.

This convention composed of men who possessed the confidence of the people—many of whom had become highly distinguished by their patriotism, virtue, and wisdom in times which tried the minds and hearts of men—undertook the arduous task. In the mild season of peace, with minds unoccupied by other subjects, they passed many months in cool, uninterrupted, and daily consultation; and finally, without having been awed by power, or influenced by any passions except love for their country, they presented and recommended to the people the plan produced by their joint and very unanimous councils.

Admit, for so is the fact, that this plan is only *recommended*, not imposed....It is not yet forgotten that well-grounded apprehensions of imminent danger induced the people of America to form the memorable [First Continental] Congress of 1774. That body recommended certain measures to their constituents, and the event proved their wisdom; yet it is fresh in our memories how soon the press began to teem with pamphlets and weekly papers against those very measures....

They who promote the idea of substituting a number of distinct confederacies in the ... plan of the convention, seem clearly to foresee that the rejection of it would put the continuance of the Union in the utmost jeopardy....I sincerely wish that it may be as clearly foreseen by every good citizen, that whenever the dissolution of the Union arrives, America will have reason to exclaim, in the words of the poet: "FAREWELL! A LONG FAREWELL TO ALL MY GREATNESS."

Mercy Otis Warren's Antifederalist Paper
"The rights of individuals ought to be the primary object of all government"

In general, Antifederalists were not as well organized as those who supported the new Constitution. Nevertheless, they published several essays in opposition to a strong national government. In particular, Antifederalists feared that the new government would be as tyrannical as the monarchy they had just overthrown. Many Antifederalists also pointed out that individual rights were not mentioned in the Constitution. They wanted a list of these fundamental liberties included with the document to prevent the government from censoring the press, conducting illegal searches and seizures, mistreating suspected criminals, and limiting other freedoms.

Although the Constitution was ratified in 1788, Antifederalists could take solace. Five out of eleven states approved the Constitution with the recommendation that amendments guaranteeing individual rights be added. By December 1791, the Bill of Rights was ratified and became law.

The following excerpt about the need for a bill of rights comes from the Antifederalist pamphlet *Observations on the New Constitution.* It was published under the pseudonym "A Columbian Patriot." Most experts now believe the author was Mercy Otis Warren, a revolutionary patriot and playwright from Massachusetts. Although she lived at a time when women were discouraged from pursuing education and politics, Warren published many political pamphlets and satires, as well as a three-volume history of the American Revolution.

Observations on the New Constitution and on the Federal and State Conventions

There is no provision by a bill of rights to guard against the dangerous encroachments of power in too many instances to be named. But I cannot pass over in silence the insecurity which we [have] with regard to warrants unsupported by evidence. The daring experiment of granting writs of assistance in a former arbitrary administration is not yet forgotten in Massachusetts. Nor can we be so ungrateful to the memory of the patriots who counteracted their operation—so soon after their manly exertions to save us from such a detestable instrument of arbitrary power—to subject ourselves to the insolence of any petty revenue officer to enter our houses, search, insult, and seize at pleasure.

We are told by a gentleman . . . "that the whole constitution is a declaration of rights." But mankind must think for themselves, and to many very judicious and discerning characters, the whole constitution with very few exceptions appears a perversion of the rights of particular states and of private citizens. . . . The rights of individuals ought to be the primary object of all government, and cannot be too securely guarded by the most explicit declarations in their favor.

—A Columbian Patriot

OLAUDAH EQUIANO (1745–1797)

Olaudah Equiano lived in Nigeria until he was 11 years old, when he was abducted from his village and sold to British slave traders. He first came to the colonies to work on a Virginia plantation but then went to various areas of the country. Equiano was so disgusted by the bigotry of even northern cities that, upon buying his freedom in 1766, he left the colonies never to return. He spent the rest of his life in London and traveled widely as a seaman.

While the revolutionary period spawned a movement to free African Americans, by the 1790s emancipation had slowed. Southerners began to realize the difficulty of controlling their slaves among a population of freed blacks. Many slaves had run away, or attempted to do so, under the guise of being freed African Americans. Therefore, in 1792, the Virginia legislature passed a law making it harder for owners to liberate their slaves. Meanwhile, cloth factories in Britain created greater demands for American cotton. That trend, combined with the 1793 invention of the cotton gin, increased the reliance on slave labor in the South.

Consequently, slavery was an integral part of white and black lifestyles throughout the country, and it was central to the national identity of that period. Ironically, just when many Americans began to accept the practice, Equiano's autobiography, first published in 1789, gave them a victim's view. The following excerpt is a clear and frank account of the horrifying conditions aboard a slave ship.

"The stench of the hold . . . was so intolerably loathsome"

The Interesting Narrative of the Life of Olaudah Equiano
Chapter 2

The first object which saluted my eyes when I arrived on the coast was the sea, and a slave ship, which was then riding at anchor and waiting for its cargo. These filled me with astonishment, which was soon converted into terror when I was carried on board. I was immediately handled and tossed up to see if I were sound by some of the crew; and I was now persuaded that I had gotten into a world of bad spirits, and that they were going to kill me. Their complexions, too, differing so much from ours, their long hair, and the language they spoke (which was very different from any I had ever heard) united to confirm me in this belief. Indeed, such were the horrors of my views and fears at the moment, that, if ten thousand worlds had been my own, I would have freely parted with them all to have exchanged my condition with that of the meanest slave in my own country. When I looked round the ship too, and saw a large furnace of copper boiling, and multitude of black people of every description chained together, every one of their countenances expression dejection and sorrow, I no longer doubted my fate; and, quite overpowered with horror and anguish, I fell motionless on the deck and fainted....

I now wished for the last friend, death, to relieve me; but soon, to my grief, two of the white men offered me eatables; and, on my refusing to eat, one of them held me fast by the hands, and laid me across, I think the windlass, and tied my feet, which the other flogged me severely. I had never experienced anything of this kind before, and although not being used to the water, ... yet, ... could I have got over the nettings, I would have jumped over the side, but I could not; and besides, the crew used to watch us very closely who were not chained down to the decks, lest we should leap into the water; and I have seen some of these poor African prisoners most severely cut, for attempting to do so, and hourly whipped for not eating. This indeed was often the case with myself.

In a little time after, amongst the poor chained men, I found some of my own nation, which in a small degree gave ease to my mind. I inquired of these what was to be done with us? They gave me to understand, we were to be carried to these white people's country to work for them. I then was a little revived, and thought, if it were no worse than working, my situation was not so desperate; but still I feared I should be put to death, the white people looked and acted in so savage a manner; for I had never seen among any people such instances of brutal cruelty; and this not only shown towards us blacks, but also to some of the whites themselves....

At last, when the ship we were in had got in all her cargo, they made ready with many fearful noises, and we were all put under deck, so that we could not see how they managed the vessel. But this disappointment was the least of my sorrow. The stench of the hold...was so intolerably loathsome, that it was dangerous to stay there for any time, and some of us had been for permitted to remain on the deck for the fresh air; but now that the whole ship's cargo were confined together, it became absolutely pestilential. The closeness of the place, and the heat of the climate, added to the number in the ship, which was so crowded that each had scarcely room to turn himself, almost suffocated us. This produced copious perspirations, so that the air soon became unfit for respiration, from a variety of loathsome smells, and brought on a sickness among the slaves, of which many died—thus falling victims to the

Investigators described the "Middle Passage" with sketches, such as the one shown here, depicting stowage aboard a slave ship in the 1780s. This well-known ship, The Brookes, carried between 450 and 600 slaves.

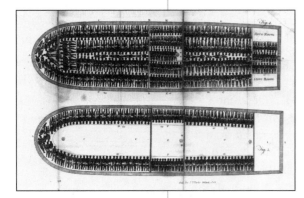

improvident avarice, as I may call it, of their purchasers. This wretched situation was again aggravated by the galling of the chains, now become insupportable, and the filth of the necessary tubs [toilets], into which the children often fell, and were almost suffocated. The shrieks of the women, and the groans of the dying, rendered the whole a scene of horror almost inconceivable.

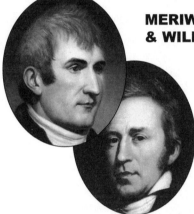

MERIWETHER LEWIS (1774–1809) & WILLIAM CLARK (1770–1838)

The story of the Lewis and Clark expedition is legendary, some might even say mythical. Nevertheless, the 8,000-mile trek presented real dangers, and the team's careful observations and diplomacy—let alone their safe return—were truly remarkable.

Both Meriwether Lewis and William Clark were born in Virginia. The two men met in 1795 while serving as officers in the army during the Indian wars in the northwest territory. In 1801, when Jefferson was elected president, Lewis became his personal secretary. In 1803, he asked Lewis to lead the "Corps of Discovery" to explore a route to the Pacific Ocean. Lewis asked Clark to co-lead the expedition.

A year later, the Corps, which included about four dozen members, set off from St. Louis. They used keelboats to haul themselves and their supplies up the Missouri River, across the plains and northward. In late 1804, the team enlisted the help of a French-Canadian trapper, Toussaint Charbonneau, and his pregnant Shoshone Indian wife, Sacajawea, to act as interpreters and guides. Sacajawea's mere presence was indispensable. When Native American tribes saw a female—and after January 1805, a female with an infant—among Lewis and Clark's party, they regarded the explorers as peaceful. Throughout the journey, many Indian tribes gave the Corps food, directions, and other supplies.

After reaching the Pacific coast in late 1805, the team returned triumphantly to St. Louis in September 1806. The expedition was considered a resounding success for many reasons. First, the adventurers had established friendly relations with Native Americans. They also sent back specimens and detailed descriptions of plants and animals for scientific study.

> *"Captain Clark saw Sacajawea . . . dance and show . . . the most extravagant joy"*

Finally, Corps members made maps and kept journals that accurately described the daunting wilderness for future traders and settlers. In short, the expedition began to chart the North American landscape and peoples, providing a basis for the identity of the expanding country.

After two editors had revised Lewis and Clark's journals, their notes were finally printed in 1814. The following excerpt describes events in August 1805. At that time, the party had reached the head-waters of the Missouri River at the present-day border between Montana and Idaho. Sacajawea had reached the lands of her tribe—the Shoshones. Recognizing many landmarks, she gave directions about which trails to take. At this point, Lewis and Clark realized they needed horses to ascend the Rocky Mountains. At the Shoshone camp, Sacajawea secured horses and guides for the explorers. A few days later, she helped Lewis and Clark avoid a disastrous loss of assistance from the natives.

The History of the Lewis and Clark Expedition
Volume II, Chapter XV, Across the Great Divide to Columbian Waters

Saturday, August 17th, 1805. On setting out at seven o'clock, Captain Clark, with Charbonneau and his wife [Sacajawea], walked on shore; but they had not gone more than a mile before Captain Clark saw Sacajawea, who was with her husband 100 yards ahead, begin to dance and show every mark of the most extravagant joy, turning round to him and pointing to several Indians, whom he now saw advancing on horse-back, sucking her fingers at the same time, to indicate that they were of her native tribe. . . .

While Sacajawea was renewing among the women the friendships of former days, Captain Clark went on, and was received by Captain Lewis and the chief, who after the first embraces and salutations were over, conducted him to a sort of a circular tent or shade of willows. . . . The moccasins of the whole party were then taken off, and after much ceremony the smoking began. After this, conference was to be opened. Glad of an opportunity of being able to converse more intelligibly, Sacajawea was sent for; she came into the tent, sat down, and was begin-ning to interpret, when, in the person of [Chief] Cameahwait, she recog-nized her brother. She instantly jumped up, and ran and embraced him, . . . weeping profusely. The chief was himself moved, though not in the same degree. After some conversation between them she resumed her seat and attempted to interpret for us; but her new situation seemed to over-power her, and she was frequently interrupted by her tears. . . .

About four o'clock the chiefs and warriors were collected and, after the customary ceremony of taking off the moccasins and smoking a pipe, we explained to them in a long harangue the purposes of our visit, making themselves the one conspicuous object of the good wishes of our government....We told them of their dependence on the will of our government for all their future supplies of whatever was necessary either for their comfort or defense; that, as we were sent to discover the best route by which merchandise could be conveyed to them, and no trade would be begun before our return, it was mutually advantageous that we should proceed with as little delay as possible; that we were under the necessity of requesting them to furnish us with horses to transport our baggage across the mountains, and a guide to show us the route; but that they would be amply remunerated for their horses, as well as for every other service that they should render us....

The speech made a favorable impression. The chief, in reply, thanked us for our expressions of friendship toward himself and his nation, and declared their willingness to render us every service....

Chapter XVI, With the Shoshones of Lehmi River

August 23rd. About three o'clock the expected [Shoshone] party arrived, consisting of fifty men, women, and children....We were ... resolved to move early in the morning....

August 24th. [After setting out six miles, the party camped for the night. However, they were not able to catch any game for dinner.] We therefore gave a little corn to those of the Indians who were actually engaged in carrying our baggage, and who had absolutely nothing to eat. We also advised Cameahwait, as we could not supply all his people with provisions, to recommend to all who were not assisting us, to go on before to their camp. This he did....

Sunday, August 25th. [But in the morning,] a few only followed his advice, the rest accompanying us at some distance on each side. We set out at sunrise, and after going seventeen miles halted for dinner, within two miles of the narrow pass in the mountains....

While at dinner we learned by means of Sacajawea that the young men who had left us this morning carried a request from the chief that the village would break camp and meet this party tomorrow, when they would all go down the Missouri into the buffalo country. Alarmed at this new caprice of the Indians, which if not counteracted, threatened to leave ourselves and our baggage on the mountains, or even if we reached the waters of the Columbia, to prevent our obtaining horses to go on further, Captain Lewis immediately called the three chiefs together. After smoking a pipe he asked them if they were men of their word, and if we could rely on their

The Lewis and Clark expedition fueled scientific and artistic interest in North American plants and animals. William Clark's journal was dotted with drawings, as shown here in the salmon trout illustration. By 1820, artists such as John James Audubon began documenting U.S. wildlife. His magpie is also shown below.

promises. They readily answered in the affirmative. He then asked if they had not agreed to assist us in carrying our baggage over the mountains. To this they also answered yes. "Why then," said he, "have you requested your people to meet us tomorrow where it will be impossible for us to trade for horses, as you promised we should? If," he continued, "you had not promised to help us in transporting our goods over the mountains, we should not have attempted it. . . . If you wish the whites to be your friends, to bring you arms, and to protect you from your enemies, you should never promise what you do not mean to perform. . . . If, therefore, you intend to keep your promise, send one of the young men immediately, to order the people to remain at the village till we arrive." The two inferior chiefs then said that they had wished to keep their word and to assist us; that they had not sent for the people, but on the contrary had disapproved of that measure, which was done wholly by the first chief. Cameahwait remained silent for some time; at last he said that he knew he had done wrong, but that, seeing his people all in want of provisions, he had wished to hasten their departure for the country where their wants might be supplied. He, however, now declared that having passed his word he would never violate it, and counter-orders were immediately sent to the village by a young man, to whom we gave a handkerchief, in order to insure dispatch and fidelity.

"there is something inexpressibly lonely in the solitude of a prairie"

WASHINGTON IRVING (1783–1859)

Washington Irving was the first American author to win international fame. He was born in New York and began his writing career by penning satirical essays on New York society. During the War of 1812, Irving wrote magazine articles about U.S. naval war heroes. However, his most famous work is The Sketchbook, *which includes "Rip Van Winkle" and "The Legend of Sleepy Hollow." With the publication of this work in 1819, many critics believe that Irving developed the short story genre.* The Sketchbook *was so popular that teachers used it in classrooms as a model of good prose writing. As a result, Irving influenced many young American writers such as Hawthorne and Longfellow.*

After working in Europe from 1815 to 1832, Washington Irving returned to the United States and immediately set off for an expedition to the west (an area now part of Oklahoma). His descriptions of buffalo hunting adventures were published in A Tour on the Prairies *in 1835. Subsequent books dealt with fur trading in Oregon and expeditions in the Rockies and Far West. Consequently, after spending seventeen years among "refined" European societies, Irving quickly became one of the most knowledgeable Americans on the West.*

This dramatic shift in perspective enabled Irving to identify typically "American" ideals and themes in these works. He celebrated the expansion of the frontier and the spirit of discovery that characterized the early nineteenth century. Drawing on his own rollicking fun on the prairies, Irving wrote, "We send our youth abroad to grow luxurious and effeminate in Europe. It appears to me that a previous tour on the prairies would be more likely to produce that manliness, simplicity, and self-dependence most in unison with our political institutions." In other words, the North American landscape helps mold better republican citizens than Europe.

Not surprisingly, Irving's western sketches yield some of the first depictions of "cowboy" icons. In the following excerpts from A Tour on the Prairies, *he describes his reliance on and attachment to his horse. Irving also illustrates the loneliness of the prairies and introduces the "dreary" howling of a wolf—subjects that readers will immediately recognize as quintessentially "American."*

A Tour on the Prairies

For my own part, I had been fortunate enough recently, by a further exchange, to get possession of the best horse in the troop; a full-blooded sorrel, of excellent bottom, beautiful form, and most generous qualities. In such situations it almost seems as if a man changes his nature with his horse. I felt quite like another being, now that I had an animal under me spirited yet gentle, docile to a remarkable degree, and easy, elastic, and rapid in all his movements. In a few days he became almost as much attached to me as a dog; would follow me when I dismounted; would come to me in the morning to be noticed and caressed; and would put his muzzle between me and my book as I sat reading at the foot of a tree. The feeling I had for this my dumb companion of the prairies gave me some faint idea of that attachment the Arab is said to entertain for the horse that has borne him about the deserts....

To one unaccustomed to it, there is something inexpressibly lonely in the solitude of a prairie; the loneliness of a forest seems nothing to it. There the view is shut in by trees, and the imagination is left free to picture some livelier scene beyond; but here we have an immense extent of landscape, without a sign of human existence. We have the consciousness of being far, far beyond the bounds of human habitation; we feel as if moving in the midst of a desert world. As my horse lagged slowly back over the scenes of our late scamper, and the delirium of the [buffalo] chase had passed away, I was peculiarly sensible to these circumstances.

The silence of the waste was now and then broken by the cry of a distant flock of pelicans, stalking like specters about a shallow pool, sometimes by the sinister croaking of a raven in the air, while occasionally a scoundrel wolf would scour off from before me, and, having attained a safe distance, would sit down and howl and whine, with tones that gave a dreariness to the surrounding solitude.

"the annihilation of our race is at hand unless we unite . . . against the common foe"

TECUMSEH (1768–1813)

The Shawnee chief Tecumseh was born in what is now Springfield, Ohio. In the early 1800s, he and his brother Chief Tenskwatawa, also known as the Prophet, opposed white settlement of Indian lands in the fertile Ohio Valley. Tired of the imposition of Christianity and white lifestyles on tribal ways, the Prophet promoted a return to traditional rituals, customs, and beliefs. In 1808, Tecumseh became the political leader of the Shawnees when he argued that the lands in the then-northwest territories belonged to all Native American tribes in common, and no particular tribe had the right to sell portions of it to the U.S. government. By 1811, Tecumseh's great charisma and oratorical skills had enabled him to unify Indian tribes along the western frontier, both north and south, in an effort to drive whites off their lands.

In 1811, after an Indian raid on a white settlement in Indiana, William Henry Harrison—governor of the territory—attacked Tecumseh's headquarters in Tippecanoe Creek, also in Indiana. At the time, Tecumseh was away recruiting warriors. Harrison's men defeated the natives and burned the town, which was located on sacred ground. Even though losses on both sides were heavy, the Battle of Tippecanoe disillusioned the Indians and weakened their confederacy. Later, during the War of 1812, Tecumseh allied himself with the British. When the great chief died in the Battle of the Thames (in Canada) in 1813, his confederacy fell apart.

The following excerpt comes from a speech Tecumseh made to the Choctaws and Chickasaws in spring of 1811, urging them to unite in an effort to win back their lands. After Tecumseh finished, a Choctaw chief delivered a differing opinion. Chief Pushmataha persuaded the two tribes that the Americans were their friends and that they should honor their treaties with them. In warning the Choctaws and Chickasaws against inaction, Tecumseh stated, "You, too, will be driven away from your native land." In that wisdom, Tecumseh himself proved to be a prophet, for the two tribes were forcibly removed to Oklahoma in the 1830s.

Tecumseh's Plea to the Choctaws and the Chickasaws

In view of questions of vast importance, have we met together in solemn council tonight.... The whites are already nearly a match for us all united, and too strong for any one tribe alone to resist; so that unless we support one another with our collective and united forces; unless every tribe unanimously combines to give check to the ambition and the avarice of the whites, they will soon conquer us apart and disunited, and we will be driven away from our native country and scattered as autumnal leaves before the wind.

But have we not courage enough remaining to defend our country and maintain our ancient independence? Will we calmly suffer the white intruders and tyrants to enslave us? Shall it be said of our race that we knew not how to extricate ourselves from the three most dreadful calamaties—folly, inactivity, and cowardice? But what need is there to speak of the past? It speaks for itself and asks, Where today is the Pequod? Where the Narragansetts, the Mohawks, Pocanokets, and many other once powerful tribes of our race? They have vanished before the avarice and oppression of the white men as snow before a summer sun. In the vain hope of alone defending their ancient possessions, they have fallen in the wars with the white men. Look abroad over their once beautiful country, and what see you now? Naught but the ravages of the pale face destroyers meet our eyes. So it will be with you Choctaws and Chickasaws! Soon your mighty forest trees, under the shade of whose wide spreading branches you have played in infancy, sported in boyhood, and now rest your wearied limbs after the fatigue of the chase, will be cut down to fence in the land which the white intruders dare to call their own. Soon their broad roads will pass over the grave[s] of your fathers, and the place of their rest will be blotted out forever. The annihilation of our race is at hand unless we unite in one common cause against the common foe. Think not, brave Choctaws and Chickasaws, that you can remain passive and indifferent to the common danger, and thus escape the common fate. Your people, too, will soon be as falling leaves and scattering clouds before their blighting breath. You, too, will be driven away from your native land ... as leaves are driven before the wintry storms.

According to the Indian Removal Act of 1830, the U.S. government offered five southeastern Native American tribes—the Choctaws, Chickasaws, Creeks, Cherokees, and Seminoles—land west of the Mississippi River in exchange for their homelands. In the 1830s, all but the Seminoles were forced to migrate to their new territories along the "Trail of Tears," so called because about one-third of these Indians perished on the long journey.

"Regiments lost their way in the fog. Men slipped in the gumbo and fell."

JOHN DOS PASSOS (1896–1970)

John Dos Passos was born in Chicago to a wealthy Portuguese-American family. After graduating from Harvard University in 1916, he joined a volunteer ambulance corps during World War I. The destruction and brutality of the war disillusioned him, so he became a radical, espousing communism for a period. During the 1920s and 1930s, he wrote novels using experimental forms to criticize American society. These avant-garde works made him famous. After World War II, however, his political philosophies changed, and his writings became more conservative. Some of his finest works of his later career were historical, including the selection shown here from The Shackles of Power: Three Jeffersonian Decades, *which was published in 1966. This excerpt narrates the Battle of New Orleans with telling detail.*

By the time British and American forces began to fight the Battle of New Orleans in January 1815, a treaty ending the War of 1812 had already been signed in December in Ghent, Flanders (now Belgium). Because the technology for travel and communication was much slower than today's, General Andrew Jackson and British commanders did not yet know the treaty had been signed. The Treaty of Ghent allowed the parties to assume the territories they controlled before the war, which is what the Americans wanted. Britain's war with France seemed finished, so the issues of unrestricted trade and impressment of American sailors were no longer relevant. Although in hindsight the Battle of New Orleans seems useless, the Americans' overwhelming victory promoted nationalism and made Jackson a hero.

The Shackles of Power: Three Jeffersonian Decades
Chapter VII, The Sevenfold Wonders of the Time

December 10 [1814], [General Andrew] Jackson was informed that the British fleet lay off the entrance to Lake Borgne. Four days later the sloops and barges of their landing parties captured the six American gunboats which were the city's only defense eastward....

Before Jackson had time to throw up defenses news came that a British force was seven miles from the city. Colonel Thornton, a veteran of Bladensburg, had pushed his barges up the bayou from Lake Borgne, surprised a company of Louisiana militia, and taken over Villeré plantation for British headquarters....

Before risking an assault the British officers decided to wait for their heavy artillery and for the arrival of Sir Edward Pakenham, who had been appointed Commander in Chief....

The delay gave Jackson two weeks to build breastworks about five miles below the city behind an abandoned canal that cut across the plain from the Mississippi to a cypress swamp. He protected his batteries with bales of cotton plundered from the merchants' warehouses.

The British allowed him another six days while they built emplacements for their artillery. They used bags of sugar which proved even less protection than the baled cotton. At the same time, they were digging a canal through the levee through which to push boatloads of troops to perform a flanking operation on the west bank of the river.

January 1, the preliminary artillery duel began. By the end of four hours superior American gunnery had silenced the British batteries. While he landed fresh guns from the fleet, General Pakenham, full of confidence in his overwhelming forces, allowed Jackson another week of grace. Jackson's breastworks were well manned now from the river to the swamp, but the militia on the west bank still lacked muskets and ammunition.

At dawn on January 8th, the redcoats were seen advancing through the white morning fog. Serried ranks firing by platoon advanced across the slimy flats. At the same time twenty-seven boatloads of British troops were crossing the Mississippi.

Regiments lost their way in the fog. Men slipped in the gumbo and fell. Shell and cannister from the American batteries plowed through the ranks. As the British emerged from the mist in front of the breastworks, American marksmanship shot them down man by man. General Pakenham was killed by a burst of grapeshot early in the day. His second in command was killed. A third major general was wounded. Scores of officers fell. By the time they retired to the camp the British had lost seven hundred killed and fourteen hundred wounded.

The American casualties were seven killed and six wounded. "This disproportion," wrote Jackson in his report, "must I know excite astonishment and may not be everywhere fully credited."

On the west bank of the Mississippi, the British made such headway that Jackson did not dare pursue the broken battalions ... back to their camp. He kept his men in their entrenchments until the British flanking party, dismayed by the loss of their generals, took to their boats. Meanwhile, expresses were galloping north with the news that New Orleans was saved.

After burning Washington in September 1814, the British sailed up the Chesapeake and bombarded Fort McHenry, near Baltimore, with cannon fire. When Francis Scott Key saw the American flag still waving the next morning, he wrote the words to the "Star Spangled Banner." Many historians view the Battle of Fort McHenry as the turning point in the war.

*B*etween the War of 1812 and the Civil War, the United States experienced dramatic growth and change in territory, population, technology, trade, and culture. The people began to think of their huge land as a nation and of themselves as Americans. However, sectional differences remained strong forces in the first half of the century—strong enough to lead to a bloody war.

The advent of canals, railroads, steamboats, and new roads increased trade among states. Thus, migrants could settle farther inland and still get their products to markets in the East. Between 1820 and 1850, immigration swelled, as European settlers sought economic opportunity. In those same years, the U.S. population grew from about 9.5 million to 23 million. Factories and urban centers flourished in the Northeast.

However, the South remained agricultural, largely unaffected by industrialization. Instead of relying on new technology, planters generally increased their productivity by adding laborers. Between 1810 and 1860, the slave population grew from a couple hundred thousand to almost 4 million.

These contrasting developments brought regional differences, or sectionalism, to a head. As the United States annexed Texas and won territory from Mexico, northern and southern states feuded over whether slavery would be legal in the new lands. Even after the passage of the Compromise of 1850, sectionalism persisted. By the time Abraham Lincoln was elected president in 1860, the southern states' threat of secession had become reality. The Civil War soon followed. The two sides battled so passionately that the war—initially expected to end in a year or two—dragged on for four devastating years. In the end, half-a-million Americans, mostly young men, had died.

Meanwhile, literature underwent many changes. Critics believe that the first classic period of American literature was born with the works of Ralph Waldo Emerson, Nathaniel Hawthorne, Herman Melville, Henry David Thoreau, and Walt Whitman. These writers identified American themes—such as self-reliance, Puritanism, morality, and democracy—which defined

Timeline

1820–21
Missouri Compromise is struck.

1830
Andrew Jackson begins forced removal of eastern Indians to the West.

1831
William Lloyd Garrison begins publishing *The Liberator*.

1835
The Alamo falls.

1840–57
Manufacturing, railroad construction, and foreign commerce boom.

1843
The Oregon Trail opens.

1845
The United States annexes Texas.

John O'Sullivan coins the phrase "Manifest Destiny."

1846
The United States goes to war against Mexico.

1848
The Women's Rights Convention is held at Seneca Falls, New York.

1850
The Compromise of 1850 is passed.

and reflected the American character. Many authors, such as Emerson, Frederick Douglass, and Margaret Fuller, were also orators. Lectures were popular entertainment during the period, and those who sought to abolish slavery or win rights for women delivered speeches to effect social change. American newspapers, already plentiful, grew dramatically in number, variety, and reach. The development of portable presses enabled printers to head west before communities had yet formed. There they published newspapers that heralded opportunities in frontier towns and encouraged settlement. Other presses were devoted to causes such as abolition or secession. During the Civil War, journalism ruled the day, as readers put aside poetry and novels in favor of news of the latest battles. American literature thus mirrored the great social changes and divisions of the era.

A Confident Nation

After the War of 1812, Americans gained confidence and pride in their nation as a spirit of unity and nationalism strengthened the union. The adoption of the U.S. Constitution established liberty and order, and the prospect for peace and economic growth stood before the nation.

Economic independence was just as important to the United States as political independence. Innovative internal improvements, such as better transportation and communication systems and a burgeoning manufacturing base, helped strengthen the country. Trade between the states increased as America experienced the first wave of the industrial revolution.

The growth of the country during the first half of the nineteenth century was extraordinary—by 1852, the U.S. population had doubled to 23 million. By the end of the 1840s, Texas and most of the American Southwest including California, Arizona, and New Mexico, were added to the country. The nation's "manifest destiny"—to stretch from the Atlantic to the Pacific Ocean—was almost complete.

The decades following the War of 1812 also brought about a renaissance in America's cultural identity. Prior to 1820, the United States had produced very few, if any, renowned writers. Many consider the years 1815 to 1861 to be the "First National Period" in American literature. Authors and poets such as James Fenimore Cooper, Nathaniel Hawthorne, Washington Irving, and Walt Whitman emerged to give America a new vision. These important writers believed that the political experiment of democracy had to be matched by radical new literature. Many literary works of the period celebrated the pioneering spirit of America, nationalism, and the strength of the individual. Others gave voice to social movements of the era such as abolition, temperance, and women's rights. New England transcendentalists led this new express of thought. Transcendentalist writers—including Ralph Waldo Emerson, Henry David Thoreau, and Margaret Fuller—embraced the meditative religions of the Orient, seeking ideas that transcended the limits of reason.

With the foundations of democracy firm, these and other artists provided the young nation with a maturing cultural identity. They helped make the nation whole, transforming a growing political and economic power into a cultural and artistic force as well.

Featured Authors

Ralph Waldo Emerson
Henry David Thoreau
Margaret Fuller
Walt Whitman
John L. O'Sullivan
Juan Nepomuceno Seguín

RALPH WALDO EMERSON (1803–1882)

Ralph Waldo Emerson has been recognized as the father of American literature, not only for his remarkable contributions as a poet, essayist, and orator, but also for the great influence he had on his contemporaries and generations of future writers. In 1825, Emerson attended Harvard Divinity School and four years later became minister of the Second Church of Boston. He soon resigned from the ministry and spent the next few years traveling in Europe. Emerson returned home and began a career as a lecturer.

Emerson was one of the leading voices in the transcendentalist movement. Transcendentalism was not a rigid belief system, but rather a loosely defined outlook on life that valued individual experience, self-reliance, and self-determination over established authority.

In 1817, Congress passed legislation to promote economic development in the United States. The federal government funded the construction of major roads and canals to connect major cities and improve trade. The Northeast became the manufacturing base of the United States. Factories were built and cities grew larger. By the 1840s, these improvements were having a major effect. The growth of its manufacturing sector strengthened America's economic performance and, consequently, its national resolve.

The following excerpt is taken from "The Young American," a lecture Emerson delivered before the Mercantile Library Association in Boston in February 1844. Emerson celebrates not only the wondrous economic and internal growth of America but also encourages the "young American" to help the country become a beacon of prosperity, morality, and justice.

"we shall yet have an American genius"

The Young American

America is beginning to assert herself to the senses and to the imagination of her children, and Europe is receding in the same degree. This, their reaction on education, gives a new importance to the internal improvements and to the politics of the country. Who has not been stimulated to reflection by the facilities now in progress of construction for travel and the transportation of goods in the United States?

This rage for road building is beneficent for America, where vast distance is so main a consideration in our domestic politics and trade....

River transportation was one of the major reasons for the rapid economic development of the United States in the nineteenth century. Steamboats, like the one pictured here, were a common sight on America's lakes and rivers.

Not only is distance annihilated, but when, as now, the locomotive and the steamboat, like enormous shuttles, shoot every day across the thousand various threads of national descent and employment, and bind them fast in one web, an hourly assimilation goes forward, and there is no danger that local peculiarities and hostilities should be preserved.

But I hasten to speak of the utility of these improvements in creating an American sentiment. An unlooked-for consequence of the railroad is the increased acquaintance it has given the American people with the boundless resources of their own soil. If this invention has reduced England to a third of its size, by bringing people so much nearer, in this country it has given a new celerity [speed] to time, or anticipated by fifty years the planting of tracts of land, the choice of water privileges, the working of mines, and other natural advantages. Railroad iron is a magician's rod, in its power to evoke the sleeping energies of land and water....

I look on such improvements, also, as directly tending to endear the land to the inhabitant. Any relation to the land, the habit of tilling it, or mining it, or even hunting on it, generates the feeling of patriotism. He who keeps shop on it, or he who merely uses it as a support to his desk and ledger, or to his manufactory, values it less. The vast majority of the people of this country live by the land and carry its quality in their manners and opinions. We in the Atlantic states, by position, have been commercial and have, as I said, imbibed easily an European culture. Luckily for us, now that steam has narrowed the Atlantic to a strait, the nervous, rocky West is intruding a new and continental element into the national mind, and we shall yet have an American genius....Without looking, then, to those extraordinary social influences which are now acting in precisely this direction, but only at what is inevitably doing around us, I think we must regard the land as a commanding and increasing power on the citizen, the sanative and Americanizing influence, which promises to disclose new virtues for ages to come....

It seems so easy for America to inspire and express the most expansive and humane spirit; new-born, free, healthful, strong, the land of the laborer, of the democrat, of the philanthropist, of the believer, of the saint, she should speak for the human race. It is the country of the future. From Washington, proverbially "the city of magnificent distances," through all its cities, states, and territories, it is a country of beginnings, of projects, of designs, and expectations....

Meantime trade had begun to appear: trade, a plant which grows wherever there is peace, as soon as there is peace, and as long as there is peace. The luxury and necessity of the noble fostered it. And as quickly as men go to foreign parts, in ships or caravans, a new order of things springs up; new command takes place, new servants and new masters. Their information, their wealth, their correspondence, have made them quite other men than left their native shore. They are nobles now, and by another patent than the king's. Feudalism had been good, had broken the power of the kings, and had some good traits of its own; but it had grown mischievous, it was time for it to die, and, as they say of dying people, all its faults came out. Trade was the strong man that broke it down, and raised a new and unknown power in its place....

The philosopher and lover of man have much harm to say of trade; but the historian will see that trade was the principle of liberty; that trade planted America and destroyed feudalism; that it makes peace and keeps peace, and it will abolish slavery. We complain of its oppression of the poor and of its building up a new aristocracy on the ruins of the aristocracy it destroyed.... Our part is plainly not to throw ourselves across the track, to block improvement, and sit till we are stone, but to watch the uprise of successive mornings, and to conspire with the new works of new days....

In every age of the world, there has been a leading nation, one of a more generous sentiment, whose eminent citizens were willing to stand for the interests of general justice and humanity, at the risk of being called, by the men of the moment, chimerical and fantastic. Which should be that nation but these states? Which should lead that movement, if not New England? Who should lead the leaders, but the Young American?...

[T]he development of our American internal resources, the extension to the utmost of the commercial system, and the appearance of new moral causes which are to modify the state, are giving an aspect of greatness to the future, which the imagination fears to open. One thing is plain for all men of common sense and common conscience, that here, here in America, is the home of man.

HENRY DAVID THOREAU (1817–1862)

Henry David Thoreau was a friend of Ralph Waldo Emerson and a fellow transcendentalist. Emerson's essay "Nature" influenced Thoreau by encouraging him to search for answers to spiritual questions in the physical or natural world. Thoreau's earliest writings were in the form of journals that contained careful observations of the natural world (indeed, some critics thought Thoreau was a botanist). This journey led

"Government is at best but an expedient"

him to live alone for two years in a cabin he built himself on Emerson's property on Walden Pond in Massachusetts. Thoreau searched the natural world for truths about spirituality and morality. He wrote Walden *(1854), an account of these experiences and self-reflections.* Walden *established Thoreau as a great literary figure and is often cited as an early influence of the modern environmentalist movement.*

Thoreau, an impassioned abolitionist, believed that government too often supported the tyranny of the majority and that the individual should never be obligated to condone unjust laws. Thoreau's classic essay, "Resistance to Civil Government" (1848) promoted passive resistance, a form of protest used to great effect in the twentieth century by Mohandas Gandhi, Martin Luther King, and antiwar protesters.

Resistance to Civil Government

I heartily accept the motto, "That government is best which governs least"; and I should like to see it acted up to more rapidly and systematically. Carried out, it finally amounts to this, which also I believe—"That government is best which governs not at all"; and when men are prepared for it, that will be the kind of government which they will have. Government is at best but an expedient; but most governments are usually, and all governments are sometimes, inexpedient....

This American government—what is it but a tradition, though a recent one, endeavoring to transmit itself unimpaired to posterity, but each instant losing some of its integrity? It has not the vitality and force of a single living man; for a single man can bend it to his will. It is a sort of wooden gun to the people themselves.... But it is not the less necessary for this; for the people must have some complicated machinery or other, and hear its din, to satisfy that idea of government which they have.

Governments show thus how successfully men can be imposed on, even impose on themselves, for their own advantage. It is excellent, we must all allow. Yet this government never of itself furthered any enterprise, but by the alacrity [speed] with which it got out of its way. *It* does not keep the country free. *It* does not settle the West. *It* does not educate. The character inherent in the American people has done all that has been accomplished; and it would have done somewhat more, if the government had not sometimes got in its way....

But, to speak practically and as a citizen, unlike those who call themselves no-government men, I ask for, not at once no government, but *at once* a better government. Let every man make known what kind of government would command his respect, and that will be one step toward obtaining it.

After all, the practical reason why, when the power is once in the hands of the people, a majority are permitted, and for a long period continue, to rule is not because they are most likely to be in the right, nor because this seems fairest to the minority, but because they are physically the strongest. But a government in which the majority rule in all cases cannot be based on justice, even as far as men understand it. Can there not be a government in which the majorities do not virtually decide right and wrong, but conscience?—in which majorities decide only those questions to which the rule of expediency is applicable? Must the citizen ever for a moment, or in the least degree, resign his conscience to the legislator? Why has every man a conscience then? I think that we should be men first, and subjects afterward. It is not desirable to cultivate a respect for the law, so much as for the right. The only obligation which I have a right to assume is to do at any time what I think right....

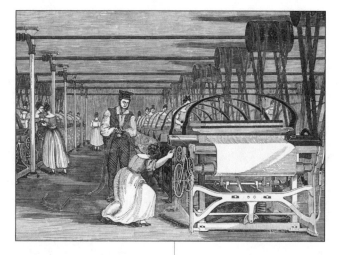

By the 1840s, the northeastern United States became the manufacturing base of the country. Textile mills sprouted up all across New England.

All men recognize the right of revolution; that is, the right to refuse allegiance to, and to resist, the government, when its tyranny or its inefficiency are great and unendurable. But almost all say that such is not the case now. But such was the case, they think, in the Revolution of '75. If one were to tell me that this was a bad government because it taxed certain foreign commodities brought to its ports, it is most probable that I should not make an ado about it, for I can do without them. [A]ll machines have their friction; and possibly this does enough good to counterbalance the evil. At any rate, it is a great evil to make a stir about it. But when the friction comes to have its machine, and oppression and robbery are organized, I say, let us not have such a machine any longer....

It is not a man's duty, as a matter of course, to devote himself to the eradication of any, even to most enormous, wrong; he may still properly have other concerns to engage him; but it is his duty, at least, to wash his hands of it, and, if he gives it no thought longer, not to give it practically his support. If I devote myself to other pursuits and contemplations, I must first see, at least, that I do not pursue them sitting upon another man's shoulders. I must get off him first, that he may pursue his contemplations too....

Unjust laws exist: shall we be content to obey them, or shall we endeavor to amend them, and obey them until we have succeeded, or shall we transgress them at once? Men, generally, under such a government as this, think that they ought to wait until they have persuaded the majority to alter them. They think that, if they should resist, the remedy would be worse than the evil. But it is the fault of the government itself that the remedy *is* worse than the evil. *It* makes it worse. Why is it not more apt to anticipate and provide for reform? Why does it not cherish its wise minority? Why does it cry and resist before it is hurt? Why does it not encourage its citizens to be on the alert to point out its faults, and *do* better than it would have them? Why does it always crucify Christ and excommunicate Copernicus and Luther, and pronounce Washington and Franklin rebels?

One would think, that a deliberate and practical denial of its authority was the only offense never contemplated by its government; else, why has it not assigned its definite, its suitable and proportionate penalty? If a man who has no property refuses but once to earn nine shillings for the State, he is put in prison for a period unlimited by any law that I know, and determined only by the discretion of those who placed him there; but if he should steal ninety times nine shillings from the State, he is soon permitted to go at large again.

If the injustice is part of the necessary friction of the machine of government, let it go, let it go: perchance it will wear smooth,—certainly the machine will wear out. If the injustice has a spring, or a pulley, or a rope, or a crank, exclusively for itself, then perhaps you may consider whether the remedy will not be worse than the evil; but if it is of such a nature that it requires you to be the agent of injustice to another, then I say, break the law. Let your life be a counter-friction to stop the machine.

"We would have every arbitrary barrier thrown down"

MARGARET FULLER (1810–1850)

Margaret Fuller has been called "the most important woman of the nineteenth century." In her short life, she was a teacher, literary critic, transcendentalist leader, and an early, influential advocate of women's rights.

Born in Cambridge, Massachusetts, Margaret Fuller became captivated by the transcendentalist movement in her 20s after she met Ralph Waldo Emerson, who became her friend, mentor, and prophet. From 1840 to 1842, Fuller edited The Dial, *a quarterly journal of transcendentalist thought. In her writing, she took ideas which began with Emerson, including doctrines of self-reliance and individualism, and applied them to women's causes.*

In 1845, Margaret Fuller's most important work, Woman in the Nineteenth Century, *was published. The book originated from Fuller's "conversations" with women whom she encouraged to think and speak freely. Fuller incorporated the material she gathered at these meetings into* Woman in the Nineteenth Century. *A classic of feminist thought,* Woman in the Nineteenth Century *helped lay the groundwork for the emerging women's rights movement.*

The institution of slavery made women more acutely aware of male dominance and oppression, leading many to become involved in the abolitionist movement. They believed that the spirit and principles behind abolitionism could also be applied to women's rights. In 1848, Elizabeth Cady Stanton and Lucretia Mott organized the first women's rights gathering, the Seneca Falls Convention in New York.

In this excerpt from Woman in the Nineteenth Century, *Fuller affirms her belief that women should assert themselves as individuals, not subordinates to men.*

Woman in the Nineteenth Century

We would have every arbitrary barrier thrown down. We would have every path laid open to Woman as freely as to Man. Were this done, and a slight temporary fermentation allowed to subside, we should see crystallizations more pure and of more various beauty. We believe the divine energy would pervade nature to a degree unknown in the history of former ages, and that no discordant collision, but a ravishing harmony of the spheres, would ensue.

Yet, then and only then will mankind be ripe for this, when inward and outward freedom for Woman as much as for Man shall be acknowledged as a *right*, not yielded as a concession. As the friend of the Negro assumes that one man cannot by right hold another in bondage, so should the friend of Woman assume that Man cannot by right lay even well-meant restrictions on Woman. If the Negro be a soul, if the woman be a soul, apparelled in flesh, to one Master only are they accountable. There is but one law for souls, and, if there is to be an interpreter of it, he must come not as man, or son of man, but as son of God.

Were thought and feeling once so far elevated that Man should esteem himself the brother and friend, but nowise the lord and tutor, of Woman,—were he really bound with her in equal worship,—arrangements as to function and employment would be of no consequence. What woman needs is not as a woman to act or rule, but as a nature to grow, as an intellect to discern, as a soul to live freely and unimpeded, to unfold such powers as were given her when we left our common home.

In 1848, women's rights advocates gathered at Seneca Falls, New York, for the Seneca Falls Convention, the first women's rights convention. Elizabeth Stanton (left) helped organize the convention. Here, she sits with Susan B. Anthony, another great women's rights advocate.

"Great is the greatest nation"

WALT WHITMAN (1819–1892)

Walt Whitman is one of America's most beloved poets. Born in Long Island, New York, Whitman, a self-educated man, worked as a teacher before moving to New York City to become a journalist. Enthralled by the city's vibrant cultural life, Whitman wrote poems and articles for popular magazines. In 1855, at the age of 36, Whitman published his own volume of poetry, Leaves of Grass, *which became an American literary classic.*

Whitman was a true patriot; his poetry celebrates America and democracy. "The United States themselves," Whitman declared in the preface to Leaves of Grass, *"are essentially the greatest poem." In* Leaves of Grass, *he embodies and writes from the perspective of all of the people of America; he is a man and a woman, a slave and a master, a lowly worker and a rich factory owner. Whitman called the third, revised edition of his poems the "New Bible" of democracy.*

"Great Are the Myths," which appeared in later editions of Leaves of Grass, *is a celebration of America—its land, ideals, and citizens.*

Great Are the Myths

Great are the myths .... I too delight in them,
Great are Adam and Eve .... I too look back and accept them;
Great the risen and fallen nations, and their poets, women, sages,
    inventors, rulers, warriors, and priests.

Great is liberty! Great is equality! I am their follower,
Helmsmen of nations, choose your craft .... where you sail, I sail,
Yours is the muscle of life or death .... yours is the perfect science ....
    in you I have absolute faith.

Great is today, and beautiful,
It is good to live in this age .... there never was any better.

Great are the plunges and throes and triumphs and falls of democracy,
Great are the reformers with their lapses and screams,
Great the daring and venture of sailors on new explorations.

Great are yourself and myself,
We are just as good and bad as the oldest and youngest or any,
What the best and worst did we could do,
What they felt .. do not we feel it ourselves?
What they wished .. do we not wish the same?

Great is youth, and equally great is old age .... great are the day and
    night;
Great is wealth and great is poverty .... great is expression and great is
    silence.

Youth large lusty loving .... youth full of grace and force and fascination,
Do you know that old age may come after you with equal grace and
    force and fascination?

Day fullblown and splendid .... day of the immense sun, and action
    and ambition and laughter,
The night follows close, with millions of suns, and sleep and restoring
    darkness.

Wealth with the flush hand fine clothes and hospitality:
But then the soul's wealth—which is candor and knowledge and
    pride and enfolding love:
Who goes for men and women showing poverty richer than wealth?

Expression of speech .. in what is written or said forget not that
    silence is also expressive,
That anguish as hot as the hottest and contempt as cold as the coldest
    may be without words,
That the true adoration is likewise without words and without kneeling.

Great is the greatest nation .. the nation of clusters of equal nations.

Great is the earth, and the way it became what it is,
Do you imagine it has stopped at this? .... and the increase abandoned?
Understand then that it goes as far onward from this as this is from the
    times when it lay in covering waters and gases.

Great is the quality of truth in man,
The quality of truth in man supports itself through all changes,
It is inevitably in the man .... He and it are in love, and never leave
    each other.

The truth in man is no dictum .... it is vital as eyesight,
If there be any soul there is truth .... If there be man or woman there is
    truth .... If there be physical or moral there is truth,
If there be equilibrium or volition there is truth .... if there be things at
    all upon the earth there is truth.

O truth of the earth! O truth of things! I am determined to press the
    whole way toward you,
Sound your voice! I scale mountains or dive in the sea after you.

Great is Language .... it is the mightiest of the sciences,
It is the fulness and color and form and diversity of the earth .... and
    of men and women .... and of all qualities and processes;
It is greater than wealth .... it is greater than buildings or ships or
    religions or paintings or music.

Great is the English speech .... What speech is so great as the English?
Great is the English brood .... What brood has so vast a destiny as the
    English?
It is the mother of the brood that must rule the earth with the new rule,
The new rule shall rule as the soul rules, and as the love and justice
    and equality in the soul rule.

Great is the law .... Great are the old few landmarks of the law ....
    they are the same in all times and shall not be disturbed.

Great are marriage, commerce, newspapers, books, freetrade, railroads,
    steamers, international mails and telegraphs and exchanges.

Great is Justice;
Justice is not settled by legislators and laws .... it is in the soul,
It cannot be varied by statutes any more than love or pride or the
    attraction of gravity can,
It is immutable .. it does not depend on majorities .... majorities or
    what not come at last before the same passionless and exact
    tribunal.

For justice are the grand natural lawyers and perfect judges .... it is in
    the soul,
It is well assorted .... they have not studied for nothing .... the great
    includes the less,
They rule on the highest grounds .... they oversee all eras and states
    and administrations.

Tocqueville in America
"I sought there the image of democracy itself"

America's democratic revolution caught the attention of many of the world's most renowned artists, intellectuals, and political leaders. Determined to see this new nation's growth and vitality for themselves, foreign visitors converged on the United States in the mid-nineteenth century. As one historian noted: "What had been a somewhat obscure, occasionally romanticized backwater of colonial exploitation became, virtually overnight, a phenomenon to be investigated, a political and moral experiment to be judged."

One foreign dignitary who was eager to examine the new democratic republic was a young French aristocrat named Alexis de Tocqueville. In 1830, Tocqueville had originally planned on traveling to America to examine new prison reforms. However, his mission soon evolved into an exhaustive study of American democracy, its institutions, and its people.

On May 11, 1831, the 25-year-old Tocqueville arrived in New York and spent the next nine months touring the country. He kept a series of notebooks in which he recorded his impressions of everything he saw and everyone he talked to. Tocqueville's notebooks eventually became *Democracy in America* (1835). *Democracy in America* was praised for its sharp, unbiased insights into American politics and society. In the book's introduction, Tocqueville explains the purpose of his mission:

I have not even pretended to judge whether the social revolution, which I believe to be irresistible, is advantageous or prejudicial to mankind. I have acknowledged this revolution as a fact already accomplished, or on the eve of its accomplishment; and I have selected the nation, from among those which have undergone it, in which its development has been the most peaceful and the most complete, in order to discern its natural consequences and to find out, if possible, the means of rendering it profitable to mankind. I confess that in America I saw more than America; I sought there the image of democracy itself, with its inclinations, its character, its prejudices, and its passions, in order to learn what we have to fear or to hope from its progress.

Democracy in America is considered by many to be one of the most comprehensive and insightful books ever written about the United States. Tocqueville's observations about religion, the press, class structure, race relations, and the role of government are revered by politicians, historians, and authors even today.

The perfect judge fears nothing ....he could go front to front before God,
Before the perfect judge all shall stand back .... life and death shall
    stand back .... heaven and hell shall stand back.

Great is goodness;

I do not know what it is any more than I know what health is .... but I know it is great.

Great is wickedness .... I find I often admire it just as much as I admire goodness:

Do you call that a paradox? It certainly is a paradox.

The eternal equilibrium of things is great, and the eternal overthrow of things is great,

And there is another paradox.

Great is life .. real and mystical .. wherever and whoever,

Great is death .... Sure as life holds all parts together, death holds all parts together;

Sure as the stars return again after they merge in the light, death is great as life.

"our manifest destiny to overspread the continent"

JOHN L. O'SULLIVAN (1813–1895)

John Louis O'Sullivan was founder and editor of the United States Magazine and Democratic Review *and later editor of the* New York Morning News. *He was one of the staunchest supporters of expanding the national boundaries of the United States. Most historians agree that O'Sullivan coined the term that stirred up nationalist and expansionist fervor among politicians and citizens in the 1840s. It was "our manifest destiny," he wrote in 1845, "to overspread the continent."*

Many used the philosophy of Manifest Destiny—which proclaimed that America's expansion was not only inevitable but divinely ordained—to justify the migration westward. Many Americans believed that the growth of the nation would inevitably foster democracy and freedom—even if expansionism led to war with Mexico. Others protested that the rhetoric of Manifest Destiny was essentially racist because it relied on notions of Latin American and Native American inferiority to whites.

The following excerpt is taken from O'Sullivan's 1845 editorial—typical of the nationalist propaganda of the times—in which he first used the phrase "manifest destiny." O'Sullivan calls for the annexation of Texas and predicts California will also soon "fall away" from Mexico.

Annexation

Texas is now ours....Her star and her stripe may already be said to have taken their place in the glorious blazon of our common nationality; and the sweep of our eagle's wing already includes within its circuit the wide extent of her fair and fertile land. She is no longer to us a mere geographical space—a certain combination of coast, plain, mountain, valley, forest, and stream. She is no longer to us a mere country on the map. She comes within the dear and sacred designation of Our Country....

Why, were other reasoning wanting, in favor of now elevating this question of the reception of Texas into the Union, out of the lower region of our past party dissensions, up to its proper level of a high and broad nationality, it surely is to be found, found abundantly, in the manner in which other nations have undertaken to intrude themselves into it, between us and the proper parties to the case, in a spirit of hostile interference against us, for the avowed object of thwarting our policy and hampering our power, limiting our greatness and checking the fulfillment of our manifest destiny to overspread the continent allotted by Providence for the free development of our yearly multiplying millions....

Texas has been absorbed into the Union in the inevitable fulfillment of the general law which is rolling our population westward; the connexion of which with that ratio of growth in population which is destined within a hundred years to swell our numbers to the enormous population of *two hundred and fifty million* (if not more), is too evident to leave us in doubt of the manifest design of Providence in regard to the occupation of this continent....

California will, probably, next fall away from the loose adhesion which, in such a country as Mexico, holds a remote province in a slight equivocal kind of dependence on the metropolis. Imbecile and distracted, Mexico never can exert any real governmental authority over such a country. The impotence of the one and the distance of the other, must make the relation one of virtual independence; unless, by stunting the province of all natural growth, and forbidding that immigration which can alone develop its capabilities and fulfill the purposes of its creation,

John Gast's Spirit of the Frontier *reflected many Americans' fervent belief that "manifest destiny"—the move to the West—was divinely ordained.*

tyranny may retain a military dominion which is no government in the legitimate sense of the term. In the case of California this is now impossible. The Anglo-Saxon foot is already on its borders. Already the advance guard of the irresistible army of Anglo-Saxon emigration has begun to pour down upon it, armed with the plough and the rifle, and marking its trail with schools and colleges, courts and representative halls, mills and meeting-houses. A population will soon be in actual occupation of California, over which it will be idle for Mexico to dream of dominion. They will necessarily become independent....Their right to independence will be the natural right of self-government belonging to

During the 1840s, thousands of settlers crossed the Great Plains, looking for adventure, fertile land, and economic opportunity.

The Oregon Trail
"Great changes are at hand"

The famous Oregon Trail was the overland route that brought the wagon trains of American emigrants to the West Coast beginning in 1843. The Oregon Trail was the only practical corridor to the West—it allowed settlers to get across the mountains. Indeed, many historians believe that, were it not for the trail, much of the American West would still be in the hands of Mexico and Canada. More than half a million people traveled west on the trail, which extended 2,000 miles. The journey was adversarial for most settlers—about 1 in 10 died along the way, and some walked the 2,000 miles barefoot.

Perhaps the most famous recounting of this journey was *The Oregon Trail* by renowned historian Francis Parkman. In 1845, Parkman, accompanied by a friend, trekked over the eastern part of the trail. They encountered storms and buffalo hunts, and met with Indians, soldiers and migrants—all recounted in vivid and compelling detail in *The Oregon Trail.* Parkman's writing was so detailed and energetic that many critics believe that he raised historical nonfiction to a literary art form. Parkman, while celebrating the beauty of the Old West, also mourns its passing. As settlers converge on the region, a new era draws nearer.

Great changes are at hand in that region. With the stream of emigration to Oregon and California, the buffalo will dwindle away, and the large wandering communities who depend on them for support must be broken and scattered. The Indians will soon be corrupted by the example of the whites, abased by whisky, and overawed by military posts; so that within a few years the traveler may pass in tolerable security through their country. Its danger and its charm will have disappeared together.

any community strong enough to maintain it—distinct in position, origin and character, and free from any mutual obligations of membership of a common political body, binding it to others by the duty of loyalty and compact of public faith....

Away, then, with all idle French talk of *balances of power* on the American Continent. There is no growth in Spanish America! Whatever progress of population there may be in the British Canadas, is only for their own early severance of their present colonial relation to the little island 3,000 miles across the Atlantic; soon to be followed by Annexation, and destined to swell the still accumulating momentum of our progress. And whosoever may hold the balance, though they should cast into the opposite scale all the bayonets and cannon, not only of France and England, but of Europe entire, how would it kick the beam against the simple, solid weight of the 250 or 300 million—and American millions— destined to gather beneath the flutter of the stripes and stars, in the fast hastening year of the Lord 1845!

JUAN NEPOMUCENO SEGUÍN (1806–1889)

Juan Nepomuceno Seguín was born into a prominent family in the city that is now called San Antonio, Texas. As a teenager in the 1820s, he came into contact with Anglo-Americans moving into the northern parts of Mexico. His family, along with other Mexican elites, welcomed the newcomers. As a young man, he publicly opposed the Mexican president and fought for the area's secession from Mexico and the formation of the Republic of Texas. After the Texas rebellion, he was elected mayor of San Antonio. However, some Anglos, who had recently moved to the area, spread rumors that he was a Mexican spy and harassed his family. Seguín was forced to move back to Mexico. There he was soon captured by authorities for his disloyalty and thrown into jail. He was then faced with a difficult choice: He could either spend the rest of his life in prison or join the Mexican army. Seguín accepted military service.

Acting on an offer from the Mexican government to cultivate land, Americans had moved to the northern parts of Mexico—regions that are part of the present-day United States and divided into states such as

"I seized a sword that galled my hand"

Texas and New Mexico. Groups of 200 or more families could settle large tracts of land if they agreed to become Mexican citizens and convert to Catholicism. By 1835, thirty-five thousand Americans lived in Texas. However, some settlers did not honor local laws, oppressed native Mexicans, and held slaves, which was illegal in Mexico.

When the Mexican government tried to regain control over the Texas area, Anglos and Hispanics living in the region rebelled. Within a year—after bloody battles, including the Alamo, in which 200 Texans, among them Davy Crockett, fought 3,000 Mexican troops—Texas gained its independence. Soon, however, the Republic of Texas sought annexation to the United States. The U.S.–Mexican War that followed tested Seguín's loyalties; he seemed to be forever divided between Texas and Mexico.

From his seat in the Texas senate, he had argued that laws be published in Spanish and English. Seguín also supported the system of slavery, which the Mexican government opposed. The Treaty of Guadalupe-Hidalgo (1848) ended the war by granting the United States massive territories that are now the states of California, New Mexico, Nevada, Utah, and Arizona in return for paying the Mexican government only $15 million. Even after the treaty was signed and Seguín was allowed to return to Texas, he spent the rest of his life moving between the two areas. Ultimately, Seguín was granted a military pension from Texas, but was denied one in Mexico, on the grounds that he was a Texas rebel.

In 1858, Seguín published Personal Memoirs, *an account of his legendary career. In the book's preface, Seguín recalls how he was slandered and endangered by his own countrymen.*

Personal Memoirs

A native of the City of San Antonio de Bexar, I embraced the cause of Texas at the report of the first cannon which foretold of her liberty; filled an honorable situation in the ranks of the conquerors of San Jacinto, and was a member of the legislative body of the Republic. I now find myself, in the very land, which in other times bestowed on me such bright and repeated evidences of trust and esteem, exposed to the attacks of scribblers and personal enemies, who, to serve, political purposes, and engender strife, falsify historical facts, which they are but imperfectly acquainted....

I have been the object of the hatred and passionate attacks of some few disorganisers, who, for a time, ruled, as masters, over the poor and oppressed population of San Antonio. They ... leagued together to exasperate and ruin me; spread against me malignant calumnies, and made use of odious machinations to sully my honor, and tarnish my well earned reputation.

A victim to the wickedness of a few men, whose imposture was favored by their origin, and recent domination over the country; a foreigner in my native land; could I be expected stoically to endure their outrages and insults? Crushed by sorrow, convinced that my death alone would satisfy my enemies, I sought for a shelter amongst those against whom I had fought; I separated from my country, parents, family, relatives and friends, and what was more, from the institutions, on behalf of which I had drawn my sword, with an earnest wish to see Texas free and happy....

Fate, however, had not exhausted its cup of bitterness. Thrown into a prison, in a foreign country, I had no alternative left, but to linger in a loathsome confinement, or to accept military service. On one hand, my wife and children, reduced to beggary and separated from me; on the other hand, to turn my arms against my own country. The alternative was sad, the struggle of feelings violent; at last the father triumphed over the citizen; I seized a sword that galled my hand. (Who amongst my readers will not understand my situation?) I served Mexico; I served her loyally and faithfully; I was compelled to fight my own countrymen, but I was never guilty of the barbarous and unworthy deeds of which I am accused by my enemies.

On March 6, 1836, the Mexican government sent 3,000 troops into San Antonio to attack Texans and American settlers. At the Alamo, 200 Texans fought 3,000 Mexican troops. Only a handful of people—mostly women and children—survived the thirteen-day assault.

Slavery and the Abolition Movement

From the 1830s to the 1860s, the economic, political, and cultural chasms between the North and South deepened. Slavery overshadowed all other political issues. A practice that sold human beings into bondage was testing the conscience of the nation and jeopardizing the very existence of the Union.

While the northern states were experiencing an industrial boom, the economy in the South remained largely agricultural, dependent upon cotton and slavery. Growing and harvesting cotton was time consuming and exhausting; planters sought slave labor as an economical way to expand their farms. Southerners resented the wealth amassed by northern businessmen from marketing the cotton crop. Northerners, on the other hand, attributed southern "backwardness" to its devotion to the "peculiar institution" of slavery.

Many northerners believed that slavery would eventually die out—but only if it was confined to the South and not permitted to take hold in new territories. However, proponents of slavery called for all lands acquired from Mexico, including California, to be thrown open to slaveholders. The Compromise of 1850 admitted California as a free state, but also implemented a stronger Fugitive Slave Law, which gave slaveholders new powers to recapture escaped slaves. Many hoped that the compromise would prevent the issue of slavery from becoming a greater source of division in the country. However, the Supreme Court ruled in *Dred Scott v. Sanford* (1857) that a slave did not become free when taken into free territory, that Congress could not bar slavery from any territory, and that blacks could not be citizens. The decision, a blow to abolitionists and a victory for slaveholders, worsened the rift between North and South.

During this sectional crisis, abolitionists promoted a universal system of morality and human rights. The motto of Frederick Douglass's newspaper, *The North Star,* summarized abolitionist views: "Right is of no sex. Truth is of no color." Historians generally credit William Lloyd Garrison—and the first issue of his influential newspaper, *The Liberator,* in 1831—with initiating the American abolitionist movement. Many abolitionists were known not only for their persuasive writings, but also for their powerful oratory. Some, such as Angelina Grimké Weld, used traditional sermons to deliver their moral messages. These men and women detailed the inhumanity of slavery and demanded an end to the system. On the other hand, conservative southern authors, such as George Fitzhugh, sought to justify the slaveholding plantation system with economic and paternal arguments.

Featured Authors

Frederick Douglass
Harriet Jacobs
Harriet Beecher Stowe
George Fitzhugh
Angelina Grimké Weld
John Greenleaf Whittier

FREDERICK DOUGLASS
(1818–1895)

Frederick Douglass, perhaps the most influential African American of the nineteenth century, was a prominent abolitionist, social reformer, orator, journalist, and author. Born a slave in Maryland, Douglass escaped from slavery when he was 20 years old. He then married Anna Murray, a free black woman, and they moved to Massachusetts to start a new life. Like many former slaves, Douglass renamed himself—from Frederick Bailey—to avoid recapture and mark his absolute break from the binds of slavery.

Douglass became an avid reader of William Lloyd Garrison's abolitionist newspaper, The Liberator. *Garrison was impressed with Douglass and encouraged him to recount his experiences as a slave to audiences. A commanding and eloquent orator, Douglass went on to address numerous abolitionist gatherings and became a tireless, lifelong advocate of racial equality.*

In 1845, Douglass published the first version of his memoirs, Narrative of the Life of Frederick Douglass. *The book depicts in graphic detail the strenuous labor in tobacco and cotton fields as well as the physical punishment which many plantation slaves endured. The volume became a best-seller and raised Douglass's profile. His freedom jeopardized, Douglass hurriedly traveled to Great Britain. Upon his return two years later, Douglass founded the abolitionist newspaper,* The North Star.

Narrative of the Life of Frederick Douglass *is one of the most famous slave narratives. Slave narratives documented slave life from the perspective of firsthand experience. These works were widely read by abolitionists, who were affected by the harrowing accounts of slave life in their pages. Not only revered as vital historical documents, slave narratives also influenced major American literary works, such as Harriet Beecher Stowe's* Uncle Tom's Cabin, *Mark Twain's* Huckleberry Finn, *and much later, Toni Morrison's* Beloved.

In the following excerpt from Narrative of the Life of Frederick Douglass, *Douglass recounts how a battle with Mr. Covey, a notorious slavebreaker, rejuvenated his spirit to live and his determination to win his freedom.*

"cowardice departed, bold defiance took its place"

Narrative of the Life of Frederick Douglass
Chapter X

On one of the hottest days of the month of August, 1833, Bill Smith, William Hughes, a slave named Eli, and myself, were engaged in fanning wheat. Hughes was clearing the fanned wheat from before the fan. Eli was turning, Smith was feeding, and I was carrying wheat to the fan. The work was simple, requiring strength rather than intellect; yet, to one entirely unused to such work, it came very hard. About three o'clock of that day, I broke down; my strength failed me....The fan of course stopped; every one had his own work to do; and no one could do the work of the other, and have his own go on at the same time.

Mr. Covey was at the house, about one hundred yards from the treading-yard where we were fanning. On hearing the fan stop, he left immediately, and came to the spot where we were....He then asked where I was. He was told by one of the hands. He came to the spot, and, after looking at me awhile, asked me what was the matter. I told him as well as I could, for I scarce had strength to speak. He then gave me a savage kick in the side, and told me to get up. I tried to do so, but fell back in the attempt. He gave me another kick, and again told me to rise. I again tried, and succeeded in gaining my feet; but, stooping to get the tub with which I was feeding the fan, I again staggered and fell.

While down in this situation, Mr. Covey took up the hickory slat with which Hughes had been striking off the half-bushel measure, and with it gave me a heavy blow upon the head, making a large wound, and the blood ran freely; and with this again told me to get up. I made no effort to comply, having now made up my mind to let him do his worst. In a short time after receiving this blow, my head grew better. Mr. Covey had now left me to my fate. At this moment I resolved, for the first time, to go to my master, enter a complaint, and ask his protection. In order to do this, I must that afternoon walk seven miles; and this, under the circumstances, was truly a severe undertaking....I succeeded in getting a considerable distance on my way to the woods, when Covey discovered me, and called after me to come back, threatening what he would do if I did not come.

I disregarded both his calls and his threats, and made my way to the woods as fast as my feeble state would allow....I had not gone far before my little strength again failed me. I could go no farther. I fell down, and lay for a considerable time. The blood was yet oozing from the wound on my head. For a time I thought I should bleed to death; and think now that I should have done so, but that the blood so matted my hair as to stop the wound. After lying there about three quarters of an hour, I nerved myself up again, and started on my way, through bogs and briers, barefooted and bareheaded, tearing my feet sometimes at nearly every step; and after a journey of about seven miles, occupying some five hours to perform it, I arrived at master's store. I then presented an appearance enough to affect any but a heart of iron....

I told him all the circumstances as well as I could, and it seemed, as I spoke, at times to affect him.... Master Thomas ridiculed the idea that there was any danger of Mr. Covey's killing me, and said that he knew Mr. Covey; that he was a good man, and that he could not think of taking me from him; that, should he do so, he would lose the whole year's wages; that I belonged to Mr. Covey for one year, and that I must go back to him....

I got no supper that night, or breakfast that morning. I reached Covey's about nine o'clock; and just as I was getting over the fence that divided Mrs. Kemp's fields from ours, out ran Covey with his cowskin, to give me another whipping. Before he could reach me, I succeeded in getting to the cornfield; and as the corn was very high, it afforded me the means of hiding....

I spent that day mostly in the woods, having the alternative before me,—to go home and be whipped to death, or stay in the woods and be starved to death. That night, I fell in with Sandy Jenkins, a slave with whom I was somewhat acquainted.... I found Sandy an old adviser. He told me, with great solemnity, I must go back to Covey; but that before I went, I must go with him into another part of the woods, where there was a certain *root,* which, if I would take some of it with me, carrying it *always on my right side,* would render it impossible for Mr. Covey, or any other white man, to whip me....

Nat Turner's Rebellion
"blood flowed in streams"

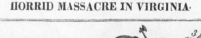

In August 1831, Nat Turner, a 31-year-old slave in Virginia, led the most famous and violent slave revolt in U.S. history. Turner and his followers trekked through several plantations, killing fifty-seven white men, women, and children. After a six-week-long manhunt, Turner was caught, convicted, and executed along with his accomplices. In his confession, Turner, a preacher and self-described prophet, explained that he had a "revelation which fully confirmed me in the impression that I was ordained for some great purpose, in the hands of the Almighty. . . . I saw white spirits and black spirits engaged in battle, and the sun was darkened— the thunder rolled in the Heavens, and blood flowed in streams." Turner's rebellion hardened antiabolitionist sentiment in the South and led to a tightening of slave codes and laws.

To please him, I at length took the root, and, according to his direction, carried it upon my right side. This was Sunday morning. I immediately started for home; and upon entering the yard gate, out came Mr. Covey on his way to meeting. He spoke to me very kindly, bade me drive the pigs from a lot near by, and passed on towards the church. Now, this singular conduct of Mr. Covey really made me begin to think that there was something in the *root* which Sandy had given me....

All went well till Monday morning. On this morning, the virtue of the *root* was fully tested. Long before daylight, I was called to go and rub, curry, and feed, the horses. I obeyed, and was glad to obey. But whilst thus engaged, whilst in the act of throwing down some blades from the loft, Mr. Covey entered the stable with a long rope; and just as I was half out of the loft, he caught hold of my legs, and was about tying me. As soon as I found what he was up to, I gave a sudden spring, and as I did so, he holding to my legs, I was brought sprawling on the stable floor.

Mr. Covey seemed now to think he had me, and could do what he pleased; but at this moment—from whence came the spirit I don't know—I resolved to fight; and, suiting my action to the resolution, I seized Covey hard by the throat; and as I did so, I rose. He held on to me, and I to him. My resistance was so entirely unexpected that Covey seemed taken all aback. He trembled like a leaf. This gave me assurance, and I held him uneasy, causing the blood to run where I touched him with the ends of my fingers. Mr. Covey soon called out to Hughes for help. Hughes came, and while Covey held me, attempted to tie my right hand. While he was in the act of doing so, I watched my chance, and gave him a heavy kick close under the ribs. This kick fairly sickened Hughes, so that he left me in the hands of Mr. Covey. This kick had the effect of not only weakening Hughes, but Covey also. When he saw Hughes bending over with pain, his courage quailed. He asked me if I meant to persist in my resistance. I told him I did, come what might; that he had used me like a brute for six months, and that I was determined to be used so no longer. With that, he strove to drag me to a stick that was lying just out of the stable door.

He meant to knock me down. But just as he was leaning over to get the stick, I seized him with both hands by his collar, and brought him by a sudden snatch to the ground. By this time, Bill came. Covey called upon him for assistance. Bill wanted to know what he could do. Covey said, "Take hold of him, take hold of him!" Bill said his master hired him out to work, and not to help to whip me; so he left Covey and myself to fight our own battle out. We were at it for nearly two hours. Covey at length let me go, puffing and blowing at a great rate, saying that if I had not resisted, he would not have whipped me half so much. The truth was, that he had not whipped me at all. I considered him as getting entirely the worst end of the bargain; for he had drawn no blood from me, but I had from him. The whole six months afterwards, that I spent with Mr. Covey, he never laid the weight of his finger upon me in anger. He would occasionally say, he didn't want to get hold of me again. "No," thought I, "you need not; for you will come off worse than you did before."

This battle with Mr. Covey was the turning-point in my career as a slave. It rekindled the few expiring embers of freedom, and revived within me a sense of my own manhood. It recalled the departed self-confidence, and inspired me again with a determination to be free. The gratification afforded by the triumph was a full compensation for whatever else might follow, even death itself.... I felt as I never felt before. It was a glorious resurrection, from the tomb of slavery, to the heaven of freedom. My long-crushed spirit rose, cowardice departed, bold defiance took its place; and I now resolved that, however long I might remain a slave in form, the day had passed forever when I could be a slave in fact. I did not hesitate to let it be known of me, that the white man who expected to succeed in whipping, must also succeed in killing me.

HARRIET JACOBS (1813–1897)

Harriet Jacobs was born a slave in North Carolina. Her mistress died when Jacobs was 11, and she was moved to the home of Dr. James Norcom, her new master. As Jacobs grew older, she was subjected to constant sexual harassment at the hands of Norcom. As a means of self-defense, Jacobs had a relationship with her white neighbor, which resulted in the births of her two children. In retaliation, Norcom sent Jacobs to work on a plantation. She soon escaped and hid with her grandmother, who was a freewoman and ran a bakery out of her home, near Norcom's house. Jacobs lived in her grandmother's cramped attic crawlspace for almost seven years, as she waited for the right moment to escape to the North.

The risks involved in trying to escape were immense; many runaways were recaptured and were tortured or killed as an example to other slaves. Thousands of slaves were successful and made the perilous journey to the North on their own or with the help of the informal network of abolitionists called "the underground railroad." As part of the "railroad" network, many escaped slaves returned to the South and risked their own reenslavement to guide others north to freedom.

Jacobs eventually found her way to the North. There, she was encouraged by friends to write her memoirs. In 1861, Jacobs (under the pen name Linda Brent) published her autobiography, Incidents in the Life of a Slave Girl, *in which she recounts in detail the years of mistreatment at*

"I resolved to leave them that night"

the hands of Dr. Norcom (Mr. Flint) and her courageous escape from
slavery. In the following excerpt, Jacobs describes the fateful night she
decided to flee Norcom's house and begin her long journey to freedom.

Incidents in the Life of a Slave Girl
XVII. The Flight

Mr. Flint was hard pushed for house servants, and rather than lose me he had restrained his malice. I did my work faithfully, though not, of course, with a willing mind. They were evidently afraid I should leave them. Mr. Flint wished that I should sleep in the great house instead of the servants' quarters. His wife agreed to the proposition, but said I mustn't bring my bed into the house, because it would scatter feathers on her carpet. I knew when I went there that they would never think of such a thing as furnishing a bed of any kind for me and my little one. I therefore carried my own bed, and now I was forbidden to use it. I did as I was ordered. But now that I was certain my children were to be put in their power, in order to give them a stronger hold on me, I resolved to leave them that night. I remembered the grief this step would bring upon my dear old grandmother; and nothing less than the freedom of my children would have induced me to disregard her advice....

I shut all the windows, locked all the doors, and went up to the third story, to wait till midnight. How long those hours seemed, and how fervently I prayed that God would not forsake me in this hour of utmost need! I was about to risk every thing on the throw of a die; and if I failed, O what would become of me and my poor children? They would be made to suffer for my fault.

At half past twelve I stole softly down stairs. I stopped on the second floor, thinking I heard a noise. I felt my way down into the parlor, and looked out of the window. The night was so intensely dark that I could see nothing. I raised the window very softly and jumped out. Large drops of rain were falling, and the darkness bewildered me. I dropped on my knees, and breathed a short prayer to God for guidance and protection. I groped my way to the road, and rushed towards the town with almost lightning speed. I arrived at my grandmother's house, but dared not see her. She would say, "Linda, you are killing me;" and I knew that would unnerve me. I tapped softly at the window of a room, occupied by a woman, who had lived in the house several years. I knew she was a faithful friend, and could be trusted with my secret. I tapped several times before she heard me. At last she raised the window, and I whispered, "Sally, I have run away. Let me in, quick." She opened the door softly, and said in low tones, "For God's sake, don't. Your grandmother is trying to buy you and de chillern. Mr. Sands was here last week. He tole her he was going away on business, but he wanted her to go ahead about buying you and de chillern, and he would help her all he could. Don't run away, Linda. Your grand-mother is all bowed down wid trouble now."

I replied, "Sally, they are going to carry my children to the plantation tomorrow; and they will never sell them to anybody so long as they have me in their power. Now, would you advise me to go back?"

"No, chile, no," answered she. "When dey finds you is gone, dey won't want de plague ob de chillern; but where is you going to hide? Dey knows ebery inch ob dis house."

I told her I had a hiding-place, and that was all it was best for her to know. I asked her to go into my room as soon as it was

The desperation that motivated many slaves to steal away is accurately captured in A Ride for Liberty, painted by Eastman Johnson in 1862.

light, and take all my clothes out of my trunk, and pack them in hers; for I knew Mr. Flint and the constable would be there early to search my room. I feared the sight of my children would be too much for my full heart; but I could not go out into the uncertain future without one last look. I bent over the bed where lay my little Benny and baby Ellen. Poor little ones! fatherless and motherless! Memories of their father came over me. He wanted to be kind to them; but they were not all to him, as they were to my womanly heart. I knelt and prayed for the innocent little sleepers. I kissed them lightly, and turned away....

Early the next morning Mr. Flint was at my grandmother's inquiring for me. She told him she had not seen me, and supposed I was at the planta-tion. He watched her face narrowly, and said, "Don't you know anything about her running off?" She assured him that she did not. He went on to say, "Last night she ran off without the least provocation. We had treated her very kindly. My wife liked her. She will soon be found and brought back. Are her children with you?" When told that they were, he said, "I am very glad to hear that. If they are here, she cannot be far off. If I find out that any of my niggers have had any thing to do with this damned business, I'll give 'em five hundred lashes." As he started to go to his father's, he turned round and added, persuasively, "Let her be brought back, and she shall have her children to live with her."

The tidings made the old doctor rave and storm at a furious rate. It was a busy day for them. My grandmother's house was searched from top to bottom. As my trunk was empty, they concluded I had taken my clothes with me. Before ten o'clock every vessel northward bound was thoroughly examined, and the law against harboring fugitives was read to all on board. At night a watch was set over the town. Knowing how distressed my grandmother would be, I wanted to send her a message; but it could not be done. Every one who went in or out of her house was closely watched. The doctor said he would take my children, unless she became responsible for them; which of course she willingly did. The next day was spent in searching. Before night, the following advertisement was posted at every corner, and in every public place for miles round:—

> "$300 REWARD! Ran away from the subscriber, an intelligent, bright, mulatto girl, named Linda, 21 years age. Five feet four inches high. Dark eyes, and black hair inclined to curl; but it can be made straight. Has a decayed spot on a front tooth. She can read and write, and in all probability will try to get to the Free States. All persons are forbidden, under penalty of the law, to harbor or employ said slave. $150 will be given to whoever takes her in the state, and $300 if taken out of the state and delivered to me, or lodged in jail.
>
> DR. FLINT."

"something
unutterably
horrible
and cruel"

HARRIET BEECHER STOWE (1811–1896)

Harriet Beecher Stowe was born June 14, 1811, the seventh child of a famous Protestant preacher. Harriet worked as a teacher and soon began writing for local and religious periodicals. During her life, she wrote poems, travel books, biographical sketches, and children's books, as well as novels.

Stowe is predominantly known for her first novel, Uncle Tom's Cabin, *published in 1852.* Uncle Tom's Cabin *focused public interest on the issue of slavery and was deeply controversial. Stowe was familiar with slavery, the antislavery movement, and the underground railroad because Kentucky, across the Ohio River from Cincinnati, Ohio, where she had lived, was a slave state. Stowe portrays not only the daily agonies of slavery, but the hypocrisy of Christian families holding slaves.*

Uncle Tom's Cabin *is unquestionably one of the most important novels in U.S. history. The book hardened militant antislavery sentiment in the North, making civil war between the North and South inevitable. President Abraham Lincoln, when introduced to Stowe at the White House in 1863, reportedly said, "So this is the little lady who made this big war."*

Long after slaves underwent separation from their families in their native lands and endured forced passage to the United States, future generations of slaves continued to face the threat of being sold away from their siblings, spouses, and children. With the rise of the cotton industry, many slaves were sold "down the river" to large plantations in the South or Southwest. The breakup of a family was one of the greatest horrors slaves faced. Many adamantly protested the separation and later risked punishment to run away in search of their relatives.

In this passage from Uncle Tom's Cabin, *Stowe examines the tormenting separation of a mother from her child at the hands of a cruel slave trader. She also interrupts the narration to directly address the reader and wryly comment on the "peculiar institution" of slavery and its relationship to Christianity. At the end of the passage, Uncle Tom, an observer, also reflects upon the slave's suffering.*

Uncle Tom's Cabin
Chapter XII, Select Incident of Lawful Trade

It was a bright, tranquil evening when the boat stopped at the wharf at Louisville. The woman had been sitting with her baby in her arms, now wrapped in a heavy sleep. When she heard the name of the place called out, she hastily laid the child down in a little cradle formed by the hollow among the boxes, first carefully spreading under it her cloak; and then she sprung to the side of the boat, in hopes that, among the various hotel-waiters who thronged the wharf, she might see her husband. In this hope, she pressed forward to the front rails, and, stretching far over them, strained her eyes intently on the moving heads on the shore, and the crowd pressed in between her and the child.

"Now's your time," said Haley, taking the sleeping child up, and handing him to the stranger. "Don't wake him up, and set him to crying, now; it would make a devil of a fuss with the gal." The man took the bundle carefully, and was soon lost in the crowd that went up the wharf.

When the boat, creaking, and groaning, and puffing, had loosed from the wharf, and was beginning slowly to strain herself along, the woman returned to her old seat. The trader was sitting there,—the child was gone!

"Why, why,—where?" she began, in bewildered surprise.

"Lucy," said the trader, "your child's gone; you may as well know it first as last. You see, I know'd you couldn't take him down south; and I got a chance to sell him to a first-rate family, that'll raise him better than you can."

The trader had arrived at that stage of Christian political perfection which has been recommended by some preachers and politicians of the north, lately in which he had completely overcome every humane weakness and prejudice. His heart was

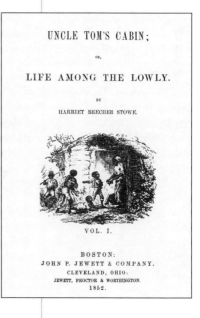

UNCLE TOM'S CABIN;

OR,

LIFE AMONG THE LOWLY.

BY

HARRIET BEECHER STOWE.

VOL. I.

BOSTON:
JOHN P. JEWETT & COMPANY.
CLEVELAND, OHIO:
JEWETT, PROCTOR & WORTHINGTON.
1852.

Slaves were bought and sold at auctions, where family members were often separated from one another.

exactly where yours, sir, and mine could be brought, with proper effort and cultivation. The wild look of anguish and utter despair that the woman cast on him might have disturbed one less practiced; but he was used to it. He had seen that same look hundreds of times. You can get used to such things, too, my friend; and it is the great object of recent efforts to make our whole northern community used to them, for the glory of the Union. So the trader only regarded the mortal anguish which he saw working in those dark features, those clenched hands, and suffocated breathings, as necessary incidents of the trade, and merely calculated whether she was going to scream, and get up a commotion on the boat; for, like other supporters of our peculiar institution, he decidedly disliked agitation.

But the woman did not scream. The shot had passed too straight and direct through the heart, for cry or tear.

Dizzily she sat down. Her slack hands fell lifeless by her side. Her eyes looked straight forward, but she saw nothing. All the noise and hum of the boat, the groaning of the machinery, mingled dreamily to her bewildered ear; and the poor, dumb-stricken heart had neither cry nor tear to show for its utter misery. She was quite calm.

The trader, who, considering his advantages, was almost as humane as some of our politicians, seemed to feel called on to administer such consolation as the case admitted of.

"I know this yer comes kinder hard, at first, Lucy," said he; "but such a smart, sensible gal as you are, won't give way to it. You see it's *necessary,* and can't be helped!"

"O! don't, Mas'r, don't!" said the woman, with a voice like one that is smothering.

"You're a smart wench, Lucy," he persisted; "I mean to do well by ye, and get ye a nice place down river; and you'll soon get another husband,—such a likely gal as you——"

"O! Mas'r, if you *only* won't talk to me now," said the woman, in a voice of such quick and living anguish that the trader felt that there was something at present in the case beyond his style of operation. He got up, and the woman turned away, and buried her head in her cloak.

The trader walked up and down for a time, and occasionally stopped and looked at her.

"Takes it hard, rather," he soliloquized, "but quiet, tho';—let her sweat a while; she'll come right, by and by!"

Tom had watched the whole transaction from first to last, and had a perfect understanding of its results. To him, it looked like something unutterably horrible and cruel, because, poor, ignorant black soul! he had not learned to generalize, and to take enlarged views. If he had only been instructed by certain ministers of Christianity, he might have thought better of it, and seen in it an everyday incident of a lawful trade; a trade which is the vital support of an institution which an American divine tells us has *"no evil but such as are inseparable from any other relations in social and domestic life."* But Tom, as we see, being a poor ignorant fellow, whose reading has been confined entirely to the New Testament, could not comfort and solace himself with views like these. His very soul bled within him for what seemed to him the *wrongs* of the poor suffering thing that lay like a crushed reed on the boxes; the reeling, living, bleeding, yet immortal *thing,* which American state law coolly classes with the bundles, and bales, and boxes, among which she is lying.

GEORGE FITZHUGH (1806–1881)

"The Southerner is the negro's friend"

George Fitzhugh, born in Port Royal, Virginia, was a small-town lawyer and journalist who would go on to earn a reputation as one of slavery's most ardent and unforgiving defenders. His two major works, Sociology for the South *(also known as* Failure of Free Society*) and* Cannibals All! *(also known as* Slaves Without Masters*), published in the 1850s, rallied southern support for slavery by extolling the virtues of the South and mocking the "chaos and anarchy" of the North.*

Slavery was defended by its proponents on various grounds. Many believed that slavery was ordained by God and that African Americans were inferior to whites and a danger to society. Others justified slavery on grounds that it was an essential instrument of the southern economy. These and other arguments established a consensus throughout the region that slavery was an integral part of the southern way of life.

Fitzhugh viewed slavery as a necessary social arrangement, a system established for the advancement of the country and benefitting everyone—weak and strong, rich and poor. As he explains in the following excerpt, Fitzhugh sees no security or contentment in the free societies of Europe and the North, where every day brings new troubles of unemployment, starvation, and injustice. In the South, he boasts, the slave enjoys food, shelter, and even friendship.

Sociology for the South

The South, quiet, contented, satisfied, looks upon all socialists and radical reformers as madmen or knaves. It is as ignorant of free society as that society is of slavery. Each section sees one side of the subject alone; each, therefore, takes partial and erroneous views of it. Social science will never take a step in advance till some Southern slave-holder, competent for the task, devotes a life-time to its study and elucidation; for slavery can only be understood by living in its midst....We should ... indignantly hurl back upon our assailants the charge, that there is something wrong and rotten in our system. From their own mouths we can show free society to be a monstrous abortion, and slavery to be the healthy, beautiful and natural being which they are trying, unconsciously, to adopt....

We would remind those who deprecate and sympathize with negro slavery, that his slavery here relieves him from a far more cruel slavery in Africa, or from idolatry and cannibalism, and every brutal vice and crime that can disgrace humanity; and that it christianizes, protects, supports and civilizes him; that it governs him far better than free laborers at the North are governed. There, wife-murder has become a mere holiday pastime; and where so many wives are murdered, almost all must be brutally treated. Nay, more: men who kill their wives or treat them brutally, must be ready for all kinds of crime, and the calendar of crime at the North proves the inference to be correct. Negroes never kill their wives. If it be objected that legally they have no wives, then we reply, that in an experience of more than forty years, we never yet heard of a negro man killing a negro woman. Our negroes are not only better off as to physical comfort than free laborers, but their moral condition is better.

But abolish Negro slavery, and how much of slavery still remains. Soldiers and sailors in Europe enlist for life; here, for five years. Are they not slaves who have not only sold their liberties, but their lives also? And they are worse treated than domestic slaves. No domestic affection and self-interest extend their ægis over them. No kind mistress, like a guardian angel, provides for them in health, tends them in sickness, and soothes their dying pillow....Wives and apprentices are slaves; not in theory only, but often in fact. Children are slaves to their parents, guardians and teachers. Imprisoned culprits are slaves. Lunatics and idiots are slaves also. Three-fourths of free society are slaves, no better treated, when their wants and capacities are estimated, than negro slaves. The masters in

Many proponents of slavery insisted that slaves in the South led a content, full life and were treated well by their owners. The savage whippings this former slave endured (top) were common on most plantations. However, the drawing (bottom) portrays the plantation as a place where whites and blacks happily coexist.

free society, or slave society, if they perform properly their duties, have more cares and less liberty than the slaves themselves....

The Southerner is the negro's friend, his only friend. Let no intermeddling abolitionist, no refined philosophy, dissolve this friendship.

ANGELINA GRIMKÉ WELD (1805–1879)

Angelina Grimké Weld and her sister Sarah Moore Grimké were outspoken antislavery and women's rights advocates. Growing up in South Carolina as daughters of a prominent judge and plantation owner, Angelina and Sarah witnessed firsthand the suffering of slaves. The sisters became fervent abolitionists and were determined to speak out against slavery.

Angelina began working with the American Anti-Slavery Society by speaking to small groups of women around New York City. Soon, interested men joined her audience. Later, Sarah joined her sister to give lectures throughout New England to mixed audiences, often facing criticism due to the public nature of their careers.

Angelina's "Appeal to the Christian Women of the South" is an evangelical sermon that preaches the sins of slavery and the redemption of emancipation. She argues that women not only have the ability to end slavery but are duty-bound, as Christians, to do so. Weld argues that southern women do have some power to fight the institution of slavery on their farms and in their communities. In this excerpt, she implores women to read, pray, speak, and act to protest slavery.

"slavery is a crime against God and man"

Appeal to the Christian Women of the South

But perhaps you will be ready to query, why appeal to *women* on this subject? We do not make the laws which perpetuate slavery. *No* legislative power is vested in *us; we* can do nothing to overthrow the system, even if we wished to do so. To this I reply, I know you do not make the laws, but I also know that *you are the wives and mothers, the sisters and daughters of those who do,* and if you really suppose *you* can do nothing to overthrow slavery, you are greatly mistaken....

1. Read then on the subject of slavery. Search the Scriptures daily, whether the things I have told you are true. Other books and papers

might be a great help to you in this investigation, but they are not necessary, and it is hardly probable that your Committees of Vigilance will allow you to have any other. The Bible then is the book I want you to read in the spirit of inquiry, and the spirit of prayer.... [I]t contains the words of Jesus, and they are spirit and life. Judge for yourselves whether *he sanctioned* such a system of oppression and crime.

2. Pray over this subject. When you have entered into your closets, and shut to the doors, then pray to your father, who seeth in secret, that he would open your eyes to see whether slavery is *sinful,* and if it is, that he would enable you to bear a faithful, open and unshrinking testimony against it, and to do whatsoever your hands find to do, leaving the consequences entirely to him.... Pray also for that poor slave, that he may be kept patient and submissive under his hard lot, until God is pleased to open the door of freedom to him without violence or bloodshed. Pray too for the master that his heart may be softened, and he made willing to acknowledge, as Joseph's brethren did, "Verily we are guilty concerning our brother," before he will be compelled to add in consequence of Divine judgment, "therefore is all this evil come upon us." ...

3. Speak on this subject. It is through the tongue, the pen, and the press, that truth is principally propagated. Speak then to your relatives, your friends, your acquaintances on the subject of slavery; be not afraid if you are conscientiously convinced it is *sinful,* to say so openly, but calmly, and to let your sentiments be known. If you are served by the slaves of others, try to ameliorate their condition as much as possible; never aggravate their faults, and thus add fuel to the fire of anger already kindled, in a master and mistress's bosom; remember their extreme ignorance, and consider them as your Heavenly Father does the *less* culpable on this account, even when they do wrong things. Discountenance *all* cruelty to them, all starvation, all corporal chastisement; these may brutalize and *break* their spirits, but will never bend them to willing, cheerful obedience.... Above all, try to persuade your husband, father, brothers, and sons, that *slavery is a crime against God and man,* and that it is a great sin to keep *human beings* in such abject ignorance; to deny them the privilege of learning to read and write....

4. Act on this subject. Some of you *own* slaves yourselves. If you believe slavery is *sinful,* set them at liberty, "undo the heavy burdens and let the oppressed go free." If they wish to remain with you, pay them wages, if not let them leave you. Should they remain teach them, and have them taught the common branches of an English education; they have minds and those minds *ought to be improved.* ...

But some of you will say, we can neither free our slaves nor teach them to read, for the laws of our state forbid it. Be not surprised when I say such wicked laws *ought to be no barrier* in the way of your duty, and I appeal to the Bible to prove this position.

Songs of Slaves
"Follow the Drinking Gourd"

Many American musical genres—such as spirituals, jazz, and blues—derive from the folk songs of black slaves. Work songs, which often involved calling and repetition, enabled slaves to work together in uniform rhythm while toiling in the fields or at machines. Lyrics typically expressed slaves' desires for freedom and religious salvation. Consequently, some work songs or spirituals helped keep up morale. Singing also helped create community, which threatened slaveholders. In fact, group chanting was discouraged because owners feared that the power of music would unite slaves in revolt against the plantation.

In some respects, slaveholders' instincts were right. Many spirituals conveyed not only religious beliefs but also a desire to escape from bondage. Some lyrics transmitted secret messages that white masters were unable to understand. A carpenter called Peg Leg Joe traveled from farm to farm and plantation to plantation, teaching slaves a song that contained clues of how to find their way northward. "Follow the Drinking Gourd" advises runaway slaves to follow the Big Dipper (the "drinking gourd"), whose North Star lights the way to freedom.

When the sun comes back and the first quail calls,
Follow the drinking gourd,
For the old man is a-waiting for to carry you to freedom
If you follow the drinking gourd.

Follow the drinking gourd,
Follow the drinking gourd,
For the old man is a-waiting for to carry you to freedom
If you follow the drinking gourd.

The riverbank will make a very good road,
The dead trees show you the way,
Left foot, peg foot traveling on
Follow the drinking gourd,

The river ends between two hills
Follow the drinking gourd,
There's another river on the other side,
Follow the drinking gourd,

When the little river meets the great big river,
Follow the drinking gourd,
For the old man is a-waiting for to carry you to freedom
If you follow the drinking gourd.

Abolitionist Harriet Tubman reportedly conducted as many as 300 slaves to freedom along the Underground Railroad.

"Through cane-brake and forest,— the hunting of men!"

JOHN GREENLEAF WHITTIER (1807–1892)

John Greenleaf Whittier was an adamant abolitionist who used poetry to express his views. Whittier's family was Quaker—a religion which did not support slavery and preached that treating anyone as property was an outrage to God. On the other hand, many Christians said that slavery occurred in the Bible and was therefore morally correct. Whittier published a number of poems before the antislavery movement had gained widespread support; therefore, he was not very popular or widely read. In fact, his beliefs put him in physical danger—he and another abolitionist were once attacked and stoned during a lecture.

Whittier's poem, "The Hunters of Men," mocks the pursuits of slave catchers. Published in 1835, the poem's irony points out contradictions in the lifestyle of southern nobility. Whittier contrasts their high-class status—demonstrated by the English pastime of hunting on horseback— with their adherence to the degrading system of slavery.

The Hunters of Men

Have ye heard of our hunting, o'er mountain and glen,
Through cane-brake and forest,—the hunting of men?
The lords of our land to this hunting have gone,
As the fox-hunter follows the sound of the horn;
Hark! the cheer and the hallo! the crack of the whip,
And the yell of the hound as he fastens his grip!
All blithe are our hunters, and noble their match,
Though hundreds are caught, there are millions to catch.
So speed to their hunting, o'er mountain and glen,
Through cane-brake and forest,—the hunting of men!

Gay luck to our hunters! how nobly they ride
In the glow of their zeal, and the strength of their pride!
The priest with his cassock flung back on the wind,
Just screening the politic statesman behind;
The saint and the sinner, with cursing and prayer,
The drunk and the sober, ride merrily there.
And woman, kind woman, wife, widow, and maid,

For the good of the hunted, is lending her aid:
Her foot's in the stirrup, her hand on the rein,
How blithely she rides to the hunting of men!

Oh, goodly and grand is our hunting to see,
In this "land of the brave and this home of the free."
Priest, warrior, and statesman, from Georgia to Maine,
All mounting the saddle, all grasping the rein;
Right merrily hunting the black man, whose sin
Is the curl of his hair and the hue of his skin!
Woe, now, to the hunted who turns him at bay!
Will our hunters be turned from their purpose and prey?
Will their hearts fail within them? their nerves tremble, when
All roughly they ride to the hunting of men?

Ho! alms for our hunters! all weary and faint,
Wax the curse of the sinner and prayer of the saint.
The horn is wound faintly, the echoes are still,
Over cane-brake and river, and forest and hill.
Haste, alms for our hunters! the hunted once more
Have turned from their flight with their backs to the shore:
What right have they here in the home of the white,
Shadowed o'er by our banner of Freedom and Right?
Ho! alms for the hunters! or never again
Will they ride in their pomp to the hunting of men!

Alms, alms for our hunters! why will ye delay,
When their pride and their glory are melting away?
The parson has turned; for, on charge of his own,
Who goeth a warfare, or hunting, alone?
The politic statesman looks back with a sigh,
There is doubt in his heart, there is fear in his eye.
Oh, haste, lest that doubting and fear shall prevail,
And the head of his steed take the place of the tail.
Oh, haste, ere he leave us! for who will ride then,
For pleasure or gain, to the hunting of men?

Civil War and Reconstruction

By the middle of the nineteenth century, the nation had developed two distinct economies and identities. In the North, the industrial revolution brought factories and urban lifestyles. Many merchants, particularly those who profited from selling U.S. goods abroad, were concentrated in northern cities. In the South, rural agriculture—relying on large plantations and a massive slave workforce—led the economy. Southern states produced much of the nation's cotton, tobacco, rice, and other staple crops for export. Tensions simmered for decades over northern traders profiting from southern-produced crops. However, in the 1850s and early 1860s, those tensions exploded over the issue of slavery.

Vocal abolitionists in the North found greater support, and their ideas began filtering into the South. Slave revolts and runaways made plantation owners fearful and angry. President Abraham Lincoln's election in 1860 increased fears that slavery would be outlawed in the South. Consequently, in 1861 eleven states seceded from the Union and formed the Confederate States of America. The two sides soon found themselves fighting a bloody, four-year-long Civil War. During the first two years, the Confederacy was more successful in battle, largely because it had superior generals. However, by 1863 the Union army began to win battles because it had more men and supplies than the South, and because Lincoln had found an effective leader in General Ulysses S. Grant.

Today, many Americans remain fascinated by the bloodiest war fought on U.S. soil. There are now more books about the Civil War than any other period of American history. However, at the time, few books were published because the nation's efforts were consumed by war. The popular poet Henry Wadsworth Longfellow wrote in his journal on April 30, 1861, "When times have such a gunpowder flavor, all literature loses its taste. Newspapers are the only reading. They are at once the record and the romance of the day." While journalists reported on the war's events, other authors took part in every facet of the war, though many did not write about their experiences until later.

After the Civil War, Reconstruction efforts concentrated on rebuilding the tattered southern infrastructure and economy, while educating former slaves. Schools for teaching African Americans reading, writing, and vocational skills began to appear. However, disagreements arose—even within the black community—over how best to raise the economic and social standing of former slaves. After Reconstruction, racial segregation and other forms of discrimination in the South further complicated those efforts. Equality for African Americans was many decades away.

Featured Authors

Herman Melville
Stephen Crane
Louisa May Alcott
John Esten Cooke
Walt Whitman
Booker T. Washington
W.E.B. DuBois

HERMAN MELVILLE (1819–1891)

Herman Melville is now regarded as one of the finest writers of American literature, but that was not always the case. By 1851, Melville had written and published his master-work, Moby Dick, *as well as several other popular short stories. Later narratives, however, were not well received, and by the Civil War, Melville had virtually disappeared from the literary scene. In April 1865, when Richmond fell to the Union, he began writing poems about events and themes of the war. Because Melville had not participated in the war firsthand, he used newspaper accounts of particular events to flesh out details. In 1866, he published the book of poetry,* Battle-Pieces and Aspects of the War.

"Portent" was the first poem in the volume. It describes the hanging of John Brown, the radical abolitionist who encouraged slave rebellion. Brown and about eighteen accomplices—black and white—tried to overtake the federal arsenal at Harper's Ferry, Virginia, in October 1859. They had planned to give the seized weapons to slaves in the area in hopes of stirring an uprising. However, Brown's raid was quickly quelled, and he was hanged for treason.

With hindsight, Herman Melville believed this incident aggravated the sectional tensions that directly led to the Civil War. Southerners feared that abolitionists would continue to foment revolt among slaves, and some began to demand secession rather than submit to what they saw as "northern outrage." Abolitionists, on the other hand, acknowledged that Brown's methods were extreme, but his ideals, upright.

Most historians agree with Melville's assessment of John Brown's raid. Sectional politics and the slavery issue dominated the presidential election of 1860. When campaigning, Abraham Lincoln was committed to stopping the spread of slavery to new territories; however, he did not seek to outlaw it in the South. Although Lincoln won the election, he had regional, not national, support. Southerners remained suspicious of Lincoln's policies. They sought to protect their way of life and insisted on the primacy of states' rights. By the time the new president took office in March 1861, seven southern states—South Carolina, Mississippi, Florida, Alabama, Georgia, Louisiana, and Texas—had seceded from the Union and formed the Confederate States of America (the Confederacy). Lincoln stepped into war as he stepped into the White House. The day after his inauguration, the Confederacy fired on Fort Sumter, in South Carolina's Charleston harbor, demanding its surrender.

"Lo, John Brown"

In light of the terrible human losses of the Civil War, Melville's "Portent" reads like a short ghost story. John Brown's body swings from the hanging post, casting a long shadow on the Shenandoah River Valley. This haunting image foreshadows the great suffering that the Civil War would ultimately inflict on that region and the nation. The meter of the poem reinforces the swinging, pendulum-like motion of Brown's corpse. The "cut" on the "crown" is literally interpreted as the wounds to the head that John Brown received during his arrest. Critics believe that these blows symbolize the first wound to the governing "crown"—or Union. In the last stanza, John Brown's beard extends beyond the "cap" or hood that was placed over his head. Blowing in the wind, his beard is likened to a meteor, a classical omen or portent of war.

The Portent
(1859)

Hanging from the beam,
Slowly swaying (such the law),
Gaunt the shadow on your green,
Shenandoah!
The cut is on the crown
(Lo, John Brown),
And the stabs shall heal no more.

Hidden in the cap
Is the anguish none can draw;
So your future veils its face,
Shenandoah!
But the streaming beard is shown
(Weird John Brown),
The meteor of war.

Many contemporaries believed that John Brown was mentally unstable, which explains Melville's phrase, "Weird John Brown."

"A burning roar filled his ears."

STEPHEN CRANE (1871–1900)

Stephen Crane led a short but highly prolific life. By his death at the age of 28 from tuberculosis, he had written about twelve volumes of poetry, articles, syndicated short stories, and novels. When Crane began writing his classic Civil War novel, The Red Badge of Courage, *in 1891, he*

had interviewed veterans but had never witnessed a battle. Nevertheless, the story contains remarkable realism about battlefront experiences— a feature that scholars explain by noting Crane's keen imagination. In 1895, when the book appeared, critics in the United States and Europe hailed The Red Badge of Courage *as a major achievement by the young author.*

Crane based The Red Badge of Courage *on events during the Battle of Chancellorsville, Virginia, in May 1863. By that time, the Civil War had raged for two years. In January of that year, President Lincoln had issued the Emancipation Proclamation, the document that freed slaves in the Confederacy, but not in slaveholding states occupied by the Union. Although it did not apply to all slaves, the Emancipation Proclamation was a symbolic move that gave both Union and Confederate soldiers a rallying point or "cause." Thereafter, compromise was impossible, and battles were fought with renewed intensity.*

The Battle of Chancellorsville was part of the Union campaign to capture the Confederate capital of Richmond, Virginia. During the first four days of May 1863, Confederate general Robert E. Lee outmaneuvered Union general Joseph Hooker. Union troops retreated, and the South won the battle though they suffered about 12,000 casualties. By this time, the Confederacy was having difficulty replacing soldiers, so it was not an absolute "victory." Historically, Chancellorsville is important because Confederate general Thomas "Stonewall" Jackson was wounded there by friendly fire. His death a few days later was another severe loss for Lee's forces.

In The Red Badge of Courage, *Henry Fleming, also called "the youth," goes into battle for the first time. Although Henry is a Union recruit, the intensely personal account of his sensations and emotions is probably similar to experiences on both sides of the conflict. Henry has self-doubts and worries that he will not have the courage to face the enemy. However, in this reading, he confronts his fears and fights, "not [as] a man but a member" and as part of "a cause."*

The Red Badge of Courage: An Episode of the American Civil War
Chapter V

He got the one glance at the foe-swarming field in front of him and instantly ceased to debate the question of his piece being loaded. Before he was ready to begin—before he had announced to himself that he was about to fight—he threw the obedient, well-balanced rifle into position and fired a first wild shot. Directly, he was working at his weapon like an automatic affair.

He suddenly lost concern for himself and forgot to look at a menacing fate. He became not a man but a member. He felt that something of which he was a part—a regiment, an army, a cause, or a country—was in a crisis. He was welded into a common personality which was dominated by a single desire. For some moments, he could not flee no more than a little finger can commit a revolution from a hand.

If he had thought the regiment about to be annihilated perhaps he could have amputated himself from it. But its noise gave him assurance. The regiment was like a fire-work that, once ignited, proceeds superior to circumstances until its blazing vitality fades. It wheezed and banded with a mighty power. He pictured the ground before it as strewn with the discomfited.

There was a consciousness always of the presence of his comrades about him. He felt the subtle battle-brotherhood more potent even than the cause for which they were fighting. It was a mysterious fraternity, born of the smoke and danger of death....

Presently he began to feel the effect of the war-atmosphere—a blistering sweat, a sensation that his eye-balls were about to crack like hot stones. A burning roar filled his ears.

Following this came a red rage. He developed the acute exasperation of a pestered animal, a well-meaning cow worried by dogs. He had a mad feeling against his rifle which could only be used against one life at a time. He wished to rush forward and strangle with his fingers. He craved a power that would enable him to make a world-sweeping gesture and brush all back. His impotency appeared to him and made his rage into that of a driven beast.

Buried in the smoke of many rifles, his anger was directed not so much against the men whom he knew were rushing toward him, as against the swirling battle-phantoms who were choking him, stuffing their smoke-robes down his parched throat. He fought frantically for respite for his senses, for air, as a babe being smothered attacks the deadly blankets.

There was a blare of heated rage, mingled with a certain expression of intentness on all faces. Many of the men were making low-toned noises with their mouths and these subdued cheers, snarls, imprecations, prayers, made a wild, barbaric song that went as an under-current of sound, strange and chant-like, with the resounding chords of the war-march. The man at the youth's elbow was babbling. In it there was something soft and tender, like the monologue of a babe. The tall soldier was swearing in a loud voice. From his lips came a black procession of curious oaths. Of a sudden, another broke out in a querulous way like a man

Confederate soldiers had no single uniform, as these men in Florida illustrate.

who has mislaid his hat. "Well, why don't they support us? Why don't they send supports? Do they think—"

The youth in his battle-sleep heard this, as one who dozes hears.

There was a singular absence of heroic poses. The men bending and surging in their haste and rage were in every impossible attitude. The steel ram-rods clanked and clanged with incessant din as the men pounded them furiously into the hot rifle-barrels. The flaps of the cartridge-boxes were all unfastened, and flapped and bobbed idiotically with each movement. The rifles, once loaded, were jerked to the shoulder and fired without apparent aim into the smoke or at one of the blurred and shifting forms which upon the field before the regiment had been growing larger and larger like puppets under a magician's hand....

The men dropped here and there like bundles. The captain of the youth's company had been killed in an early part of the action. His body lay stretched out in the position of a tired man resting, but upon his face there was an astonished and sorrowful look as if he thought some friend had done him an ill turn. The babbling man was grazed by a shot that made the blood stream widely down his face. He clapped both hands to his head. "Oh!" he said, and ran. Another grunted suddenly as if he had been struck by a club in the stomach. He sat down and gazed ruefully. In his eyes there was mute, indefinite reproach. Farther up the line a man, standing behind a tree, had had his knee-joint splintered by a ball. Immediately, he had dropped his rifle and gripped the tree with both arms. And there he remained, clinging desperately, and crying for assistance that he might withdraw his hold upon the tree.

At last, an exultant yell went along the quivering line. The firing dwindled from an uproar to a last vindictive popping. As the smoke slowly eddied away, the youth saw that the charge had been repulsed. The enemy were scattered into reluctant groups. He saw a man climb to the top of the fence, straddle the rail and fire a parting shot. The waves had receded, leaving bits of dark debris upon the ground.

Some in the regiment began to whoop frenziedly. Many were silent. Apparently, they were trying to contemplate themselves.

After the fever had left his veins, the youth thought that at last he was going to suffocate. He became aware of the foul atmosphere in which he had been struggling. He was grimy and dripping like a laborer in a foundry. He grasped his canteen and took a long swallow of the warmed water.

A sentence with variations went up and down the line. "Well, we've helt 'em back. We've helt 'em back; derned if we haven't." The men said it blissfully, leering at each other with dirty smiles.

Visual reporting of the Civil War relied on sketches. Artists such as Winslow Homer and Alfred and William Waud perched themselves near battlefields where they drew images to send to a newspaper. Another artist at the newspaper office would use the sketch to carve an engraving that would then be used on the printing presses. The sketch shown here depicts Union general Philip Sheridan's ride in 1864.

The youth turned to look behind him and off to the right and off to the left. He experienced the joy of a man who at last finds leisure in which to look about him.

Under foot, there were a few ghastly forms, motionless. They lay twisted in fantastic contortions. Arms were bent and heads were turned in incredible ways. It seemed that the dead men must have fallen from some great height to get into such positions. They looked to be dumped out upon the ground from the sky.

"their fortitude seemed contagious"

LOUISA MAY ALCOTT (1833–1888)

Louisa May Alcott is best known for her popular children's novel, Little Women. *However, she also wrote novels for adults, thrillers, and autobiographical sketches. In December 1862, Alcott volunteered to serve as a Civil War nurse in a Union hospital in Washington, D.C. She worked there only six weeks before she caught typhoid fever and had to return home. The experience, nevertheless, gave her inspiration for her literary breakthrough. In 1863, she published her autobiographical essay "Hospital Sketches" in a Boston paper, marking her first success.*

With men off fighting, women's roles expanded during the Civil War. First, they carried on the work that men would have normally done at home; women toiled in factories and ran farms and businesses. In addition, they supported the war effort by sewing uniforms, feeding soldiers, and raising money for medical supplies. As the war continued, women also began to take on a larger share of nursing on both sides of the conflict. Historians estimate that more than 3,000 women cared for the sick and wounded during the Civil War.

As Alcott learned firsthand, the work of Civil War nurses was grueling and disturbing. The following excerpt describes the arrival of wounded soldiers from the Battle of Fredericksburg, Virginia, in December of 1862—another conflict in the Union campaign to capture Richmond. Although Union general Ambrose Burnside had an advantage in troop number, his opponent, General Robert E. Lee, held strategic positions on the high ground behind Fredericksburg. After the North occupied the town, they attempted to charge the Confederate line, losing thousands of men to artillery fire from the Confederate stronghold on Marye's Heights. After a humiliating defeat, Union troops retreated.

Alcott's writing proves that the horrors of war were not all faced on the battlefields, but rather, some were encountered in hospitals and convalescent camps. In the following excerpt from "Hospital Sketches," Tribulation Periwinkle, a prim spinster, describes a typical day in a makeshift Civil War hospital. Unprepared for the realities of nursing, Trib expresses surprise about the tasks she must perform. Throughout the humorous narration, Alcott warmly praises the heroism of Union soldiers and sympathizes with their great physical suffering.

Hospital Sketches
Chapter III, A Day

"*THEY'VE* come! They've come! Hurry up, ladies—you're wanted."

"Who have come? The rebels?" . . .

"Bless you, no child; it's the wounded from Fredericksburg; forty ambulances are at the door, and we shall have our hands full in fifteen minutes."

"What shall we have to do?"

"Wash, dress, feed, warm and nurse them for the next three months, I dare say. Eighty beds are ready, and we were getting impatient for the men to come. Now you will begin to see hospital life in earnest. . . . Come to me in the ball-room when you are ready; the worst cases are always carried there, and I shall need your help." . . .

The first thing I met was a regiment of the vilest odors that ever assaulted the human nose, and took it by storm. . . . [A]nd the worst of this affliction was, every one had assured me that it was a chronic weakness of all hospitals, and I must bear it. I did, armed with lavender water, with which I so besprinkled myself and premises, that, like my friend, Sairy, I was soon known among my patients as "the nurse with the bottle." . . . I progressed by slow stages up stairs and down, till the main hall was reached, and I paused to take breath and a survey. There they were! "our brave boys," as the newspapers justly call them, for cowards could hardly have been so riddled with shot and shell, so torn and shattered, nor have borne suffering for which we have no name, with an uncomplaining fortitude, which made one glad to cherish each as a brother. In they came, some on stretchers, some in men's arms, some feebly staggering along propped on rude crutches, and one lay stark and still with covered face, as a comrade gave his name to be recorded before they carried him away to the dead house. All was hurry and confusion; the hall was full of these wrecks of humanity, for the most exhausted could not reach a bed till duly ticketed and registered. . . .

The sight of several stretchers, each with its legless, armless, or desperately wounded occupant, entering my ward, admonished me that I was there to work, not to wonder or weep; so I corked up my feelings, and

Many Civil War nurses (shown above) worked for the United States Sanitary Commission, an organization founded by Elizabeth Blackwell, the first female medical doctor in the United States.

returned to the path of duty.... Forty beds were prepared, many already tenanted by tired men who fell down anywhere, and drowsed till the smell of food roused them. Round the great stove was gathered the dreariest group I ever saw—ragged, gaunt and pale, mud to the knees, with bloody bandages untouched since put on days before; many bundled up in blankets, coats being lost or useless; and all wearing that disheartened look which proclaimed defeat, more plainly than any telegram of the [Union general] Burnside blunder. I pitied them so much, I dared not speak to them, though, remembering all they had been through since the rout at Fredericksburg, I yearned to serve the dreariest of them all. Presently, Miss Blank ...put basin, sponge, towels, and a block of brown soap into my hands, with these appalling directions:

"Come, my dear, begin to wash as fast as you can. Tell them to take off socks, coats, and shirts, scrub them well, put on clean shirts, and the attendants will finish them off, and lay them in bed."

If she had requested me to shave them all, or dance a horn-pipe on the stove funnel, I should have been less staggered; but to scrub some dozen lords of creation at a moment's notice, was really—really—. However, there was no time for nonsense, and, having resolved when I came to do everything I was bid, I drowned my scruples in my washbowl, clutched my soap manfully, and, assuming a businesslike air, made a dab at the first dirty specimen I saw....

Having done up our human wash, and laid it out to dry, the second syllable of our version of the word war-fare was enacted with much success. Great trays of bread, meat, soup and coffee appeared; and both nurses and attendants turned waiters, serving bountiful rations to all who could eat....

All having eaten, drank, and rested, the surgeons began their rounds; and I took my first lesson in the art of dressing wounds. It wasn't a festive scene, by any means; for Dr. P., whose aid I constituted myself, fell to work with a vigor which soon convinced me that I was a weaker vessel, though nothing would have induced me to confess it then. He had served in the Crimea, and seemed to regard a dilapidated body very much as I should have regarded a damaged garment; and, turning up his cuffs, whipped out a very unpleasant looking housewife, cutting, sawing, patching and piecing, with the enthusiasm of an accomplished surgical seamstress; explaining the process, in scientific terms, to the patient, meantime; which, of course, was immensely cheering and comfortable. There was an uncanny sort of fascination in watching him, as he peered and probed into the mechanism of those wonderful bodies, whose mysteries he understood so well. The more intricate the wound, the better he liked it. A poor private, with both legs off, and shot through the lungs, possessed more attractions for him than a dozen generals, slightly scratched in some "masterly retreat."...

The amputations were reserved till the morrow, and the merciful magic of ether was not thought necessary that day, so the poor souls had to bear their pains as best they might. It is all very well to talk of the patience of a woman; and far be it from me to pluck that feather from her cap, for, heaven knows, she isn't allowed to wear many; but the patient endurance of these men, under trials of the flesh, was truly wonderful; their fortitude seemed contagious, and scarcely a cry escaped them, though I often longed to groan for them, when pride kept their white lips shut, while great drops stood upon their foreheads, and the bed shook with the irrepressible tremor of their tortured bodies.

Photography on the Battlefields

The technology of photography was in its infancy during the Civil War. Each shot required lengthy set-up time, and the negative had to be developed immediately after the photograph was taken. This process was extremely delicate if the photograph were taken outdoors. In that event, a developing wagon (shown here) was used as a dark room. This cumbersome process did not lend itself to "snapshots." Therefore, photography during the Civil War was rarely used to capture battle scenes. Instead, early photographers needed controlled environments and unmoving subjects. They took portraits of soldiers, generals, and others on the front lines. Sometimes photographers took pictures of battlefields after the shooting stopped, showing ambulance corps at work and dead bodies. One of the most famous civil war photographers was Mathew Brady, who created striking portraits of General Robert E. Lee, General Ulysses S. Grant, and President Abraham Lincoln.

"The Virginians still advance."

JOHN ESTEN COOKE (1830–1886)

John Esten Cooke—sometimes referred to as "the Sir Walter Scott of the southern border"—was a Virginia novelist, poet, and historian. A fierce secessionist, Cooke had already written two best-selling novels by the time the Civil War began. He enlisted in the Confederate Army and served first under General J.E.B. Stuart, then under General Robert E. Lee until the surrender at Appomattox. In addition to three Civil War novels, Cooke went on to write his memoirs in The Wearing of the Grey *and a biography of General Lee.*

In his 1869 novel Mohun, *Cooke gives a particularly vivid description of the Battle of Gettysburg, the bloody conflict that most historians think marked the turning point in the Civil War. Riding on victories in Fredericksburg and Chancellorsville, General Lee rationalized that an attack in Union territory was essential.*

Lee marched through Maryland and set up camps in southern Pennsylvania while a large Union force, led by General George Meade, moved in. On the first two days of fighting around Gettysburg—July 1 and 2, 1863—Lee's troops seriously weakened Union positions north and west of the city. However, Lee believed that to win the battle, he needed to capture the Union stronghold on Cemetery Ridge, south of the city. On July 3, he ordered the ill-fated Pickett's Charge. Confederate soldiers marched across flat farmland to attack the center of the Union line at its high ground on the ridge. However, artillery fire from the ridge crippled Pickett's men, and after battling through the first Union line, they were engulfed by Federal troops. Holding onto their positions, Union troops forced Lee's army to withdraw, but with catastrophic losses on both sides. The Union lost 23,000 men to casualties; Confederates lost 28,000—an overall casualty rate of 30 percent, making it the bloodiest battle on U.S. soil.

In the following excerpt from his novel Mohun, *Cooke's description of Gettysburg not only vividly illustrates the military maneuvers of the battle but also praises the valor of Lee's Army of Northern Virginia. Cooke's reverent tone conveys his allegiance to the Confederacy and the loyalty that many secessionist soldiers felt toward their families and their states. Robert E. Lee once wrote the reason for his joining the Confederate Army. "With all my devotion to the Union and the feeling of loyalty and duty of an American citizen, I have not been able to raise my hand against my relatives, my children, my home. I have therefore resigned my commission in the [Federal] Army...."*

Mohun
The Charge of the Virginians

It is the third of July, 1863. Lee's line of battle, stretching along the crest of Seminary Ridge, awaits the signal for a new conflict with a carelessness as great as on the preceding day. The infantry are laughing jesting, cooking their rations, and smoking their pipes. The ragged cannoneers, with flashing eyes, smiling lips, and faces blackened with powder, are standing in groups, or lying down around the pieces of artillery. Near the centre of the line a gray-headed officer, in plain uniform, and entirely unattended, has dismounted, and is reconnoitering the Federal position through a pair of field-glasses.

It is Lee and he is looking toward Cemetery Heights. . . .

Lee gazes for some moments through his glasses at the long range bristling with bayonets. Not a muscle moves; he resembles a statue. Then he lowers the glasses, closes them thoughtfully, and his calm glance passes along the lines of his army. You would say that this glance penetrates the forest; that he sees his old soldiers, gay, unshrinking, unmoved by the reverses of [Confederate general] Longstreet [on the previous day], and believing in themselves and in him! . . . The face of the great commander suddenly flushes. He summons a staff officer and utters a few words in calm and measured tones. The order is given. The grand assault is about to begin. . . .

Pickett's division of Virginia troops has been selected for the hazardous venture, and they prepare for the ordeal in the midst of a profound silence. Since the morning scarce a gunshot has been heard. Now and then only, a single cannon, like a signal-gun, sends its growl through the hills. . . .

At one o'clock the moment seems to have arrived. Along the whole front of Hill and Longstreet, the southern artillery all at once bursts forth. One hundred and forty-five cannon send their threatening thunder across the peaceful valley. From Cemetery Heights, eighty pieces reply to them; and for more than an hour these two hundred and twenty-five cannon tear the air with their harsh roar, hurled back in crash after crash from the rocky ramparts. That thunder is the most terrible yet heard in the war. It stirs the coolest veterans. . . .

Suddenly the Federal fire slackens, and then ceases . . . Lee's guns also cease firing. The hour has come.

The Virginians, under [General George E.] Pickett, form in double line in the edge of the woods, where Lee's centre is posted. These men are ragged and travelworn, but their bayonets and gunbarrels shine like silver. From the steel hedge, as the men move, dart lightnings. . . .

At the word, they move out, shoulder to shoulder, at common time. Descending the slope, they enter on the valley, and move steadily toward the heights.

Robert E. Lee was one of the most revered and beloved generals on either side of the Civil War. A Confederate general once said that he would follow Lee into battle blindfolded.

The advance of the column, with its battle-flags floating proudly, and its ranks closed up and dressed with the precision of troops on parade, is a magnificent spectacle. Old soldiers, hardened in the fires of battle, and not given to emotion, lean forward watching the advance of the Virginians with fiery eyes. You would say, from the fierce clutch of the gaunt hands on the muskets, that they wish to follow; and many wish that.

The column is midway the valley, and beginning to move more rapidly, when suddenly the Federal artillery opens.

The ranks are swept by round shot, shell, and canister. Bloody gaps appear, but the line closes up, and continues to advance. The fire of the Federal artillery redoubles. All the demons of the pit seem howling, roaring, yelling, and screaming. The assaulting column is torn by a whirlwind of canister, before which men fall in heaps mangled, streaming with blood, their bosoms torn to pieces, their hands clutching the grass, their teeth biting the earth. The ranks, however, close up as before, and the Virginians continue to advance.

From common time, they have passed to quick time—now they march at the double-quick. That is to say, they run. They have reached the slope; the enemy's breastworks are right before them; and they dash at them with wild cheers.

They are still three hunded yards from the Federal works, when the real conflict commences, to which the cannonade was but child's play. Artillery has thundered, but something more deadly succeeds it—the sudden crash of musketry. From behind a stone wall the Federal infantry rise up and pour a galling fire into the charging column. It has been accompanied to this moment by a body of other troops, but those troops now disappear, like dry leaves swept off by the wind. The Virginians still advance.

Amid a concentrated fire of infantry and artillery, in their front and on both flanks, they pass over the ground between themselves and the enemy; ascend the slope; rush headlong at the breastworks; storm them; strike their bayonets into the enemy, who recoil before them, and a wild cheer rises, making the blood leap in the veins of a hundred thousand men.

The Federal works are carried and the troops are wild with enthusiasm. With a thunder of cheers they press upon the flying enemy toward the crest.

Alas! as the smoke drifts, they see what is enough to dishearten the bravest. They have stormed the first line of works only! Beyond, is another and stronger line still. Behind it swarm the heavy reserves of the enemy, ready for the death-struggle. But the column cannot pause. It is "do or die." In their faces are thrust the muzzles of muskets spouting flame. Whole ranks go down in the fire. The survivors close up, utter a fierce cheer, and rush straight at the second tier of works.

Then is seen a spectacle which will long be remembered with a throb of the heart by many. The thinned ranks of the Virginians are advancing, unmoved, into the very jaws of death. They go forward—and are annihilated. At every step death meets them. The furious fire of the enemy, on both flanks and in their front, hurls them back, mangled and dying. The brave Garnett is killed while leading on his men. Kemper is lying on the earth maimed for life. Armistead is mortally wounded at the moment when he leaps upon the breastworks:—he waves his hat on the point of his sword, and staggers, and falls. Of fifteen field officers, fourteen have fallen. Three-fourths of the men are dead, wounded, or prisoners. The Federal infantry has closed in on the flanks and rear of the Virginians—whole corps assault the handful—the little band is enveloped, and cut off from succor—they turn and face the enemy, bayonet to bayonet, and die.

When the smoke drifts away, all is seen to be over. It is a panting, staggering, bleeding remnant only of the brave division that is coming back so slowly yonder. They are swept from the fatal hill—pursued by yells, cheers, cannon-shot, musket-balls, and canister. As they doggedly retire before the howling hurricane, the wounded are seen to stagger and fall. Over the dead and dying sweeps the canister. Amid volleys of musketry and the roar of cannon, all but a handful of Pickett's Virginians pass into eternity.

Blacks in Blue

Many African Americans volunteered to serve behind the lines during the Civil War, but Congress did not allow them to become soldiers until 1862. During the last two years of the war, almost 200,000 African Americans, mostly slaves freed by the Emancipation Proclamation, served as soldiers in the Union army. Once enlisted, black soldiers fought in segregated units that were led by white officers. They were paid less than whites and performed manual labor.

However, African-American troops fought heroically in several major battles. For example, the Massachusetts 54th Colored Regiment, headed by Colonel Robert Gould Shaw, led the courageous charge of Fort Wagner, South Carolina, in 1863. The troops were greatly outnumbered and faced heavy artillery fire from the high walls of the fort. The memorial to Shaw and the Massachusetts 54th, completed in 1897 by Augustus St. Gaudens, is shown here with Massachusetts 54th veterans. Art historians now consider St. Gaudens's memorial to be one of the best sculptural works of the nineteenth century. African-Americans' military service helped increase the federal government's commitment to the emancipation of slaves as a permanent policy.

"O Captain! my Captain!"

WALT WHITMAN (1819–1892)

Walt Whitman lived in Washington, D.C., during the Civil War and served for three years as a visitor and "consolant" to wounded soldiers. As a visitor, Whitman often wrote letters home to soldiers' loved ones. Walt Whitman traveled occasionally to the battlefront, where he witnessed another side of the war. Throughout these experiences, Whitman kept a rough diary written on scraps of paper in his pockets. He later wrote, "The real war will never get into the books," though scholars believe that Whitman intended to shape his diary into a Civil War account. Instead, he wrote poems documenting war and its aftermath. Several are thought to be among the best poetry in U.S. literature.

As a Washington resident, Walt Whitman noted in his journals that he often saw President Abraham Lincoln. "I see the President almost every day, as I happen to live where he passes to and from his [summer] lodgings out of town. . . . I see very plainly Abraham Lincoln's dark brown face, with the deep-cut lines, the eyes always, to me, with a deep latent sadness in the expression. We have got so that we exchange bows, and very cordial ones." Whitman practically deified Lincoln. A Yankee, Whitman particularly valued the president's devotion to the Union.

On April 9, 1865, Confederate general Robert E. Lee surrendered to General Ulysses S. Grant at Appomattox, Virginia, and the Civil War officially ended. However, secessionist feelings did not immediately subside. Five days later, while President Lincoln was attending a play at Ford's Theater in Washington, D.C., a southern sympathizer, John Wilkes Booth, shot Lincoln in the back of the head. He died the next morning. The news was devastating to those in the North. Historians estimate that about one-third of the Union population turned out to mourn the president along the funeral train's journey to Illinois.

The following poem, written by Walt Whitman in 1865, captures the grief many felt for their martyred leader. Likening the Union to a ship, Whitman characterizes Abraham Lincoln as a beloved captain. The narrator, a shipmate, is in shock, unable to comprehend the loss.

O Captain! My Captain!

O Captain! my Captain! our fearful trip is done,
The ship has weather'd every rack, the prize we sought is won,
The port is near, the bells I hear, the people all exulting,

While follow eyes the steady keel, the vessel grim and daring;
    But O heart! heart! heart!
        O the bleeding drops of red,
            Where on the deck my Captain lies,
                Fallen cold and dead.

O Captain! my Captain! Rise up and hear the bells;
Rise up—for you the flag is flung—for you the bugle trills,
For you bouquets and ribbon'd wreaths—for you the shores a-crowding,
For you they call, the swaying mass, their eager faces turning;
    Here Captain! dear father!
        This arm beneath your head!
            It is some dream that on the deck,
                You've fallen cold and dead.

My Captain does not answer, his lips are pale and still,
My father does not feel my arm, he has no pulse nor will,
The ship is anchor'd safe and sound, its voyage closed and done,
From fearful trip the victor ship comes in with object won;
    Exult O shores, and ring O bells!
        But I with mournful tread,
            Walk the deck my Captain lies,
                Fallen cold and dead.

Walt Whitman imagined such complexity in Lincoln's face and character that he argued a portrait capturing Lincoln's likeness had never been created. Mathew Brady took this photo in 1864.

BOOKER T. WASHINGTON (1856?–1915)

From the late 1800s up until World War I, Booker T. Washington was the most influential spokesperson for African Americans. Washington was born a slave. His mother was a slave, and his father was an unidentified white man. After the Civil War, Washington was able to satisfy his "intense longing" to read and write by working his way through the Hampton Normal and Agricultural Institute in Virginia. Washington started a teaching career, and in 1891, he founded the Tuskegee Institute in Alabama, an all-black vocational school. He became an adviser to the president and a leading public figure.

Before Booker T. Washington gained prominence, the Thirteenth, Fourteenth, and Fifteenth Amendments to the Constitution were ratified.

"dignify and glorify common labour"

These amendments outlawed slavery, granted citizenship to African Americans, and gave black men the vote. Although they resulted in great voter turnout, these amendments did not create immediate social change for African Americans. In 1880, for example, 90 percent of all southern blacks were employed in farming or domestic-service positions—the same work they had performed as slaves.

Following Reconstruction, the South instituted a system of separation, or segregation, of the races by passing so-called Jim Crow laws. Separate facilities, such as drinking fountains, restrooms, and waiting areas, reminded southern blacks each day of their "inferior" status. In 1896, the Supreme Court ruled in Plessy v. Ferguson *that segregation in public places was legal as long as "separate but equal" facilities were provided. In practice, however, black facilities were rarely "equal" to those of whites.*

Rather than confront the discrimination of the period, Washington focused on trying to improve prospects for blacks by building vocational schools where they could learn trades and skills. In 1895, he made a now-famous speech at the Atlanta Exposition, urging African Americans to work hard and get along with whites. In the same speech, he asked whites to help blacks advance themselves. This speech became known as the Atlanta Compromise, and his nonconfrontational philosophy brought him fame.

Up from Slavery
Chapter XIV, The Atlanta Exposition Address

Mr. President and Gentlemen of the Board
of Directors and Citizens.

One-third of the population of the South is of the Negro race. No enterprise seeking the material, civil, or moral welfare of this section can disregard this element of our population and reach the highest success....

To those of my race who depend on bettering their condition in a foreign land or who underestimate the importance of cultivating friendly relations with the Southern white man, who is their next-door neighbor, I would say: "Cast down your bucket where you are"—cast it down in making friends in every manly way of the people of all races by whom we are surrounded.

Cast it down in agriculture, mechanics, in commerce, in domestic service, and in the professions. And in this connection it is well to bear in mind that whatever other sins the South may be called to bear, when it comes to business, pure and simple, it is in the South that the Negro is given a man's chance in the commercial world, and in nothing is this

Exposition more eloquent than in emphasizing this chance. Our greatest danger is that in the great leap from slavery to freedom we may overlook the fact that the masses of us are to live by the productions of our hands, and fail to keep in mind that we shall prosper in proportion as we learn to dignify and glorify common labor and put brains and skill into the common occupations of life; shall prosper in proportion as we learn to draw the line between the superficial and the substantial, the ornamental gewgaws of life and the useful. No race can prosper until it learns that there is as much dignity in tilling a field as in writing a poem. It is at the bottom of life we must begin, and not at the top. Nor should we permit our grievances to overshadow our opportunities....

The wisest among my race understand that the agitation of questions of social equality is the extremest folly, and that progress in the enjoyment of all the privileges that will come to us must be the result of severe and constant struggle rather than of artificial forcing. No race that has anything to contribute to the markets of the world is long in any degree ostracized. It is important and right that all privileges of the law be ours, but it is vastly more important that we be prepared for the exercises of these privileges. The opportunity to earn a dollar in a factory just now is worth infinitely more than the opportunity to spend a dollar in an opera-house.

In conclusion, may I repeat that nothing in thirty years has given us more hope and encouragement, and drawn us so near to you of the white race, as this opportunity offered by the Exposition.... I pledge that in your effort to work out the great and intricate problem which God has laid at the doors of the South, you shall have at all times the patient, sympathetic help of my race; only let this be constantly in mind, that ... far above and beyond material benefits will be that higher good, that, let us pray God, will come, in a blotting out of sectional differences and racial animosities and suspicions.... This, this, coupled with our material prosperity, will bring into our beloved South a new heaven and a new earth.

W.E.B. DuBOIS (1868–1963)

A vocal supporter of racial equality, W.E.B. DuBois attended Fisk and Harvard Universities as well as the University of Berlin. He became a professor in Philadelphia and Atlanta, and his writings about black life in the United States were published widely. Besides writing essays, fiction, poetry, and scholarly works, DuBois helped establish the National

"Mr. Washington represents . . . adjustment and submission."

Association for the Advancement of Colored People (NAACP) and edited its journal, The Crisis, for many years.

DuBois argued that education—specifically higher education—was the key to the social and economic advancement of African Americans. During Reconstruction, the federal government and northern reformers helped to educate former slaves. Thousands of black men and women of all ages enrolled in classes and sought skills—such as reading and writing—that they had been denied under slavery. The Freedmen's Bureau established over 4,000 schools, including some colleges and universities, to train teachers, ministers, and other professionals who could take on leadership roles. By the late nineteenth century, DuBois was disturbed because this aid was diminishing. In addition, he harshly criticized legalized segregation. Noting the emergence of the Ku Klux Klan and lynching parties, DuBois believed that African Americans had not yet come close to attaining social, economic, and political equality.

Publishing the book The Souls of Black Folk *in 1903 brought DuBois fame. In the following excerpt, DuBois argues against Booker T. Washington's philosophy. In the same book, he predicted that "the problem of the Twentieth Century is the problem of the color line."*

The Souls of Black Folk
III. Of Mr. Booker T. Washington and Others

Easily the most striking thing in the history of the American Negro since 1876 is the ascendancy of Mr. Booker T. Washington. It began at the time when war memories and ideals were rapidly passing; a day of astonishing commercial development was dawning; a sense of doubt and hesitation overtook the freedmen's sons,—then it was that his leading began. Mr. Washington came, with a simple definite program, at the psychological moment when the nation was a little ashamed of having bestowed so much sentiment on Negroes, and was concentrating its energies on Dollars....

Mr. Washington represents in Negro thought the old attitude of adjustment and submission; but adjustment at such a peculiar time as to make his program unique. This is an age of unusual economic development, and Mr. Washington's program naturally takes an economic cast, becoming a gospel of Work and Money to such an extent as apparently almost completely to overshadow the higher aims of life. Moreover, this is an age when the more advanced races are coming in closer contact with the less developed races, and the race-feeling is therefore intensified; and Mr. Washington's program practically accepts the alleged inferiority of the Negro races. Again, in our own land, the reaction from the sentiment of war time has given impetus to race-prejudice against Negroes, and

Mr. Washington withdraws many of the high demands of Negroes as men and American citizens. . . .

Mr. Washington distinctly asks that black people give up, at least for the present, three things,—

First, political power,

Second, insistence on civil rights,

Third, higher education of Negro youth—and concentrate all their energies on industrial education, the accumulation of wealth, and the conciliation of the South. This policy has been courageously and insistently advocated for over fifteen years, and has been triumphant for perhaps ten years. As a result of this tender of the palm-branch, what has been the return? In these years there have occurred:

1. The disfranchisement of the Negro.

2. The legal creation of a distinct status of civil inferiority for the Negro.

3. The steady withdrawal of aid from institutions for the higher training of the Negro.

These movements are not, to be sure, direct results of Mr. Washington's teachings; but his propaganda has, without a shadow of a doubt, helped their speedier accomplishment. The question then comes: Is it possible, and probable, that nine millions of men can make effective progress in economic lines if they are deprived of political rights, made a servile caste, and allowed only the most meager chance for developing their exceptional men? If history and reason give any distinct answer to these questions, it is an emphatic No. . . .

The black men of America have a duty to perform, a duty stern and delicate,—a forward movement to oppose a part of the work of their greatest leader. So far as Mr. Washington preaches Thrift, Patience, and Industrial Training for the masses, we must hold up his hands and strive with him. . . . But so far as Mr. Washington apologizes for injustice, North or South, does not rightly value the privilege and duty of voting, belittles the emasculating effects of caste distinctions, and opposes the higher training and ambition of our brighter minds,—so far as he, the South, or this Nation, does this,—we must unceasingly and firmly oppose them. By every civilized and peaceful method we must strive for the rights which the world accords to men, clinging unwaveringly to those great words which the sons of the Fathers would fain forget: "We hold these truths to be self-evident: That all men are created equal; that they are endowed by their Creator with certain unalienable rights; that among these are life, liberty, and the pursuit of happiness."

African Americans gained vocational skills at segregated schools such as Tuskegee Institute. Tuskegee students (shown below) conduct experiments in a chemistry lab.

1865 1919

From the end of the Civil War to the end of World War I, the United States underwent a second wave of industrialization that transformed the nation's economy, landscape, and identity. In a rapid transition, residents in New England and parts of the Midwest found themselves working in urban factories, rather than rural farms. White migration, mining, and railroad expansion brought fundamental changes to the Great Plains and Far West. Although the United States was not the first country to industrialize, it implemented these changes with amazing speed. By the early twentieth century, America was among the wealthiest and strongest nations in the world.

In the second half of the nineteenth century, immigrants poured into the country to help construct rail lines, settle the frontier, and work in factories. Transcontinental train service, telegraphs, and telephones—along with successful attempts to relocate Native American tribes—meant that the East and West Coasts of the United States were united. Interstate commerce grew and the economy with it. Because of increased economic influence, U.S. relations with other countries grew more important. In addition, the government began to build colonies overseas to find greater markets for its goods and to protect international trade routes. American scholars, authors, and artists traveled abroad—particularly to Europe—and became part of an international exchange of ideas. In short, America's stature in diplomacy, commerce, and intellectual arenas provided a springboard to global dominance.

Finally, assuming its role as an international power, the United States entered World War I in 1917. President Woodrow Wilson's war declaration called for American support to make the world "safe for democracy." When World War I ended in 1918, millions of soliders and civilians lay dead, yet "the war to end all wars" did not lead to lasting peace.

Professional writers grew in popularity through the growth of magazines, dime novels, and their increased

1855
The first skeleton-framed skyscraper is built.

1858
Prospectors discover gold in Colorado.

1867
Russia sells Alaska to the United States.

1868
Brooklyn Bridge construction begins.

1881
Andrew Carnegie opens his steel plant in Pennsylvania.

1885
Southern and eastern Europeans begin to come to the United States.

1889
Whites begin to settle Oklahoma Indian Territory.

1890
The National American Women's Suffrage Association is founded.

1893
The Chicago World's Fair opens, highlighting technological progress.

readership. These authors responded to the era's overwhelming changes in a variety of ways. Some longed for their old lifestyles and regional customs, while others revered the awesome power of technology. Some portrayed the grim reality of immigrant ghettos and the stifling mores of wealthy socialites. Progressives campaigned against political corruption and the exploitation of workers; others rallied for women's suffrage. During World War I, many American authors became disillusioned with "progress." As a whole, these views provide insight into the wealth of experiences that characterized this period of stunning social change.

1898
President McKinley sends American forces to fight the Spanish American War in the Philippines, the first time American troops fight outside the Western Hemisphere.

1899
The United States annexes the Philippine Islands.

1900
In Manhattan, more than 40,000 tenements house 1.5 million people.

1909
The National Association for the Advancement of Colored People is founded.

1913
Woodrow Wilson becomes president and advocates "internationalism," a new approach to foreign affairs.

1914
Archduke Ferdinand is assassinated, sparking World War I.

1919
The Treaty of Versailles ends World War I.

1920
The Nineteenth Amendment is ratified, guaranteeing women the right to vote.

The Closing of the Frontier

Just before the Civil War, writers all across the United States began telling stories about people and places they knew well. They sensed that new industry and floods of immigrants would change their lifestyles and cultures, so they wrote to preserve their heritage.

In the West, train tracks and trestles as well as large-scale mining were beginning to scar the once-pristine landscape. These technologies—combined with aggressive government policies—encouraged white migration and settlement of the vast plains, the Rocky Mountains, and the West Coast. In their wake, native peoples and wildlife faltered. The government removed countless tribes from their ancestral lands, by force and by treaty, to make way for railroad and mining ventures. By the 1890s the frontier officially closed. Many writers who had traveled or lived in the area were afraid of losing the rugged spirit of the "Old West," so they immortalized pioneers, cowboys, Indians, and the American bison as cultural icons.

This literary movement is called "local color," and it was the first sign of a new writing philosophy—realism. Realists found truth and meaning in ordinary life. Unlike previous generations, writers such as Willa Cather, Bret Harte, and Hamlin Garland believed that their own landscapes were subjects for great literature. Their works were often nostalgic, humorous, or critical.

Although many regional writers reacted against technology, it directly helped their careers. In 1865 there were only 700 magazines in the United States, but by the turn of the century there were 5,000. The rapid growth of magazines and newspapers enabled many to be full-time writers and journalists. Trains, telegraphs, and telephones helped fuel readers' interest in the varied regions of this vast country. At the same time, those technologies created an insatiable hunger for land that nearly destroyed many native peoples.

Technology was therefore a double-edged sword. Citizens could quickly and easily experience the abundance of the United States through high-speed travel, immediate telecommunications, and burgeoning literature. But many writers sensed the nation was losing part of its identity—its varied cultures, flora, and fauna—for that privilege.

Featured Authors

Willa Cather
Bret Harte
Nat Love
Hamlin Garland
Black Elk

WILLA CATHER (1873–1947)

Willa Cather—one of America's most popular storytellers of the prairie frontier—was a life-long pioneer. When she was 9 years old, her family moved from Virginia to Nebraska, a set-ting that featured prominently in her fiction. Later, Cather helped push back the frontier for women in education and literature. She attended the University of Nebraska and devoted her career to writing when these pursuits were reserved largely for men. In 1908, Cather became the managing editor of McClure's Magazine *and spent the rest of her life in New York City. By 1947, she had penned thirteen novels and sixty short stories, many of them portraying accomplished, indepen-dent female characters like herself. Time and again, Cather's work probed broad pioneering themes—starting over or blazing new trails.*

Willa Cather's home state of Nebraska was first organized as a terri-tory before the Civil War in the 1854 Kansas-Nebraska Act. Thereafter, settlers began moving to the Great Plains in increasing numbers. To encourage the migration of families, the 1862 Homestead Act granted free land to both men and women. Consequently, a woman in the West could control the title to her own land. In practice, however, the Homestead Act proved a failure. Most Americans who did not already own land were too poor to become farmers—even when they could get land for free. Moving, building a house, and buying farming tools such as plows and wagons often proved too costly. Those who managed such feats often found homesteading a backbreaking, lonely, and financially unrewarding experience. Frequent droughts, floods, and blizzards made agriculture in Nebraska exceedingly difficult in the nineteenth century.

Cather published her novel O Pioneers! *in 1913, after she had moved to New York City and agricultural advances had begun to tame the harsh frontier of Nebraska. In this work, Cather draws on her child-hood experiences on the desolate plains and describes the landscape and the difficulties early settlers faced in farming. Her story focuses on the Bergson family, immigrants from Sweden who own land on the Divide, an area in Nebraska near the Kansas border. This reading intro-duces Alexandra, the eldest child of the Bergson family who will soon take control of the farm. By the end of the novel, Alexandra's tenacity and intelligence win out over male jealousy and the seemingly insur-mountable odds of "the wild land." Meanwhile, Cather helps mold the ideal of the pioneer spirit, giving readers insight into their motivations, hardships, and dreams.*

> *"[The land] was like a horse that . . . runs wild and kicks things to pieces."*

O Pioneers!
Part I: The Wild Land, Chapter 2

On one of the ridges of that wintry waste stood the low log house in which John Bergson was dying. The Bergson homestead was easier to find than many another, because it overlooked Norway Creek, a shallow, muddy stream that sometimes flowed, and sometimes stood still, at the bottom of a winding ravine with steep, shelving sides overgrown with brush and cottonwoods and dwarf ash. This creek gave a sort of identity to the farms that bordered upon it. Of all the bewildering things about a new country, the absence of human landmarks is one of the most depressing and disheartening. The houses on the Divide were small and were usually tucked away in low places; you did not see them until you came directly upon them. Most of them were built of sod itself, and were only the unescapable ground in another form. The roads were but faint tracks in the grass, and the fields were scarcely noticeable. The record of the plow was insignificant, like the feeble scratches on stone left by prehistoric races, so indeterminate that they may, after all, be only the markings of glaciers, and not a record of human strivings.

In eleven long years John Bergson had made but little impression upon the wild land he had come to tame. It was still a wild thing that had its ugly moods; and no one knew when they were likely to come, or why. Mischance hung over it. Its Genius was unfriendly to man. The sick man was feeling this as he lay looking out of the window, after the doctor had left him, on the day following Alexandra's trip to town. There it lay outside his door, the same land, the same lead-colored miles. He knew every ridge and draw and gully between him and the horizon. To the south, his plowed fields; to the east, the sod stables, the cattle corral, the pond—and then the grass.

Bergson went over in his mind the things that held him back. One winter his cattle had perished in a blizzard. The next summer one of his plow horses broke its leg in a prairie-dog hole and had to be shot. Another summer he lost his hogs from cholera, and a valuable stallion died from a rattlesnake bite. Time and again his crops had failed. He had lost two children, boys, that came between Lou and Emil, and there had been the cost of sickness and death. Now, when he had at last struggled out of debt, he was going to die himself. He was only forty-six, and had, of course, counted upon more time.

Bergson had spent his first five years on the Divide getting into debt, and the last six getting out. He had paid off his mortgages and had ended pretty much where he began, with the land. He owned exactly six hundred and forty acres of what stretched outside his door....

John Bergson had the Old-World belief that land, in itself, is desirable. But this land was an enigma. It was like a horse that no one knows how to break to harness, that runs wild and kicks things to pieces. He had an idea that no one understood how to farm it properly, and this he often discussed with Alexandra.

Their neighbors, certainly, knew even less about farming than he did. Many of them had never worked on a farm until they took up their homesteads. They had been *handwerkers* at home; tailors, locksmiths, joiners, cigarmakers, etc. Bergson himself had worked in a shipyard.

For weeks, John Bergson had been thinking about these things.... He counted the cattle over and over. It diverted him to speculate as to how much weight each of the steers would probably put on by spring. He often called his daughter in to talk to her about this. Before Alexandra was twelve years old, she had begun to be a help to him, and as she grew older he had come to depend more and more upon her resourcefulness and good judgment.... It was Alexandra who read the papers and followed the markets, and who learned by the mistakes of their neighbors. It was Alexandra who could always tell about what it had cost to fatten each steer, and who could guess the weight of a hog before it went on the scales closer than John Bergson himself....

Alexandra, her father often said to himself, was like her grandfather; which was his way of saying she was intelligent.... In his daughter, John Bergson recognized the strength of will, and the simple direct way of thinking things out, that had characterized his father in his better days. He would much rather, of course, have seen this likeness in one of his sons, but it was not a question of choice. As he lay there day after day, he had to accept the situation as it was, and to be thankful that there was one among his children to whom he could entrust the future of his family and the possibilities of his hard-won land....

After a trip to the West, writer Margaret Fuller wrote that it was generally men's choice to migrate, and women followed "as women will, doing their best for affection's sake but too often in heartsickness and weariness." While Fuller's account was often true, many women adapted well to western life as farmers, ranchers, and bronco busters. A settler on the Great Plains (shown above) gathers buffalo chips for fuel.

BRET HARTE (1836–1902)

Bret Harte, born in Albany, New York, became famous for his fiction and poetry about the final settlement of the American frontier. His greatest literary successes occurred after he became editor of The Overland Monthly, *a magazine in San Francisco, in 1868.*

At that time, San Francisco's population was nearly 250,000, and it was the commercial heart of the Pacific Coast. Since the mid-1850s, Chinese immigrants had begun settling in

"Thar isn't her match in the county."

the West Coast region to help build railroads. With trails blazed by early settlers and railways, independent prospectors came to the Rockies between the 1850s and 1870s to mine for gold and silver. These trends brought changes to the westernmost areas of the country. With each new discovery of precious metals, permanent settlers joined the rush of prospectors, who helped populate new towns in California, Colorado, Montana, and Nevada. In short, the Far West was becoming less "wild," and regional writers such as Bret Harte helped preserve and mythologize American notions of cowboys, saloons, and bandits of the "Old West."

Harte wrote the following poem, "Chiquita," in the form of a one-sided conversation in a western dialect. The speaker is a horse trader, extolling the virtues of the horse at hand, Chiquita, to the reader. The narrator also addresses his horse handler, Jack. Besides emphasizing the importance of a good horse in the rugged landscape of the West, the speaker's story reveals much about his own character—a western stereotype—the not-so-reliable horse dealer.

Frederic Remington was most famous for his illustrations, paintings, and sculptures depicting cowboys, Indians, and western battle scenes. Like many regional writers of the late nineteenth century, Remington romanticized and mythologized life in the Wild West.

Chiquita

Beautiful! Sir, you may say so. Thar isn't her
      match in the county.
Is thar, old gal,—Chiquita, my darling, my beauty?
Fell of that neck, sir,—thar's velvet! Whoa! Steady,
      —ah, will you, you vixen!
Whoa! I say. Jack, trot her out; let the gentleman
      look at her paces.

Morgan!—She ain't nothin' else, and I've got the
      papers to prove it.
Sired by Chippewa Chief, and twelve hundred dollars
      won't buy her.
Briggs of Tuolumne owned her. Did you know Briggs
      of Tuolumne?—
Busted hisself in White Pine, and blew out his brains
      down in 'Frisco?
Hedn't no savey—hed Briggs. Thar, Jack! that'll
      do,—quit that foolin'!
Nothin' to what she kin do, when she's got her work
      cut out before her.
Hosses is hosses, you know, and likewise, too, jockeys
      is jockeys;
And 't ain't ev'ry man as can ride as knows what a
      hoss has got in him.

Know the old ford on the Fork, that nearly got
 Flanigan's leaders?
Nasty in daylight, you bet, and a mighty rough ford in
 low water!
Well, it ain't six weeks ago that me and the Jedge and
 his nevey
Struck for that ford in the night, in the rain, and the
 water all around us;

Up to our flanks in the gulch, and Rattlesnake Creek,
 just a bilin',
Not a plank left in the dam, and nary a bridge on the
 river.
I had the gray, and Jedge has his roan, and his
 nevey, Chiquita;
And after us trundled the rocks jest loosed from the top
 of the canyon.

Lickity, lickity, switch, we came to the ford, and
 Chiquita
Buckled right down to her work, and afore I could yell
 to her rider,
Took water jest at the ford, and there was the Jedge
 and me standing,
and twelve hundred dollars of hoss-flesh afloat and a
 driftin' to thunder!

Would ye b'lieve it? that night that hoss, that ar' filly,
 Chiquita,
Walked herself into her stall and stood there, all quiet
 and dripping:
Clean as a beaver or rat, with nary a buckle of harness,
Just as she swam the Fork, —that hoss, that ar' filly,
 Chiquita.

That's what I call a hoss! and—What did you say?
 —Oh, the nevey?
Drownded, I reckon,—leastways, he never kem back
 to deny it.
Ye see the derned fool had no seat,—ye couldn't have
 made him a rider;
And then, ye know, boys will be boys, and hosses—
 well, hosses is hosses!

*"for that day
I was the hero
of Deadwood"*

NAT LOVE (1854–1921)

*Nat Love was born into slavery in Tennessee.
After the Civil War—at the age of 15—he headed
to Dodge City, Kansas, to "rustle up" opportunity.
He soon joined a team of Texas cowboys and
became an expert in identifying livestock brands.
In 1876, Love won a roping and shooting contest
in Deadwood, South Dakota, where he earned his
nickname, "Deadwood Dick." After years of driving cattle and fighting
Indians on the trail, Love's job was made obsolete by trains that could
transport herds to market faster. Consequently, in 1890, he became a
porter for the luxury Pullman sleeping cars, the only railroad job then
open to African Americans. Love enjoyed the railroad job for the same
reason he did the cowboy life: it allowed him to see more of the world.
In his autobiography, published in 1907, he wrote, "I have seen a large
part of America, and am still seeing it, but the life of a hundred years
would be all too short to see our country. America, I love thee...."*

*Nat Love's autobiography reminds readers that whites were not the
only players in the settlement of the West. As many as 5,000 black cowboys drove cattle along the western trails. In addition, historians report
that about 20 percent of the western cavalry that fought the Plains
Indians were African American.*

*Love's work details those violent clashes with Indians in the west-
ern United States. By the 1860s, railroads, mining, and frontier settlement
had created great demands for Native American lands. Though the government negotiated treaties with each tribe or "nation," in practice the
treaties were not honored—by the government, gold prospectors, settlers,
or tribal members. In 1867, the federal government decided to confine
all the Plains tribes to two reservations—one in Dakota Territory and the
other in Oklahoma.*

*Faced with the loss of their hunting grounds and their ways of life,
many tribes saw no alternative but to fight, even though they knew their
chances for success were small. The following selection from Love's
autobiography describes events during the summer of 1876, particularly
the Battle of Little Big Horn in southern Montana. There General George
Custer and 264 of his troops met their deaths against Sioux and
Cheyenne Indians.*

*Love writes with a bias toward the U.S. government and General
Custer. However, from today's perspective, the government's policy was
questionable. Gold had been discovered in the Black Hills, and the government was intent on removing the native tribes from that area, even*

though an earlier treaty had granted them hunting rights to that land. According to the Sioux religion, the Black Hills were sacred, so the western Sioux refused to give up their rights to that property. Consequently, the government resorted to force. The Plains Indians' victory at Little Big Horn was unusual and short lived. Within a few months the warriors surrendered and were forced onto reservations.

The Life and Adventures of Nat Love, Better Known in the Cattle Country as Deadwood Dick
Chapter XIII

In the spring of 1876, orders were received at the home ranch [in Arizona] for three thousand head of three-year-old steers to be delivered near Deadwood, South Dakota. This being one of the largest orders we had ever received at one time, every man around the ranch was placed on his mettle to execute the order in record time.

Cowboys mounted on swift horses were dispatched to the farthest limits of the ranch with orders to round up and run in all the three-year-olds on the place, and it was not long before the ranch corrals began to fill up with the long horns as they were driven by the several parties of cowboys; as fast as they came in we would cut out, under the bosses' orders such cattle as were to make up our herd.

In the course of three days we had our herd ready for the trail and we made our preparations to start on our long journey north. Our route lay through New Mexico, Colorado, and Wyoming, and as we had heard rumors that the Indians were on the war path and were kicking up something of a rumpus in Wyoming, Indian Territory, and Kansas, we expected trouble before we again had the pleasure of sitting around our fire at the home ranch. Quite a large party was selected for this trip owing to the size of the herd and the possibility of trouble on the trail from the Indians. We, as usual, were all well armed and had as mounts the best horses our ranch produced, and in taking the trail we were perfectly confident that we could take care of our herd and ourselves through anything we were liable to met. We had not been on the trail long before we met other outfits, who told us that General Custer was out after the Indians and that a big fight was expected when the Seventh U.S. Cavalry, General Custer's command, met the Crow tribe and other Indians under the leadership of Sitting Bull, Rain-in-the-Face, Old Chief Joseph, and other chiefs of lesser prominence, who had for a long time been terrorizing the settlers of that section and defying the Government.

As we proceeded on our journey it became evident to us that we were only a short distance behind the soldiers. When finally the Indians and soldiers met in the memorable battle or rather massacre in the Little

Early Miners in the West
"Some of the blowing dust was gold."

Prospecting for gold and silver was a "get-rich-quick" scheme. Lured by tales of gold nuggets the size of a man's fist, prospectors rushed to and helped build new mining towns. In reality, however, the metals were less plentiful than the hardships and violence of the frontier. Often the towns faded quickly. However, in some cases such as Virginia City, Nevada, mining towns prospered with the discoveries of their resources. Ironically, while individual prospectors found most large deposits, big corporations mined those areas and gained the lion's share of the wealth. Nevertheless, prospectors and settlers helped those areas to become territories of the United States government, and they helped to create considerable literature about the magic, riches, and excitement of the West. "A Peck of Gold" by Robert Frost tells readers how indelibly the precious ore permeates the Western conscience.

A Peck of Gold

Dust always blowing about the town
Except when sea fog laid it down.
And I was one of the children told
Some of the blowing dust was gold.

All the dust the wind blew high
Appeared like gold in the sunset sky.
But I was one of the children told
Some of the dust was really gold.

Such was life in the Golden Gate.
Gold dusted all we drank and ate.
And I was one of the children told
We all must eat our peck of gold.

Big Horn Basin on the Little Big Horn River in northern Wyoming, we were only two days behind them, or within 60 miles, but we did not know that at the time or we would have gone to Custer's assistance....

The Custer Battle was June 25, 1876. The battle commenced on Sunday afternoon and lasted about two hours. That was the last of General Custer and his Seventh Cavalry. How I know this so well is because we had orders from one of the Government scouts to go in camp, that if we went any further North we were liable to be captured by the Indians.

We arrived in Deadwood in good condition without having had any trouble with the Indians on the way up. We turned our cattle over to their new owners at once, then proceeded to take in the town. The next morning, July 4th, the gamblers and mining men made up a purse of $200 for a roping contest between the cowboys that were then in town. . . . It did not take long to arrange the details for the contest and contestants, six of them being colored cowboys, including myself. Our trail boss was chosen to pick out the mustangs from a herd of wild horses just off the range, and he picked out twelve of the most wild and vicious horses that he could find.

The conditions of the contest were that each of us who were mounted was to rope, throw, tie, bridle and saddle, and mount the particular horse picked for us in the shortest time possible. The man accomplishing the feat in the quickest time to be declared the winner.

It seems to me that the horse chosen for me was the most vicious of the lot. Everything being in readiness, the [Colt] "45" cracked and we all sprang forward together, each of us making for our particular mustang.

I roped, threw, tied, bridled, saddled, and mounted my mustang in exactly nine minutes from the crack of the gun. The time of the next nearest competitor was twelve minutes and thirty seconds. This gave me the record and championship of the West, which I held up to the time I quit the business in 1890, and my record has never been beaten. It is worthy of passing remark that I never had a horse pitch with me so much as that mustang, but I never stopped sticking my spurs in him and using my quirt on his flanks until I proved his master. Right there the assembled crowd named me Deadwood Dick and proclaimed me champion roper of the western cattle country.

The roping contest over, a dispute arose over the shooting question with the result that a contest was arranged for the afternoon, as there happened to be some of the best shots with rifle and revolver in the West present that day. . . .

The range was measured off 100 and 250 yards for the rifle and 150 for the Colt 45. At this distance a bulls eye about the size of an apple was put up. Each man was to have 14 shots at each range with the rifle and 12 shots with the Colts 45. I placed every one of my 14 shots with the rifle in the bulls eye with ease, all shots being made from the hip; but with the 45 Colts I missed it twice, only placing 10 shots in the small circle, Stormy Jim being my nearest competitor, only placing 8 bullets in the bulls eye clear, the rest being quite close, while with the 45 he placed 5 bullets in the charmed circle. This gave me the championship of rifle

The Indians' victory at the Battle of Little Big Horn was unusual among the Indian Wars of the late nineteenth century. The painting shown here dramatizes "Custer's last stand."

and revolver shooting as well as the roping contest, and for that day I was the hero of Deadwood.... [A]s it was the busy season,... our outfit began to make preparations to return to Arizona....

Everything now being in readiness with us we took the trail homeward bound, and left Deadwood in a blaze of glory. On our way home we visited the Custer battle field in the Little Big Horn Basin.

There was ample evidence of the desperate and bloody fight that had taken place a few days before. We arrived home in Arizona in a short time without further incident, except that on the way back we met and talked with many of the famous Government scouts of that region, among them Buffalo Bill (William F. Cody), Yellow Stone Kelley, and many others of that day.... [A] finer or braver body of men never lived than these scouts of the West....

The name of Deadwood Dick was given to me by the people of Deadwood, South Dakota, July 4, 1876, after I had proven myself worthy to carry it, and after I had defeated all comers in riding, roping, and shooting, and I have always carried the name with honor since that time.

"Go tell the caporal that a vaquero has been killed"

A MEXICAN FOLK BALLAD

Ranching was a way of life in Old Mexico—today's American Southwest—long before the United States gained the territory. In fact, Mexican vaqueros, *or cattle drivers, preceded the U.S. adoption of the cowboy role and identity. Not surprisingly, in the 1860s many of the cowboys en route to Dodge City, Kansas, were Mexican and Mexican-American.*

Latino cowboys eased the monotony of the trail with ballad-style folk songs called "corridos," which were usually sung with a guitar accompaniment. The songs were composed anonymously and handed down through word of mouth. Although corridos *flourished in the American Southwest and border lands between 1865 and 1915, their origins have been traced to Medieval Spain. Following is a* corrido *in English translation that dates from the 1860s. In the Spanish original, words rhymed, and the meter, or rhythm, was regular. Nevertheless, the English lyrics emphasize the Latinos' excellence, as well as their pride, in swimming and horsemanship.*

Kansas I

When we left for Kansas with a great herd of cattle,
ah, what a long trail it was! I was not sure I would survive.

The *caporal* would tell us, as if he was going to cry,
"Watch out for that bunch of steers; don't let them get past you."

Ah, what a good horse I had! He did nothing but gallop.
And, ah, what a violent cloudburst! I was not sure I would come back.

Some of us asked for cigarettes, others wanted something to eat;
and the *caporal* would tell us, "So be it, it can't be helped."

By the pond at Palomas a vicious steer left the herd.
and the *caporal* lassoed it on is honey-colored horse.

Go tell the *caporal* that a vaquero has been killed;
all he left was his leather jacket hanging on the rails of the corral.

We got to the Salado River, and we swam our horses across;
an American was saying, "Those men are as good as drowned."

I wonder what the man thought, that we came to learn, perhaps;
why, we're from the Rio Grande, where the good swimmers are from.

And then Kansas came in sight, and the *caporal* tells us,
"We have finally made it, we'll soon have them in the corral."

Back again in San Antonio, we all bought ourselves good hats,
and this is the end of the singing of the stanzas about the trail drivers.

HAMLIN GARLAND (1860–1940)

Hamlin Garland was born just before the Civil War to a family in West Salem, Wisconsin. For the first twenty-four years of his life, he toiled without success on prairie farms from Wisconsin to Iowa and the Dakotas. Finally giving up on the elusive "land of plenty," Garland moved to Boston in 1884. In the 1890s, he began writing sketches of the midwestern landscape he left behind. His works through the early 1900s provide grim, realistic details about the hardship and bitter disappointment of many midwestern frontier settlers.

"And their bones / Lie white on the flame-charred sod"

Throughout the mid-1800s, a striking feature of the midwestern plains was the great herds of American bison, or buffalo. In the mid-1860s, 13 to 15 million buffalo roamed the Plains. However, gangs of railroad laborers slaughtered thousands to feed themselves while building the Union Pacific Railroad. Buffalo hunting became a popular sport, and railroad companies organized train tours, even allowing hunters to gun down the animals from slow-moving railroad cars. In 1871, industry had found a way to make use of buffalo hides, so about 9 million buffalo were killed in the next three years. All of these practices led to the virtual extinction of these great herds by the early 1880s.

Buffalo meat, hides, and bones were the mainstays of tribal life on the Plains, and their destruction was closely related to U.S. government policies toward Indian nations. After decades of relocation and faithless treaties with the federal government, the slaughter of the buffalo was one of the final blows to the Plains Indians—leaving them without food, homes, or purpose. Stripped of their independence, the Native American tribes became more reliant upon the U.S. government for their territory, food, supplies, and culture. This weakening of Plains tribes meant that whites could expand even farther into what was then Native American land. In 1889, the Indian Territory of Oklahoma was opened to white settlement, and by the 1890s, the frontier officially closed.

The following poem is Hamlin Garland's eulogy to the buffalo.

The Passing of the Buffalo

Going, the wild things of our land.
Passing, the antelope and the buffalo.
They have gone with the sunny sweep
Of the untracked plain.
They have passed away with the untrammeled
Current of our streams.

With the falling trees they fell,
With the autumn grasses they rotted,
And their bones
Lie white on the flame-charred sod,
Mixed with the antlers of the elk.

For centuries they lay down and rose
In peace and calm content.
They were fed by the rich grass
And watered by sunny streams.

A Plains Indian Song

"Let your hoofs / Thunder over us!"

Most Native American literature in the nineteenth century was not written. For centuries their literary traditions were oral—including storytelling, speechmaking at formal events, ritual chants, and song. Written forms of nineteenth century Indian literature were either interpreted and documented by others or published by a few Native Americans.

The following Chippewa song, translated by Alice Corbin, probably was performed with a ritual dance. Even without the dancers' movements or the drums and rattles that would have accompanied this song, the words tell us about the prominence of the buffalo to the Chippewa Indian's existence. It addresses the buffalo as a powerful, revered presence.

This song represents a culture that the federal government and white settlers misunderstood and sought to "assimilate" in the late nineteenth century. The Dawes Severalty Act of 1887 was designed to separate individuals from their tribes and make each nuclear family independent farmers, like white settlers. Missionaries and schools also aimed to "civilize" Native Americans by converting them to Christianity and white ways. These trends, combined with the buffalo slaughter and reservation policies, devastated tribal life in the United States.

Buffalo Dance

Strike ye our land
With curved horns!
Now with cries
Bending our bodies,
Breathe fire upon us;
Now with feet
Trampling the earth,
Let your hoofs
Thunder over us!
Strike ye our land
With curved horns!

The plover called to them
Out of the shimmering air,
The hawk swooped above them,
The blackbirds sat on their backs
In the still afternoons;
In the cool mud they wallowed,
Rolling in noisy sport.

The slaughter of the buffalo in the 1870s and 1880s marked the end of traditional tribal life for the Plains Indians. The immense pile of buffalo bones (shown above) suggests the vast numbers that were killed at one time.

They lived through centuries of struggle—
In swarming millions—till the white man came.
The snows of winter were terrible,
The dry wind was hard to bear,
But the breath of man, the smoke
Of his gun were more fatal.

They fell by the thousands.
They melted away like smoke.
Mile by mile they retreated westward;
Year by year they moved north and south
In dust-brown clouds;

Each year they descended upon the plains
In endless floods;
Each winter they retreated to the hills
Of the south.
Their going was like the ocean current,
But each spring they stopped a little short—
They were like an ebbing tide.
They came at last to meager little bands
That never left the hills—
Crawling in somber files from canyon to canyon—
Now they are gone!

"A people's dream died there."

BLACK ELK (1862–1950)

The Indian Wars of the 1800s were fueled by misunderstanding as well as by greed. In some cases, U.S. troops mishandled situations that ended in tragedy. One of the most well-known of these incidents was the Massacre at Wounded Knee.

In December 1890, U.S. cavalry troops approached Chief Big Foot and his tribe of Minneconjou Sioux Indians. At that time, Big Foot was dying of pneumonia, and Sioux Territory had been reduced so often that the tribe was already devastated. The U.S. government, however, suspected the tribe was armed for revolt, so U.S. troops were ordered to relocate them to Wounded Knee Creek, South Dakota, and disarm them. Once at Wounded Knee, the soldiers confiscated all weapons. However, in trying to disarm a young Indian who was deaf, confusion and gunfire broke out. U.S. troops fired their guns and cannons on all members of the tribe. When the firing ceased, Big Foot was dead, and more than half of his 400 men, women, and children were killed or seriously wounded.

The best-known account of the Massacre at Wounded Knee was told by a Sioux Holy Man named Black Elk. In 1931, John Neihardt interviewed Black Elk about his life, and Neihardt published Black Elk Speaks *the following year. This excerpt vividly describes the massacre, but it also eloquently conveys the Sioux tribe's despair and the loss of the belief system that once held the tribe together.*

Black Elk Speaks
Chapter XXIII

It was now near the end of the Moon of Popping Trees, and I was twenty-seven years old (December 1890). We heard that Big Foot was coming down from the Badlands with nearly four hundred people. Some of these were from Sitting Bull's band. They had run away when Sitting Bull was killed, and joined Big Foot on Good River. There were only about a hundred warriors in this band, and all the others were women and children and some old men. They were all starving and freezing, and Big Foot was so sick [with pneumonia] that they had to bring him along in a pony drag. They had all run away to hide in the Badlands, and they were coming in now because they were starving and freezing. When they crossed Smoky Earth River, they followed up Medicine Root Creek to its head. Soldiers were over there looking for them. The soldiers had everything and were not freezing and starving. Near Porcupine Butte the soldiers came up to the Big Foots, and they surrendered and went along with the soldiers to Wounded Knee Creek....

It was in the evening when we heard that the Big Foots were camped over there with the soldiers....It was the next morning (December 29, 1890) that something terrible happened.

Chapter XXIV

That evening before it happened, I went in to Pine Ridge ..., and while I was there, soldiers started for where the Big Foots were. These made about five hundred soldiers that were there next morning. When I saw them starting I felt that something terrible was going to happen. That night I could hardly sleep at all. I walked around most of the night.

In the morning I went out after my horses, and while I was out I heard shooting off toward the east, and I knew from the sound that it must be wagon-guns (cannon) going off. The sounds went right through my body, and I felt that something terrible would happen.

When I reached camp with the horses, a man rode up to me and said: "Hey-hey-hey! The people that are coming are fired on! I know it!"

I saddled up my buckskin and put on my sacred shirt. It was one I had made to be worn by no one but myself. It had a spotted eagle out-stretched on the back of it, and the daybreak star was on the left shoulder, because when facing south that shoulder is toward the east....

I painted my face all red, and in my hair I put one eagle feather for the One Above.

It did not take me long to get ready, for I could still hear the shooting over there.

I started out alone on the road that ran across the hills to Wounded Knee. I had no gun. I carried only the sacred bow of the west that I had seen in my great vision. I had gone only a little way when a band of young men came galloping after me....

We rode fast, and there were about twenty of us now. The shooting was getting louder. A horseback from over there came galloping very fast toward us, and he said: "Hey-hey-hey! They have murdered them!" Then he whipped his horse and rode away faster toward Pine Ridge.

In a little while we had come to the top of the ridge where, looking to the east, you can see for the first time the monument and the burying ground on the little hill where the church is. That is where the terrible thing started. Just south of the burying ground on the little hill a deep dry gulch runs about east and west, very crooked, and it rises westward to nearly the top of the ridge where we were.... We stopped on the ridge not far from the head of the dry gulch. Wagon-guns were still going off over there on the little hill.... There was much shooting down yonder, and there were many cries, and we could see cavalrymen scattered over the hills ahead of us. Cavalrymen were riding along the gulch and shooting into it, where the women and children were running away and trying to hide in the gullies and the stunted pines.

A little way ahead of us, just below the head of the dry gulch, there were some women and children who were huddled under a clay bank, and some cavalrymen were there pointing guns at them.

We stopped back behind the ridge, and I said to the others: "Take courage. These are our relatives. We will try to get them back." Then we all sang a song which went like this:

"A thunder being nation I am, I have said.

A thunder being nation I am, I have said.

You shall live.

You shall live.

You shall live.

You shall live."

Then I rode over the ridge and the others after me, and we were crying: "Take courage! It is time to fight!" The soldiers who were guarding our relatives shot at us and then ran away fast, and more cavalrymen on the other side of the gulch did too. We got our relatives and sent them across the ridge to the northwest where they would be safe.

I had no gun, and when we were charging, I just held the sacred bow out in front of me with my right hand. The bullets did not hit us at all....

By now many other Lakotas, who had heard the shooting, were coming up from Pine Ridge, and we all charged on the soldiers. They ran eastward where the trouble began. We followed down along the dry gulch, and what we saw was terrible. Dead and wounded women and children and little babies were scattered all along there where they had been trying to run away. The soldiers had followed along the gulch, as they ran, and murdered them in there. Sometimes they were in heaps because they had huddled together, and some were scattered all along. Sometimes bunches of them had been killed and torn to pieces where the wagon-guns hit them....

Shown above is Big Foot, the great Sioux chief, lying dead in the snow after the Massacre at Wounded Knee, South Dakota, in 1890.

When we drove the soldiers back, they dug themselves in, and we were not enough people to drive them out from there. In the evening they marched off up Wounded Knee Creek, and then we saw all that they had done there.

Men and women and children were heaped and scattered all over the flat at the bottom of the little hill where the soldiers had their wagon-guns, and westward up the dry gulch all the way to the high ridge, the dead women and children and babies were scattered.

When I saw this I wished that I had died too, but I was not sorry for the women and children. It was better for them to be happy in the other world....

Chapter XXV

I did not know then how much was ended. When I look back now from this high hill of my old age, I can still see the butchered women and children lying heaped and scattered all along the crooked gulch as plain as when I saw them with eyes still young. And I can see that something else died there in the bloody mud, and was buried in the blizzard. A people's dream died there. It was a beautiful dream.

And I, to whom so great a vision was given in my youth,—you see me now a pitiful old man who has done nothing, for the nation's hoop is broken and scattered. There is no center any longer, and the sacred tree is dead.

Artists Render Industrialization and Urbanization

Many American historians view the late nineteenth century in terms of technology and science, identifying the dynamism that helped drive the massive social changes of the period. Railroads changed the landscape and revolutionized transportation for commerce, migration, and pleasure. Railroads also gave momentum to inventions, such as an efficient process to produce steel, airbrakes, electrical engines, and refrigeration. As the nation's first "big business," railroads also presaged a new economic reality—one dominated by massive industries with great financial and political power. Factories drew farmers to cities and millions of immigrants into the country, sparking rapid urban growth. By 1920, more than half the population lived in cities, and more than 50 percent of the labor force was working in manufacturing and transportation. Even though the statistics and trends are tidy, industrialization and urbanization were not sterile processes conducted in laboratories. They took place amid real people and played out in their daily lives. Sensitive to these effects, writers and artists showed a variety of personal perspectives on the scientific wonders and evils of the day.

Some authors were awestruck by great technological feats, such as the completion of the transcontinental railroad in 1869 and the Brooklyn Bridge in 1883. Their positive portrayals helped Americans to value "progress" and technological advances as great influences on society. Others, such as Rebecca Harding Davis, interpreted factories and their effects on the average worker as bleak, destructive forces. Such depictions laid the groundwork for social reformers and labor organizers in the Progressive Era. From among their ranks, immigrants found spokespersons, such as Abraham Cahan, who eloquently described the trials and opportunities in their new land. The immigrant experience revisited the question "Who is an American?" This new perspective both reinforced and undercut the American belief in success based on merit—that self-made people can rise from rags to riches and compete equally in U.S. society. In contrast, wealthy socialites, such as Edith Wharton, also found voices to immortalize their conventions and lifestyles. These reflections were typically conservative, preserving the social stratification of the era and reinforcing class distinctions. Finally, poet Carl Sandburg viewed urban life itself, acknowledging its drawbacks but praising its dynamism, strength, and raw energy. As a whole, these accounts give personal insight into the nation's stunning transformation into an urban manufacturing power.

Featured Authors

Bret Harte
Rebecca Harding Davis
Edith Wharton
Hart Crane
Abraham Cahan
Carl Sandburg

BRET HARTE (1836–1902)

*Born in Albany, New York, Bret Harte became
famous for his fiction and poetry about the
American frontier. He migrated to Oakland,
California, in 1854, and in 1868, he became
editor of* The Overland Monthly, *a San
Francisco magazine. About that time, he
enjoyed his greatest literary success.*

*"This is what
the Engines
said, | Unreported
and unread."*

Harte's migration to the West Coast in the 1850s would have taken
place only partly on trains. That was because, at that time, large sections
of the West, particularly areas beyond the Mississippi River, were pass-
able only by coach or wagon. However, May 1869 marked a milestone
in American industrial development. That month, the tracks of the
Central Pacific and Union Pacific Railroads met near Promontory, Utah,
bridging nearly 2,000 miles of rough terrain from Omaha, Nebraska, to
San Francisco. Fulfilling the dream of many western businessmen, the
transcontinental railroad was complete. California miners and importers
now had a faster way to send their freight to manufacturing and retail
areas in the Midwest and East. Passengers were able to cross the plains
and mountains of the West in six days, rather than the four to six months
it took pioneers in covered wagons. The industrial development of the
Great Plains and the Far West had begun in earnest.

Bret Harte's perspective as a Yankee who moved west enables him
to write an amusing dialog of regional rivalry in his poem, "What the
Engines Said." Harte imagines what the two railroad engines would
have said when they met face to face that day in Utah. The poem
stresses the optimism of the day and the greatness of the regions that
the transcontinental railroad tracks connect. The competition that Harte
describes relates also to the construction of the railroad itself. The
government promised each railroad company payments based on the
amount of track they laid, touching off a feverish and sometimes dangerous competition. Thousands of Americans, many of them Chinese and
Irish immigrants and Civil War veterans, provided the backbreaking
labor required to build trestles, blast tunnels through mountains, and
drive spikes in the desert. Harte's optimism, though it was shared by
many at the time, does not mention those who gave their lives for the
railroad's construction.

What the Engines Said

*Opening of the Pacific Railroad,
May 12, 1869*

What was it the Engines said,
Pilots touching,—head to head
Facing on the single track,
Half a world behind each back?
This is what the Engines said,
Unreported and unread.

With a prefatory screech,
In a florid Western speech,
Said the Engine from the WEST:
"I am from Sierra's crest;
And if altitude's a test,
Why, I reckon, it's confessed
That I've done my level best."

Said the Engine from the EAST:
"They who work best talk the least.
S'pose you whistle down your brakes;
What you've done is no great shakes,—
Pretty fair,—but let our meeting
Be a different kind of greeting.
Let those folks with champagne stuffing,
Not their Engines, do the *puffing*.

In May 1869, officials celebrated the completion of the transcontinental railroad at Promontory, Utah. This event ushered in a new wave of industrial development in the Great Plains and Far West.

"Listen! Where Atlantic beats
Shores of snow and summer heats;
Where the Indian autumn skies
Paint the woods with wampum dyes,—
I have chased the flying sun,
Seeing all he looked upon,
Blessing all that he has blessed,
Nursing in my iron breast
All his vivifying heat,
All his clouds about my crest;
And before my flying feet
Every shadow must retreat."

Said the Western Engine, "Phew!"
And a long, low whistle blew.
"Come, now, really that's the oddest

Talk for one so very modest.
You brag of your East! *You* do?
Why, *I* bring the East to *you!*
All the Orient, all Cathay,
Find through me the shortest way;
And the sun you follow here
Rises in my hemisphere.
Really,—if one must be rude,—
Length, my friend, ain't longitude."

Said the Union: "Don't reflect, or
I'll run over some Director."
Said the Central: "I'm Pacific;
But, when riled, I'm quite terrific.
Yet today we shall not quarrel,
Just to show these folks this moral,
How two Engines—in their vision—
Once have met without collision."

This is what the Engines said,
Unreported and unread;
Spoken slightly through the nose,
With a whistle at the close.

REBECCA HARDING DAVIS (1831–1910)

A pioneering author in both subject matter and literary style, Rebecca Harding Davis was a newspaper journalist, novelist, and short story writer. She submitted her work about immigrant factory workers, "Life in the Iron Mills," to the leading magazine of the day, the Atlantic Monthly, *in 1861. At that time, few writers portrayed industrialization with such keen realism and foresight.* Atlantic *editor James Field immediately published the story in the April edition. Despite writing 10 novels and more than 100 shorter works, Rebecca Harding Davis was relatively unknown by the time she died in 1910. A new edition of her classic tale, "Life in the Iron Mills," renewed interest in her work in the 1970s.*

During industrialization, iron was an important resource in the development of new railroads, bridges, and skyscrapers. However, these structures needed steel—a stronger, tougher form of iron. Mass production of steel was very expensive until the invention of the Bessemer process in the 1850s. The new process combined carbon, silicon, and

"unsleeping engines groan and shriek"

manganese with molten iron (called crude iron or pig iron) to create steel. With this process and new uses for steel, iron production boomed from 920,000 tons in 1860 to 10.3 million tons in 1900.

"Life in the Iron Mills" has been called visionary because, in 1861, industrialization in many parts of the country was only just beginning, and pollution was virtually unknown. While many authors were still elated about the progress that industrialization heralded, Davis depicted factories as a malignant force that polluted the environment and tortured the souls of individuals who worked in them. Her story focuses on a family of Welsh immigrants—Deborah, a cotton mill worker, and her cousin Hugh, the young iron mill worker. The following selection describes Deborah leaving her cotton mill job for the night, going home to make dinner, and then delivering food to Hugh, who is making pig iron at the furnace.

Life in the Iron Mills (or The Korl Woman)

One rainy night, about eleven o'clock, a crowd of half-clothed women stopped outside of the cellar-door. They were going home from the cotton-mill.

"Good-night, Deb," said one, a mulatto, steadying herself against the gas-post. She needed the post to steady her. So did more than one of them....

Deborah groped her way into the cellar, and, after considerable stumbling, kindled a match, and lighted a tallow dip, that sent a yellow glimmer over the room. It was low, damp,—the earthen floor covered with a green, slimy moss,—a fetid air smothering the breath. Old Wolfe lay asleep on a heap of straw, wrapped in a torn horse-blanket. He was a pale, meek little man, with a white face and red rabbit-eyes. The woman Deborah was like him; only her face was even more ghastly, her lips bluer, her eyes more watery. She wore a faded cotton gown and a slouching bonnet. When she walked, one could see that she was deformed, almost a hunchback....

[Deborah makes dinner and calls to a young girl, Janey, to see if she is home. Janey awakes and tells Deborah that Hugh has not been home yet and is due to work until morning.]

The woman [Deborah] sprang up, and hastily began to arrange some bread and flitch [rank salt pork] in a tin pail, and to pour her own measure of ale into a bottle. Tying on her bonnet, she blew out the candle.

"Lay ye down, Janey dear," she said, gently, covering her with the old rags. "Hur can eat the potatoes, if hur's hungry." [Janey then asks the question:]

"Where are ye goin', Deb? The rain's sharp."

"To the mill, with Hugh's supper."

"Let him bide till th' morn. Sit ye down."

"No, no,"—sharply pushing her off. "The boy'll starve."

She hurried from the cellar, while the child wearily coiled herself up for sleep. The rain was falling heavily, as the woman, pail in hand, emerged from the mouth of the alley, and turned down the narrow street, that stretched out, long and black, miles before her. Here and there a flicker of gas lighted an uncertain space of muddy footwalk and gutter; the long rows of houses, except an occasional lager-bier shop, were closed; now and then she met a band of mill-hands skulking to or from their work.

Not many even of the inhabitants of a manufacturing town know the vast machinery of system by which the bodies of workmen are governed, that goes on unceasingly from year to year. The hands of each mill are divided into watches that relieve each other as regularly as the sentinels of an army. By night and day the work goes on, the unsleeping engines groan and shriek, the fiery pools of metal boil and surge. Only for a day in the week, in half-courtesy to public censure, the fires are partially veiled; but as soon as the clock strikes midnight, the great furnaces break forth with renewed fury, the clamor begins with fresh, breathless vigor, the engines sob and shriek like "gods in pain."

As Deborah hurried down through the heavy rain, the noise of these thousand engines sounded through the sleep and shadow of the city like far-off thunder. The mill to which she was going lay on the river, a mile below the city-limits. It was far, and she was weak, aching from standing twelve hours at the spools. Yet it was her almost nightly walk to take this man his supper, though at every square she sat down to rest, and she knew she should receive small word of thanks.

Perhaps, if she had possessed an artist's eye, the picturesque oddity of the scene might have made her step stagger less, and the path seem shorter; but to her the mills were only "summat deilish to look at by night."

The road leading to the mills had been quarried from the solid rock, which rose abrupt and bare on one side of the cinder-covered road, while the river, sluggish and black, crept past on the other. The mills for rolling iron are simply immense tent-like roofs, covering acres of ground, open on every side. Beneath these roofs Deborah looked in on a city of fires, that burned hot and fiercely in the night. Fire in every horrible form: pits of flame waving in the wind; liquid metal-flames writhing in tortuous streams through the sand; wide caldrons filled with boiling fire, over which bent ghastly wretches stirring the strange brewing; and though all, crowds of half clad men, looking like revengeful ghosts in the red light, hurried, throwing masses of glittering fire. It was like a street in Hell. Even Deborah muttered as she crept through, "'T looks like t' Devil's place!" It did,—in more ways than one.

"an opportunity to show off pretty dresses and graceful attitudes"

EDITH WHARTON (1862–1937)

Edith Wharton was born into wealthy Manhattan society, a world that she drew upon in many of her more than forty literary works. The 1920 publication of her classic novel Age of Innocence *earned her a Pulitzer Prize—the first to be awarded to a woman. Focusing on the upper-crust subjects Wharton knew so well,* Age of Innocence *tells the story of a love triangle amid the traditional mores of New York's high society in the early 1870s. As a writer, she supplemented her girlhood memories with research in fashion, interior décor, and other areas to ensure accuracy in describing period scenery and details. Wharton's accuracy extends to relationships, and she is widely praised for her insightful description and analysis of social customs of the "old money" families of the period.*

In the last quarter of the nineteenth century, big businesses, including railroads, steel, and oil, made a few Americans—such as J.P. Morgan, Andrew Carnegie, and John D. Rockefeller—extraordinarily rich. Many moderately wealthy Americans invested in the stock market, compounding their riches until the economic downturn of the 1890s. While poor immigrants toiled in factories that some called sweatshops, the upper classes found new diversions. Those with leisure time visited new museums, art galleries, opera houses, and symphonies in New York and Boston. Golf and tennis emerged as new sports for the upper classes. Finally, rich Americans traveled—both to upscale resort areas in the United States and to foreign destinations, often in Europe and the Middle East.

In the following scene from the Age of Innocence, *Newland Archer has been married to May—a peer among his social set—for a little over a year. The narrator describes the summer home of one of Archer's friends in Newport, Rhode Island, and the Newport Archery Club competing on the lawn. Wharton's depiction of the setting conjures a mental image almost as detailed as a painting. While the scene illustrates the leisure activities of wealthy urbanites on vacation, it also suggests the emptiness that Archer vaguely detects in his obligations and pursuits.*

The Age of Innocence
Chapter XXI

The small bright lawn stretched away smoothly to the big bright sea.

The turf was hemmed with an edge of scarlet geranium and coleus, and cast-iron vases painted in chocolate color, standing at intervals along the winding path that led to the sea, looped their garlands of petunia and ivy geranium above the neatly raked gravel.

Halfway between the edge of the cliff and the square wooden house (which was also chocolate-colored, but with the tin roof of the verandah striped in yellow and brown to represent an awning) two large targets had been placed against a background of shrubbery. On the other side of the lawn, facing the targets, was pitched a real tent, with benches and garden-seats about it. A number of ladies in summer dresses and gentlemen in gray frock-coats and tall hats stood on the lawn or sat upon the benches; and every now and then a slender girl in starched muslin would step from the tent, bow in hand, and speed her shaft at one of the targets, while the spectators interrupted their talk to watch the result.

Artist Childe Hassam belongs to the American Impressionist school. Like their European counterparts, Impressionists in the United States often chose to paint wealthy subjects and their pursuits. In Hassam's The Victorian Chair *(1906), viewers sometimes detect boredom or alienation in this well-to-do young woman.*

Newland Archer, standing on the verandah of the house, looked curiously down upon this scene. On each side of the shiny painted steps was a large blue china flower-pot on a bright yellow china stand. A spiky green plant filled each pot, and below the verandah ran a wide border of blue hydrangeas edged with more red geraniums. Behind him, the French windows of the drawing rooms through which he had passed gave glimpses, between swaying lace curtains, of glassy parquet floors islanded with chintz *poufs,* dwarf armchairs, and velvet tables covered with trifles in silver.

The Newport Archery Club always held its August meeting at the Beauforts'. The sport, which had hitherto known no rival but croquet, was beginning to be discarded in favor of lawn tennis; but the latter game was still considered too rough and inelegant for social occasions, and as an opportunity to show off pretty dresses and graceful attitudes the bow and arrow held their own.

Archer looked down with wonder at the familiar spectacle. It surprised him that life should be going on in the old way when his own reactions to it had so completely changed. It was Newport that had first brought home to him the extent of the change. In New York, during the previous winter, after he and May had settled down in the new greenish-yellow house with the bow-window and the Pompeian vestibule, he had dropped back with relief into the old routine of the office, and the renewal of this daily activity had served as a link with his former self. Then there had been the pleasurable excitement of choosing a showy gray stepper for May's brougham (the Wellands had given the carriage), and the abiding occupation and interest of arranging his new library, which, in spite of family doubts and disapprovals, had been carried out as he had dreamed, with a dark embossed paper, Eastlake bookcases and "sincere" armchairs and tables. At the Century he had found Winsett again, and at the Knickerbocker [men's clubs] the fashionable young men of his own set; and what with the hours dedicated to the law and those given to dining out or entertaining friends at home, with an occasional evening at the Opera or the play, the life he was living had still seemed a fairly real and inevitable sort of business.

But Newport represented the escape from duty into an atmosphere of unmitigated holiday-making. Archer had tried to persuade May to spend the summer on a remote island off the coast of Maine (called, appropriately enough, Mount Desert), where a few hardy Bostonians and Philadelphians were camping in "native" cottages, and whence came reports of enchanting scenery in a wild, almost trapper-like existence amid woods and waters.

But the Wellands always went to Newport, where they owned one of the square boxes on the cliffs, and their son-in-law could adduce no good reason why he and May should not join them there. As Mrs. Welland rather tartly pointed out, it was hardly worth while for May to have worn herself out trying on summer clothes in Paris if she was not to be allowed to wear them; and this argument was of a kind to which Archer had as yet found no answer.

"we have seen night lifted in thine arms"

HART CRANE (1899–1932)

Hart Crane led a short life scarred by family strife and an inability to support himself as a poet. Nevertheless, his brief writing career produced complex works that are now regarded as classic modern literature. Among them are a series of fifteen poems that make up The Bridge, *written during the 1920s and published in 1930. Like*

Walt Whitman's effort to summarize the great breadth and diversity of the United States, The Bridge *represents Crane's attempt to describe the variety of New York City. Among its compelling images of urban life, the first poem of the book, "Proem: To Brooklyn Bridge," looms large.*

Construction of the Brooklyn Bridge was widely esteemed as the greatest technological feat of its age. Engineer John Roebling had perfected the steel cable suspension bridge in other cities, so he became the designer for the proposed bridge across the East River that would connect the boroughs of Manhattan and Brooklyn. Constructed between 1869 and 1883 at a cost of $15 million, the Brooklyn Bridge took a human toll as well. Twenty-seven men died in its construction, including John Roebling. When the Brooklyn Bridge opened in May 1883, it was the longest suspension bridge in the country.

In addition to the engineering miracle, many observers found great beauty in the precision of the cables strung from monumental towers. Since its completion, admirers and authors have made connections between the bridge and American values—including national pride; a belief in "progress" and technology for social improvement; and its simple, practical aesthetic.

Hart Crane's poem "Proem: To Brooklyn Bridge" was written in 1926. At that time, poets (many of whom are termed "modernists") tried to develop new forms to express themselves. Crane developed this complex poem from his many associations, presenting the bridge from a number of almost-dizzying perspectives. The Brooklyn Bridge that emerges from this poem is often interpreted as an optimistic metaphor for urban technological achievements and perfect beauty.

Proem: To Brooklyn Bridge

How many dawns, chill from his rippling rest
The seagull's wings shall dip and pivot him,
Shedding white rings of tumult, building high
Over the chained bay waters Liberty—

Then, with inviolate curve, forsake our eyes
As apparitional as sails that cross
Some page of figures to be filed away;
—Till elevators drop us from our day ...

I think of cinemas, panoramic sleights
With multitudes bent toward some flashing scene
Never disclosed, but hastened to again,
Foretold to other eyes on the same screen;

In 1899, fashionable New York residents strolled across the Brooklyn Bridge. Pedestrians in those days were awed by the monumental towers and the brilliant symmetry of the cables.

And Thee, across the harbor, silver-paced
As though the sun took step of thee, yet left
Some motion ever unspent in thy stride,—
Implicitly thy freedom staying thee!

Out of some subway scuttle, cell or loft
A bedlamite speeds to thy parapets,
Tilting there momently, shrill shirt ballooning,
A jest falls from the speechless caravan.

Down Wall, from girder into street noon leaks,
A rip-tooth of the sky's acetylene;
All afternoon the cloud-flown derricks turn . . .
The cables breathe the North Atlantic still.

And obscure as that heaven of the Jews,
They guerdon . . . Accolade thou dost bestow
Of anonymity time cannot raise:
Vibrant reprieve and pardon thou dost show.

O harp and altar, of the fury fused,
(How could mere toil align thy choiring strings!)
Terrific threshold of the prophet's pledge,
Prayer of pariah, and the lover's cry,—

Again the traffic lights that skim thy swift
Unfractioned idiom, immaculate sigh of stars,
Beading thy path—condense eternity:
And we have seen night lifted in thine arms.

Under thy shadow by the piers I waited;
Only in darkness is thy shadow clear.
The City's fiery parcels all undone,
Already snow submerges an iron year . . .

O Sleepless as the river under thee,
Vaulting the sea, the prairies' dreaming sod,
Unto us lowliest sometime sweep, descend
And of the curveship lend a myth to God.

ABRAHAM CAHAN (1860–1951)

"the taste of mutual estrangement"

Born to a devout Jewish family in Lithuania, Abraham Cahan fled Russian oppression and arrived in the United States in 1882. Like many eastern European immigrants at the time, he found work in dingy and dangerous clothing factories, commonly called sweat-shops, where he gained insight into the labor issues that he later championed. In 1897 Cahan helped found, and for fifty years was the editor of, an influential Yiddish newspaper, Forward. *In addition, he authored several novels. His first novella,* Yekl: A Tale of the New York Ghetto, *was published in 1896. William Dean Howells— editor of* Harper's Magazine, *literary critic, and a prolific writer him-self—hailed* Yekl *as the harbinger of a "new New York." Today, some argue that Cahan is the "father" of Jewish-American literature.*

In the late nineteenth century, immigrants provided the additional labor that booming industry needed. Historians estimate that between 1866 and 1915, about 25 million foreigners entered the country. Beside the pull of economic opportunities, there were other factors causing the flood of immigrants to the United States. Many refugees suffered politi-cal or religious persecution in their home countries. Some were peas-ants in eastern and southern Europe who faced grinding poverty brought by industrialization in those areas.

By working largely in factories, these newcomers helped fuel the industrial changes of the period. Because many immigrants settled in cities, sometimes in crowded ghettos, they were a major force in rapid urbanization. In addition, they brought their native cultures, which were at first ridiculed for being "different" from earlier immigrants. Popular prejudice soared, as many established Americans feared they would lose their jobs to new immigrants who often worked for lower wages. Some citizens believed that these new immigrants would not assimilate. However, their cultural contributions have given much depth and rich-ness to U.S. society.

Abraham Cahan was one such contributor. His novella Yekl *takes its title from the Yiddish name of the main character. Yekl is a recent immigrant who works in a New York sweatshop. He lives in the ghetto of the lower east side of Manhattan. At the beginning of the story, he has already "moved up" from sewing trousers to making jackets. Yekl has also taken an English name (Jake) and speaks broken English, indica-tions of his cultural assimilation in the three years since his arrival in America. During that time, Jake has saved money, and he has just sent for his family to join him. This scene depicts Yekl's meeting with his wife (Gitl) and son (Yosselé) when they first arrive at Ellis Island, the processing station for newly arriving immigrants. His perception of Gitl indicates that he has adopted some of the American prejudice against newcomers, and seeing his fine American clothes, she finds him strange, too. Their reactions show the cultural chasm that the two must overcome if the family is to survive intact.*

Yekl: A Tale of the New York Ghetto
Chapter 4, The Meeting

A few weeks later, on a Saturday morning, Jake, with an unfolded telegram in his hand, stood in front of one of the desks at the Immigration bureau of Ellis Island. He was freshly shaven and clipped, smartly dressed in his best clothes and ball shoes, and, in spite of the sickly expression of shamefacedness and anxiety which distorted his features, he looked younger than usual.

All the way to the island he had been in a flurry of joyous anticipation. The prospect of meeting his dear wife and child and, incidentally, of showing off his swell attire to her, had thrown him into a fever of impatience. But on entering the big shed he had caught a distant glimpse of Gitl and Yosselé through the railing separating the detained immigrants from their visitors, and his heart had sunk at the sight of his wife's uncouth and un-American appearance. She was slovenly dressed in a brown jacket and skirt of grotesque cut, and her hair was concealed under a voluminous wig of a pitch-black hue. This she had put on just before leaving the steamer, both "in honor of the Sabbath" and by way of sprucing herself up for the great event. Since Yekl had left home she had gained considerably in the measurement of her waist. The wig, however, made her seem stouter and shorter than she would have appeared without it. It also added at least five years to her looks. But she was aware neither of this nor of the fact that in New York even a Jewess of her station and orthodox breeding is accustomed to blink at the wickedness of displaying her natural hair, and that none but an elderly matron may wear a wig without

From Ellis Island, new immigrants gaze at the Statue of Liberty in New York Harbor, suggesting their optimism and their belief in American principles, such as freedom and equality.

being the occasional target for snowballs or stones. She was naturally dark of complexion, and the nine or ten days spent at sea had covered her face with a deep bronze, which combined with her prominent cheek bones, inky little eyes, and, above all, the smooth black wig, to lend her resemblance to a squaw.

Jake had no sooner caught sight of her than he had averted his face, as if loth [loath] to rest his eyes on her, in the presence of the surging crowd around him, before it was inevitable. He dared not even survey the crowd to see whether it contained any acquaintance of his, and he vaguely wished that her release were delayed indefinitely.

Presently the officer behind the desk took the telegram from him, and in another little while Gitl, hugging Yosselé with one arm and a bulging parcel with the other, emerged from a side door.

"Yekl!" she screamed out in a piteous high key, as if crying for mercy.

"Dot'sh alla right!" he returned in English, with a wan smile and unconscious of what he was saying. His wandering eyes and dazed mind were striving to fix themselves upon the stern functionary and the questions he bethought himself of asking before finally releasing his prisoners. The contrast between Gitl and Jake was so striking that the officer wanted to make sure—partly as a matter of official duty and partly for the fun of the thing—that the two were actually man and wife.

"*Oi* a lamentation upon me! He shaves his beard!" Gitl ejaculated to herself as she scrutinized her husband, "Yosselé, look! Here is *taté!*"

But Yosselé did not care to look at taté. Instead, he turned his frightened little eyes—precise copies of Jake's—and buried them in his mother's cheek.

When Gitl was finally discharged she made to fling herself on Jake. But he checked her by seizing both loads from her arms. He started for a distant and deserted corner of the room, bidding her follow. For a moment the boy looked stunned, then he burst out crying and fell to kicking his father's chest with might and main, his reddened little face appealingly turned to Gitl. Jake continuing his way tried to kiss his son into toleration, but the little fellow proved too nimble for him. It was in vain that Gitl, scurrying behind, kept expostulating with Yosselé: "Why, it is taté!" Taté was forced to capitulate before the march was brought to an end.

At length, when the secluded corner had been reached, and Jake and Gitl had set down their burdens, husband and wife flew into mutual embrace and fell to kissing each other. The performance had an effect of something done to order, which, it must be owned, was far from being belied by the state of their minds at the moment. Their kisses imparted the taste of mutual estrangement to both. In Jake's case the sensation was quickened by the strong steerage odors which were emitted by Gitl's person, and he involuntarily recoiled.

The Statue of Liberty

"Give me your tired, your poor . . ."

The Statue of Liberty was a gift from France to the United States to celebrate their friendship, which was established during the American Revolution, and to recognize the U.S. centennial anniversary. Created by sculptor Frédéric Auguste Bartholdi between 1876 and 1884, the Statue of Liberty was one of the great symbolic artworks of the late nineteenth century. (Part of the unfinished sculpture is shown in this photo taken in Bartholdi's workshop.) However, the monumental statue was not complete until the American people raised money for its eighty-nine-foot pedestal. Jewish-American poet Emma Lazarus wrote her now famous work, "The New Colossus," in 1883 to help raise those funds. Portraying the United States as a haven for immigrants, the poem was inscribed on the statue's pedestal in 1903.

The poem's title refers to "the colossus" of classical Greek times—a bronze monument of the sun god poised over Rhodes harbor. Lazarus hails the "new colossus"—the Statue of Liberty overlooking New York Harbor—as a symbol of the humane generosity of U.S. immigration policy.

The New Colossus

Not like the brazen giant of Greek fame,
With conquering limbs astride from land to land;
Here at our sea-washed, sunset gates shall stand
A mighty woman with a torch, whose flame
Is the imprisoned lightning, and her name
Mother of Exiles. From her beacon-hand
Glows world-wide welcome; her mild eyes command
The air-bridged harbor that twin cities frame.
"Keep, ancient lands, your storied pomp!" cries she
With silent lips. "Give me your tired, your poor,
Your huddled masses yearning to breathe free,
The wretched refuse of your teeming shore.
Send these, the homeless, tempest-tost to me,
I lift my lamp beside the golden door!"

"You look like a *poritz* [Yiddish word for nobleman]," she said shyly.
"How are you? How is mother?"

"How should she be? So, so. She sends you her love," Gitl mumbled out.
"How long was father ill?"

"Maybe a month. He cost us health enough."

He proceeded to make advances to Yosselé, she appealing to the child in his behalf. For a moment the sight of her, as they were both crouching before the boy, precipitated a wave of thrilling memories on Jake and made him feel in his own environment. Presently, however, the illusion took wing and here he was, Jake the Yankee, with his bonnetless, wigged, dowdyish little greenhorn by his side! That she was his wife, nay, that he was a married man at all, seemed incredible to him. The sturdy, thriving urchin had at first inspired him with pride; but as he now cast another side glance at Gitl's wig he lost all interest in him, and began to regard him, together with his mother, as one great obstacle dropped from heaven, as it were, in his way.

Gitl, for her part, was overcome with a feeling akin to awe. She, too, could not get herself to realize that this stylish young man—shaved and dressed as in Povodye is only some young nobleman—was Yekl, her own Yekl, who had all these three years never been absent from her mind. And while she was once more examining Jake's blue diagonal cutaway, glossy stand-up collar, the white four-in-hand necktie, coquettishly tucked away in the bosom of his starched shirt, and, above all, patent leather shoes, she was at the same time mentally scanning the Yekl of three years before. The latter alone was hers, and she felt like crying to the image to come back to her and let her be *his* wife.

CARL SANDBURG (1878–1967)

A proponent of simple, accessible poetry, Carl Sandburg was perhaps the most popular poet of the 1920s and 1930s. Sandburg's verse does not rhyme, and his meter is often irregular. His native Midwest informed the bulk of his work, in which he emphasized ordinary people and places. Sandburg's first published poem was also his most critically acclaimed. In 1914, "Chicago" appeared in Chicago-based Poetry *magazine, ushering in a new surge of artistic activity in the region. Midwesterners such as Sandburg, Theodore Dreiser, Frank Lloyd Wright, and others believed that Chicago, as the foremost city in America's "heartland," should be a major cultural force.*

"City of the Big Shoulders"

By the late nineteenth century, Chicago had become a major industrial, transportation, and urban center. Increasing immigrant settlement combined with technological changes brought enormous growth. By the mid-1850s, Chicago had become a hub for thousands of miles of railroad track. Midwestern farmers—and later western miners and businessmen via the transcontinental railroad—sent their products to the East through Chicago, making it, as Sandburg wrote, "the nation's freight handler." Ranchers and farmers sent cattle and hogs to Chicago on railroad cars, so that city became the center for the meat packing industry.

Carl Sandburg's "Chicago" praises the city by using the metaphor of a strong laborer or boxer—a tough, coarse bruiser. Though he mentions several unpleasant aspects of urban life, including hunger and crime, his pride in the city is evident in its energetic activity and raw power.

Chicago

Hog Butcher for the World,
Tool Maker, Stacker of Wheat,
Player with Railroads and the Nation's Freight Handler;
Stormy, husky, brawling,
City of the Big Shoulders:
They tell me you are wicked and I believe them, for I have seen
     your painted women under the gas lamps luring the farm boys.
And they tell me you are crooked and I answer: Yes, it is true I
     have seen the gunman kill and go free to kill again.
And they tell me you are brutal and my reply is: On the faces of
     woman and children I have seen the marks of wanton hunger.
And having answered so I turn once more to those who sneer at this
     my city, and I give them back the sneer and say to them:
Come and show me another city with lifted head singing so proud
     to be alive and coarse and strong and cunning.
Flinging magnetic curses amid the toil of piling job on job, here is a
     tall bold slugger set vivid against the little soft cities;
Fierce as a dog with tongue lapping for action, cunning as a savage
     Pitted against the wilderness,
          Bareheaded,
          Shoveling,
          Wrecking,
          Planning,
          Building, breaking, rebuilding,
Under the smoke, dust all over his mouth, laughing with white
     teeth,

Chicago World's Fair of 1893

The World's Columbian Exposition, held in Chicago in 1893, officially celebrated the 400th anniversary of Christopher Columbus's voyages. In practical terms, however, it praised American culture and society. A major international event, the fair attracted about 27 million visitors from many countries.

World's fairs traditionally allowed manufacturers to promote their products, exhibiting the latest in consumer goods, technology, and urban planning. The Chicago World's Fair was no exception. Largely through such expositions in the 1800s, Americans came to idealize "progress" and technological invention.

The Chicago World's Fair influenced architecture and the arts as well. Chief architect Daniel Burnham planned the buildings of White City in the monumental Beaux Arts style, a design that many civic buildings have used ever since. World's fairs, emphasizing exhibits and education, also encouraged the development of science and art museums in cities across the nation. In addition, some historians believe that the Chicago World's Fair helped encourage the great outpouring of arts and culture in that city.

The Palace of Fine Arts embodied the Beaux Arts architectural style of White City in the 1893 Chicago World's Fair. Designed to be temporary, these grand buildings were destroyed after the fair concluded.

Under the terrible burden of destiny laughing as a young man
    laughs,
Laughing even as an ignorant fighter laughs who has never lost a
    battle,
Bragging and laughing that under his wrist is the pulse, and under
    his ribs the heart of the people,
       Laughing!
Laughing the stormy, husky, brawling laughter of Youth, half-
    naked, sweating, proud to be Hog Butcher, Tool Maker, Stacker
    of Wheat, Player with railroads and Freight Handler to the
    Nation.

Social Critics and Reformers

American history is full of individuals agitating for change. However, between the end of the Civil War and World War I, writers and lecturers poured forth ideas for improving society from a particularly deep well. Reformers highlighted issues as diverse as women's suffrage, racial injustice, government corruption, inferior housing, and the exploitation of workers. Society's underpinnings shifted with the freeing of slaves, massive immigration, and vast industrialization. The convergence of these changes in urban areas produced friction and inevitable conflict. Nevertheless, the insight and eloquence of U.S. writers were crucial to articulating problems and offering solutions.

Predating the Civil War, activism for women's rights continued until 1920, when women finally won the vote nationwide with passage of the Nineteenth Amendment to the Constitution. Champions of women's rights included visionary writers and speakers such as Frances Harper and Elizabeth Cady Stanton.

The economic depression of the 1890s produced new tensions and another tide of critical thought. Industrialists had become powerful and greedy. They offered poor working conditions and very low wages. Politicians became corrupted by bribes from wealthy corporations. Poverty and disease were rampant in squalid inner cities. Urban housing was in short supply. To combat these and other ills, a broad social reform campaign—the Progressive Era—emerged between 1895 and 1920. Progressives looked to government to counteract social problems and protect the common good. They successfully campaigned for legislation to protect child workers and break up powerful corporate monopolies.

Authors had a particularly strong influence on progressive reforms. Through exposés in national magazines, investigative journalists such as Lincoln Steffens and Upton Sinclair brought stories of wrongdoing to the masses. President Theodore Roosevelt coined a new term when he called such writers "muckrakers." He used the word to describe their tendency to rake "muck" or look at the underside of life.

Despite their successes, progressives were not able to protect the rights of African Americans who endured terrorism and segregation during this period. In thousands of cases, black men would not exercise the right to vote because of intimidation and violence. Mark Twain's novel about racism, *Huckleberry Finn*, pricked the conscience of Americans when it appeared in the mid 1880s. Later, muckrakers took up the cause of antilynching legislation.

In short, the Progressive era illustrates the complex relationship between literature, government, and social change. The writings of critics and reformers helped the U.S. democracy remain a vibrant competion of ideas and principles.

Featured Authors

Frances E. Watkins Harper
Elizabeth Cady Stanton
Mary Wilkins Freeman
Samuel L. Clemens
Lincoln Steffens
Upton Sinclair

FRANCES E. WATKINS HARPER (1825–1911)

Born to free parents in Baltimore, Frances Ellen Watkins Harper received a good education and went on to become a teacher and an ardent spokesperson for the abolition of slavery, women's suffrage, and temperance. Her travel and lecture schedules were grueling, yet she made time for prolific writing. Harper's activist mind-set spilled over into her publications, which included novels, essays, and newspaper columns. However, she is best remembered for her politically charged poetry. In fact, some critics believe that Frances Harper created the genre of African-American protest poetry. Throughout her life, she combined her courageous activism, religious faith, and idealism to work toward social improvement for all.

Before Harper took to the abolitionist lecture circuit in 1853, the women's suffrage movement had been born with the 1848 Seneca Falls Convention. However, by 1861, women's rights activists had agreed to take up the cause of abolition. According to some historians, this fateful decision cost the women's movement valuable momentum. At the time, however, women's leaders believed that their cause—liberty and equality for all—was the same as that of abolitionists. Women also had a practical strategy. Forging alliances with well-known abolitionists such as Frederick Douglass and William Lloyd Garrison would win them publicity and lobbying power in Congress. In fact, Douglass attended the Seneca Falls Convention, and he helped win passage of Resolution 9, the most controversial resolution in the convention's Declaration of Sentiments. After his speech, which stated that women should be given the vote, Resolution 9 passed by a slim margin. To illustrate the strength of abolitionist and feminist loyalties, Frederick Douglass's newspaper proclaimed "truth is of no sex" in its motto.

Frances Harper delivered her well-known "We Are All Bound Up Together" speech to the Eleventh Women's Rights Convention in 1866, marking her earliest contribution to the national women's rights effort. At this event, she took the lectern alongside other famous suffragists, such as Elizabeth Cady Stanton, Lucretia Mott, and Susan B. Anthony. The speech illustrates the broad platform of the women's rights movement. In addition to suffrage, women worked for equal protection under law, as well as education, property, divorce, and reproductive rights.

"justice is not fulfilled so long as woman is unequal before the law"

We Are All Bound Up Together

I feel I am something of a novice upon this platform. Born of a race whose inheritance has been outrage and wrong, most of my life had been spent in battling those wrongs. But I did not feel as keenly as others that I had these rights, in common with other women, which are now demanded. About two years ago, I stood within the shadows of my home. A great sorrow had fallen upon my life. My husband had died suddenly, leaving me a widow, with four children, one my own, and the others stepchildren. I tried to keep my children together. But my husband died in debt; and before he had been in the grave three months, the administrator had swept away the very milk-crocks and wash tubs from my hands. I was a farmer's wife and made butter for the Columbus market; but what could I do, when they had swept all away? They left me one thing—and that was a looking-glass! Had I died instead of my husband, how different would have been the result! By this time he would have had another wife, it is likely; and no administrator would have gone into his house, broken up his home, and sold his bed, and taken away his means of support.

I took my children in my arms, and went out to seek my living. While I was gone; a neighbor to whom I had once lent five dollars, went before a magistrate and swore that he believed I was a non-resident, and laid an attachment on my very bed. And I went back to Ohio with my orphan children in my arms, without a single feather bed in this wide world, that was not in the custody of the law. I say, then, that justice is not fulfilled so long as woman is unequal before the law.

We are all bound up together in one great bundle of humanity, and society cannot trample on the weakest and feeblest of its members without receiving the curse in its own soul. You tried that in the case of the negro. You pressed him down for two centuries; and in so doing you crippled the moral strength and paralyzed the spiritual energies of the white men of the country. When the hands of the black were fettered, white men were deprived of the liberty of speech and the freedom of the press. Society cannot afford to neglect the enlightenment of any class of its members. . . .

This grand and glorious revolution which has commenced, will fail to reach its climax of success, until throughout the length and brea[d]th of the American Republic, the nation shall be so color-blind, as to know

Frances Harper pointed out differences between white and black women in her "Bound Up Together" speech. She said, "You white women speak of rights. I speak of wrongs. . . . Let me go tomorrow morning and take my seat in one of your street cars . . . and the conductor will put up his hand and stop the car rather than let me ride." Photographer Alfred Steiglitz captured The Terminal, an image of a New York streetcar, in 1892.

no man by the color of his skin or the curl of his hair. It will then have no privileged class, trampling upon and outraging the unprivileged classes, but will be then one great privileged nation, whose privilege will be to produce the loftiest manhood and womanhood that humanity can attain.

ELIZABETH CADY STANTON (1815–1902)

Elizabeth Cady Stanton is commonly regarded as the intellectual of the women's rights movement. Her brilliant writing was a major force in the earliest efforts to articulate the injustices against women and document their demands. Stanton helped plan the Seneca Falls Convention, which was held in her hometown in upstate New York. She authored the Declaration of Sentiments—the document approved at Seneca Falls—and coauthored a multivolume history of the American women's movement. In addition, she wrote hundreds of letters and documents seeking support for equal rights. The obligation of raising seven children, however, meant that she could not travel as much as her colleagues, particularly Susan B. Anthony. Stanton and Anthony met in 1851 and tirelessly worked together for women's rights for fifty years. Sadly, when they died in 1902 and 1906 respectively, women still had not won the right to vote.

Historians attribute that failure to many factors, but they often cite a split among women's rights activists. When new constitutional amendments were proposed after the Civil War, feminists took two distinct positions. The conservative faction, led by Lucy Stone, supported the Fourteenth and Fifteenth Amendments, which granted citizenship to former slaves and voting rights to black men. Outraged at what she perceived as betrayal by her abolitionist allies, Elizabeth Cady Stanton refused to support the amendments because they did not include women's suffrage. In 1869, Stanton formed the National Women's Suffrage Association (NWSA) and became its president. That same year, Lucy Stone and others formed the American Women's Suffrage Association (AWSA).

Under Stanton and Anthony, the NWSA took what were then extreme measures. For example, in 1872, Susan B. Anthony registered and voted in a presidential election in Rochester, New York, arguing that the Fourteenth Amendment gave her that right. Her arrest did not lead

"we will be heard"

to a trial or appeal in federal court, as she and her lawyer had hoped. That women's rights activists resorted to such "radicalism" indicates not only their determination, but also the deep-seated opposition they faced.

The following excerpt from Stanton's autobiography details her efforts to include a women's rights speaker at the nation's centennial anniversary celebration, held in Philadelphia in 1876. When denied a place on the program, a group of Stanton's NWSA followers charged the platform. This story illustrates the difficulty women's groups faced in being heard, much less followed, in the sexist culture of the late nineteenth century.

Eighty Years and More: Reminiscences 1815–1897
Chapter XIX, The Spirit of '76

Then [in 1876] it was thought pre-eminently proper that a Woman's Declaration of Rights should be issued. Days and nights were spent over that document. After many twists from our analytical tweezers, with a critical consideration of every word and sentence, it was at last, by a consensus of the competent, pronounced very good. Thousands were ordered to be printed, and were folded, put in envelopes, stamped, directed, and scattered. Miss [Susan B.] Anthony, Mrs. [Matilda Joslyn] Gage, and I worked sixteen hours, day and night, pressing everyone who came in, into the service, and late at night carrying immense bundles to be mailed. With meetings, receptions, and a succession of visitors, all of whom we plied with woman suffrage literature, we felt we had accomplished a great educational work....

Here we had many prolonged discussions as to the part we should take, on the Fourth of July, in the public celebration. We thought it would be fitting for us to read our Declaration of Rights immediately after that of the Fathers was read, as an impeachment of them and their male descendants for their injustice and oppression. Ours contained as many counts, and quite as important, as those against King George in 1776. Accordingly, we applied to the authorities to allow us seats on the platform and a place in the programme of the public celebration, which was to be held in the historic old Independence Hall. As General Hawley was in charge of the arrangements for the day, I wrote him as follows:

"1431 CHESTNUT STREET, July 1, 1876.
"GENERAL HAWLEY.

"*Honored Sir:* As President of the National Woman's Suffrage Association, I am authorized to ask you for tickets to the platform, at Independence Hall, for the celebration on the Fourth of July. We should like to have seats for at least one representative woman from each State.

We also ask your permission to read our Declaration of Rights immediately after the reading of the Declaration of Independence of the Fathers is finished. Although these are small favors to ask as representatives of one-half of the nation, yet we shall be under great obligations to you if granted.

"Respectfully Yours,

"ELIZABETH CADY STANTON."

To this I received the following reply:

"U.S.C.C. HEADQUARTERS, July 2.

"MRS. ELIZABETH CADY STANTON.

"*Dear Madam*: I send you, with pleasure, half a dozen cards of invitation. As the platform is already crowded, it is impossible to reserve the number of seats you desire. I regret to say it is also impossible for us to make any change in the programme at this late hour. We are crowded for time to carry out what is already proposed.

"Yours Very Respectfully,

"JOSEPH R. HAWLEY,

"President, U.S.C.C."

With this rebuff, Mrs. [Lucretia] Mott and I decided that we would not accept the offered seats, but would be ready to open our own convention called for that day, at the First Unitarian church, where the Rev. William H. Furness had preached for fifty years. But some of our younger coadjutors decided that they would occupy the seats and present our Declaration of Rights. They said truly, women will be taxed to pay the expenses of this celebration, and we have as good a right to that platform and to the ears of the people as the men have, and we will be heard.

That historic Fourth of July dawned at last, one of the most oppressive days of that heated season. Susan B. Anthony, Matilda Joslyn Gage, Sara Andrews Spencer, Lillie Devereux Blake, and Phoebe W. Couzins made their way through the crowds under the broiling sun of Independence Square, carrying the Woman's Declaration of Rights. This Declaration had been handsomely engrossed by one of their number and signed by the oldest and most prominent advocates of woman's enfranchisement. Their tickets of admission proved an "open sesame" through the military barriers, and, a few moments before the opening of the ceremonies, these women found themselves within the precincts from which most of their sex were excluded.

The Declaration of 1776 was read by Richard Henry Lee of Virginia, about whose family clusters so much historic fame. The moment he

Around the turn of the century, a new generation of college-educated women undertook the fight for voting rights. Like early suffragists, they faced strong opposition from men. The 1909 cartoon, depicting a sympathetic father trying to care for babies on election day, demonstrates men's continued opposition to women's suffrage. The 1914 photo shows an activist trying to gain male support for women's voting rights.

finished reading was determined upon as the appropriate time for the presentation of the Woman's Declaration. Not quite sure how their approach might be met, not quite certain if, at this final moment, they would be permitted to reach the presiding officer, those ladies arose and made their way down the aisle. The bustle of preparation for the Brazilian hymn covered their advance. The foreign guests and the military and civil officers who filled the space directly in front of the speaker's stand, courteously made way, while Miss Anthony, in fitting words, presented the Declaration to the presiding officer. Senator Ferry's face paled as, bowing low, with no word he received the Declaration, which thus became part of the day's proceedings. The ladies turned, scattering printed copies as they deliberately walked down the platform. On every side eager hands were outstretched, men stood on seats and asked for them, while General Hawley, thus defied and beaten in his audacious denial to women of the right to present their Declaration, shouted, "Order, order!"

Passing out, these ladies made their way to a platform, erected for the musicians, in front of Independence Hall. Here, under the shadow of Washington's statue, back of them the old bell that proclaimed "liberty to all the land and all the inhabitants thereof," they took their places, and, to a listening, applauding crowd, Miss Anthony read the Woman's Declaration. During the reading of the Declaration, Mrs. Gage stood beside Miss Anthony and held an umbrella over her head, to shelter her friend from the intense heat of the noonday sun. And thus in the same hour, on opposite sides of old Independence Hall, did the men and women express their opinions of the great principles proclaimed on the natal day of the Republic.

"Men git in a good many places . . . jest because they push in ahead of women."

MARY WILKINS FREEMAN (1852–1930)

Born in Raldolph, Massachusetts, Mary Wilkins left college after one year and took up writing to support her needy family. Wilkins's writing talents enabled her to support herself as a single woman until she married Dr. Charles Freeman at the age of 49. Mary Freeman's labor of love—and profit—ultimately produced children's books, poetry, plays, novels, and fifteen volumes of her best work, short stories. Most of her writing focused on the rural New England she knew so well.

After the Civil War, demographics changed those areas. Most men had either died in the war, settled on cheap land in the West, or taken jobs in cities. Rural New England became poor and dominated by single women. It was a small leap, then, to Freeman's fictional matriarchal landscape. Her humorous stories were populated by impoverished but strong-willed—if eccentric—women. Although her characters and situations strike readers as funny, critics admire Freeman's work because she lovingly crafted her characters. Her stories found broad audiences in newspapers and magazines during the 1880s, and her first collection of short stories was published in 1887. Her second, A New England Nun and Other Stories, *appeared in 1891.*

Mary Freeman's popular stories reflect a change in attitudes and policies toward women. In 1890, the two women's organizations led by Elizabeth Cady Stanton and Lucy Stone finally merged to form the National American Women's Suffrage Association (NAWSA). By that time, American women had experienced some gains. In many states, married women were granted property rights and equal guardianship over children. About 30 percent of college students were women. In 1890, Wyoming had been admitted into the Union with its women's suffrage intact. Throughout that decade, the NAWSA embarked on a long, state-by-state campaign to win voting rights for women in federal elections. In 1896, Utah became a state and enfranchised women; Idaho granted suffrage to women that same year.

At the dawn of the twentieth century, a new generation of women's suffrage leaders continued to lobby, demonstrate, and press for federal legislation for another two decades. Seventy-two years after Seneca Falls, the Nineteenth Amendment granting universal women's suffrage was finally ratified in August 1920.

Women's persistence is foreshadowed in Freeman's short story "A Church Mouse," which tells of a homeless woman, Hetty Fifield, who campaigns for the job as sexton (caretaker) of her local meetinghouse. The simple, direct manner of the protagonist's speech and the "outrageousness" of her requests throw the deacon off balance and ultimately wear him down. By the end of this excerpt, readers can foresee that the deacon will not easily get Hetty to quit her meetinghouse residence. "A Church Mouse"—a title heavy with irony—appeared in the collection A New England Nun and Other Stories.

A Church Mouse

"I NEVER heard of a woman's bein' saxton."

"I dun' know what difference that makes; I don't see why they shouldn't have women saxtons as well as men saxtons, for my part, nor nobody else neither. They'd keep dusted 'nough sight cleaner. I've seen the dust layin' on my pew thick enough to write my name in a good many times, an' I ain't said nothin' about it. An' I ain't going' to say nothin' now again Joe Sowen, now he's dead an' gone. He did jest as well as most men do. Men git in a good many places where they don't belong, an' where they set as awkward as a cow on a hen-roost, jest because they push in ahead of women. I ain't blamin' 'em; I s'pose if I could push in I should, jest the same way. But there ain't no reason that I can see, nor nobody else neither, why a woman shouldn't be saxton."

Hetty Fifield stood in the rowen hay-field before Caleb Gale. He was a deacon, the chairman of the selectmen, and the rich and influential man of the village. One looking at him would not have guessed it. There was nothing imposing about his lumbering figure in his calico shirt and baggy trousers. However, his large face, red and moist with perspiration, scanned the distant horizon with a stiff and reserved air; he did not look at Hetty.

"How'd you go to work to ring the bell?" said he. "It would have to be tolled, too, if anybody died."

"I'd jest as lief [rather] ring that little meetin'-house bell as to stan' out here and jingle a cow-bell," said Hetty; "an' as for tollin', I'd jest as soon toll the bell for Methusaleh, if he was livin' here! I'd laugh if I ain't got strength 'nough for that."

"It takes a kind of a knack."

"If I ain't got as much knack as old Joe Sowen ever had, I'll give up the ship."

"You couldn't tend the fires."

"Couldn't tend the fires—when I've cut an' carried in all the wood I've burned for forty year! Couldn't keep the fires a-goin' in them two little wood-stoves!"

"It's consider'ble work to sweep the meetin'-house."

"I guess I've done 'bout as much work as to sweep that little meetin'-house, I ruther guess I have."

"There's one thing you ain't thought of."

"What's that?"

"Where'd you live? All old Sowen got for bein' saxton was twenty dollar a year, an' we couldn't pay a woman so much as that. You wouldn't have enough to pay for your living' anywheres."

"Where am I goin' to live whether I'm saxton or not?"

Caleb Gale was silent.

There was a wind blowing, the rowen hay drifted round Hetty like a brown-green sea touched with ripples of blue and gold by the asters and golden-rod. She stood in the midst of it like a May-weed that had gathered a slender toughness through the long summer; her brown cotton gown clung about her like a wilting leaf, outlining her harsh little form.

She was as sallow as a squaw, and she had pretty black eyes; they were bright, although she was old. She kept them fixed upon Caleb. Suddenly she raised herself upon her toes; the wind caught her dress and made it blow out; her eyes flashed. "I'll tell you where I'm goin' to live," said she. *"I'm goin' to live in the meetin'-house."*

Caleb looked at her. *"Goin' to live in the meetin'-house!"*

The pioneering social worker Jane Addams founded a settlement house, called Hull House, in the immigrant slums of Chicago in 1889. Settlement houses provided community services, such as child care (shown here) for working mothers and vocational classes. As such services sprang up across the nation's cities, settlement workers—mostly college-educated women—became reform leaders.

"Yes, I be."

"Live in the meetin'-house!"

"I'd like to know why not."

"Why—you couldn't—live in the meetin'-house. You're crazy."

Caleb flung out the rake which he was holding, and drew it in full of rowen. Hetty moved around in front of him, he raked imperturbably; she moved again right in the path of the rake, then he stopped. "There ain't no sense in such talk."

"All I want is jest the east corner of the back gall'ry, where the chimbly goes up. I'll set up my cookin' stove there, an' my bed, an' I'll curtain it off with my sunflower quilt, to keep off the wind."

"A cookin'-stove an' a bed in the meetin'-house!"

"Mis' Grout she give me that cookin'-stove, an' that bed I've allers slept on, before she died. She give 'em to me before Mary Anne Thomas, an' I moved 'em out. The air settin' out in the yard now, an' if it rains that stove an' that bed will be spoilt. It looks some like rain now. I guess you'd better give me the meetin'-house key right off."

"You don't think you can move that cookin'-stove an' that bed into the meetin'-house—I ain't goin' to stop to hear such talk."

"My worsted-work, all my mottoes I've done, an' my wool flowers, air out there in the yard."

Caleb raked. Hetty kept standing herself about until he was forced to stop, or gather her in with the rowen hay. He looked straight at her, and scowled; the perspiration trickled down his cheeks. "If I go up to the house can Mis' Gale git me the key to the meetin'-house?" said Hetty.

"No, she can't."

"Be you goin' up before long?"

"No, I ain't." Suddenly Caleb's voice changed: it had been full of stubborn vexation, now it was blandly argumentative. "Don't you see it ain't no use talkin' such nonsense, Hetty? You'd better go right along, an' make up your mind it ain't to be thought of."

"Where be I goin' tonight, then?"

"Tonight?"

"Yes; where be I a-goin'?"

"Ain't you got any place to go to?"

"Where do you s'pose I've got any place? Them folks air movin' into Mis' Grout's house, an' they as good as told me to clear out. I ain't got no folks to take me in. I dun' know where I'm goin'; mebbe I can go to your house?"

Caleb gave a start. "We've got company to home," said he, hastily. "I'm 'fraid Mis' Gale wouldn't think it was convenient."

Hetty laughed. "Most everybody in the town has got company," said she.

Caleb dug his rake into the ground as if it were a hoe, then he leaned on it, and stared at the horizon. There was a fringe of yellow birches on the edge of the hay-field; beyond them was a low range of misty blue hills. "You ain't got no place to go to, then?"

"I dun' know of any. There ain't no poor-house here, an' I ain't got no folks."

Caleb stood like a statue. Some crows flew cawing over the field. Hetty waited. "I s'pose that key is where Mis' Gale can find it?" she said, finally.

Caleb turned and threw out his rake with a jerk. "She knows where 'tis; it's hangin' up behind the settin'-room door. I s'pose you can stay there tonight, as long as you ain't got no other place. We shall have to see what can be done."

Hetty scuttled off across the field. "You mustn't take no stove nor bed into the meetin'-house," Caleb called after her; "we can't have that, nohow."

Hetty went on as if she did not hear.

"He ain't no bad nigger, gentlemen"

SAMUEL L. CLEMENS (1835–1910)

The life of Samuel L. Clemens, who wrote using the pen name Mark Twain, has become legendary. His stint as a Mississippi riverboat pilot and his adventures as a prospector and journalist in the Wild West are well known. Clemens's literary achievements and quick wit made him a beloved celebrity, both in the United States and abroad. Though his life may seem a catalog of successes, he also endured tragedy and misfortune. Clemens suffered the deaths of his wife and two daughters and made bad investments that eventually led to bankruptcy. The same author who wrote humorous works

about childhood innocence, such as Tom Sawyer, *later penned bitter satires. Whatever his tone or subject, Mark Twain's career as a humorist was largely based on his insightful critiques and exaggerated portrayals of human foibles and social conventions—including racism and ignorance.*

Many critics acknowledge that Twain wrote the great American novel when he published Huckleberry Finn. *Ernest Hemingway said, "All modern American literature comes from one book by Mark Twain called* Huckleberry Finn. . . . *It's the best book we've had. . . . There was nothing before. There has been nothing so good since." That* Huckleberry Finn *continues to fall in and out of favor with censors illustrates to a small degree the discomfort and debate it ignited when it was first published in the United States in 1885. Its antebellum Missouri setting enabled Clemens to use the pre–Civil War treatment of slaves to indict the racism of his day.*

After the Civil War, terrorism against former slaves became a tragically common occurrence. Racist organizations formed in the South to intimidate black voters and frighten them away from the polls. In thousands of cases, African Americans were tortured and hanged (or lynched) without due legal process. Their offenses were often slight or completely manufactured by racist mobs. Violence against blacks bred increased fears of a backlash. Terrorist perpetrators commonly justified their actions by accusing victims of plotting riots or raping white women. In reality, violence was usually committed not only to carry out vigilante justice but also to reassert white power. The terrorism and lynching of African Americans became an important issue for progressive journalists, such as Ida B. Wells-Barnett and W.E.B. DuBois, one of the founders of the National Association for the Advancement of Colored People. In spite of their condemnation and activism, the lynching of African Americans continued until the 1960s.

Consequently, the following selection from Huckleberry Finn *reverberated with U.S. audiences in the late 1880s. At this point in the story, the runaway slave, Jim, has just been apprehended. After crafting Jim as a sympathetic character throughout the length of the novel, Twain subjects him to verbal and physical abuse and threats of lynching. Only the doctor's praise of Jim's upright actions spares Jim's life at the hands of the mob. Jim's best friend and coconspirator in the escape, Huck Finn, chooses not to speak up for Jim's better treatment, illustrating Huck's moral weakness and hypocrisy. These flaws are particularly repugnant in light of Jim's silence about their alliance, which protects Huck. In giving his narrator these indefensible foibles, Mark Twain assails the racism and hypocrisy of society at large.*

Huckleberry Finn
Chapter XLII, Why They Didn't Hang Jim

I followed the men to see what they was going to do with Jim, and the old doctor and Uncle Silas followed after Tom into the house. The men was very huffy and some of them wanted to hang Jim for an example to all the other niggers around there, so they wouldn't be trying to run away like Jim done, and making such a raft of trouble and keeping a whole family scared most to death for days and nights. But the others said, don't do it, it wouldn't answer at all; he ain't our nigger and his owner would turn up and make us pay for him, sure. So that cooled them down a little, because the people that's always the most anxious for to hang a nigger that hain't done just right is always the very ones that ain't the most anxious to pay for him when they've got their satisfaction out of him.

They cussed Jim considerble, though, and give him a cuff or two side the head once in a while, but Jim never said nothing and he never let on to know me, and they took him to the same cabin and put his own clothes on him and chained him again, and not to no bed-leg this time but to a big staple drove into the bottom log, and chained his hands, too, and both legs, and said he warn't to have nothing but bread and water to eat after this till his owner come, or he was sold at auction because he didn't come in a certain length of time, and filled up our hole, and said a couple of farmers with guns must stand watch around about the cabin every night, and a bulldog tied to the door in the day-time; and about this time they was through with the job and was tapering off with a kind of genrl good-by cussing, and then the old doctor comes and takes a look and says:

"Don't be no rougher on him than you're obleeged to, because he ain't a bad nigger. When I got to where I found the boy [Tom Sawyer] I see I couldn't cut the bullet out without some help, and he warn't in no condition for me to leave to go and get help; and he got a little worse and a little worse, and after a long time he went out of his head and wouldn't let me come a-nigh him any more, and said if I chalked his raft he'd kill me, and no end of wild foolishness like that, and I see I couldn't do anything at all with him; so I says, I got to

E.W. Kemble illustrated the first edition of Huckleberry Finn. *Drawings helped readers visualize the growing friendship and intimacy of Jim and Huck. News of terrorism against African Americans contrasted sharply with such idealized images at the turn of the twentieth century.*

have *help* somehow; and the minute I says it out crawls this nigger from somewheres and says he'll help, and he done it, too, and done it very well. Of course I judged he must be a runaway nigger, and there I *was*! and there I had to stick right straight along all the rest of the day and all night. I was a fix, I tell you! I had a couple of patients with the chills, and of course I'd of liked to run up to town and see them, but I dasn't, because the nigger might get away, and then I'd be to blame; and yet never a skiff come close enough for me to hail. So there I had to stick plumb until daylight this morning; and I never see a nigger that was a better nuss or faithfuler, and yet he was resking his freedom to do it, and was all tired out, too, and I see plain enough he'd been worked main hard lately. I liked the nigger for that; I tell you, gentlemen, a nigger like that is worth a thousand dollars—and kind treatment, too. I had everything I needed, and the boy was doing as well there as he would 'a' done at home, better, maybe, because it was so quiet; but there I *was*, with both of 'm on my hands, and there I had to stick till about dawn this morning; then some men in a skiff come by, and as good luck would have it the nigger was setting by the pallet with his head propped on his knees sound asleep; so I motioned them in quiet, and they slipped up on him and grabbed him and tied him before he knowed what he was about, and we never had no trouble. And the boy being in a kind of a flighty sleep, too, we muffled the oars and hitched the raft on, and towed her over very nice and quiet, and the nigger never made the least row nor said a word from the start. He ain't no bad nigger, gentlemen; that's what I think about him."

Somebody says:

"Well, it sounds very good, doctor, I'm obleeged to say."

Then the others softened up a little, too, and I was mighty thankful to that old doctor for doing Jim that good turn; and I was glad it was according to my judgment of him, too; because I thought he had a good heart in him and was a good man the first time I see him. Then they all agreed that Jim had acted very well, and was deserving to have some notice took of it, and reward. So every one of them promised, right out and hearty, that they wouldn't cuss him no more.

Then they come out and locked him up. I hoped they was going to say he could have one or two of the chains took off, because they was rotten heavy, or could have meat and greens with his bread and water; but they didn't think of it and I reckoned it warn't best for me to mix in, but I judged I'd get the doctor's yarn to Aunt Sally somehow or other.

"public enterprise became private greed"

LINCOLN STEFFENS (1866–1936)

A few years after graduating from the University of California in 1899, Lincoln Steffens took on editorial roles at McClure's Magazine, *where he published his famous muckraking articles exposing corruption in city governments. He compiled this series of articles, each examining a particular city, into his 1904 book,* The Shame of the Cities.

To prevent readers from becoming depressed, Steffens wrote in the introduction, "But there is hope, not alone despair, in the commercialism of our politics. If our political leaders are to be always a lot of political merchants, they will supply any demand we may create. All we have to do is to establish a steady demand for good government." This quotation summarizes the philosophy of progressive journalists—that exposure of injustice and corruption would bring about reforms in government, institutions, and social relations. Therefore, while their focus might seem negative, progressive journalists published their exposés to advance their optimistic vision of a better society.

As more and more people moved into cities in the late 1800s and early 1900s, they overburdened the urban infrastructure. For example, housing was inadequate. This population trend, as well as industrial expansion and technological change, strained city governments. They could not provide enough water, sewers, electricity, police and fire stations, schools, and other services. Political "bosses" and their machines—or informal political networks—became sophisticated players in and manipulators of this frustrating mayhem. With grafts, bribes, and kickbacks, they got the seemingly impossible done. Bosses won popular support with voters by treating constituents to special favors, such as throwing lavish parties or developing facilities such as public parks. Few people complained about the corruption because bosses knew the needs of their voters and could help individuals with their everyday problems.

However, around the turn of the century, progressive reformers became increasingly concerned about urban issues. When examining city problems such as homelessness, overcrowding, unsanitary conditions, or industrial greed, progressives often looked to government action as a solution. Investigators soon realized that municipal governments ran on unacceptable levels of corruption. Because of bribes and kickbacks, citizens paid dearly for goods and services. Reformers such as Lincoln Steffens demanded a more ethical system of local government to effectively combat increasing urban ills.

Steffens's article "Tweed Days in St. Louis" appeared in the October 1902 edition of McClure's Magazine *before being published in book form in 1904. The term "tweed" refers to the notorious William Marcy "Boss" Tweed, who ran a corrupt political ring in New York between 1869 and 1871.*

The Shame of the Cities
Tweed Days in St. Louis

St. Louis, the fourth city in size in the United States, is making two announcements to the world: one that it is the worst-governed city in the land; the other that it wishes all men to come there (for the World's Fair) and see it. It isn't our worst-governed city; Philadelphia is that. But St. Louis is worth examining while we have it inside out....

The corruption of St. Louis came from the top. The best citizens—the merchants and big financiers—used to rule the town, and they ruled it well. They set out to outstrip Chicago. The commercial and industrial war between these two cities was at one time a picturesque and dramatic spectacle such as is witnessed only in our country. Business men were not mere merchants and the politicians were not mere grafters; the two kinds of citizens got together and wielded the power of banks, railroads, factories, the prestige of the city, and the spirit of its citizens to gain business and population. And it was a close race. Chicago, having the start, always led, but St. Louis had pluck, intelligence, and tremendous energy. It pressed Chicago hard. It excelled in a sense of civic beauty and good government; and there are those who think yet it might have won. But a change occurred. Public spirit became private spirit, public enterprise became private greed.

Along about 1890, public franchises and privileges were sought, not only for legitimate profit and common convenience, but for loot. Taking but slight and always selfish interest in the public councils, the big men misused politics. The riff-raff, catching the smell of corruption, rushed into the Municipal Assembly, drove out the remaining respectable men, and sold the city—its streets, its wharves, its markets, and all that it had—to the now greedy business men and bribers. In other words, when the leading men began to devour their own city, the herd rushed into the trough and fed also.

So gradually has this occurred that these same citizens hardly realize it. Go to St. Louis and you will find the habit of civic pride in them; they still boast. The visitor is told of the wealth of the residents, of the financial strength of the banks, and of the growing importance of the industries, yet he sees poorly paved, refuse-burdened streets, and dusty or mud-covered alleys; he passes a ramshackle fire-trap crowded with the sick,

Jacob Riis: Progressive Photographer

The photograph Five Cents a Spot *appeared in Jacob Riis's* book How the Other Half Lives. *He described the unauthorized tenement in shocking terms. "What squalor and degradation inhabit these dens the health officers know. . . . In a room not thirteen feet either way slept twelve men and women, two or three in bunks set in a sort of alcove, the rest on the floor. . . . Most of the men were lodgers, who slept there for five cents a spot."*

America's first photojournalist, Jacob Riis, came to the United States from Denmark in 1870. After trying several occupations, he eventually became a newspaper reporter in New York City. Drawing on his own experiences as a struggling immigrant in the slums, he decided to document the poverty and despair of that life. In 1878, Riis used new technology—small, portable cameras and flashlights, called "pistol lights"—to photograph slums at night. He set out with other amateur photographers, capturing snapshots of people sleeping in small, cramped spaces. The rudimentary design of his lighting system was imperfect; he once accidentally set a tenement on fire and had to snuff out the flame himself. Nevertheless, in 1890, he published his images and stories in the bestselling book *How the Other Half Lives.* Theodore Roosevelt, then a rising politician, read the work and became a close friend. Between 1890 and 1923, Riis published more than a dozen books, influencing reform in housing and child labor laws, as well as the creation of public parks. His brilliant use of the camera—with its stark representation of facts—revealed the need for social change and made Riis the forerunner of American documentary photography.

and learns that it is the City Hospital; he enters the "Four Courts," and his nostrils are greeted by the odor of formaldehyde used as a disinfectant, and insect powder spread to destroy vermin; he calls at the new City Hall, and finds half the entrance boarded with pine planks to cover up the unfinished interior. Finally, he turns a tap in the hotel, to see liquid mud flow into wash-basin or bath-tub.

The St. Louis charter vests legislative power of great scope in a Municipal Assembly, which is composed of a council and a House of Delegates. Here is a description of the latter by one of Mr. Folk's [the district attorney's] grand juries:

"We have had before us many of those who have been, and most of those who are now, members of the House of Delegates. We found a number of these utterly illiterate and lacking in ordinary intelligence, unable to give a better reason for favoring or opposing a measure than a desire to act with the majority. In some, no trace of mentality or morality could be found; in others, a low order of training appeared, united with base cunning, groveling instincts, and sordid desires. Unqualified to respond to the ordinary requirements of life, they are utterly incapable of comprehending the significance of an ordinance, and are incapacitated, both by nature and training, to be the makers of laws. The choosing of such men to be legislators makes a travesty of justice, sets a premium on incompetency, and deliberately poisons the very source of the law."

These creatures are well organized. They had a "combine"—a legislative institution—which the grand jury described as follows:

"Our investigation, covering more or less fully a period of ten years, shows that, with few exceptions, no ordinance has been passed wherein valuable privileges or franchises are granted until those interested have paid the legislators the money demanded for action in the particular case. Combines in both branches of the Municipal Assembly are formed by members sufficient in number to control legislation. To one member of this combine is delegated the authority to act for the combine, and to receive and to distribute to each member the money agreed upon as the price of his vote in support of, or in opposition to, a pending measure. So long has this practice existed that such members have come to regard the receipt of money for action on pending measures as a legitimate perquisite of a legislator." ...

In order to insure a regular and indisputable revenue, the combine of each house drew up a schedule of bribery prices for all possible sorts of grants, just such a list as a commercial traveler takes out on the road with him. There was a price for a grain elevator, a price for a short switch; side tracks were charged for by the linear foot, but at rates which varied according to the nature of the ground taken; a street improvement cost so much; wharf space was classified and precisely rated. As there was a scale for favorable legislation, so there was one for defeating bills. It made a difference in the price if there was opposition, and it made a difference whether the privilege asked was legitimate or not. But nothing was passed free of charge.

UPTON SINCLAIR (1878–1968)

Upton Sinclair was a prolific writer, ultimately publishing fifty novels, twenty nonfiction works, as well as essays, plays, and juvenile books. However, he remains best known for The Jungle, *a muckraking exposé of the Chicago meatpacking industry. Critics believe this novel began a new genre—the*

"cursing Durham's with all the power of his soul"

"contemporary historical novel." In other words, he analyzed contemporary events and situations through fiction. Sinclair's trailblazing work reportedly influenced other successful authors, such as John Steinbeck and John Dos Passos.

In November and December of 1904, Sinclair investigated the filthy working conditions in Chicago's slaughterhouses. In 1905, he published a serialized version of his findings in a socialist weekly, Appeal to Reason. A year later, The Jungle was released in book form. As an official member of the Socialist Party of America, Sinclair intended to portray the fundamental injustice of capitalist society—the oppression of the lower classes through "wage slavery" or the exploitation of workers. He put forth socialism as the answer to the problem. Instead, the public and politicians focused on the issues of meat inspection and food safety. As a direct result of Sinclair's novel, Congress passed in 1906 the Beef Inspection Act and the first Pure Food and Drug Act, which forbade the manufacture and sale of adulterated and fraudulently labeled products. These regulations were the kinds of governmental reforms that most progressives championed.

The Jungle follows its fictional character, Jurgis Rudkus, from Lithuania to his new home in Packingtown in Chicago. The story traces his disillusionment with America's promise of "the good life," culminating with tragic events such as the deaths of his wife and son and his imprisonment. Late in the novel, Jurgis joins a socialist movement and finds new hope.

In the following excerpt, Jurgis loses the "blinders" of a naive immigrant. He begins to hear about corrupt practices from reliable sources, such as his father, Antanas. Antanas's age prevents him from getting any but the most degrading, filthy work. Even then, Antanas gets his job only by agreeing to give his contact one-third of his wages (an example of graft). Moreover, Jurgis witnesses unethical and gruesome practices himself.

The Jungle
Chapter 5

Jurgis would find out these things for himself if he stayed there [in Durham's meatpacking plant] long enough; it was the men who had to do all the dirty jobs, and so there was no deceiving them; and they caught the spirit of the place, and did like all the rest. Jurgis had come there, and thought he was going to make himself useful, and rise and become a skilled man; but he would soon find out his error—for nobody rose in Packingtown by doing good work. You could lay that down for a rule—if you met a man who was rising in Packingtown, you met a knave.

The Ashcan School: Realists in Art

Around the turn of the century, a group of artists, now called the Ashcan School, took inspiration from the gritty reality of urban life, particularly New York City. Robert Henri, the leader of the movement, told his followers, "Paint what you see. Paint what is real to you." As a result, artists such as John Sloan, George Luks, and George Bellows portrayed American subjects rather than those found in European art. Perhaps the most sensational of these was Bellows's series of boxing paintings, which have a raw, brutal energy. Although boxing was illegal in New York City, prizefights occurred anyway, attracting crowds of all class backgrounds. Ashcan artists considered themselves progressives and tried to bring a social conscience—as well as an American artistic sensibility—to their works.

That man who had been sent to Jurgis's father by the boss, *he* would rise; the man who told tales and spied upon his fellows would rise; but the man who minded his own business and did his work—why, they would 'speed him up' till they had worn him out, and then they would throw him into the gutter.

Jurgis went home with his head buzzing. Yet he could not bring himself to believe such things—no, it could not be so. Tamouszius [Jurgis's colleague] was simply another of the grumblers. He was a man who spent all his time fiddling; and he would go to parties at night and not get home till sunrise, and so of course he did not feel like work. Then, too, he was a puny little chap; and so he had been left behind in the race, and that was why he was sore. And yet so many strange things kept coming to Jurgis's notice every day.

He tried to persuade his father to have nothing to do with the offer. But old Antanas had begged until he was worn out, and all his courage was gone; he wanted a job, any sort of a job. So the next day he went and found the man who had spoken to him, and promised to bring him a third of all he earned; and that same day he was put to work in Durham's cellars. It was a 'pickle room', where there was never a dry spot to stand upon, and so he had to take nearly the whole of his first week's earning to buy him a pair of heavy-soled boots. He was a

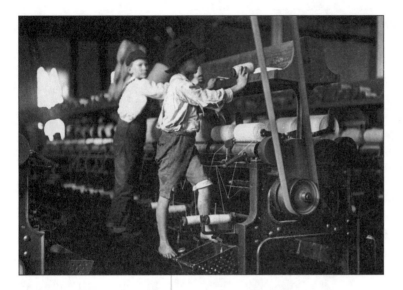

Lewis Hine trained as a sociologist then used his camera to document the evils of child labor. Beginning in 1909, Hine published several "photo stories" about children working long hours in dangerous mines and factories. In this photo, young boys work at spinning machines in a textile mill in Macon, Georgia. Hine's vivid documentation of exploited children helped establish child labor and worker safety laws at state and local levels.

'squeedgie' man; his job was to go about all day with a long-handled mop, swabbing the floor. Except that it was damp and dark, it was not an unpleasant job, in summer.

Now, Antanas Rudkus was the meekest man that God ever put on earth; and so Jurgis found it a striking confirmation of what the men all said that his father had been at work only two days before he came home as bitter as any of them, and cursing Durham's with all the power of his soul. For they had set him to cleaning out the traps; and the family sat round and listened in wonder while he told them what that meant. It seemed that he was working in the room where the men prepared the beef for canning, and the beef had lain in vats full of chemicals, and men with great forks speared it out and dumped it into trucks, to be taken to the cooking room. When they had speared out all they could reach, they emptied the vat on the floor, and then with shovels scraped up the balance and dumped it into the truck. This floor was filthy, yet they set Antanas with his mop slopping the 'pickle' into a hole that connected with a sink, where it was caught and used over again forever; and if that were not enough there was a trap in the pipe, where all the scraps of meat and odds and ends of refuse were caught, and every few days it was the old man's task to clean these out, and shovel their contents into one of the trucks with the rest of the meat! ...

All of these were sinister incidents; but they were trifles compared to what Jurgis saw with his own eyes before long. One curious thing he had noticed, the very first day, in his profession of shoveller of guts; which was the sharp trick of the floor bosses whenever there chanced to come a 'slunk' calf. Any man who knows anything about butchering knows that the flesh of a cow that is about to calve or has just calved is not fit for food. A good many of these came every day to the packing houses, and, of course, if they had chosen, it would have been an easy matter for the packers to keep them till they were fit for food. But for the saving of time and fodder, it was the law that cows of that sort came along with the others, and whoever noticed it would tell the boss, and the boss would start up a conversation with the government inspector, and the two would stroll away. So in a trice the carcass of the cow would be cleaned out, and the entrails would have vanished. It was Jurgis's task to slide them into the trap, calves and all, and on the floor below they took out these 'slunk' calves, and butchered them for meat, and used even the skins of them.

One day a man slipped and hurt his leg; and that afternoon, when the last of the cattle had been disposed of, and the men were leaving, Jurgis was ordered to remain and do some special work which this injured man had usually done. It was late, almost dark, and the government inspectors had all gone, and there were only a dozen or two men on the floor. That day they had killed about four thousand cattle, and these cattle had come in freight trains from far States, and some of them had got hurt. There were some with broken legs and some with gored sides; there were some that had died, from what cause no one could say; and they were all to be disposed of, here in darkness and silence. 'Downers', the men called them; and the packing house had a special elevator upon which they were raised to the killing beds, where the gang proceeded to handle them with an air of businesslike nonchalance which said plainer than any words that it was a matter of everyday routine. It took a couple of hours to get them out of the way, and in the end Jurgis saw them go into the chilling rooms with the rest of the meat, being carefully scattered here and there so that they could not be identified. When he came home that night he was in a very sombre mood, having begun to see at last how those might be right who had laughed at him for his faith in America.

Americans Abroad and World War I

In 1880, the sultan of Turkey closed the Turkish diplomatic mission to the United States, believing it to be a waste of money on a second-rate nation. But only twelve years later, every major world power except Austria-Hungary had established an embassy in Washington, D.C. Between 1890 and 1920, the once-isolationist United States emerged onto the world stage, developing a powerful military force and actively pursuing a foreign policy to rival any nation.

The nineteenth century had seen a dramatic division of the world into far-flung empires controlled by European countries. In the years prior to the First World War, several factors motivated the United States to experiment with imperialism. Proponents of U.S. intervention abroad based their arguments on ideologies of Manifest Destiny and Social Darwinism (applying evolutionary biological principles to human society). Growing spheres of influence throughout the world caused government officials and other powerful Americans to worry about security and trade. As a result, many argued that the time had come for the United States to enter the race as well. Most important, U.S. merchants, farmers, and industrialists clamored for new international markets for the tremendous abundance of goods produced by the rapid industrialization of the United States. Many Americans concurred with Indiana senator Albert Beveridge when he prophesied that "American factories are making more than the American people can use; American soil is producing more than we can consume. Fate has written our policy for us; the trade of the world must and shall be ours."

In the thirty years before its entry into World War I in 1917, the United States sent military troops or diplomatic policymakers to Cuba, Puerto Rico, the Philippines, China, and Mexico. For the first time, America's leading philosophers, policymakers, artists, and writers were broadly engaged in international affairs. The nation's decision to enter World War I, its victory a year later, and President Woodrow Wilson's attempts at ensuring peace cemented the United States' position as a world power, bringing with it both the triumphs and the perils of global engagement.

Novelist Henry James documented the encounters between Americans and Europeans with a flair not seen before in American literature. In her Pulitzer Prize–winning novel *One of Ours,* author Willa Cather explored the impact of the far-off conflict on a Nebraska family whose son leaves home to fight. Poet E.E. Cummings, a father of the modernist literary movement, darkly documented the despair and death the war produced and concluded—as many poets of battle had before him—that war is an awful, futile affair.

Featured Authors

Henry James
Rudyard Kipling
Ernest Crosby
José de Diego
Willa Cather
E.E. Cummings

HENRY JAMES (1843–1916)

Henry James was born in New York in 1843 to intellectually curious and artistic parents. James and his siblings grew up surrounded by many of the most famous thinkers and artists of the mid-nineteenth century. (His brother William became one of the first important American psychologists.) When James's family moved to Europe in 1855, his education as a citizen of the world began. There, Henry James fell in love with the "old ways," and his fascination with the American experience abroad would form the basis for many of the stories and novels he produced in his lifetime. Though James spent most of his life abroad, he is considered a master of the American novel form.

Henry James was not alone in his cosmopolitan lifestyle. By the late 1800s, steamship travel had made transatlantic crossings possible for many Americans, especially newly wealthy industrialists. Many were eager to take in the sights and sounds of Europe, others to show off their recently acquired riches. For the first time, Americans were contributing significantly to the international worlds of art, culture, and ideas, which had long been dominated by European taste and influence. Many of James's novels feature an American protagonist encountering the pleasures and perils of the Old World. For James, this "international experience" often produced a collision between American innocence, honesty, and activism, and European knowledge, artifice, and corruption.

In James's famous novel The Portrait of a Lady, *Isabel Archer is an intelligent, curious, independent-minded young American woman, who comes to Europe to explore both the continent and her own identity. In the following scene, Isabel's friend (American journalist Henrietta Stackpole) has come to England to visit. The encounter between Henrietta, an outspoken and opinionated woman, and Isabel's kind cousin Ralph Touchett, a wealthy American expatriate devoted to European ways, symbolizes the conflict between the Old and New that occurred as Americans began to venture out into the larger world.*

"He's what's called a cosmopolite"

The Portrait of a Lady
Chapter X

The train presently arrived, and Miss Stackpole, promptly descending, proved, as Isabel had promised, quite delicately, even though rather provincially, fair. She was a neat, plump person, of medium stature, with a round face, a small mouth, a delicate complexion, a bunch of light brown ringlets at the back of her head and a peculiarly open, surprised-looking eye. The most striking point in her appearance was the remarkable fixedness of this organ, which rested without impudence or defiance, but as if in conscientious exercise of a natural right, upon every object it happened to encounter. It rested in this manner upon Ralph himself, a little arrested by Miss Stackpole's gracious and comfortable aspect, which hinted that it wouldn't be so easy as he had assumed to disapprove of her. She resulted, she shimmered, in fresh, dove-colored draperies, and Ralph saw at a glance that she was as crisp and new and comprehensive as a first issue before the folding. From top to toe she had probably no misprint. She spoke in a clear, high voice—a voice not rich but loud; yet after she had taken her place with her companions in Mr. Touchett's carriage she struck him as not all in the large type, the type of horrid 'headings', that he had expected. She answered the enquiries made of her by Isabel, however, and in which the young man ventured to join, with copious lucidity; and later, in the library at Gardencourt [the family's English estate], when she had made the acquaintance of Mr. Touchett (his wife not having thought it necessary to appear) did more to give the measure of her confidence in her powers.

'Well, I should like to know whether you consider yourselves American or English,' she broke out. 'If once I knew I could talk to you accordingly.'

'Talk to us anyhow and we shall be thankful,' Ralph liberally answered. . . .

'I don't suppose that you're going to undertake to persuade me that *you're* an American,' she said.

'To please you I'll be an Englishman, I'll be a Turk!'

'Well, if you can change about that way you're very welcome,' Miss Stackpole returned.

'I'm sure you understand everything and that differences of nationality are no barrier to you,' Ralph went on.

Miss Stackpole gazed at him still. 'Do you mean the foreign languages?'

'The languages are nothing. I mean the spirit—the genius.'

'I'm not sure that I understand you,' said the correspondent of the *Interviewer;* 'but I expect I shall before I leave.'

'He's what's called a cosmopolite,' Isabel suggested.

'That means he's a little of everything and not much of any. I must say I think patriotism is like charity—it begins at home.'

'Ah, but where does home begin, Miss Stackpole?' Ralph enquired.

'I don't know where it begins, but I know where it ends. It ended a long time before I got here.' . . .

'What does he do for a living?' she asked of Isabel the evening of her arrival. 'Does he go round all day with his hands in his pockets?'

'He does nothing,' smiled Isabel; 'he's a gentleman of large leisure.'

'Well, I call that a shame—when I have to work like a carconductor,' Miss Stackpole replied. 'I should like to show him up.'

'He's in wretched health; he's quite unfit for work,' Isabel urged.

'Pshaw! don't you believe it. I work when I'm sick,' cried her friend. Later, when she stepped into the boat on joining the water party, she remarked to Ralph that she supposed he hated her and would like to drown her.

'Ah no,' said Ralph, 'I keep my victims for a slower torture. And you'd be such an interesting one!'

'Well, you do torture me; I may say that. But I shock all your prejudices; that's one comfort.'

'My prejudices? I haven't a prejudice to bless myself with. There's intellectual poverty for you.'

'The more shame to you; I've some delicious ones. Of course I spoil your flirtation, or whatever it is you call it, with your cousin; but I don't care for that, as I render her the service of drawing you out. She'll see how thin you are.'

'Ah, do draw me out!' Ralph exclaimed. 'So few people will take the trouble.'

Miss Stackpole, in this undertaking, appeared to shrink from no effort; resorting largely, whenever the opportunity offered, to the natural expedient of interrogation. On the following day the weather was bad, and in the afternoon the young man, by way of providing indoor amusement, offered to show her the pictures. Henrietta strolled through the long gallery in his society, while he pointed out its principal ornaments and mentioned the painters and subjects. Miss Stackpole looked at the pictures in perfect silence, committing herself to no opinion, and Ralph was gratified by the fact that she delivered herself none of the little ready-made ejaculations of delight of which the visitors to Gardencourt were so frequently lavish. This young lady indeed, to do her justice, was but little addicted to the use of conventional terms; there was something earnest and inventive in her tone, which at times, in its strained delibera-tion, suggested a person of high culture speaking a foreign language. Ralph Touchett subsequently learned that she had at one time officiated

James McNeill Whistler was an American artist who lived and painted abroad. The subject of this 1883 portrait, titled Arrangement in Flesh Color and Black: Portrait of Theodore Duret, was a European art collector and critic.

"Modernist" Art for a Modern World

Painter Georgia O'Keeffe's 1917 watercolor Evening Star No. VI.

As early as 1907, the American photographer Alfred Stieglitz had been exhibiting a new style of painting, known as Abstract art, by both European and American artists. In 1913, the now-famous Armory Show was held at the 69th Regional Armory Building in New York City, the first major U.S. showing of this new modern style. Such European greats as Picasso and Matisse were there, as were many young American painters experimenting in the new mode. More than 1,300 works were displayed. Traditional critics, and much of the art-viewing public, found the paintings shocking and confusing. Abstract art ignored the conventions of representational art—the traditional scenes of history, portraiture, and landscape—and instead purposefully distorted color and form.

Stieglitz continued to cultivate these artists from his studio in New York. One of the most famous of the Stieglitz group was painter Georgia O'Keeffe. Though O'Keeffe is best known for her paintings of flowers and southwestern scenes, much of her work is abstract in style.

The modern art of the first few decades of the twentieth century would form the basis for future artistic revolutions. The interplay between American and European artists at this crucial time mimicked the dialogue in literature, politics, and ideas that was already criss-crossing the globe. Modernist art was international art—befitting of America's emergence onto the global stage.

as art-critic to a journal of the other world; but she appeared, in spite of this fact, to carry in her pocket none of the small change of admiration. Suddenly, just after he had called her attention to a charming Constable, she turned and looked at him as if he himself had been a picture.

'Do you always spend your time like this?' she demanded.

'I seldom spend it so agreeably.'

'Well, you know what I mean—without any regular occupation.'

'Ah,' said Ralph, 'I'm the idlest man living.'

Miss Stackpole directed her gaze to the Constable again, and Ralph bespoke her attention for a small Lancret hanging near it, which represented a gentleman in a pink doublet and hose and a ruff, leaning against the pedestal of a statue of a nymph in a garden and playing the guitar to two ladies seated on the grass. 'That's my ideal of a regular occupation,' he said.

Miss Stackpole turned to him again, and, though her eyes had rested upon the picture, he saw she had missed the subject. She was thinking of something much more serious. 'I don't see how you can reconcile it to your conscience.'

'My dear lady, I *have* no conscience!'

'Well, I advise you to cultivate one. You'll need it the next time you go to America.'

'I shall probably never go again.'

'Are you ashamed to show yourself?'

Ralph meditated with a mild smile. 'I suppose that if one has no conscience one has no shame.'

'Well, you've got plenty of assurance,' Henrietta declared. 'Do you consider it right to give up your country?'

'Ah, one doesn't give up one's country any more than one gives up one's grandmother. They're both antecedent to choice—elements of one's composition that are not to be eliminated.'

'I suppose that means that you've tried and been worsted. What do they think of you over here?'

'They delight in me.'

'That's because you truckle to them.'

'Ah, set it down a little to my natural charm!' Ralph sighed.

'I don't know anything about your natural charm. If you've got any charm it's quite unnatural. It's wholly acquired—or at least you've tried hard to acquire it, living over here. I don't say you've succeeded. It's a charm that I don't appreciate, anyway. Make yourself useful in some way, and then we'll talk about it.'

'Well, now, tell me what I shall do,' said Ralph.

'Go right home, to begin with.'

'Yes, I see. And then?'

'Take right hold of something.'

'Well, now, what sort of thing?'

'Anything you please, so long as you take hold. Some new idea, some big work.'

'Is it very difficult to take hold?' Ralph enquired.

'Not if you put your heart into it.'

'Ah, my heart,' said Ralph. 'If it depends on my heart—!'

'Haven't you got a heart?'

'I had one a few days ago, but I've lost it since.'

'You're not serious,' Miss Stackpole remarked; 'that's what's the matter with you.'

"Take up the White Man's burden"

RUDYARD KIPLING (1865–1936)
ERNEST CROSBY (1856–1907)

Between 1890 and the 1930s, the United States intervened militarily and diplomatically in many places around the globe—from Asia and the Pacific to Latin America and the Caribbean. This level of involvement abroad came from a nation that had prided itself on its policies of isolation. But the lure of ripe foreign markets, the need to protect U.S. interests and security, and the tempting examples of European countries creating their own outrageously profitable colonial empires across the seas proved too hard for Americans to resist. Over the course of a few decades, America's empire builders, led by globally minded presidents like William McKinley and Theodore Roosevelt, pursued their own brand of imperialism. Its success was based on a confluence of people and ideologies: elitist, often racist "civilizing" rhetoric fueled by notions of Social Darwinism and "survival of the fittest"; power- and profit-hungry capitalists and political leaders; and a continuation of the philosophy of Manifest Destiny.

U.S. imperialism began in the Pacific. In 1893, American soldiers, under the guise of protecting the national interest, helped a group of white foreigners—mostly U.S. businessmen—overthrow Hawaii's constitutional monarch, Queen Liluokalani. Five years later, the United States annexed the island without the consent of the Hawaiian people. That same year, a long-brewing war between Spain and its Latin American colony, Cuba, broke out. The American public, fueled by a rash of dubious "yellow journalism" reportage and by outrage at the supposed Spanish destruction of the USS Maine, *clamored for war. Four months after the United States entered the conflict, they had won it, with surprisingly little bloodshed. Ironically, the Treaty of Paris, which formally ended the war, resulted in Spain's ceding Puerto Rico, Guam, the Philippines, and control of Cuba to the United States. Many saw this situation as directly contradictory to the traditional American principles of self-government and isolationism. The same month the treaty was ratified, fighting broke out in the Philippine Islands, where angry Filipinos, who had wrongly assumed they would be free to rule themselves after Spain's defeat, attacked U.S. soldiers.*

The United States also repeatedly intervened overseas for financial reasons. In 1903, the U.S. government acquired land at the top of Columbia to build and control what became the Panama Canal. The canal allowed thousands of ships bearing both imports and exports to pass more swiftly from ocean to ocean. In the Far East, American diplomats were busy securing access to markets for U.S. goods. Secretary of State John Hay championed an Open Door policy, which successfully kept the vast country of China from becoming parceled off into competing spheres of influence, controlled by European powers.

Not everyone supported such aggressive actions. Some U.S. policymakers feared losing American lives in foreign lands; others believed that empire-building inherently contradicted the very nature of a democratic republic. Still others argued that those who claimed to be working to civilize and Christianize foreign lands were merely masked profit-seeking capitalists, eager to exploit natural resources far from U.S. shores.

Published in McClure's Magazine in February 1899, Rudyard Kipling's poem "The White Man's Burden" provided fuel for the fire at a critical moment in the country's imperial experiment. Kipling, a British author who lived in colonial India, had seen the processes and consequences of imperialism firsthand, and he warned of its dangers as well as its glories. His racism and elitism, common to the times, are also evident in the work.

Publication of the poem triggered an enormous response in the United States, both in support of and against American imperialism. Writer Ernest Crosby, a pacifist and president of the Anti-Imperialist League of New York, parodied Kipling's poem in a New York Times editorial he titled "The Real 'White Man's Burden.'" The two poems presented here, highlight the numerous, complex issues—race, destiny, money, position, and power—that marked the Age of Imperialism in the United States.

The White Man's Burden
by Rudyard Kipling

Take up the White Man's burden—
 Send forth the best ye breed—
Go, bind your sons to exile
 To serve your captives' need;
To wait, in heavy harness,
 On fluttered folk and wild—
Your new-caught sullen peoples,
 Half devil and half child.

Take up the White Man's burden—
    In patience to abide,
To veil the threat of terror
    And check the show of pride;
By open speech and simple,
    An hundred times made plain,
To seek another's profit
    And work another's gain.

Take up the White Man's burden—
    The savage wars of peace—
Fill full the mouth of Famine,
    And bid the sickness cease;
And when your goal is nearest
    (The end for others sought)
Watch sloth and heathen folly
    Bring all your hope to nought.

Take up the White Man's burden—
    No iron rule of kings,
But toil of serf and sweeper—
    The tale of common things.
The ports ye shall not enter,
    The roads ye shall not tread,
Go, make them with your living
    And mark them with your dead.

Take up the White Man's burden,
    And reap his old reward—
The blame of those ye better
    The hate of those ye guard—
The cry of hosts ye humour
    (Ah, slowly!) toward the light:—
"Why brought ye us from bondage,
    Our loved Egyptian night?"

Take up the White Man's burden—
    Ye dare not stoop to less—
Nor call too loud on Freedom
    To cloak your weariness.
By all ye will or whisper,
    By all ye leave or do,
The silent sullen peoples
    Shall weigh your God and you.

Take up the White Man's burden!
    Have done with childish days—
The lightly-proffered laurel,
    The easy ungrudged praise:
Comes now, to search your manhood
    Through all the thankless years,
Cold, edged with dear-bought wisdom,
    The judgment of your peers.

9964—The Philippines, Porto Rico and Cuba—Uncle Sam's Burden
(With apologies to Mr. Kipling.)

This image, from a stereoview published in 1899, shows Uncle Sam as a United States soldier carrying a "burden" of small children representing the Phillipines, Puerto Rico, and Cuba.

The Real "White Man's Burden"
by Ernest Crosby

Take up the White Man's burden;
    Send forth your sturdy sons,
And load them down with whisky
    And Testaments and guns.
Throw in a few diseases
    To spread in tropic climes,
For there the healthy niggers
    Are quite behind the times.

And don't forget the factories.
    On those benighted shores
They have no cheerful iron-mills
    Nor eke department stores.
They never work twelve hours a day,
    And live in strange content,
Altho they never have to pay
    A single cent of rent.

Take up the White Man's burden,
    And teach the Philippines
What interest and taxes are
    And what a mortgage means.
Give them electrocution chairs,
    And prisons, too, galore,
And if they seem inclined to kick,
    Then spill their heathen gore.

They need our labor question, too,
    And politics and fraud,
We've made a pretty mess at home;

Let's make a mess abroad.
And let us ever humbly pray
   The Lord of Hosts may deign
To stir our feeble memories,
   Lest we forget—the Maine.

Take up the White Man's burden;
   To you who thus succeed
In civilizing savage hoards
   They owe a debt, indeed;
Concessions, pensions, salaries,
   And privilege and right,
With outstretched hands you raise to bless
   Grab everything in sight.

Take up the White Man's burden,
   And if you write in verse,
Flatter your Nation's vices
   And strive to make them worse.
Then learn that if with pious words
   You ornament each phrase,
In a world of canting hypocrites
   This kind of business pays.

"You, the all powerful Gentlemen of the North."

JOSÉ DE DIEGO (1867–1918)

José de Diego, a Puerto Rican poet and revolutionary, wrote verse meant to inspire and encourage his fellow Puerto Ricans as they struggled with 400 years of colonial rule, first by Spain and then later by the United States. His poems, composed in Spanish and often illuminating issues of political liberation and cultural rebirth, are considered among the greatest in Puerto Rican literature.

As a result of the United States' quick victory over Spain in the Spanish-American War, the U.S. government suddenly acquired an overseas empire. Important questions arose about how Spain's former colonies, now in the hands of the U.S. military, would be governed, and who would do the governing. For Puerto Rico, the answer came in 1900 when the United States Congress passed the Foraker Act, which estab-

*lished a civilian government on the island and declared it a U.S. territory.
In 1917, President Woodrow Wilson signed the Jones Act, making all
Puerto Ricans U.S. citizens. In 1952, Puerto Ricans voted for and
received commonwealth status with the United States—a status they
maintain at the beginning of the twenty-first century.*

José de Diego's beautiful poem Hallelujahs, *written in Spanish and
printed here in an English translation, challenged the United States—
whom Diego sarcastically called "the gentlemen of the North"—to allow
Puerto Ricans to control their own destiny. Throughout the poem, Diego
outlines a long history of political oppression and colonial rule, and
points out the hypocrisies in the words and actions of the island's northern neighbors. For today's Puerto Ricans who believe that their island
should become fully independent from the United States, the poem's
message still resounds.*

Hallelujahs

Gentlemen from the powerful, bountiful North,
Our island is part of the world.

Our Caribbean island is part of the Americas.

In the Beginning, God raised our island from the sea,
when its waters were clear and undisturbed.

And, after centuries, coming from the East,
the Arawaks inhabited the island.

And, centuries after, quaking the seas, the Spanish
ships arrived.

Mighty ships, cursed with being Latin.

That day your Puritan ships did battle, our Spanish
fleet were no match; tiny.

That day, when the Spanish people sank, ships and all,
in the seas of the Americas.

That day when you came in your splendor,
You, the all powerful Gentlemen of the North.

The destruction of the USS Maine *in Havana Harbor on February 15, 1898, killed more than 250 American soldiers. Outraged, the American public believed the Spanish had orchestrated the explosion. "Remember the* Maine *and the hell with Spain!" became the country's battle cry. On April 25, Congress declared war on Spain.*

Forgive, Gentlemen, the heavens and earth,
for having made this island, long before
the war …

Forgive, that so many of us were born,
before the United States.

Born in the Americas, with nothing,
but the kindness of God.

We are not the strongest, nor are we the
    masters,
but we are sons of the *Conquistadors*.

We know the mysteries of philosophy
and of the Art of Holy Poetry

But we know nothing, in our land of the Sun,
of the government practiced in Tammany Hall.

Nor do we understand your creative doctrines,
that placed the Philippines within the boundaries of
California.

Forgive, Gentlemen, if we seem perplexed,
of your concept of the Right of the People.

We shun concepts that would reduce us to an Island of
Thieves.

We shun, despite your historical reversals, the language and the
spirit of the Anglo people.

We speak another language, with other thoughts,
with the power of the spirit
and the power of the wind.

And we have been telling you for a long time,

over and over,

to go to the Devil
and leave us with God.

WILLA CATHER (1873–1947)

The factors that gave rise to the First World War (1914–18) are a complicated web of alliances that gradually drew one nation after another into armed conflict. Officially, the war began on August 14, 1914, when German troops invaded Belgium to reach France. Two months earlier, while visiting Serbia, Austrian archduke Franz Ferdinand and his wife had been assassinated by a Serbian nationalist. This incident set into motion a chain of events that would eventually leave the whole of Europe, from the British Isles to Russia, at war.

Competition among European nations—driven by nationalism, imperialism, and the rise of militarism—had produced a complex alliance system. Most European countries had signed treaties of assistance with one another, pledging to defend their partners should they be attacked. And so following the archduke's assassination, Austria-Hungary declared war on Serbia, who had allied with Russia, who summarily declared war on Austria. Germany, Austria-Hungary's ally, then declared war on Russia and a few days later on France—Russia's ally. When Germany invaded Belgium, Great Britain entered the war on the side of France and Russia.

In 1914, most Americans supported the United States' commitment to neutrality. Still, millions of naturalized U.S. citizens maintained strong ties to the countries of their birth and thus closely followed the news of the war. Many Americans opposed the fighting for pacifist reasons; others feared that, if the United States were dragged in, too many American lives would be lost on a continent too far away.

Gradually, Americans developed sympathy for the British and French cause, especially as stories of German atrocities, circulated by the British press, mounted. Some Americans felt a general kinship and commonality with their British ancestors. More important, the United States traded with Britain and France much more extensively than they did with Germany.

When German U-boats responded to a British naval blockade by declaring unrestricted submarine warfare on all ships, the United States was forced to end its neutral stance and enter the war on the side of Great Britain and France. In April 1917, a reluctant President Woodrow Wilson, who just months earlier had tried to bring about a "peace without victory," delivered his war resolution before Congress. Wilson

> "Something new, and certainly evil, was at work among mankind."

pledged that the world would "be made safe for democracy." By May, Congress had passed the Selective Service Act to draft American men into military service. The United States was going to war 3,000 miles from home.

Willa Cather's Pulitzer Prize–winning novel One of Ours, published in 1922, tells the story of Claude Wheeler, a Nebraska farmboy who decides that he will fight against Germany. Cather uses Claude and his family as a way to explore the impact that America's increasing international engagement was having on the heartland, from the initial rumors of war—which prompt the Wheelers and many of their neighbors to dig out old maps to locate the far-away places dominating the news—to the complicated and uncomfortable story of German neighbors, longtime friends, whose loyalties are falsely called into question because of their heritage. In the following scenes, Claude and his mother discuss the German army's advances in France and the growing sense that this "Great War" is unlike any previous one.

One of Ours
Chapter IX

Enid and Mrs. Royce had gone away to the Michigan sanatorium where they spent part of every summer, and would not be back until October. Claude and his mother gave all their attention to the war dispatches. Day after day, through the first two weeks of August, the bewildering news trickled from the little towns out into the farming country.

About the middle of the month came the story of the fall of the forts at Liège [Belgium], battered at for nine days and finally reduced in a few hours by siege guns brought up from the rear,—guns which evidently could destroy any fortifications that ever had been, or ever could be constructed. Even to these quiet wheat-growing people, the siege guns before Liège were a menace; not to their safety or their goods, but to their comfortable, established way of thinking. They introduced the greater-than-man force which afterward repeatedly brought into this war the effect of unforseeable natural disaster, like tidal waves, earthquakes, or the eruption of volcanoes.

On the twenty-third came the news of the fall of the forts at Namur; again giving warning that an unprecedented power of destruction had broken loose in the world. A few days later the story of the wiping out of the ancient and peaceful seat of learning at Louvain made it clear that this force was being directed toward incredible ends. By this time, too, the papers were full of accounts of the destruction of civilian populations. Something new, and certainly evil, was at work among mankind.

Nobody was ready with a name for it. None of the well-worn words descriptive of human behaviour seemed adequate. The epithets grouped about the name of "Attila" were too personal, too dramatic, too full of old, familiar human passion.

One afternoon in the first week of September Mrs. Wheeler was in the kitchen making cucumber pickles, when she heard Claude's car coming back from Frankfort. In a moment he entered, letting the screen door slam behind him, and threw a bundle of mail on the table.

"What do you think, Mother? The French have moved the seat of government to Bordeaux! Evidently, they don't think they can hold Paris."

British troops move into place at dusk for the Battle of Broodseinde.

Mrs. Wheeler wiped her pale, perspiring face with the hem of her apron and sat down in the nearest chair. "You mean that Paris is not the capital of France anymore? Can that be true?"

"That's what it looks like. Though the papers say it's only a precautionary measure."

She rose. "Let's go up to the map. I don't remember exactly where Bordeaux is...."

Claude followed her to the sitting-room, where her new map hung on the wall above the carpet lounge. Leaning against the back of a willow rocking-chair, she began to move her hand about over the brightly coloured, shiny surface murmuring, "Yes, there is Bordeaux, so far to the south; and there is Paris."

Claude, behind her, looked over her shoulder. "Do you suppose they are going to hand over their city to the Germans, like a Christmas present? I should think they'd burn it first, the way the Russians did Moscow. They can do better than that now, they can dynamite it!"

"Don't say such things." Mrs. Wheeler dropped into the deep willow chair, realizing that she was very tired, now that she had left the stove and the heat of the kitchen. She began weakly to wave the palm leaf fan before her face. "It's said to be such a beautiful city. Perhaps the Germans will spare it, as they did Brussels. They must be sick of destruction by now. Get the encyclopaedia and see what it says. I've left my glasses downstairs."

Claude brought a volume from the bookcase and sat down on the lounge. He began: "*Paris, the capital city of France and the Department of the Seine,*—Shall I skip the history?"

"No. Read it all."

He cleared his throat and began again: *"At its first appearance in history, there was nothing to foreshadow the important part which Paris was to play in Europe and in the world,"* etc.

Mrs. Wheeler rocked and fanned, forgetting the kitchen and the cucumbers as if they had never been. Her tired body was resting, and her mind, which was never tired, was occupied with the account of early religious foundations under the Merovingian kings. Her eyes were always agreeably employed when they rested upon the sunburned neck and catapult shoulders of her red-headed son.

Claude read faster and faster until he stopped with a gasp.

"Mother, there are pages of kings! We'll read that some other time. I want to find out what it's like now, and whether it's going to have any more history." He ran his finger up and down the columns. "Here, this looks like business. *Defences: Paris, in a recent German account of the greatest fortresses of the world, possesses three distinct rings of defences"*—here he broke off. "Now, what do you think of that? A German account, and this is an English book! The world simply made a mistake about the Germans all along. It's as if we invited a neighbour over here and showed him our cattle and barns, and all the time he was planning how he would come at night and club us in our beds."

Mrs. Wheeler passed her hand over her brow. "Yet we have had so many German neighbours, and never one that wasn't kind and helpful."

"I know it. Everything Mrs. Erlich ever told me about Germany made me want to go there. And the people that sing all those beautiful songs about women and children went into Belgian villages and—"

"Don't, Claude!" his mother put out her hands as if to push his words back. "Read about the defences of Paris; that's what we must think about now. I can't but believe there is one fort the Germans didn't put down in their book, and that it will stand. We know Paris is a wicked city, but there must be many God-fearing people there, and God has preserved it all these years. You saw in the paper how the churches are full all day of women praying." She leaned forward and smiled at him indulgently. "And you believe those prayers will accomplish nothing, son?"

Claude squirmed, as he always did when his mother touched upon certain subjects. "Well, you see, I can't forget that the Germans are praying, too. And I guess they are just naturally more pious than the French." Taking up the book he began once more: *"In the low ground again, at the narrowest part of the great loop of the Marne,"* etc.

Claude and his mother had grown familiar with the name of that river, and with the idea of its strategic importance, before it began to stand out in black headlines a few days later. . . .

Since the men were all afield, Mrs. Wheeler now went every morning to the mailbox at the crossroads, a quarter of a mile away, to get yesterday's Omaha and Kansas City papers which the carrier left. In her eagerness she opened and began to read them as she turned homeward, and her feet, never too sure, took a wandering way among sunflowers and buffaloburrs. One morning, indeed, she sat down on a red grass bank beside the road and read all the war news through before she stirred, while the grasshoppers played leap-frog over her skirts, and the gophers came out of their holes and blinked at her. That noon, when she saw Claude leading his team to the water tank, she hurried down to him without stopping to find her bonnet, and reached the windmill breathless.

"The French have stopped falling back, Claude. They are standing at the Marne. There is a great battle going on. The papers say it may decide the war. It is so near Paris that some of the army went out in taxi-cabs."

Claude drew himself up. "Well, it will decide about Paris, anyway, won't it? How many divisions?"

"I can't make out. The accounts are so confusing. But only a few of the English are there, and the French are terribly outnumbered. Your father got in before you, and he has the papers upstairs."

"They are twenty-four hours old. I'll go to Vicount tonight after I'm done work, and get the Hastings paper."

In the evening, when he came back from town, he found his father and mother waiting up for him. He stopped a moment in the sitting-room. "There is not much news, except that the battle is on, and practically the whole French army is engaged. The Germans outnumber them five to three in men, and nobody knows how much in artillery. General Joffre says the French will fall back no farther." He did not sit down, but went straight upstairs to his room.

Mrs. Wheeler put out the lamp, undressed, and lay down, but not to sleep. Long afterward, Claude heard her gently closing a window and he smiled to himself in the dark. His mother, he knew, had always thought of Paris as the wickedest of cities, the capital of a frivolous, wine-drinking, Catholic people, who were responsible for the massacre of St. Bartholomew and for the grinning atheist, Voltaire. For the last two weeks, ever since the French began to fall back in Lorraine, he had noticed with amusement her growing solicitude for Paris.

It was curious, he reflected, lying wide awake in the dark: four days ago the seat of government had been

John Singer Sargent's mural-sized painting Gassed *(shown below) is a haunting depiction of the horrors of poison gas warfare, as blinded soldiers follow one another on the battlefield.*

The New Weapons of War

World War I was a modern war in every sense, including the use of sophisticated new weaponry. These deadly new weapons included a German canon—nicknamed "Big Bertha" after the wife of a German munitions maker—that could hurl 1,800 pound shells from seventy-five miles. Machine guns fired more than 600 rounds of ammunition every minute. In April 1915, at the Battle of Ypres, German forces first used tubes of poison gas to fell their enemy. The chlorine fog suffocated two entire French divisions.

The powerfully lethal combination of tanks and airplanes ushered in a new era of "mechanized warfare." Tanks were large, slow-moving vehicles that ran on treads and were built of steel, enabling them to deflect bullets. By 1917, British forces were using large numbers of tanks to drive through enemy defenses, clearing the way for infantry soldiers. Initially, airplanes were too unreliable to be used in combat. Early dogfights consisted of pilots sitting in open cockpits, shooting at each other with pistols. But by war's end, larger, more powerful airplanes were being used for strategic, targeted bombing.

moved to Bordeaux,—with the effect that Paris seemed suddenly to have become the capital, not of France, but of the world! He knew he was not the only farmer boy who wished himself tonight beside the Marne. The fact that the river had a pronounceable name, with a hard Western "r" standing like a keystone in the middle of it, somehow gave one's imagination a firmer hold on the situation. Lying still and thinking fast, Claude felt that even he could clear the bar of French "politeness"—so much more terrifying than German bullets—and slip unnoticed into that outnumbered army. One's manners wouldn't matter on the Marne tonight, the night of the eighth of September, 1914. There was nothing on earth he would so gladly be as an atom in that wall of flesh and blood that rose and melted and rose again before the city which had meant so much through all the centuries—but had never meant so much before. Its name had come to have the purity of an abstract idea. In great sleepy continents, in land-locked harvest towns, in the little islands of the sea, for four days men watched that name as they might stand out at night to watch a comet, or see a star fall.

E.E. CUMMINGS (1894–1962)

E.E. Cummings is one of a group of American poets, including Ezra Pound and Gertrude Stein, who began a modern revolution in American poetry from their expatriate community in Paris. The son of a Unitarian minister, Cummings grew up in Boston, graduating from Harvard just as World War I was erupting in Europe. He joined a volunteer ambulance corps but saw little action. Instead, he was arrested and imprisoned for several months after a suspicious French censor confiscated some of Cummings's mail. After the war, Cummings returned to the literary freedom of Paris, participating in an international artistic movement that dramatically reshaped American poetry.

Though the United States officially entered the Great War in early 1917, the mobilization of troops and the transportation of both personnel and equipment to the European fronts was an enormous undertaking. Thousands of young men were drafted, sent to be trained, and shipped off to battle. Pervasive changes in the routines of daily life affected all Americans as most available resources were funneled toward the war effort. While new recruits trained at military bases around the country, citizens planted victory gardens, rationed such valuable commodities as metals and wheat, and contributed private boats and ships to the massive naval buildup. Under President Woodrow Wilson's direction, numerous regulatory agencies were created to oversee the wartime economy as well as to develop war propaganda meant to help promote the cause, encourage military and civilian service, and coordinate the sales of war bonds.

Along with such efforts came disturbing wartime violations of civil liberties. Americans became increasingly, sometimes violently intolerant of foreign-born and even native-born Americans of German descent. These unfortunate incidents ran the gamut from the silliness of attempts to rename all things German—sauerkraut became liberty cabbage, dachshund dogs became liberty pups—to the frightening, such as the passage and enforcement of the Espionage (1917) and Sedition (1918) Acts, which made it illegal for American citizens to criticize the government or Allied war effort.

By May of 1918, the German army was a mere fifty miles from Paris. But with the arrival and aggressive use of American troops—known as "doughboys"—the Allies began to repel German advances. By November, the German armies had begun to mutiny. On the eleventh hour of the

"who rushed like lions to the roaring slaughter"

215

Isadora Duncan and the Birth of Modern Dance

Isadora Duncan is considered one of the founding mothers of modern dance. Born Angela Duncan in San Francisco, California, Isadora grew up a poetic, artistic, free-spirited child. She made her professional debut in Chicago in 1899, and then took her bold, new dance style to Europe where she quickly became known as one of the most talented and avant-garde artists of her time.

As with other emerging modern art movements, Isadora Duncan's dancing was a dramatic turn away from the traditional. Instead of the formal classical ballets performed by large ensembles that had dominated most of the Western world's stages in the nineteenth century, Duncan's "modern" dance was often performed solo, employing free-flowing robes as costumes, and bare or sandaled feet. She looked to Classical Greek sculpture for form and style and danced to the music of romantic composers. Her performances concentrated heavily on the upper body and torso as "the generating force" for all movement, and she celebrated the natural design of the body with emotionally expressive gestures, including an emphasis on athleticism through running, skipping, and jumping.

Isadora Duncan's personal life was as unconventional as her professional life. A great believer in love but not in marriage, she gave birth to two children, both of whom drowned in a tragic accident in 1913. Duncan spent much of her life trying to bring the principles of modern dance to young people, opening various schools throughout Europe.

Duncan's legacy to the world of dance is a great one. Sadly, she died in as dramatic a fashion as she had lived, when, in 1927, the long scarf she was wearing became tangled in the wheel of the sportscar in which she was riding.

eleventh day of the eleventh month, the commander in charge of the Allied forces called for the guns to be silenced. Along the miserable miles of trenches, exhausted soldiers from both sides crept out, embracing one another and celebrating the end of the worst armed conflict the world had yet seen. More than 20 million people had died in the four years of fighting. The United States lost more than 325,000, but European losses of both troops and civilians were incomparably devastating. Russia alone lost 9 million people; Germany more than 7 million.

The destruction of the war—and the terrifying capacity of the new weapons that had been used to wage it—haunted those who survived. Though America and its allies had emerged victorious and powerful from this global conflict, they had certainly paid a price.

In the following poem, published in 1926, E.E. Cummings expresses the irony of war: that to be victorious, terrible loss must be suffered. And, he challenges much of the patriotic zealotry and jingoistic rhetoric that had fueled the dramatic emergence of the United States onto the world stage in the beginning of the twentieth century, through colonization, war, and trade. Cummings's use of free verse and his nontraditional punctuation, capitalization, and word breaks characterize his style, one that helped to shape the course of modern poetry in the twentieth century.

next to of course god america i

"next to of course god america i
love you land of the pilgrims' and so forth oh
say can you see by the dawn's early my
country 'tis of centuries come and go
and are no more what of it we should worry
in every language even deafanddumb
thy sons acclaim your glorious name by gorry
by jingo by gee by gosh by gum
why talk of beauty what could be more beautiful than these heroic happy dead
who rushed like lions to the roaring slaughter
they did not stop to think they died instead
then shall the voice of liberty be mute?"

He spoke. And drank rapidly a glass of water

UNIT 4 • DEMOCRACY AND ADVERSITY

1919 1945

*I*n the twenty-five years following the end of World War I, the United States endured dramatic changes of fortune on its roller-coaster ride from riches and material excess to severe economic depression and back to world economic and military dominance. During these tumultuous years, paradigms shifted and literary forms changed dramatically.

At first, the 1920s were marked by great wealth. Large companies grew bigger. Mass marketing and consumer loans enabled middle-class citizens to own automobiles and modern household conveniences. Art of all types flourished, as wealthy consumers and patrons grew in number. Between the world wars, many authors sought new themes and modes of expression. For example, African Americans developed their own literary forms and messages, inspired by black music and experiences.

With the stock market crash of 1929, however, boom times came to an abrupt halt. Within a few years, millions of Americans had lost their jobs and homes in the Great Depression. Desperate for new economic leadership, voters elected President Franklin Roosevelt in 1932. His promise to make a "new deal" with the American people led to the creation of federal agencies and programs to give people jobs, economic assistance, and hope. Writers, dramatists, visual artists, and photographers all benefited from government programs to support the arts and enrich American culture. At the same time, intellectuals rallied for economic equality. An outgrowth of this trend was "reportage," a literary form that created emotional appeals to win audiences over to an author's political views. Despite activist writings and dozens of new social programs, the economy remained depressed throughout the 1930s.

However, the emergence of foreign enemies changed the economic picture once again. As Nazi Germany and imperialist Japan rose to power in the 1930s and early 1940s, the United States was ultimately drawn into the Second World War. Military contractors geared up for wartime production, kick-starting the economy and giving

---

1923
Ku Klux Klan membership reaches its peak.

1925
F. Scott Fitzgerald publishes *The Great Gatsby*.

1927
The first motion picture with sound, *The Jazz Singer*, is released.

1929
The New York stock market crashes, and the Great Depression begins.

1930
President Herbert Hoover signs the Hawley-Smoot Tariff Act.

1931
Japan seizes Manchuria.

1932
American voters elect President Franklin Roosevelt.

1933
Adolf Hitler comes to power in Germany.

U.S. workers and soldiers a renewed sense of national pride and purpose. Arts and literature, too, found new passion and energy, much of it borne of American ideals and war-related issues—such as freedom, human rights, heroism, racism, and equality. The literature of World War II is varied and rich, but war's extraordinary events lend themselves particularly well to nonfiction, including colorful journalism and moving autobiography.

In short, the upheavals following World War I gave rise to enormous social and economic changes. Whether molding those changes or reacting to them, American authors forged unyielding events into enduring cultural artifacts.

1935
President Roosevelt signs legislation for his Second New Deal.

1939
John Steinbeck publishes *The Grapes of Wrath.*

1941
Japan attacks Pearl Harbor, and the United States enters World War II.

1942
The U.S. government orders Japanese Americans living on the West Coast to move to "relocation centers."

1943
Race riots break out in Detroit, Harlem, and dozens of other U.S. cities.

1944
Allies land in Normandy, France.

1945
Germany surrenders.

The United States drops two atomic bombs on Japanese cities, and Japan surrenders.

The Jazz Age

The 1920s were a golden era. The postwar economy grew and optimism reigned. F. Scott Fitzgerald—a great novelist of the period—captured the mood in his 1937 essay, "Early Success." He wrote, "The uncertainties of 1919 were over—there seemed little doubt about what was going to happen—America was going on the greatest, gaudiest spree in history.... The whole golden boom was in the air—its splendid generosities, its outrageous corruptions and the torturous death struggle of the old America in prohibition."

Prohibition was the common term for a constitutional amendment that outlawed the manufacture, sale, and transportation of alcoholic beverages. Enacted nationwide in 1920, the policy was generally unsuccessful. Few abstained from drinking—even the politicians who supported its passage—and the laws were not enforced. Prohibition produced corruption and a huge business for organized crime.

The "splendid generosities" Fitzgerald mentioned came from the great wealth generated after World War I. In 1920, for the first time in U.S. history, more people lived in urban than in rural areas. In cities, people took factory jobs or office work that earned them higher wages than they earned on the farm. They then spent their new wealth on houses, cars, and other material goods. A consumer culture emerged. Consequently, the owners of some big businesses, such as Henry Ford, became millionaires. Few anticipated the impending stock market crash of 1929.

Despite the general optimism of American society, young people were disillusioned by the brutality of World War I and vowed to be different from previous generations. A youth culture flowered for the first time in American history. New customs in dating, fashion, drinking, music, and dancing arose. Young women felt more powerful after gaining the right to vote; they displayed their new sophistication in "flapper" dress and "bobbed" hairstyles.

The decade's wealth empowered African Americans as well. World War I had encouraged a huge migration of blacks to northern cities for factory work. The heavy concentration of African Americans in New York—and their relative wealth compared with those in the South—led to a great explosion in black art and culture. New York's Harlem hosted one of the greatest artistic movements in American history, the Harlem Renaissance. African-American theater, dance, visual art, literature, and music matured there. Black musical forms such as jazz and blues filled clubs across the country and lent the decade its nickname: "The Jazz Age."

Featured Authors

F. Scott Fitzgerald
Dorothy Parker
Upton Sinclair
Toni Morrison
Langston Hughes
Zora Neale Hurston

F. SCOTT FITZGERALD
(1896–1940)

Perhaps no other writer is more closely identified with the "roaring 20s" than F. Scott Fitzgerald. He not only wrote insightfully about the decade, but participated wholeheartedly in its parties, drinking, and other lavish excesses.

Fitzgerald was born in Minnesota and attended Princeton University before joining the army. At the age of 24, he published his first novel, This Side of Paradise—*a story about college students. As a young author focusing on youthful themes, Fitzgerald became a spokesperson for the new postwar generation.* This Side of Paradise *quickly became a best seller. That same year—1920—he married a wealthy southern belle, Zelda Sayre. Fitzgerald soon became disappointed by the emptiness of his materialistic existence, and—even though he reveled in the extravagance of the decade—the theme of disillusionment recurs in his work.*

However, in general, wealth and optimism reigned in the 1920s. After World War I, Americans wanted to buy goods that they had been unable or unwilling to buy during the war. They bought big ticket items, such as houses and cars. Business boomed, and unemployment dropped. American prosperity resulted in U.S. citizens holding about 40 percent of the world's total wealth in the 1920s.

Many Americans skated along in these "good times" and were disinterested in politics. Consequently, few politicians proposed major policy changes. Nevertheless, the temperance movement had succeeded in outlawing the manufacture, sale, and transport of alcoholic beverages nationwide by 1920. However, it was a hollow law—most people, especially those in the cities, continued to frequent "speakeasies," or saloons. Few of these establishments were shut down even though officials were well aware of their locations. Prohibition created new business for gangsters, who made millions of dollars providing illegal alcohol to meet the continued demand. In some cities, rich crime bosses paid off government officials to ignore the alcohol trade.

Fitzgerald's novel, The Great Gatsby, *illustrates the wealth and immorality of the era. Published in 1925, it is commonly regarded as his masterpiece. The main character, Jay Gatsby, is a rich but mysterious resident of Long Island. Gatsby's neighbor, Nick Carraway, narrates the story of Gatsby's attempt to renew his love for Daisy, now married to another rich man.*

"Laughter is easier minute by minute"

In the following selection, Carraway attends a lavish party at Gatsby's house. Although the partygoers accept Gatsby's hospitality and expensive entertainment, they speculate openly about their host's mysterious past. Their suspicions suggest the immorality and hollow materialism that F. Scott Fitzgerald criticizes. Although the author never explains exactly how Gatsby got his money, several scenes suggest that he might have had criminal connections. However, the book's tragic ending— Gatsby's loss of Daisy and his life—concludes that the rich are their own "mob"—reckless, unprincipled, and insular.

The Great Gatsby
Chapter III

There was music from my neighbor's house through the summer nights. In his blue gardens men and girls came and went like moths among the whisperings and the champagne and the stars. At high tide in the afternoon I watched his guests diving from the tower of his raft, or taking the sun on the hot sand of his beach while his two motor-boats slit the waters of the Sound, drawing aquaplanes over cataracts of foam. On week-ends his Rolls-Royce became an omnibus, bearing parties to and from the city between nine in the morning and long past midnight, while his station wagon scampered like a brisk yellow bug to meet all trains. And on Mondays eight servants, including an extra gardener, toiled all day with mops and scrubbing-brushes and hammers and garden-shears, repairing the ravages of the night before....

At least once a fortnight a corps of caterers came down with several hundred feet of canvas and enough colored lights to make a Christmas tree of Gatsby's enormous garden. On buffet tables, garnished with glistening hors d'oeuvre, spice baked hams crowded against salads of harlequin designs and pastry pigs and turkeys bewitched to a dark gold. In the main hall a bar with a real brass rail was set up, and stocked with gins and liquors and with cordials so long forgotten that most of his female guests were too young to know one from another.

By seven o'clock the orchestra has arrived, no thin five-piece affair, but a whole pitful of oboes and trombones and saxophones and viols and cornets and piccolos, and low and high drums. The last swimmers have come in from the beach now and are dressing up-stairs; the cars from New York are parked five deep in the drive, and already the halls and salons and verandas are gaudy with primary colors, and hair shorn in strange new ways, and shawls beyond the dreams of Castile. The bar is in full swing, and floating rounds of cocktails permeate the garden outside, until the air is alive with chatter and laughter, and casual innuendo and

The Growth of Film

The entertainment industry thrived in the prosperity of the "Jazz Age." Although the first motion pictures were produced around 1900, film grew into popular entertainment—and an artistic medium—in the 1920s. Aiming for broad audiences, most movies portrayed hackneyed, shallow plot themes such as crime, romance, adventure, and high society. However, as directors and actors plumbed the new technology, some created enduring works and roles.

Silent films dominated the decade until "talkies"—movies with soundtracks—appeared in 1927. That year, in step with the jazz era, the first on-screen voice that audiences heard was Al Jolson's in *The Jazz Singer*.

Today many regard Charlie Chaplin as the greatest movie star of the 1920s. His comic yet sensitive portrayal of a tramp with ill-fitting clothes, a bowler hat, mustache, and cane endeared him to generations. In 1921, after seeing Charlie Chaplin's film *The Kid,* author Hart Crane tried to put into words Chaplin's "pantomime, so beautiful, and so full of eloquence." Conveying the complex comic-sadness of the tramp character, Crane wrote in the poem "Chaplinesque" that "we have seen / The moon in lonely alleys make / A grail of laughter of an empty ash can."

introductions forgotten on the spot, and enthusiastic meetings between women who never knew each other's names.

The lights grow brighter as the earth lurches away from the sun, and now the orchestra is playing yellow cocktail music, and the opera of voices pitches a key higher. Laughter is easier minute by minute, spilled with prodigality, tipped out at a cheerful word....

I believe that on the first night I went to Gatsby's house I was one of the few guests who had actually been invited. People were not invited—they went there. They got into automobiles which bore them out to Long Island, and somehow they ended up at Gatsby's door. Once there they were introduced by somebody who knew Gatsby, and after that they conducted themselves according to the rules of behavior associated with amusement parks. Sometimes they came and went without having met Gatsby at all, came for the party with a simplicity of heart that was its own ticket of admission....

As soon as I arrived I made an attempt to find my host, but the two or three people of whom I asked his whereabouts stared at me in such an amazed way, and denied so vehemently any knowledge of his movements, that I slunk off in the direction of the cocktail table—the only place in the garden where a single man could linger without looking purposeless and alone.

I was on my way to get roaring drunk from sheer embarrassment when Jordan Baker came out of the house and stood at the head of the marble steps, leaning a little backward and looking with contemptuous interest down into the garden.

Welcome or not, I found it necessary to attach myself to someone before I should begin to address cordial remarks to the passers-by.

"Hello!" I roared, advancing toward her. . . .

With Jordan's slender golden arm resting in mine, we descended the steps and sauntered about the garden. A tray of cocktails floated at us through the twilight, and we sat down at a table with the two girls in yellow and three men, each one introduced to us as Mr. Mumble.

"Do you come to these parties often?" inquired Jordan of the girl beside her. . . .

"I like to come," Lucille said. "I never care what I do, so I always have a good time. When I was here last I tore my gown on a chair, and he asked me my name and address—inside of a week I got a package from Croirier's with a new evening gown in it." . . .

"There's something funny about a fellow that'll do a thing like that," said the other girl eagerly. "He doesn't want any trouble with *any*body."

"Who doesn't?" I inquired.

"Gatsby. Somebody told me——"

The two girls and Jordan leaned together confidentially.

"Somebody told me they thought he killed a man once."

A thrill passed over all of us. The three Mr. Mumbles bent forward and listened eagerly.

"I don't think it's so much *that*," argued Lucille sceptically; "it's more that he was a German spy during the war."

One of the men nodded in confirmation.

"I heard that from a man who knew all about him, grew up with him in Germany," he assured us positively.

"Oh, no," said the first girl, "it couldn't be that, because he was in the American army during the war." As our credulity switched back to her she leaned forward with enthusiasm. "You look at him sometimes when he thinks nobody's looking at him. I bet he killed a man."

She narrowed her eyes and shivered. Lucille shivered. We all turned and looked around for Gatsby. It was testimony to the romantic speculation he inspired that there were whispers about him from those who had found little that it was necessary to whisper about in this world.

DOROTHY PARKER (1893–1967)

Dorothy Parker was a witty journalist who personified the vivacity and liberalism of youth culture in the 1920s. Her brash cynicism and independence became a prototype for young women of the postwar generation who sought to forge new roles.

And rip the hearts of men in half"

Throughout her career, Parker enjoyed success as a poet, playwright, critic, and screenwriter. However, she achieved her greatest critical acclaim as an author of short stories. While working as a theater critic for Vanity Fair *magazine, Parker helped form a literary circle, known as the Algonquin Round Table. She joined other journalists, playwrights, and performers in New York's Algonquin Hotel for lunches enlivened by clever conversation. There she sharpened her biting humor. One of Parker's often-quoted book reviews stated, "This is not a novel to be tossed aside lightly. It should be thrown aside with great force." Her caustic remarks lost her many friends and, reportedly, a few jobs.*

Parker was not the only woman speaking out in the 1920s. After women gained the right to vote nationwide in 1920, they experienced a kind of "liberation." Young women, in particular, adopted habits and fads that their elders believed disgraceful—smoking, drinking, "bobbing" their hair, shortening their hemlines, wearing lipstick, and dancing the Charleston. Compared with earlier generations, women had unprecedented privacy with men, who took them out on "dates" in cars. Previously, men had "called on," or visited, women at home. However, women's traditional roles in families and in the workplace changed little during the 1920s. In the political realm, they rarely voted in unified blocks to demonstrate political power.

In 1926, Dorothy Parker published her collection of poetry, Enough Rope, *which became a best seller. It included the following poem, "Song of Perfect Propriety." With heavy irony, Parker claims to be a "little" woman "writing little verse"—an act of "perfect propriety." However, her wishes and images are hardly that of a "respectable" young lady. Indeed, they reflect a deep frustration with sexual inequality and dainty women's roles of the period.*

Song of Perfect Propriety

Oh, I should like to ride the seas,
    A roaring buccaneer;
A cutlass banging at my knees,
    A dirk behind my ear.
And when my captives' chains would clank
    I'd howl with glee and drink,
And then fling out the quivering plank
    And watch the beggars sink.

I'd like to straddle gory decks,
    And dig in laden sands,
And know the feel of throbbing necks
    Between my knotted hands.
Oh, I should like to strut and curse
    Among my blackguard crew ...
But I am writing little verse,
    As little ladies do.

Oh, I should like to dance and laugh
    And pose and preen and sway,
And rip the hearts of men in half,
    And toss the bits away.
I'd like to view the reeling years
    Through unastonished eyes,
And dip my finger-tips in tears,
    And give my smiles for sighs.

I'd stroll beyond the ancient bounds,
    And tap at fastened gates,
And hear the prettiest of sounds—
    The clink of shattered fates.
My slaves I'd like to bind with thongs
    That cut and burn and chill ...
But I am writing little songs,
    As little ladies will.

Artists, designers, and photographers—as much as social forces—helped mold the "flapper" icon that dominated the 1920s. John Held Jr. illustrated this magazine cover with his classic interpretation of a flapper.

COSMO HAMILTON'S *New Serial* "Daughters of Folly
McCLURE'S
August   25 Cents

UPTON SINCLAIR (1878–1968)

Upton Sinclair became a full-time writer at the age of 22 and spent much of his long career writing novels with strong political agendas. Sinclair became a member of the Socialist Party of America in 1904, and he penned several progressive—or "muckraking"—books that exposed corruption, the exploitation of workers, and other scandals. One of his later works criticized Henry Ford, auto industry pioneer and the icon of "roaring '20s" individualism, wealth, and materialism.

Henry Ford did not invent the automobile. However, his clever development of mass production and marketing enabled him to become one of the richest men in America. Because he divided labor on a moving assembly line, Ford produced cars ever faster and made them available to more and more consumers. The cost of a Ford auto steadily declined from $850 in 1908 to less than $300 in 1926. This trend, combined with the rising wealth of everyday citizens, marked the rise of the American car culture in the 1920s. By 1929, half of American households owned at least one automobile, sometimes called a flivver or Tin Lizzy. The boom in the auto industry led the economic surge of the decade.

The following excerpt from Sinclair's historical fiction novel, The Flivver King, *is set after the election of Calvin Coolidge in 1924. President Coolidge had a "hands-off" or* laissez-faire *approach to the U.S. economy, making him a friend of big business. Meanwhile, organized crime rings were also becoming rich from the inability, or unwillingness, of law enforcement officials to uphold prohibition. Few important gangster "bosses" were arrested, and some, such as Chicago's Al "Scarface" Capone, were practically celebrities.*

The Flivver King, published in 1937, juxtaposes Henry Ford's rise to wealth and fame with one of his factory workers, Abner Shutt. In this selection, Shutt and his family symbolize average Americans—and their rising standard of living—in the mid-1920s. The oldest son, Johnny, is earning promotions and higher wages for his skilled labor. Hank, the second son, is a gangster involved in alcohol trafficking. All seem to be cruising along in the "good times" of the 1920s. During the 1930s, however, the Shutts lose their jobs and symbolize the weakness of the "everyman" in the face of economic depression.

"American ingenuity had solved . . . poverty"

The Flivver King

Happy times were here again. American industry, adopting Henry Ford's policy of mass production and low prices, was making it possible for everybody to have his share of everything. The newspapers, the statesmen, the economists, all agreed that American ingenuity had solved the age-old problem of poverty. There could never be another depression. It was "the New Capitalism."

Henry had a seemingly inexhaustible market for his cars. He was employing more than two hundred thousand men, paying in wages a quarter of a billion dollars a year. He had developed fifty-three different industries, beginning alphabetically with aeroplanes and ending with wood-distillation. He bought a broken-down railroad and made it pay; he bought coal-mines and trebled their production. He perfected new processes—the very smoke which had once poured from his chimneys was now made into automobile parts.

The Shutt family was a part of this vast empire, and they were on the way up. Five days in the week, rain or shine, winter or summer, Abner's flivver came chugging to the Highland Park [Ford] plant; he had a better one now, for the price was down to $300, and any working-man with a job could get one on monthly payments. Johnny had a brand new one of him [sic] own, which made the Shutts a "two-car family"—a great distinction, according to the motor-car ads.

Johnny, ever serious and hard-working, had finished at school and gone to work as a welder, a skilled job which paid him eight seventy-five a day. In less than a year he had become a subforeman, and was raised to nine fifty. That was what training did for you.

Strange and unexpected as it might seem, the second son was also "getting his." Hank did not have any title, and did not boast about his job, except to a few inmates. But he had the "dough," as he called it, also the "mazuma," and the "jack," and the "kale." He wore silk shirts and ties to match, razor-edged trousers, shiny new shoes, and an air of ease and confidence. He would come home and slip his mother a bill, and tell her to get something to make life easier for her; he would give his old grandpop a dollar or two to keep him in tobacco. He was a good-hearted fellow.

Hank would say he was working for the best people in Detroit; those whose names were in the blue-books and their pictures in the society columns. Right after the war

The Ford Model T, first manufactured in 1908, changed the fabric of American life. By the 1920s, Henry Ford's assembly lines were pumping out thousands of affordably priced Tin Lizzies every day. Shown here is a Model A, manufactured in the late 1920s.

the American people had plumped for prohibition; but these best people were taking the liberty of disregarding an inconvenient law. Right across a narrow river from Detroit lay a free country, well stocked with Canadian whiskeys and West Indian rums and French wines; the business of ferrying these products across the river at night was a lucrative one, and the job of moving them into the interior and hiding them before dawn, called for quick-witted young fellows who knew how to handle a truck, also an automatic or sawed-off shotgun in an emergency.

TONI MORRISON (1931–)

Toni Morrison is among the most famous of contemporary American authors. Although she has been an editor, playwright, and critic, she is best known for her seven novels about the black experience. Morrison's literary achievements have been recognized with many awards, including a Pulitzer Prize, which she won in 1988 for Beloved. *In 1993, she became the first African American to be honored with a Nobel Prize in literature.*

Morrison's life began in Lorain, Ohio, where she was born to parents who had migrated from the South—her father from Georgia and her mother from Alabama. Her parents were part of a much larger movement of African Americans that is sometimes called the "Great Migration." During Reconstruction, many former slaves slowly began to migrate to northern urban centers. That trend increased significantly between 1890 and 1910, when about 200,000 African Americans moved northward. Then, during World War I, factory representatives actively recruited southern blacks to come work in northern cities, and the tide of migrants became a flood. Historians estimate that 500,000 blacks settled in the North between 1914 and 1919.

Although blacks who moved to northern cities were not treated "equally" with whites, as a whole, their lives improved dramatically over what they had known in the South. The booming economy enabled blacks to prosper. They earned living wages, sent their children to decent schools, and voted. In larger cities such as New York, Philadelphia, and Chicago, African Americans built their own civic groups, cultural centers, and publications. As black migration continued in the 1920s, the number of African Americans in New York City more than doubled. In the 1920s, Harlem—a ghetto in New York City— became the largest black community in the nation.

"the City . . . danced with them"

As a result of these migration trends, Harlem became the center of a great movement in black culture called the "Harlem Renaissance." All forms of art thrived. Jazz, which had begun with black musicians in New Orleans in the late 1800s, spread across the country with the migration of African-American musicians. Jazz became so popular that it became synonymous with the decade—the "jazz age." Consequently, African Americans strongly influenced cultural life in the United States.

Morrison, who studied literature under the tutelage of a Harlem Renaissance writer, set her 1992 novel Jazz *in Harlem during the 1920s. The novel's structure mimics features of the jazz musical form. Morrison's rambling, improvisational tone treats language as a "malleable toy"—the same way that jazz musicians improvise melodies and tempo. Similar to jazz musicians' trading of improvisational "solos," Morrison's characters take turns narrating the events. In the following excerpt from* Jazz, *the author refers back to events in 1906, when the main characters, Joe and Violet Trace, first moved from Virginia to New York City. Morrison suggests that their optimism and excitement were probably shared by millions of African-American migrants, including those who continued to move northward throughout the 1920s.*

Jazz

Violet and Joe left Tyrell, a railway stop through Vesper County [Virginia], in 1906, and boarded the colored section of the Southern Sky. When the train trembled approaching the water surrounding the City, they thought it was like them: nervous at having gotten there at last, but terrified of what was on the other side. Eager, a little scared, they did not even nap during the fourteen hours of a ride smoother than a rocking cradle. The quick darkness in the carriage cars when they shot through a tunnel made them wonder if maybe there was a wall ahead to crash into or a cliff hanging over nothing. The train shivered with them at the thought but went on and sure enough there was ground up ahead and the trembling became the dancing under their feet. Joe stood up, his fingers clutching the baggage rack above his head. He felt the dancing better that way, and told Violet to do the same.

They were hanging there, a young country couple, laughing and tapping back at the tracks, when the attendant came through, pleasant but unsmiling now that he didn't have to smile in this car full of colored people.

"Breakfast in the dining car. Breakfast in the dining car. Good morning. Full breakfast in the dining car." He held a carriage blanket over his arm and from underneath it drew a pint bottle of milk, which he placed in the hands of a young woman with a baby asleep across her knees. "Full breakfast."

He never got his way, this attendant. He wanted the whole coach to file into the dining car, now that they could. Immediately, now that they were out of Delaware and a long way from Maryland there would be no green-as-poison curtain separating the colored people eating from the rest of the diners. The cooks would not feel obliged to pile extra helpings on the plates headed for the curtain; three lemon slices in the iced tea, two pieces of coconut cake arranged to look like one—to take the sting out of the curtain; homey it up with a little extra on the plate. Now, skirting the City, there were no green curtains; the whole car could be full of colored people and everybody on a first-come first-serve basis. If only they would....

Joe and Violet wouldn't think of it—paying money for a meal they had not missed and that required them to sit still at, or worse, separated by, a table. Not now. Not entering the lip of the City dancing all the way. Her hip bones rubbed his thigh as they stood in the aisle unable to stop smiling. They weren't even there yet and already the City was speaking to them. They were dancing. And like a million others, chests pounding, tracks controlling their feet, they stared out the windows for the first sight of the City that danced with them, proving already how much it loved them. Like a million more they could hardly wait to get there and love it back.

Some were slow about it and traveled from Georgia to Illinois, to the City, back to Georgia, out to San Diego and finally, shaking their heads, surrendered themselves to the City. Others knew right away that it was for them, this City and no other. They came on a whim because there it was and why not? They came after much planning, many letters written to and from, to make sure and know how and how much and where. They came for a visit and forgot to go back to tall cotton or short. Discharged with or without honor, fired with or without severance, dispossessed with or without notice, they hung around for a while and then could not imagine themselves anywhere else. Others came because a relative or hometown buddy said, Man, you best see this place before you die; or, We got room now, so pack your suitcase and don't bring no high-top shoes.

However they came, when or why, the minute the leather of their soles

The Harlem Renaissance lured many African-American painters to New York City, including Jacob Lawrence, who arrived in 1930. Shown here is a work from his series, The Migration of the Negro. This panel, which depicts race riots in East St. Louis, was painted in the 1940s.

In the 1920s, Harlem's Cotton Club hosted some of the country's best jazz musicians, many of them black. However, well-heeled whites made up most of the audience.

hit the pavement—there was no turning around. Even if the room they rented was smaller than the heifer's stall and darker than a morning privy, they stayed to look at their number, hear themselves in an audience, feel themselves moving down the street among hundreds of others who moved the way they did, and who, when they spoke, regardless of the accent, treated language like the same intricate malleable toy designed for their play....

The wave of black people running from want and violence crested in the 1870s; the '80s, the '90s but was a steady stream in 1906 when Joe and Violet joined it. Like the others, they were country people, but how soon country people forget. When they fall in love with a city, it is forever, and it is like forever. As though there never was a time when they didn't love it. The minute they arrive at the train station or get off the ferry and glimpse the wise streets and the wasteful lamps lighting them, they know they are born for it. There, in a city, they are not so much new as themselves: their stronger, riskier selves. And in the beginning when they first arrive, and twenty years later when they and the City have grown up, they love that part of themselves so much they forget what loving other people was like—if they ever knew, that is. I don't mean they hate them, no, just that what they start to love is the way a person is in the City; the way a schoolgirl never pauses at a stoplight but looks up and down the street before stepping off the curb; how men accommodate themselves to tall buildings and wee porches; what a woman looks like moving in a crowd; or how shocking her profile is against the backdrop of the East River. The restfulness in kitchen chores when she knows the lamp oil or the staple is just around the corner and not seven miles away; the amazement of throwing open the window and being hypnotized for hours by people on the street below....

That kind of fascination, permanent and out of control, seizes children, young girls, men of every description, mothers, brides, and barfly women, and if they have their way and get to the City, they feel more like themselves, more like the people they always believed they were. Nothing can pry them away from that; the City is what they want it to be: thriftless, warm, scary and full of amiable strangers. No wonder they forget pebbly creeks and when they do not forget the sky completely think of it as a tiny piece of information about the time of day or night.

LANGSTON HUGHES (1902–1967)

Langston Hughes is probably the best-known author of the Harlem Renaissance. He was born in Joplin, Missouri, but lived in Kansas, Illinois, Ohio, and Mexico before settling in Harlem in 1921. An incredibly versatile writer, he created work in every genre, including short stories, novels, plays, musicals, autobiography, history, and essays. However, Hughes is most famous for his voluminous poetry. In fact, some critics believe that he is the single most influential black poet in American literature. His poems stress racial pride and use the rhythms of African-American music—such as spirituals, jazz, and blues.

The music termed "the blues" began with Negro work songs and spirituals in the South. In the early twentieth century, black musicians began drawing on this heritage, publishing and performing songs with melancholy lyrics and unusual "blues" notes (flatted thirds and sevenths). As in work songs, repetition and calling were also important blues features.

W.C. Handy, a musician and band leader, is credited with being the "Father of the Blues" because he carefully noted local black folk songs and transcribed them. His composition, "The Memphis Blues," published in 1912, is widely accepted as the first song to have the word "blues" in it. Later, black author Ralph Ellison characterized the blues as "an impulse to keep the painful detail and episodes of a brutal existence alive in one's aching consciousness." As more musicians composed and performed the blues, its popularity spread throughout the country. By the 1920s, blues music had reached its "classic" period.

Langston Hughes believed that music was the major art form within the African-American community. This appreciation led to his writing the first poem to make use of the blues form. "The Weary Blues" appeared in a New York newspaper in 1923 and launched Hughes's literary career. Two years later, his first collection of poetry, also called The Weary Blues, *was published. The poem's speaker is walking down Lenox Avenue, a street in Harlem, when he hears a blues musician sing and play the piano. The poem mimics the structure of a blues song—using calls such as "O Blues!" and "Sweet Blues!" and refrains of "He did a lazy sway" and "I got the Weary Blues / And I can't be satisfied."*

> *"He played that sad raggy tune like a . . . fool."*

Trumpeter and vocalist Louis Armstrong is considered a father of jazz and blues. In the 1920s, he recorded with many classic blues singers such as Ma Rainey and Bessie Smith.

The Weary Blues

Droning a drowsy syncopated tune,
Rocking back and forth to a mellow croon,
    I heard a Negro play.
Down on Lenox Avenue the other night
By the pale dull pallor of an old gas light
      He did a lazy sway . . .
      He did a lazy sway . . .
To the tune o' those Weary Blues.
With his ebony hands on each ivory key
He made that poor piano moan with melody.
    O Blues!
Swaying to and fro on his rickety stool
He played that sad raggy tune like a musical fool.
    Sweet Blues!
Coming from a black man's soul.
    O Blues!
In a deep song voice with a melancholy tone
I heard that Negro sing, that old piano moan—
  "Ain't got nobody in all this world,
  Ain't got nobody but ma self.
  I's gwine to quit ma frownin'
  And put ma troubles on the shelf."
Thump, thump, thump, went his foot on the floor.
He played a few chords then he sang some more—
    "I got the Weary Blues
    And I can't be satisfied.
    Got the Weary Blues
    And can't be satisfied—
    I ain't happy no mo'
    And I wish that I had died."
And far into the night he crooned that tune.
The stars went out and so did the moon.
The singer stopped playing and went to bed
While the Weary Blues echoed through his head.
He slept like a rock or a man that's dead.

ZORA NEALE HURSTON
(1891–1960)

The most successful female writer to grow out of the Harlem Renaissance, Zora Neale Hurston settled in New York City in 1925. After she earned her degree from Barnard College, Hurston went on to document African-American folklore and to write short stories, novels, and her autobiography. Some critics believe that her insightful depictions of black life helped promote racial understanding.

The 1920s were trying times for race relations. The concentration of blacks in northern urban ghettoes intensified segregation and discrimination. In the early 1920s, the Ku Klux Klan (KKK) recruited thousands of new members. KKK members routinely intimidated, abused, and lynched African Americans. In response, some African Americans fought back. In the early 1920s, Marcus Garvey won thousands of followers by advocating the return of U.S. blacks to Africa. Black women had an even more arduous struggle against sexism and poverty as well.

Zora Neale Hurston published her classic novel Their Eyes Were Watching God *in 1937. The story chronicles the complex life of Janie Crawford, an African-American woman. Hurston's masterful use of dialect lends authenticity to Janie and her struggles. In the following scene, 16-year-old Janie and her grandmother confront the realities of being a poor black orphan on the verge of womanhood.*

"De nigger woman is de mule uh de world"

Their Eyes Were Watching God
Chapter 2

Oh to be a pear tree—*any* tree in bloom! With kissing bees singing of the beginning of the world! She [Janie] was sixteen. She had glossy leaves and bursting buds and she wanted to struggle with life but it seemed to elude her. Where were the singing bees for her? Nothing on the place nor in her grandma's house answered her. She searched as much of the world as she could from the top of the front steps and then went on down to the front gate and leaned over to gaze up and down the road. Looking, waiting, breathing short with impatience. Waiting for the world to be made.

Through pollinated air she saw a glorious being coming up the road. In her former blindness she had known him as shiftless Johnny Taylor,

Boom times for business fueled great building projects throughout the 1920s. Symbols of national pride, skyscrapers rose in large cities, especially Manhattan. William Van Alen designed the Chrysler Building (shown here), which was completed in 1928. Art and design critics regard it as one of the most graceful architectural achievements of the period.

tall and lean. That was before the golden dust of pollen had beglamored his rags and her eyes.

In the last stages of Nanny's sleep, she dreamed of voices. Voices far-off but persistent, and gradually coming nearer. Janie's voice. Janie talking in whispery snatches with a male voice she couldn't quite place. That brought her wide awake. She bolted upright and peered out of the window and saw Johnny Taylor lacerating her Janie with a kiss.

"Janie!"

The old woman's voice was so lacking in command and reproof, so full of crumbling dissolution,—that Janie herself believed that Nanny had not seen her. So she extended herself outside of her dream and went inside of the house. That was the end of her childhood.

Nanny's head and face looked like the standing roots of some old tree that had been torn away by the storm. Foundation of ancient power that no longer mattered. The cooling palma christi leaves that Janie had bound about her grandma's head with a white rag had wilted down and become part and parcel of the woman. Her eyes didn't bore and pierce. They diffused and melted Janie, the room and the world into one comprehension.

"Janie, youse uh 'oman, now, so—"

"Naw, Nanny, naw Ah ain't no real 'oman yet."

The thought was too new and heavy for Janie. She fought it away.

Nanny closed her eyes and nodded a slow, weary affirmation many times before she gave it voice.

"Yeah, Janie, youse got yo' womanhood on yuh. So Ah mout ez well tell yuh whut Ah been savin' up for uh spell. Ah wants to see you married right away."

"Me, married? Naw, Nanny, no ma'am! Whut Ah know 'bout uh husband?"

"Whut Ah seen just now is plenty for me, honey, Ah don't want no trashy nigger, no breath-and-britches, lak Johnny Taylor usin' yo' body to wipe his foots on."

Nanny's words made Janie's kiss across the gatepost seem like a manure pile after a rain.

"Look at me, Janie. Don't set dere wid yo' head hung down. Look at yo' ole grandma!" Her voice began snagging on the prongs of her feelings. "Ah don't want to be talkin' to you lak dis. Fact is Ah done been on mah knees to mah Maker many's de time askin' *please*—for Him not to make de burden too heavy for me to bear."

"Nanny, Ah just—ah didn't mean nothin' bad."

"Dat's what makes me skeered. You don't mean no harm. You don't even know where harm is at. Ah'm ole now. Ah can't be always guidin' yo' feet from harm and danger. Ah wants to see you married right away."

"Who Ah'm goin' tuh marry off-hand lak dat? Ah don't know nobody."

"De Lawd will provide. He know Ah done bore de burden in de heat uh de day. Somebody done spoke to me 'bout you long time ago. Ah ain't said nothin' 'cause dat wasn't de way Ah placed you. Ah wanted huh to school out and pick from a higher bush and a sweeter berry. But dat ain't yo' idea, Ah see."

"Nanny, who—who dat been askin' you for me?"

"Brother Logan Killicks. He's a good man, too."

"Naw, Nanny, no ma'am! Is dat whut he been hanging' round here for? He look like some old skullhead in de grave yard."

The older woman sat bolt upright and put her feet to the floor, and thrust back the leaves from her face.

"So you don't want to marry off decent like, do yuh? You just wants to hug and kiss and feel around with first one man and then another, huh? You wants to make me suck the same sorrow yo' mama did, eh? Mah ole head ain't gray enough. Mah back ain't bowed enough to suit yuh!"

The vision of Logan Killicks was desecrating the pear tree, but Janie didn't know how to tell Nanny that. She merely hunched over and pouted at the floor.

"Janie."

"Yes, ma'am."

"You answer me when Ah speak. Don't you set dere poutin' wid me after all Ah done went through for you!"

She slapped the girl's face violently, and forced her head back so that their eyes met in struggle. With her hand uplifted for the second blow she saw the huge tear that welled up from Janie's heart and stood in each eye. She saw the terrible agony and the lips tightened down to hold back the cry and desisted. Instead she brushed back the heavy hair from Janie's face and stood there suffering and loving and weeping internally for both of them.

"Come to yo' Grandma, honey. Set in her lap lak yo' use tuh. Yo' Nanny wouldn't harm a hair uh yo' head. She don't want nobody else to do it neither if she kin help it. Honey de white man is de ruler of everything as fur as Ah been able tuh find out. Maybe it's some place way off in de ocean where de black man is in power, but we don't know nothin' but what we see. So de white man throw down de load and tell de nigger man tuh pick it up. He pick it up because he have to, but he don't tote it. He hand it to his womenfolks. De nigger woman is de mule uh de world as fur as Ah can see. Ah been praying fuh it tuh be different wid you. Lawd, Lawd, Lawd!"

For a long time she sat rocking with the girl held tightly to her sunken breast. Janie's long legs dangled over one arm of the chair and the long braids of her hair swung low on the other side. Nanny half sung, half sobbed a running chant-prayer over the head of the weeping girl.

"Lawd have mercy! It was a long time on de way but Ah reckon it had to come. Oh Jesus! Do, Jesus! Ah done de best Ah could.

The Great Depression and the New Deal

The stock market crash of October 29, 1929, marked the beginning, though not the cause, of the Great Depression. The crash merely drew attention to economic imbalances that had grown since the end of World War I. Tax laws favoring the rich enabled wealthy speculators to force up the prices of stocks and real estate. At the same time, workers and farmers earned a smaller and smaller share of the nation's wealth. In addition, credit flowed too freely. Consumers bought goods on credit and later found themselves without much income during the downturn. Many were unable to pay for their old purchases or make new ones to fuel economic growth. The first president during the Great Depression, Herbert Hoover, was unsuccessful in turning the tide. Rather, he signed the 1930 Hawley-Smoot Tariff Act, raising duties on imported goods, which historians think added to the economic decline.

By 1932, an election year, millions of Americans were unemployed. Having been evicted from their homes, an unprecedented number lived in squalid shantytowns and faced starvation. The mounting severity of the crisis demanded new thinking and new leadership. After twelve years of Republican presidents, U.S. voters elected Democrat Franklin Roosevelt on his platform to make a "New Deal" with the American people. He had no firm answers, but rather stressed bold experimentation until a solution was found. President Roosevelt and Congress passed a host of new laws designed to create jobs, help displaced farmers, and alleviate suffering. Although the New Deal did provide some relief, the nation struggled through hard times during the entire decade of the 1930s.

Among intellectual circles, radical ideas had also taken hold. As the income gap between rich and poor increased, academics and writers began to question the capitalist economic system. Witnessing greed and excess, the collapse of the stock market, and finally the shattered lives of the unemployed, intellectuals rallied for change. Much of this criticism took the form of socialist or Marxist ideologies, which advocate economic security for all members of society.

Consequently, much of the literature, music, and visual art of the 1930s reveals leftist sentiments. Authors such as John Steinbeck highlighted the struggles of downtrodden characters against forces more powerful than themselves. Meanwhile, hundreds of authors, including Richard Wright and Ralph Ellison, worked for the Works Progress Administration, a New Deal relief program. They interviewed ordinary individuals and documented their stories, thus creating a social history project of immense scope and power. Photographers, visual artists, and dramatists also gained jobs through the federal government. Thanks to their efforts, the Great Depression has been vividly recorded for future generations.

Featured Authors

John Dos Passos
Clifford Odets
Meridel LeSueur
John Steinbeck
Ralph Ellison
Genevieve Taggard

JOHN DOS PASSOS (1896–1970)

After graduating from Harvard University in 1916, John Dos Passos served as an ambulance driver in France and Italy during World War I. Disillusioned by his experiences in the Great War, Dos Passos joined the Communist Party for a time. Although he later became more conservative, Dos Passos is best known for his early novels of the 1920s and 1930s. In those books he developed new literary techniques to reveal problems and promote change.

Dos Passos's most famous work is U.S.A—three ambitious novels that portray life in the country between 1900 and 1930. Characterized as a "national epic," U.S.A criticizes what Dos Passos viewed as the materialism and shallowness of American society in a new literary form. Borrowing techniques from the film industry, he interrupts his stories with what he calls "newsreels," featuring newspaper headlines, songs, and famous quotations to reveal hypocrisy and highlight various political events of the period.

The last novel of the trilogy, The Big Money, *was published in 1936. The final newsreel in that book, excerpted below, focuses on the economic decline of the late 1920s. It includes three main themes: negative economic trends, positive assurances of politicians, and tension between the classes depicted in labor struggles.*

The topics in this selection identify one of the main causes of the Great Depression—the unequal distribution of wealth. In the 1920s, industries consolidated. By 1929, 200 corporations controlled nearly half the country's corporate assets. The wealthiest Americans became even more rich. As a result, there was too little money in the hands of working people, who, as the majority of consumers, fueled economic growth.

The first line of the excerpt refers to the stock market crash of October 29, 1929, or Black Tuesday, the event that marked the onset of the Great Depression. That month, the value of stocks on the New York Stock Exchange fell by 37 percent. With this disastrous economic news, Dos Passos juxtaposes political rhetoric such as "MARKET SURE TO RECOVER" and "REAL VALUES UNHARMED." The final quotation, which begins "the President declared," was likely spoken by former president Calvin Coolidge in 1929. Its inclusion probably demonstrates Dos Passos's view that the upper classes and politicians were out of touch with the economic troubles underlying the period.

"President sees prosperity near"

On Black Tuesday—October 29, 1929—crowds gathered outside banks and stock market offices on Wall Street in New York City. Share prices had plummeted 25 percent from the previous day, sparking a panic.

In contrast to those statements, the newsreel employs a folk song (in italics) about the plight of lower class workers. Supporting the song are excerpts about various labor strikes—news that contradicts the pacifying assurances of American politicians.

The Big Money
Newsreel LXVIII

WALL STREET STUNNED ...

MARKET SURE TO RECOVER FROM SLUMP

DECLINE IN CONTRACTS

POLICE TURN MACHINE GUNS ON COLORADO
MINE STRIKERS KILL 5 WOUND 40

sympathizers appeared on the scene just as thousands of office workers were pouring out of the buildings at the lunch hour. As they raised their placard high and started an indefinite march from one side to the other, they were jeered and hooted not only by the office workers but also by workmen on a building under construction....

We leave our home in the morning
We kiss our children goodbye ...

U.S. CHAMBER OF COMMERCE URGES CONFIDENCE

REAL VALUES UNHARMED

While we slave for the bosses
Our children scream an' cry
But when we draw our money
Our grocery bills to pay

PRESIDENT SEES PROSPERITY NEAR

Not a cent to spend for clothing
Not a cent to lay away

STEAMROLLER IN ACTION AGAINST MILITANTS

MINERS BATTLE SCABS

But we cannot buy for our children
Our wages are too low
Now listen to me you workers
Both you women and men
Let us win for them the victory
I'm sure it ain't no sin

CARILLON PEALS IN SINGING TOWER

the President declared it was impossible to view the increased advantages for the many without smiling at those who a short time ago expressed so much fear lest our country might come under the control of a few individuals of great wealth.

CLIFFORD ODETS (1906–1963)

Clifford Odets grew up in the Bronx, New York, with parents who had immigrated from eastern Europe. After ten years of trying to make a living by acting, he turned to playwriting, the endeavor that brought him success. Odets's first production, Waiting for Lefty, *was staged in 1935 to great critical and popular acclaim. Though he continued to write stageplays and screenplays into the 1950s, his later works were not as popularly received as* Waiting for Lefty. *Consequently, Odets remains closely associated with the Depression era.*

While Clifford Odets was a struggling actor in the 1920s, much of the nation's economic growth was spurred by consumer spending on cars, home appliances, furniture, and other products. Most people bought these items with installment loans rather than paying for them outright. Eventually, consumers' buying power ran out of steam, and they were overburdened with debt, unable to make new purchases. With consumer demand low, businesses faltered and had to reduce salaries or lay off workers entirely. Those same workers did not have enough money to make their monthly payments. Many people came home to find their purchases had been hauled away—repossessed by the bank.

As the Great Depression continued, workers in many assembly line industries began to organize to improve salaries and working conditions.

"Get brass toes . . . and know where to kick!"

Between 1933 and 1941, union membership grew from 3 million to more than 8 million, thanks in part to labor-friendly government legislation. During that decade, the sit-down strike became common. Instead of walking out of factories, union members went to the plant but did not work. Instead they sat down. This tactic prevented companies from hiring strike breakers to take the place of strikers.

Waiting for Lefty is a one-act play that includes several scenes framed within a labor union meeting. In the end, the characters attending the meeting call for a strike. The following scene between Joe, a taxi driver, and his wife Edna dramatizes the effect that the ailing economy had on families. The character called Fatt and the seated men, referred to at the beginning and end of the scene, are the disgruntled workers.

Waiting for Lefty
I. Joe and Edna

The lights fade out and a white spot picks out the playing space within the space of seated men. The seated men are very dimly visible in the outer dark, but more prominent is FATT smoking his cigar and often blowing the smoke in the lighted circle.

A tired but attractive woman of thirty comes into the room, drying her hands on an apron. She stands there sullenly as JOE comes in from the other side, home from work. For a moment they stand and look at each other in silence.

JOE: Where's all the furniture, honey?
EDNA: They took it away. No installments paid.
JOE: When?
EDNA: Three o'clock.
JOE: They can't do that.
EDNA: Can't? They did it.
JOE: Why, the palookas, we paid three-quarters.
EDNA: The man said read the contract.
JOE: We must have signed a phoney....
EDNA: It's a regular contract and you signed it.
JOE: Don't be so sour, Edna.... (Tries to embrace her.)
EDNA: Do it in the movies, Joe—they pay Clark Gable big money for it.
JOE: This is a helluva house to come home to. Take my word!
EDNA: Take MY word! Whose fault is it?
JOE: Must you start that stuff again?
EDNA: Maybe you'd like to talk about books?
JOE: I'd like to slap you in the mouth!
EDNA: No you won't.

JOE: (sheepishly): Jeez, Edna, you get me sore some time....

EDNA: But just look at me—I'm laughing all over!

JOE: Don't insult me. Can I help it if times are bad? What the hell do you want me to do, jump off a bridge or something?

EDNA: Don't yell. I just put the kids to bed so they won't know they missed a meal. If I don't have Emmy's shoes soled tomorrow, she can't go to school. In the meantime let her sleep.

JOE: Honey, I rode the wheels off the chariot today. I cruised around five hours without a call. It's conditions.

EDNA: Tell it to the A&P!

JOE: I booked two-twenty on the clock. A lady with a dog was lit ...she gave me a quarter tip by mistake. If you'd only listen to me—we're rolling in wealth.

EDNA: Yeah? How much?

JOE: I had "coffee and—" in a beanery. (Hands her silver coins.) A buck four.

EDNA: The second month's rent is due tomorrow.

JOE: Don't look at me that way, Edna.

EDNA: I'm looking through you, not at you.... Everything was gonna be so ducky! A cottage by the waterfall, roses in Picardy. You're a four-star-bust! If you think I'm standing for it much longer, you're crazy as a bedbug.

JOE: I'd get another job if I could. There's no work—you know it.

EDNA: I only know we're at the bottom of the ocean.

JOE: What can I do?

EDNA: Who's the man in the family, you or me?

JOE: That's no answer. Get down to brass tacks. Christ, gimme a break, too! A coffee and java all day. I'm hungry, too. Babe. I'd work my fingers to the bone if—

EDNA: I'll open a can of salmon.

JOE: Not now. Tell me what to do!

EDNA: I'm not God!

JOE: Jeez, I wish I was a kid again and didn't have to think about the next minute.

EDNA: But you're not a kid and you do have to think about the next minute. You got two blondie kids sleeping in the next room. They need food and clothes. I'm not mentioning anything else—But we're stalled like a flivver in the snow. For five years I laid awake at night listening to my heart pound. For God's sake, do something, Joe, get

In 1936, a new kind of labor strike took hold. By "sitting down" on the job, union members discouraged bosses from bringing in strike breakers to take their place. Shown here are workers striking in an auto plant in Michigan.

wise. Maybe get your buddies together, maybe go on strike for better money. Poppa did it during the war and they won out. I'm turning into a sour old nag.

JOE: (defending himself): Strikes don't work!

EDNA: Who told you?

JOE: Besides that means not a nickel a week while we're out. Then when it's over they don't take you back.

EDNA: Suppose they don't. What's to lose?

JOE: Well, we're averaging six–seven dollars a week now.

EDNA: That just pays for the rent.

JOE: That is something, Edna.

EDNA: It isn't. They'll push you down to three and four a week before you know it. Then you'll say, "That's somethin'," too!

JOE: There's too many cabs on the street, that's the whole damn trouble.

EDNA: Let the company worry about that, you big fool! If their cabs didn't make a profit, they'd take them off the streets. Or maybe you think they're in business just to pay Joe Mitchell's rent!

JOE: You don't know a-b-c, Edna.

EDNA: I know this—your boss is making suckers outa you boys every minute. Yes, and suckers out of all the wives and the poor innocent kids who'll grow up with crooked spines and sick bones. Sure, I see it in the papers, how good orange juice is for kids. But damnit our kids get colds one on top of the other. They look like little ghosts. Betty never saw a grapefruit. I took her to the store last week and she pointed to a stack of grapefruits. "What's that!" she said. My God, Joe—the world is supposed to be for all of us. . . .

[Joe and Edna continue to fight. Edna threatens to leave Joe for her old boyfriend Bud Haas, who has a better job than Joe. In anger, Joe threatens to physically hurt Edna.]

EDNA: You don't scare me that much! (Indicates a half inch on her finger.)

JOE: This is what I slaved for!

EDNA: Tell it to your boss.

JOE: He don't give a damn for you or me!

EDNA: That's what I say.

JOE: Don't change the subject!

EDNA: This is the subject, the exact subject! Your boss makes this subject. I never saw him in my life, but he's putting ideas in my head a mile a minute. He's giving your kids that fancy disease called the rickets. He's making a jelly-fish outa you and putting wrinkles in my face. This is the subject every inch of the way! He's throwing me into Bud Haas' lap. When in hell will you get wise—

JOE: I'm not so dumb as you think! But you are talking like a red.

EDNA: I don't know what that means. But when a man knocks you down you get up and kiss his fist! You gutless piece of baloney.

JOE: One man can't—

EDNA: (with great joy): I don't say one man! I say a hundred, a thousand, a whole million, I say. But start in your own union. Get those hack boys together! Sweep out those racketeers like a pile of dirt! Stand up like men and fight for the crying kids and wives. Goddamnit! I'm tired of slavery and sleepless nights.

JOE: (with her): Sure, sure! . . .

EDNA: Yes. Get brass toes on your shoes and know where to kick!

JOE: (suddenly jumping up and kissing his wife full on the mouth): Listen, Edna, I'm goin' down to 174th Street to look up Lefty Costello. Lefty was saying the other day . . . (He suddenly stops.) How about this Haas guy?

EDNA: Get out of here!

JOE: I'll be back! (Runs out. For a moment EDNA stands triumphant. There is a blackout and when the regular lights come up, JOE MITCHELL is concluding what he has been saying):

JOE: You guys know this stuff better than me. We gotta walk out!

(Abruptly he turns and goes back to his seat.)

Blackout

MERIDEL LeSUEUR (1900–1996)

Born to politically active parents in Iowa, Meridel LeSueur made a long career of writing short stories, novels, and articles, many of them with feminist or socialist slants. She began writing fiction in the 1920s, while she acted in Hollywood silent films. In the 1930s, LeSueur became active in the labor movement and other liberal causes. Today she is regarded as an astute chronicler of women's problems and achievements.

By 1932, the Great Depression had brought terrible suffering to millions of Americans. The mood of the country—particularly in cities, where unemployment and hunger had hit hardest—was of absolute despair. Unable to pay rent or mortgage, thousands were evicted from their homes. Many homeless families built shacks along the outskirts of large cities. Less commonly known is that approximately 3 million of the 13 million unemployed Americans were women. Often men left their families in search of work, and women needed to find jobs.

Disillusioned with President Herbert Hoover's inability to improve the economy, voters in November 1932 elected Franklin Roosevelt on his

"The street . . . now becomes a mart"

platform to institute a "New Deal." At the center of the New Deal was a belief that the federal government should go to greater lengths to protect the needy and promote the public good.

About that time, Meridel LeSueur began writing articles that documented the lives of poverty-stricken Americans in the Midwest. She and other liberal activists described what they saw as the worst effects of the capitalist system—financial inequality, exploitation of workers, and the plight of women and minorities. They relayed their stories in the form of "reportage," a new literary genre. A type of biased journalism, reportage used a "three-dimensional" narration style, intended to help readers see, feel, and "experience" the event. Borrowing characteristics from short stories, reportage features strong characterization and heightened detail for persuasive effect. "Women on the Breadlines" is LeSueur's first work of reportage. It appeared in the communist journal, The New Masses, *in 1932.*

Women on the Breadlines

I am sitting in the city free employment bureau. It's the women's section. We have been sitting here now for four hours. We sit here every day, waiting for a job. There are no jobs. Most of us have had no breakfast. Some have had scant rations for over a year. Hunger makes a human being lapse into a state of lethargy, especially city hunger. Is there any place else in the world where a human being is supposed to go hungry amidst plenty without an outcry, without protest, where only the boldest steal or kill for bread, and the timid crawl the streets, hunger like the beak of a terrible bird at the vitals?

We sit looking at the floor. No one dares think of the coming winter. There are only a few more days of summer. Everyone is anxious to get work to lay up something for that long siege of bitter cold. But there is no work. Sitting in the room we all know it. That is why we don't talk much. We look at the floor dreading to see that knowledge in each other's eyes. There is a kind of humiliation in it. We look away from each other. . . .

So we sit hour after hour, day after day, waiting for a job to come in. There are many women for a single job. A thin sharp woman sits inside a wire cage looking at a book. For four hours we have watched her looking at that book. She has a hard little eye. In the small bare room there are half a dozen women sitting on the benches waiting. . . .

This is a domestic employment bureau. Most of the women who come here are middle-aged, some have families, some have raised their families and are now alone, some have men who are out of work. Hard times and the man leaves to hunt for work. He doesn't find it. He drifts on. The woman probably doesn't hear from him for a long time. She expects it. She isn't surprised. She struggles alone to feed the many

Dorothea Lange: Stories in a Frame
"I saw . . . the hungry and desperate mother"

As part of the Second New Deal, the Farm Security Administration (FSA) was charged with helping farmers and migrant workers during the Great Depression. The FSA Historical Section employed about a dozen photographers to help document the suffering of rural Americans. The photographers' efforts were intended to stir sympathy and support for relief programs.

In seven years, FSA photographers traveled hundreds of thousands of miles and amassed more than 250,000 negatives. They dealt with challenging circumstances on the road. Equipment failed in extreme weather conditions, and moisture sometimes spoiled film. However, FSA photographers produced some of the finest social documentary images to date. Some became artists in their own right.

Today, one of the best-known FSA photographers is Dorothea Lange, who worked for the project for five years until 1940. Many art historians admire her ability to capture a story in a single frame; others appreciate the surprising intimacy her portraits share. In her biography, *Photographs of a Lifetime*, Lange relates the story behind her most famous portrait, *Migrant Mother*, captured in March 1936.

> It was raining, the camera bags were packed, and I had on the seat beside me in the car the results of my long trip, the box containing all those rolls and packs of exposed film ready to mail back to Washington. . . . Sixty-five miles an hour for seven hours would get me home to my family that night, and my eyes were glued to the wet and gleaming highway that stretched out ahead. . . .
>
> I was on my way and barely saw a crude sign with pointing arrow which flashed by at the side of the road, saying PEA PICKERS CAMP. But out of the corner of my eye, I did see it. . . . Having well convinced myself for twenty miles that I could continue on, I did the opposite. Almost without realizing what I was doing, I made a U-turn on the empty highway. . . . I was following instinct, not reason; I drove into that wet soggy camp and parked my car like a homing pigeon.
>
> I saw and approached the hungry and desperate mother, as if drawn by a magnet. I do not remember how I explained my presence or my camera to her, but I do remember she asked me no questions. . . . She told me her age, that she was 32. She said that they had been living on frozen vegetables from the surrounding fields, and birds that the children killed. She had just sold tires from her car to buy food. There she sat in that lean-to tent with her children huddled around her, and seemed to know that my pictures might help her, and so she helped me. There was a sort of equality about it.

mouths. Sometimes she gets help from the charities.... If she's proud then she starves silently, leaving her children to find work, coming home after a day's searching to wrestle with her house, her children.

Some such story is written on the faces of all these women....

A girl we have seen every day all summer went crazy yesterday at the YW. She went into hysterics, stamping her feet and screaming.

She hadn't had work for eight months. "You've got to give me something," she kept saying. The woman in charge flew into a rage that probably came from days and days of suffering on her part, because she is unable to give jobs, having none. She flew into a rage at the girl and there they were facing each other in a rage both helpless, helpless. This woman told me once that she could hardly bear the suffering she saw, hardly hear it, that she couldn't eat sometimes and had nightmares at night.

So they stood there, the two women, in a rage, the girl weeping and the woman shouting at her. In the eight months of unemployment she had gotten ragged, and the woman was shouting that she would not send her out like that. "Why don't you shine your shoes?" she kept scolding the girl, and the girl kept sobbing and sobbing because she was starving....

Sitting here waiting for a job, the women have been talking in low voices about the girl Ellen. They talk in low voices with not too much pity for her, unable to see through the mist of their own torment. "What happened to Ellen?" one of them asks. She knows the answer already. We all know it.

A young girl who went around with Ellen tells about seeing her last evening back of a cafe downtown, outside the kitchen door, kicking, showing her legs so that the cook came out and gave her some food and some men gathered in the alley and threw small coin on the ground for a look

Many homeless Americans during the Great Depression lived in shantytowns on the outskirts of cities. Such sites were often called "Hoovervilles" to criticize President Herbert Hoover's economic policies.

at her legs. And the girl says enviously that Ellen had a swell breakfast and treated her to one too, that cost two dollars....

"I guess she'll go on the street now," a thin woman says faintly, and no one takes the trouble to comment further. Like every commodity now the body is difficult to sell and the girls say you're lucky if you get fifty cents.

It's very difficult and humiliating to sell one's body.

Perhaps it would make it clear if one were to imagine having to go out on the street to sell, say, one's overcoat. Suppose you have to sell your coat so you can have breakfast and a place to sleep, say, for fifty cents. You decide to sell your only coat. You take it off and put it on your arm. The street, that has before been just a street, now becomes a mart, something entirely different. You must approach someone now and admit you are destitute and are now selling your clothes, your most intimate possessions. Everyone will watch you talking to the stranger showing him your overcoat, what a good coat it is. People will stop and watch curiously. You will be quite naked on the street. It is even harder to try to sell one's self, more humiliating. It is even humiliating to try to sell one's labor. When there is no buyer.

JOHN STEINBECK (1902–1968)

Pulitzer Prize winner and Nobel laureate John Steinbeck wrote several classic works of American literature. He typically spotlighted poor, oppressed characters in his novels and short stories, many of which were set in his native state of California. Raised in the fertile Salinas Valley, Steinbeck absorbed a love for the land that produced richly detailed descriptions of place and time. Between 1937 and 1939, he lived and worked with Oklahoma migrants looking for farm work. Based on that experience he wrote his master-piece, The Grapes of Wrath. *The novel details the migration of the Joad family, tenant farmers fleeing the Oklahoma Dust Bowl. A year after its 1939 publication,* The Grapes of Wrath *won Steinbeck the Pulitzer Prize. He continued to publish well into the 1960s, but Steinbeck remains best known for his early works from the Depression years.*

In the decade preceding the Great Depression, farmers in the Great Plains plowed up millions of acres of semi-arid grasslands to plant crops like corn, wheat, and cotton. From the early to mid-1930s, with little grass and few trees to secure the topsoil, drought and wind produced dust storms from Texas to North Dakota—a region that came to be called the "Dust Bowl." The southern plains were hardest hit by the agricultural disaster. Thousands of farmers and sharecroppers left their land in search of better lives in California. Such migrants were collectively known as "Okies," in reference to Oklahomans who left their homes.

With the institution of President Franklin Roosevelt's Second New Deal in 1935, Congress created the Resettlement Administration to help poor farmers. By 1937, this program was replaced by the Farm Security Administration (FSA). The FSA loaned about $1 billion to help tenant farmers buy property. However, many former tenant farmers had become migrant workers and did not meet residency requirements for the entitle-ment. Some simply lacked information about the programs.

"If the dust only wouldn't fly."

The following excerpt from The Grapes of Wrath *details a common way that farmers were forced to vacate their property by landlords or lenders. Steinbeck portrays the economic system as a "monster."*

The Grapes of Wrath
Chapter Five

The owners of the land came onto the land, or more often a spokesman for the owners came. They came in closed cars, and they felt the dry earth with their fingers, and sometimes they drove big earth augers into the ground for soil tests. The tenants, from their sun-beaten dooryards, watched uneasily when the closed cars drove along the fields. And at last the owner men drove into the dooryards and sat in their cars to talk out of the windows. The tenant men stood beside the cars for a while, and then squatted on their hams and found sticks with which to mark the dust.

In the open doors the women stood looking out, and behind them the children—corn-headed children, with wide eyes, one bare foot on top of the other bare foot, and the toes working. The women and the children watched their men talking to the owner men. They were silent.

Some of the owner men were kind because they hated what they had to do, and some of them were angry because they hated to be cruel, and some of them were cold because they had long ago found that one could not be an owner unless one were cold. And all of them were caught in something larger than themselves. Some of them hated the mathematics that drove them, and some were afraid, and some worshiped the mathematics because it provided a refuge from thought and from feeling. If a bank or a finance company owned the land, the owner man said, The Bank—or the Company—needs—wants—insists—must have—as though the Bank—or the Company were a monster, with thought and feeling, which had enslaved them. These last would take no responsibility for the banks or the companies because they were men and slaves, while the banks were machines and masters all at the same time. Some of the owner men were a little proud to be slaves to such cold and powerful masters. The owner men sat in the cars and explained. You know the land is poor. You've scrabbled at it long enough, God knows.

The squatting tenant men nodded and wondered and drew figures in the dust, and yes, they knew, God knows. If the dust only wouldn't fly. If the top would only stay on the soil, it might not be so bad.

Steinbeck described the terrible dust storms that plagued the Midwest as follows: "Men and women huddled in their houses, and they tied handkerchiefs over their noses when they went out, and wore goggles to protect their eyes. . . ." Here, a family seeks shelter.

The owner men went on leading to their point: You know the land's getting poorer. You know what cotton does to the land; robs it, sucks all the blood out of it.

The squatters nodded—they knew, God knew. If they could only rotate the crops they might pump blood back into the land.

Well, it's too late. And the owner men explained the workings and the thinkings of the monster that was stronger than they were. A man can hold land if he can just eat and pay taxes; he can do that.

Yes, he can do that until his crops fail one day and he has to borrow money from the bank.

But—you see, a bank or a company can't do that, because those creatures don't breathe air, don't eat side-meat. They breathe profits; they eat the interest on money. If they don't get it, they die the way you die without air, without side-meat. It is a sad thing, but it is so. It is just so.

The squatting men raised their eyes to understand. Can't we just hang on? Maybe the next year will be a good year. God knows how much cotton next year. And with all the wars—God knows what price cotton will bring. Don't they make explosives out of cotton? And uniforms? Get enough wars and cotton'll hit the ceiling. Next year, maybe. They look up questioningly.

We can't depend on it. The bank—the monster has to have profits all the time. It can't wait. It'll die. No, taxes go on. When the monster stops growing it dies. It can't stay one size.

Soft fingers began to tap the sill of the car window, and hard fingers tightened on the restless drawing sticks. In the doorways of the sun-beaten tenant houses, women sighed and then shifted feet so that the one that had been down was now on top, and the toes working. Dogs came sniffing near the owner cars and wetted on all four tires one after another. And chickens lay in the sunny dust and fluffed their feathers to get the cleansing dust down to the skin. In the little sties the pigs grunted inquiringly over the muddy remnants of the slops.

The squatting men looked down again. What do you want us to do? We can't take less share of the crop—we're half starved now. The kids are hungry all the time. We got no clothes, torn an' ragged. If all the neighbors weren't the same, we'd be ashamed to go to meeting.

And at last the owner men came to the point. The tenant system won't work any more. One man on a tractor can take the place of twelve or fourteen families. Pay him a wage and take all the crop. We have to do it. We don't like to do it. But the monster's sick. Something's happened to the monster.

But you'll kill the land with cotton.

We know. We've got to take cotton quick before the land dies. Then we'll sell the land. Lots of families in the East would like to own a piece of land.

Highway 66 was the primary route "Dust Bowl" refugees took to California. Lured by tales of pretty white houses in orange groves, thousands of migrants, like the ones shown here, sold their belongings, left their homes, and drove west in old—often unreliable—cars.

The tenant men looked up alarmed. But what'll happen to us? How'll we eat?

You'll have to get off the land. The plows'll go through the dooryard.

And now the squatting men stood up angrily. Grampa took up the land, and he had to kill the Indians and drive them away. And Pa was born here, and he killed weeds and snakes. Then a bad year came and he had to borrow a little money. An' we was born here. There in the door—our children born here. And Pa had to borrow money. The bank owned the land then, but we stayed and we got a little bit of what we raised.

We know that—all that. It's not us, it's the bank. A bank isn't like a man. Or an owner with fifty thousand acres, he isn't like a man either. That's the monster.

Sure, cried the tenant men, but it's our land. We measured it and broke it up. We were born on it , and we got killed on it, died on it. Even if it's no good, it's still ours. That's what makes it ours—being born on it, working it, dying on it. That makes ownership, not a paper with numbers on it.

We're sorry. It's not us. It's the monster. The bank isn't like a man.

Yes, but the bank is only made of men.

No, you're wrong there—quite wrong there. The bank is something else than men. It happens that every man in a bank hates what the bank does, and yet the bank does it. The bank is something more than men, I tell you. It's the monster. Men made it, but they can't control it.

The tenants cried, Grampa killed Indians, Pa killed snakes for the land. Maybe we can kill banks—they're worse than Indians and snakes. Maybe we got to fight to keep our land, like Pa and Grampa did.

And now the owner men grew angry. You'll have to go.

But it's ours, the tenant men cried. We——

No. The bank, the monster owns it. You'll have to go.

We'll get our guns, like Grampa when the Indians came. What then?

Well—first the sheriff, and then the troops. You'll be stealing if you try to stay, you'll be murderers if you kill to stay. The monster isn't men, but it can make men do what it wants.

But if we go, where'll we go? How'll we go? We got no money.

We're sorry, said the owner men. The bank, the fifty-thousand-acre owner can't be responsible. You're on land that isn't yours. Once over the line maybe you can pick cotton in the fall. Maybe you can go on relief. Why don't you go on west to California? There's work there, and it never gets cold. Why, you can reach out anywhere and pick an orange. Why there's always some kind of crop to work in. Why don't you go there? And the owner men started their cars and rolled away.

Woody Guthrie: Activist Songwriter
"California is a garden of Eden"

In the 1930s, music—like literature and art—was used to make a social statement. Woody Guthrie, a self-taught musician, was the first to use the folk ballad to spotlight the oppressed and call for change. Born in Oklahoma in 1912, he led a colorful life, which included hopping a train in his early teens and performing music for cash. In the 1930s, Guthrie, like many other victims of the Dust Bowl, was forced to leave his home in Texas and travel from state to state looking for opportunity. His experiences among migrant workers inspired him to compose many works and ultimately become heavily involved in the labor movement. By the end of his prolific life in 1967, he had written about a thousand songs. According to music critics, Guthrie's politically charged lyrics have influenced several contemporary musicians, including Bob Dylan and Bruce Springsteen.

The following song, "(If You Ain't Got the) Do Re Mi" was recorded in 1940 on Guthrie's album *Dust Bowl Ballads*. It describes the disappointment of migrants when they find life in California as hard as that on the Great Plains.

Lots of folks back East, they say, leavin' home every day,
Beatin' the hot old dusty way to the California line.
'Cross the desert sands they roll, getting out of that old dust bowl,
They think they're going to a sugar bowl, but here's what they find—
Now, the police at the port of entry say,
"You're number fourteen thousand for today."

CHORUS:
Oh, if you ain't got the do-re-mi, folks, if you ain't got the do-re-mi,
Why, you better go back to beautiful Texas, Oklahoma, Kansas, Georgia, Tennessee.
California is a garden of Eden, a paradise to live in or see;
But believe it or not, you won't find it so hot
If you ain't got the do-re-mi.

If you want to buy you a home or farm, that can't do nobody harm,
Or take your vacation by the mountains or sea.
Don't swap your old cow for a car, you'd better stay right where you are,
You'd better take this little tip from me.
'Cause I look through the want ads every day
But the headlines on the papers always say:

[Chorus]

*"the Lawd
made all
men equal"*

RALPH ELLISON (1914–1994)

*Unable to be categorized easily, the works of
Ralph Ellison have confounded critics and
enlightened readers for decades. Born in
Oklahoma City, Ellison studied music at the
Tuskegee Institute in Alabama before turning his
hand to writing. In 1936, he moved to New York
City, then the center of the African-American liter-
ary world. However, many rich literary patrons from the 1920s had lost
their money in the Great Depression and could no longer afford to
encourage young writers. Without a patron, Ellison began documenting
folklore for the Federal Writer's Project of the Works Progress Administration (WPA) in 1939. Most critics agree that the interviews he conducted
with African Americans in Harlem gave him material and insights for his
classic novel,* The Invisible Man, *published in 1952.*

*Ellison's move to New York coincided with President Roosevelt's
Second New Deal. As part of that plan, in 1935 Congress instituted the
WPA, a program that invested $5 billion in job creation. During the next
eight years, the WPA restored the dignity of unemployed Americans by
giving jobs to about 8.5 million, including laborers, students, teachers,
writers, dramatists, musicians, and artists. Through the Federal Writers
Project, authors composed travel guides and documented folklore.*

*Ellison conducted this WPA interview—sometimes titled "Colonial
Park" or "Eli Luster"—in Harlem in 1939. Although the subject's name,
Eli Luster, is fictitious, his voice conveys a realistic "slice-of-life" monologue. Ellison mimics the speaker's dialect and colloquialisms, lending
authenticity to the subject's ideas and values. While many intellectuals
and writers of the Great Depression took an interest in liberal ideologies,
many ordinary Americans had more conservative notions about how
equality between races and classes would be achieved. Eli Luster takes
a Christian view of equality and predicts that the Apocalypse, or God's
dramatic intervention, will put sinful matters right.*

Colonial Park

It's too bad about them two submarines. They can experiment an'
everything, but they cain't go but so far. Then God steps in. . . . Take back
in 1912. They built a ship called the *Titanic*. Think they built it over in
England; I think that was where it was built. Anyway, they said it couldn't
sink. It was for all the big rich folks: John Jacob Astor—all the big aristo-

crats. Nothing the color of this could git on the boat. Naw suh! Didn't want nothing look like me on it. One girl went down to go with her madam and they told her she couldn't go. They didn't want nothing look like this on there. They told the madam, "You can go, but she cain't." The girl's madam got mad and told 'em if the girl didn't go she wasn't going. And she didn't neither. Yessuh, she stayed right here.

Well, they got this big boat on the way over to England. [In reality, the *Titanic* was sailing toward the United States when it sank.] They said she couldn't sink—that was man talking....Had the richest folks in the world on it just having a big tune. Got over near England, almost ready to dock, and ups and hits an iceberg, and sank! That was the boat they said was so big it couldn't sink. They didn't want nothing look like this on it, no sir! And don't you think that woman wasn't glad she stuck by that girl. She was plenty glad. Man can go only so far. Then God steps in. Sho, they can experiment around. They can do a heap. They can even make a man. But they cain't make him breathe....

God's the only one can give life. God made all this, and he made it for everybody. And he made it equal. This breeze and these green leaves out here is for everybody. The same sun's shining down on everybody. This breeze comes from God and man can't do nothing about it. I breathe the same air old man Ford and old man Rockefeller breathe. They got all the money and I ain't got nothing, but they got to breathe the same air I do.

Man cain't make no man....For nineteen hundred years man's had things his way. He's been running the world to suit hisself....Adam an' Eve sinned in the Garden and God left the world to itself. Men been running it like they want to. They been running it like they want to for nineteen hundred years. Rich folks done took all the land. They got all the money. Men down to the City Hall making fifty thousand dollars a year and nothing like this cain't even scrub the marble floors or polish the brass what they got down there.

Old man Ford and J. P. Morgan got all the money and folks in this part cain't even get on relief. But you just watch: the Lawd made all men equal and pretty soon now it's gonna be that way again. I'm a man. I breathe the same air old man Ford breathes cause God made man equal. God formed man in his own image....One drop of God's blood made all the nations in the world: Africans, Germans, Chinamen, Jews, Indians; all come from one drop of God's blood. God took something outa Adam and made woman, he made Eve....Eve started having children. Some of 'em was black and some of 'em was white. But they was all equal. God didn't know no color; we all the same. All he want from man is his heart thumping the blood. Them what take advantage of skin like this got to come by God. They gonna pay.

They tell me 'bout George Washington. He was the first president this country ever had. First thing I heard was he said to keep us look like this down in the cornfield. He tole 'em, "don't let 'em have no guns. You ain't to let 'em have no knife. Don't let 'em have nothing." He tole 'em if they wanted to have a strong nation to keep us down. He said if ever they git guns in they hands they'll rise up and take the land; don't let 'em have nothing. But he didn't say nothing about no pick and ax!

They been carrying out what he said. God didn't say nothing. That was just man's idea and here in this country they been carrying out what old man George Washington said. But God's time is coming. Today you hear all these folks got millions of dollars talking 'bout God. They ain't fooling nobody, though. They even got IN GOD WE TRUST on all the silver money. But it don't mean nothing. This sun and air is God's. It don't belong to nobody and cain't no few get it all to theyself. People around this park can have all they want. But you wait. God's gonna straighten it all out.

Look at the dust blowing in the wind. That's the way all the money they got gonna be. You see things, folks they call white, but man ain't got no idea of how white God gon' make things. Money won't be worth no more'n that dust blowing on the ground. Won't be no men down to Washington making fifty thousand dollars a week and folks cain't hardly make eighteen dollars a month. Everybody'll be equal, in God's time.

"Something spoke in my patriot heart."

GENEVIEVE TAGGARD (1894–1948)

An accomplished poet, Genevieve Taggard was well recognized during her lifetime. Her first volume of poetry was published in 1922. Thereafter, Taggard's literary career expanded to include editing a poetry anthology and writing a biography of Emily Dickinson. Like many authors in the 1930s, Taggard was a staunch liberal, supporting, among other causes, the advancement of minorities.

Those views were shared by President Roosevelt's wife, Eleanor Roosevelt. Her influence helped open doors in the Roosevelt administration to African Americans. For example, Mary McLeod Bethune—an educator and a friend of Mrs. Roosevelt—was appointed to head a new department in the National Youth Administration, the Office of Minority Affairs. However, segregation remained a primary feature of American life during the Great Depression.

In 1939, the famous operatic singer Marian Anderson was denied access to perform at the concert hall of the Daughters of the American Revolution (DAR) in Washington, D.C. Many believed this decision was made because she was black. Outraged, Eleanor Roosevelt canceled her membership in the DAR and helped coordinate Anderson's Easter concert on the steps of the Lincoln Memorial instead. Noted for her singing of spirituals, Anderson herself devoted much time to the civil rights crusade.

"Proud Day," published in 1939, is Taggard's response to Anderson's triumphant Lincoln Memorial performance. She notes the setting and the gaze of Lincoln's statue not only to paint the event itself, but also to allude to slavery and the fierce war that was waged over it. That spirituals helped African Americans endure and overcome slavery was another moving parallel in this historic concert. The images and associations of Anderson's performance were so powerful that Martin Luther King Jr. would decide to give his now-famous "I Have a Dream" speech on the very same spot twenty-four years later.

Marian Anderson's 1939 Easter concert on the Lincoln Memorial steps was a powerful event not only because of the grand setting, but also because of her personal stand for civil rights.

Proud Day

Our sister sang on the Lincoln steps. Proud day.
We came to hear our sister sing. Proud day.
Voice out of depths, poise with memory.
What goodness, what splendor lay long under foot!
Our sister with a lasso of sorrow and triumph
Caught America, made it listen. Proud day.

The peaceful Lincoln sat so still. Proud day.
Waiting the Republic to be born again. Proud day.
Never, never forget how the dark people rewarded us
Giving out of their want and their little freedom
This blazing star. This blazing star.
Something spoke in my patriot heart. Proud day.

orld War II

Mired in the Great Depression of the 1930s, U.S. leaders were more concerned with issues at home than with those abroad. Meanwhile, terrible events were unfolding in Europe and the Far East. German chancellor Adolf Hitler was aggressively annexing neighboring territories, while Italian dictator Benito Mussolini was expanding his reach in southeastern Europe and northern Africa. In 1937, Japanese troops stormed China, revealing their own imperial ambitions. By the time the United States formally entered World War II in December 1941, Hitler controlled most of Europe, and Japan's military machine had moved across Southeast Asia and the western Pacific. President Franklin Roosevelt faced the overwhelming task of fighting a two-front war on an unprecedented scale.

By the early 1940s, preparation for this massive conflict had lifted the nation out of its economic depression. When millions of U.S. troops left the country, wartime production demanded more workers and opened up well-paying, skilled jobs to women and minorities for the first time.

Despite valiant civilian and military contributions by all groups, on the homefront racism took sinister forms. About 100,000 Japanese Americans were forcibly removed from their homes and held in internment camps for most of the war. Race riots flared, as black workers began to demand better working and living conditions.

By September 1945, American military and economic might had won the day. The victory, however, came with high costs and responsibilities. Altogether about 290,000 Americans died in combat, and more than 670,000 were wounded. Included in the billions of dollars Congress spent on defense was a massive effort to develop the atomic bomb. The decision to use two such devices against Japan brought a swift end to the war, but the advent of nuclear weapons opened a Pandora's box of horror, anxiety, and nuclear proliferation for decades to come.

Featured Authors

E.B. White
Leon Uris
Jeanne Wakatsuki Houston
James D. Houston
Countee Cullen
Martha Gellhorn
Elie Wiesel
John Hersey

For today's readers, the literature of World War II is as varied as the men and women who lived through the conflict. Some soldiers, such as Leon Uris, came back and wrote novels about battlefront drama. African-American writer Countee Cullen noted the irony in America's fight against racism abroad when segregation, poll taxes, and race riots persisted in the United States. War correspondents, such as Martha Gellhorn, reported on conflict from the front lines, while columnists at home, such as E.B. White, commented on American attitudes. Many minorities recounted wartime persecution and atrocities in arresting autobiographies, such as those written by Jeanne Wakatsuki Houston and Elie Wiesel. These authors give penetrating insight into the enormous scale of military conflict, heroism, and human suffering that characterized the twentieth century's last world war.

E.B. WHITE (1899–1985)

Elwyn Brooks White was born in Mount Vernon, New York, and graduated from Cornell University in 1921. A journalist, essayist, and stylist, White is well known for his children's books, particularly Charlotte's Web. *For more than forty years, he wrote columns and articles for magazines such as the* New Yorker *and* Harper's Magazine. *In 1979, E.B. White revised the famous style book,* Elements of Style, *which was originally written by his professor, William Strunk Jr. White's unique voice is known for its simple grace and bemused observations.*

While White was writing his column for Harper's Magazine, *World War II was gearing up in Europe. In 1938, German dictator Adolf Hitler annexed Austria under the pretense of uniting all Germans under one nation. He then overtook a mostly German populated region of Czechoslovakia, called the Sudetenland. Flouting his promise to British and French leaders that the Sudetenland would be his last territorial conquest, Hitler invaded the rest of Czechoslovakia within six months. When Adolf Hitler invaded Poland on September 1, 1939, Great Britain and France declared war on Germany.*

The first year of World War II in Europe was disastrous. In the spring of 1940, Hitler overtook Denmark, Norway, Belgium, and the Netherlands. In June, France fell to Germany, and German bombs were raining on England.

The following essay by E.B. White appeared in July of 1940, when President Franklin Roosevelt was having secret meetings with British prime minister Winston Churchill to discuss an alliance. White criticizes the general mood of some Americans regarding events in Europe and voices his support for freedom, a theme that would echo in Roosevelt's State of the Union address in January 1941. During that famous speech, Roosevelt helped turn isolationist Americans in favor of war by describing basic human rights—ideas that would later become the foundation of the United Nations. He said, "In future days, which we seek to make secure, we look forward to a world founded upon four essential human freedoms. The first is freedom of speech and expression—everywhere in the world. The second is freedom of every person to worship God in his own way—everywhere in the world. The third is freedom from want ... everywhere in the world. The fourth is freedom from fear ... anywhere in the world."

"I am in love with freedom"

Freedom

I have often noticed on my trips up to the city that people have recut their clothes to follow the fashion. On my last trip, however, it seemed to me that people had remodeled their ideas too—taken in their convictions a little at the waist, shortened the sleeves of their resolve, and fitted themselves out in a new intellectual ensemble copied from a smart design out of the very latest page of history. It seemed to me they had strung along with Paris a little too long.

I confess to a disturbed stomach. I feel sick when I find anyone adjusting his mind to the new tyranny that is succeeding abroad. Because of its fundamental strictures, fascism does not seem to me to admit of any compromise or any rationalization, and I resent the patronizing air of persons who find in my plain belief in freedom a sign of immaturity. If it is boyish to believe that a human being should live free, then I'll gladly arrest my development and let the rest of the world grow up.

I shall report some of the strange remarks I heard in New York. One man told me that he thought perhaps the Nazi ideal was a sounder ideal than our constitutional system "because have you ever noticed what fine alert young faces the young German soldiers have in the newsreel?" He added:"Our American youngsters spend all their time at the movies— they're a mess." That was his summation of the case, his interpretation of the new Europe. Such a remark leaves me pale and shaken. If it represents the peak of our intelligence, then the steady march of despotism will not receive any considerable setback at our shores.

Another man informed me that our democratic notion of popular government was decadent and not worth bothering about—"because England is really rotten and the industrial towns there are a disgrace." That was the only reason he gave for the hopelessness of democracy; and he seemed mightily pleased with himself, as though he were more familiar than most with the anatomy of decadence, and had detected subtler aspects of the situation than were discernible to the rest of us.

Another man assured me that anyone who took *any* kind of government seriously was a gullible fool. You could be sure, he said, that there is nothing but corruption "because of the way Clemenceau acted at Versailles." He said it didn't make any difference really about this war. It was just another war. Having relieved himself of this majestic bit of reasoning, he subsided.

Another individual, discovering signs of zeal creeping into my blood, berated me for having lost my detachment, my pure skeptical point of view. He announced that he wasn't going to be swept away by all this nonsense, but would prefer to remain in the role of innocent bystander, which he said was the duty of any intelligent person. (I noticed, however, that he phoned later to qualify his remark, as though he had lost some of his innocence in the cab on the way home.)

Those are just a few samples of the sort of talk that seemed to be going round—talk that was full of defeatism and disillusion and sometimes of a too studied innocence. Men are not merely annihilating themselves at a great rate these days, but they are telling one another enormous lies, grandiose fibs. Such remarks as I heard are fearfully disturbing in their cumulative effect. They are more destructive than dive bombers and mine fields, for they challenge not merely one's immediate position but one's main defenses. They seemed to me to issue either from persons who could never have really come to grips with freedom, so as to understand her, or from renegades. Where I expected to find indignation, I found paralysis, or a sort of dim acquiescence, as in a child who is dully swallowing a distasteful pill. I was advised of the growing anti-Jewish sentiment by a man who seemed to be watching the phenomenon of intolerance not through tears of shame but with clear intellectual gaze, as through a well-ground lens.

The least a man can do at such a time is to declare himself and tell where he stands. I believe in freedom with the same burning delight, the same faith, the same intense abandon that attended its birth on this continent more than a century and a half ago. I am writing my declaration rapidly, much as though I were shaving to catch a train. Events abroad give a man a feeling of being pressed for time. Actually I do not believe I am pressed for time, and I apologize to the reader for a false impression that may be created. I just want to tell, before I get slowed down, that I am in love with freedom and that it is an affair of long standing and that it is a fine state to be in, and that I am deeply suspicious of people who are beginning to adjust to fascism and dictators merely because they are succeeding in war. From such adaptable natures a smell rises. I pinch my nose.

For as long as I can remember I have had a sense of living somewhat freely in a natural world. I don't mean I enjoyed freedom of action, but my existence seemed to have the quality of freeness. I traveled with secret papers pertaining to a divine conspiracy. Intuitively I've always been aware of the vitally important pact that a man has with himself, to be all things to himself, and to be identified with all things, to stand self-reliant, taking advantage of his haphazard connection with a planet, riding his luck, and following his bent with the tenacity of a hound. My first and greatest love affair was with this thing we call freedom, this lady of infinite allure, this dangerous and beautiful and sublime being who restores and supplies us all.

It began with the haunting intimation (which I presume every child receives) of his mystical inner life; of God in man; of nature publishing herself through the "I." This elusive sensation is moving and memorable. It comes early in life: a boy, we'll say, sitting on the front steps on a summer night, thinking of nothing in particular, suddenly hearing as with a new perception and as though for the first time the pulsing sound of crickets, overwhelmed with the novel sense of identification, with the natural company of insects and grass and night, conscious of a faint answering cry to the universal perplexing question: "What is 'I'?" Or a little girl, returning from the grave of a pet bird and leaning with her elbows on the windowsill, inhaling the unfamiliar draught of death, suddenly seeing herself as part of the complete story. Or an older youth, encountering for the first time a great teacher who by some chance word or mood awakens something and the youth beginning to breathe as an individual and conscious of strength in his vitals. I think the sensation must develop in many men as a feeling of identity with God—an eruption of the spirit caused by allergies and the sense of divine existence as distinct from mere animal existence. This is the beginning of the affair with freedom.

But a man's free condition is of two parts: the instinctive freeness he experiences as an animal dweller on a planet, and the practical liberties he enjoys as a privileged member of human society. The latter is, of the two, more generally understood, more widely admired, more violently challenged and discussed. It is the practical and apparent side of freedom. The United States, almost alone today, offers the liberties and the privileges and the tools of freedom. In this land the citizens are still invited to write their plays and books, to paint their pictures, to meet for discussion, to dissent as well as to agree, to mount soapboxes in the public square, to enjoy education in all subjects without censorship, to hold court and judge one another, to compose music, to talk politics with their neighbors without wondering whether the secret police are listening, to exchange ideas as well as goods, to kid the government when it needs kidding, and to read real news of real events instead of phony news manufactured by a paid agent of the state. This is a fact and should give every person pause.

"How long had we been in the mud?"

LEON URIS (1924–)

Born in Baltimore, Leon Uris has traveled widely and has written many best-selling novels. In early 1942, shortly after World War II broke out, Uris quit high school and joined the U.S. Marine Corps. His first novel, Battle Cry, *published in 1953, drew heavily on his World War II experiences as a radio*

operator in the Pacific theater. Uris went on to write other historical fiction novels, most of them expansive and action-filled. His stories often center on oppressed peoples, including those in Israel and Ireland.

On December 7, 1941, Japanese warplanes dealt a crushing blow to U.S. military installations at Pearl Harbor, on the Hawaiian island of Oahu. The next day, the United States declared war on Japan. On December 11, Germany and Italy declared war on the United States, and Congress acknowledged a state of war with those Axis powers.

After Pearl Harbor, the United States and its allies rationalized that they needed to concentrate on defeating Germany first. However, in the summer of 1942, while allied planes were bombing German cities, American forces won an important victory over the Japanese fleet at Midway Island. Thereafter, U.S. troops began a coordinated island-hopping campaign across the Pacific to protect Australia from Japanese occupation while moving into position to attack Japan itself. One of the first efforts by U.S. land forces was an attempt to evict the Japanese from the Solomon Islands, off the northeast coast of Australia.

Between August 1942 and February 1943, U.S. forces mounted a series of land, sea, and air battles on the island of Guadalcanal in the Solomons. After six long months, U.S. troops took the island, inflicting heavy losses on the Japanese.

The following excerpt from Leon Uris's first novel, Battle Cry, *vividly illustrates the experiences of a company of marine radio operators during this long siege in the jungles of Guadalcanal.*

Battle Cry
Part 3, Chapter 7

January 19, 1943

How long had we been in mud? Only six days? We were up to our asses in mud. It was turning evening and the rain would be coming soon to make more mud. It was nearly knee deep in this ravine. The hills were slick and slimy, the air was heavy and putrid with the smell of dead Japs. You could smell one a mile away. The whiskerino contest was off to a good start, only you couldn't see the whiskers for the mud. Mud caked in so thick on the face and body and the fast-rotting dungarees that it not only seemed the uniform of the day but our very flesh covering.

The drive had been slow, radio operation almost nil. We only used one set, a TBX, to Regiment. Regiment's code was Topeka; we were Topeka White. Due to the snail's pace and the terrain, telephone squad carried most of the load in keeping communications. My boys were used as pack mules. They assisted the telephone men when needed. Mostly, they made several trips a day to the beach supply dump, over glassy ridges,

American success in the Pacific theater was linked to the code used by Navajo Indians serving as radio operators. During the war, the Japanese military never did decipher the code, based on the unwritten Navajo language. Shown here are Navajo "code talkers" operating a radio in Bougainville, an island east of Papua, New Guinea.

two miles to the coast. Back again in blistering sun, carrying five-gallon cans of water, dragged with curses back to the CP [command post]. It was a lifeline. They packed heavy boxes of ammunition, C-ration, D-ration, the chocolate candy bars that tasted like Ex-Lax but held enough vitamins to sustain a man for a day. They walked, limped, and crawled the tortuous miles back and forth to the dump like a line of ants, worn and beaten but coming back again for another load.

At darkness they'd crawl in holes in the mud to sleep until their round of guard duty—attempt to sleep with swarms of bugs all around, and the hated anopheles zinging down and biting into the flesh. And even as the mosquitoes bit and sucked blood, the Marines couldn't raise a dead-tired arm to slap them off.

We hadn't seen a Jap, not a live one. Only the dead with their terrible stench. The riflemen left them there for us to bunk with. But live ones were there. You could feel them all about, peeking at you from the treetops . . . from the brush . . . watching your every move.

In the hole at night you'd huddle next to your mate to stop the shakes. Getting malaria? Hell no, just shaking wet and the mud sliding around in your boondockers. Too beat out to think, even about home. Hard to sleep . . . the jungle was alive with silence. It took time before you could tell a land crab from a Jap. Doc Kyser emptied a whole drum from his tommy gun into a bush one night, and it was a land crab. After a while you don't mind them crawling over you. You reached automatically for your knife and stabbed it and put it outside the foxhole. If you piled up more land crabs than the next foxhole, you might win a couple cigarettes on a bet.

Thirst . . . always the hunger for water. Our water was salted and made your stomach rebel. Once in a while you got that vision of a long cool beer floating by. Nothing to do but lick your lips with your thick dry tongue and try to forget it.

How long had we been in the mud? Only six days.

We pulled into the new CP and waited for the rain to sink us deeper.
"O.K., you guys, dig in."
"Where the hell we going to dig? We're already in."
"On the slopes where it is dry, asshole."
Lieutenant Bryce approached the Feathermerchant, who was on his knees hacking the earth with a pick as Danny shoveled.
"Ski," Bryce said.
"Yes."

Poster Art of World War II

The United States government used poster art during World War II as part of its propaganda campaign at home. Posters encouraged people to enlist in the armed forces, work in factories, buy war bonds, and keep sensitive military information to themselves. One witty aphorism reminded Americans that "Loose lips sink ships." Posters also encouraged public support by painting enemies as merchants of death. Artist Thomas Hart Benton designed *The Sowers* (shown here) to bring war's dark reality to citizens at home. It shows fascists as evil monsters, tossing human skulls to the ground.

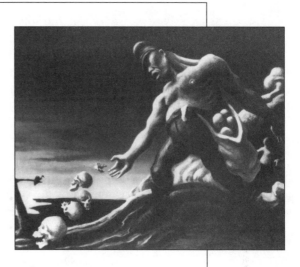

"After you finish your hole, dig me in." He unfolded a stretcher he was carrying. "Fix my hole so this fits in."

Zvonski threw down the trenching tool and arose. "Dig your own goddam hole, Lieutenant. I been lugging water cans for eleven hours."

"Don't address me by rank," Bryce hissed nervously. "There is no rank up here. You want a sniper to hear you?"

"I sure do."

"I'll have you courtmartialed for this!"

"Like hell you will. Sam says we all dig our own holes. So start digging—and don't dig too close around here."

Bryce turned and left. Ski went over to Gunner Keats. "Bryce got a stretcher from sick bay to sleep on, Jack," he said.

"The dirty . . . mind your own business, Ski," he answered and took off after Bryce.

There was a swish overhead of an artillery shell. It landed and exploded on our reverse slope.

"Say, ain't the Tenth firing kind of late in the day?"

"Probably just lining up for effect."

Another shell landed, hitting the top of the ridge some two hundred yards away.

"Crazy bastards, don't they know we're down here?"

Huxley rushed to the switchboard. "Contact the firing officer at once. They're coming too close." Another shell crashed, sending us all flopping into the mud. It hit on our side of the hill.

"Hello," Huxley roared as another dropped almost in us, "this is Topeka White. You men are coming in right on our C.P."

"But sir," the voice at the other end of the line answered, "we haven't fired since morning."

"Holy Christ!" the Major yelled. "Hit the deck, it's Pistol Pete!"

We scattered but the Jap 108s found us in their sights. We crawled deep in the mire, behind trees and rocks. Our foxholes hadn't been dug yet. *Swish...Whom! Whom!* WHOM! They roared in and the deck bounced and mud and hot shrapnel splattered everywhere.

Andy and Ski spotted a small cave on the hillside and dashed for it. They hung onto their helmets and braced their backs against the wall. There, opposite them, sat a Jap soldier. He was dead. His eyes had been eaten out by the swarms of maggots which crawled through his body. The stink was excruciating. "I'm getting out of here," Ski said.

Andy jerked him back in. "Hang on, Ski. They're blasting the hell outa us. Go on, put your head down and puke." A concussion wave caused the Jap to buckle over. He dropped, broken in half by rot. Ski put his head down and vomited.

Spanish Joe crawled through the muck to Sister Mary. He put his arm about Marion and held him.

"Why didn't you stay where you were? You're safer there."

"I...I...want somebody to look at," he whined.

Highpockets was on his feet scanning the sky. He was the only man standing. He waded through the mire as though his feet were a pair of plungers. "Move over to the other slope, you people," he shouted to one group. He made his way to the switchboard, shouting commands as he went. "Give me the Tenth...firing officer...LeForce, go to the ridge and see if you can spot them. Hello, this is Topeka White...Pete is right on us ...can you give us some help? I'll have a spotter up there in a minute."

"Hit the deck, Sam!" WHOM!

"Hello, this is Huxley, Topeka White...about two thousand yards to our left. Hello, this is Topeka ..."

It was dark before we crawled out. Two hours of it. We dug in and fell off to sleep, not even bothering to stab land crabs.

JEANNE WAKATSUKI HOUSTON (1934–) & JAMES D. HOUSTON (1933–)

Jeanne Wakatsuki Houston is a second generation Japanese American. She grew up in southern California and spent three and a half years in Manzanar War Relocation Center (in eastern California's Owens Valley) with her family between 1942 and 1945. She went on to study at San Jose State College, where she met her husband James D. Houston. A

novelist, Houston helped his wife articulate her experiences in the book
Farewell to Manzanar: A True Story of Japanese American Experience
during and after the World War II Internment. *Together they published
her classic autobiography in 1973, a time when few people knew the full
story of the U.S. government's wartime treatment of Japanese Americans.*

*In February 1942, President Franklin Roosevelt signed Executive
Order 9066, which allowed the War Department to declare "military
areas" in western states. Through the executive order, the War Department
could exclude anyone from these areas (primarily along the West Coast)
who might threaten the war effort. After the bombing of Pearl Harbor,
hostilities toward Japanese Americans ran high, and many politicians
feared that they might serve as spies for the Japanese government. With
Executive Order 9066, the federal government forced more than 100,000
Japanese Americans to leave their homes. Many had to sell off their
possessions cheaply or leave them behind. Without any evidence that
the evacuees were spies, the government relocated them to internment
camps farther inland and kept most of them imprisoned behind barbed
wire until the war was nearly over. A majority of the internees were U.S.
born, or second generation Americans.*

In the 1944 Supreme Court case Korematsu v. United States, *the
Court upheld the relocation order, agreeing with the government that it
was a national security measure. In the December 1944 case* Ex Parte
Endo, *the Court overturned its previous ruling, stating that it was illegal
to intern loyal Japanese Americans. At that point, the camps began
to disband.*

In the following excerpt from Farewell to Manzanar, *Jeanne
Wakatsuki Houston describes her arrival at Manzanar, a relocation
camp in the desert of California. She was about 7 years old at the time.*

Farewell to Manzanar
Chapter 2, Shikata Ga Nai

The name Manzanar meant nothing to us when we left Boyle Heights.
We didn't know where it was or what it was. We went because the government ordered us to. And, in the case of my older brothers and sisters,
we went with a certain amount of relief. They had all heard stories of
Japanese homes being attacked, of beatings in the streets of California
towns. They were as frightened of the Caucasians as Caucasians were
of us. Moving, under what appeared to be government protection, to an
area less directly threatened by the war seemed not such a bad idea at
all. For some it actually sounded like a fine adventure.

Our pickup point was a Buddhist church in Los Angeles. It was very
early, and misty, when we got there with our luggage. Mama had bought

The photographer Ansel Adams recorded stunning images of Manzanar internment camp in the fall of 1943. Adams later donated his negatives to the Library of Congress so that this sad chapter of American history would be forever preserved and remembered.

heavy coats for all of us. She grew up in eastern Washington and knew that anywhere inland in early April would be cold. I was proud of my new coat, and I remember sitting on a duffel bag trying to be friendly with the Greyhound driver. I smiled at him. He didn't smile back. He was befriending no one. Someone tied a numbered tag to my collar and to the duffel bag (each family was given a number, and that became our official designation until the camps closed), someone else passed out box lunches for the trip, and we climbed aboard....

We rode all day. By the time we reached our destination, the shades were up. It was late afternoon. The first thing I saw was a yellow swirl across a blurred, reddish setting sun. The bus was being pelted by what sounded like splattering rain. It wasn't rain. This was my first look at something I would soon know very well, a billowing flurry of dust and sand churned up by the wind through Owens Valley.

We drove past a barbed-wire fence, through a gate, and into an open space where trunks and sacks and packages had been dumped from the baggage trucks that drove out ahead of us. I could see a few tents set up, the first rows of black barracks, and beyond them, blurred by sand, rows of barracks that seemed to spread for miles across this plain. People were sitting on cartons or milling around, with their backs to the wind, waiting to see which friends or relatives might be on this bus. As we approached, they turned or stood up, and some moved toward us expectantly. But inside the bus no one stirred. No one waved or spoke. They just stared out the windows, ominously silent. I didn't understand this. Hadn't we finally arrived, our whole family intact? I opened a window, leaned out, and yelled happily. "Hey! This whole bus is full of Wakatsukis!"

Outside, the greeters smiled. Inside there was an explosion of laughter, hysterical, tension-breaking laugher that left my brothers choking and whacking each other across the shoulders.

We had pulled up just in time for dinner. The mess halls weren't completed yet. An outdoor chow line snaked around a half-finished building that broke a good part of the wind. They issued us army mess kits, the round metal kind that fold over, and plopped in scoops of canned Vienna sausage, canned string beans, steamed rice that had been cooked too long, and on top of the rice a serving of canned apricots. The Caucasian servers were thinking that the fruit poured over rice would make a good dessert. Among the Japanese, of course, rice is never eaten with sweet foods, only with salty or savory foods. Few of us could eat such a mixture. But at this point no one dared protest. It would have been impolite. I was horrified when I saw the apricot syrup seeping through my little mound of rice. I opened my mouth to complain. My mother jabbed me in the back to keep quiet. We moved on through the line and joined the others squatting in the lee of half-raised walls, dabbing courteously at what was, for almost everyone there, an inedible concoction.

COUNTEE CULLEN (1903–1946)

Raised in a middle class family in New York, Countee Cullen earned his B.A. in 1925 from New York University and his M.A. in 1926 from Harvard. After graduating, he went on to become a teacher in New York public schools and a literary editor for Opportunity *maga- zine. A part of the Harlem Renaissance liter- ary movement, Cullen wrote in many genres but is best known as a poet. He was unusual among Harlem Renaissance authors because, instead of developing new "black" forms of poetry, he chose to use tradi- tional forms. Thus, Cullen ensured himself a broad audience, including whites, to whom he could drive home his themes of racial inequality.*

Feelings of racism and resentment reached a boiling point during World War II. Waves of African-American migrants came from the rural South to northern cities to work in factories; longstanding bigotry soon erupted into violence. Attacks on blacks and other minorities grew into full-fledged riots in 1942, and by 1943, riots occurred in virtually every major U.S. city. The Detroit riots of June 1943 reportedly left twenty-five blacks and nine whites dead. Many more were injured. In response to these events, a new militancy took hold among black leaders. Noting that African-American men and women still endured segregation in the South—and that they served in segregated units in the U.S. armed forces—black leaders found it ironic that their nation was fighting racism in Europe. In short, they wanted to use the war-related goal of "fighting racism" to help bring social justice to their own country.

The following poem by Countee Cullen points out the double stan- dard U.S. policymakers applied toward racism at home and abroad. Cullen writes directly to "the land," or the United States, in a literary device called an "apostrophe." An apostrophe is an address to an inanimate object or person to express intense emotion. He likens bigotry to a

"The kiss of hate and bigotry"

"worm" that divides the nation and undermines its best efforts to defeat racism overseas.

Apostrophe to the Land

O land of mine, O land I love,
    A Worm gnaws at your root;
Unless that worm you scotch, remove,
    Peace will not be the fruit.
Let Hirohito be dethroned,
    With Hitler gibbet-high,
Let Mussolini, bloody, stoned,
    Be spaded deep in lye;

Destroy these three by rope or pyre,
    By poison, rack, or blade,
By every destruction dire
    The Christian mind has made;

Yet while the Worm remains to gorge
    Upon the nation's tree,
There is no armor we may forge
    To fit Peace perfectly.

Rend, rend the Swastika in twain,
    The Rising Sun deform;
But our flag, shall it remain
    The garment of the Worm?

Is there no hand to lift it free
    Of that miasmic kiss;
The kiss of hate and bigotry,
    The seal of prejudice?

Is there no knight of burning zeal,
    No gifted Galahad,
In accents of redemptive steel
    To cry, "Rejoice! Be glad!"?

Goliath's David long is dust;
    From what heroic sperm
Shall come the deep and valiant thrust
    To slay the loathely Worm?

The little men with slanting eyes,
    They know our pedigree,
They know the length of the Worm that lies
    Under the lynching tree.

The men with strides that ape the geese,
    They know the nation's thorn:
How one man will his brother fleece,
    And hold his hue in scorn.
From Berlin, Rome, and Tokyo,
    The gibing flashes run:
"That land's good picking for the crow,
    Whose people are not one."

Not till the poll tax perishes
    With peons of the South,
And all that hatred cherishes
    With blatant, twisted mouth;

Not till the cheated cropper thrive
    And draw his first free breath
(Though court and custom still contrive
    His legalistic death);

Not till the hedges fall, the moats
    Be mirrors for the stars,
And fair hands drop from darker throats
    Shall we extinguish Mars.

O land of mine, O land I love,
    The Worm gnaws at your root;
Unless that Worm you scotch, remove,
    Peace will not be the fruit.

The Tuskegee Airmen were graduates of the first U.S. Army flight school for blacks, located in Tuskegee, Alabama. About 1 million African Americans served in the military during World War II. As in previous wars, blacks served in segregated units under white officers.

"there could not be so many ships in the world"

MARTHA GELLHORN (1908–1998)

In a literary career that spanned six decades, Martha Gellhorn distinguished herself early as one of the world's first female war correspondents. After writing a novel about the Great Depression, she began her journalism career in 1937, covering the Spanish civil war for the magazine Collier's Weekly. *Around that time, she met Ernest Hemingway. Although she would later resent being associated with the famous author, she married Hemingway in 1940 and left him in 1945. Because they both served as World War II correspondents, their writing became a source of competition and argument between them. Hemingway reportedly resented the fact that his wife "scooped" him on the D-Day landings by stowing aboard a hospital ship and going ashore as a stretcher-bearer. Her exciting career included going on night bombing raids over Germany with British pilots and witnessing the liberation of Dachau concentration camp. She later covered the Vietnam War, the Arab-Israeli war of 1967, and the U.S. invasion of Panama in 1989. Beside her illustrious war correspondence, Gellhorn wrote a number of novels and short stories.*

Between July 1943 and June 1944, British and American forces in Europe bombed German cities and attacked what Winston Churchill termed "the soft underbelly of the Axis" in Italy. On June 6, two days after capturing Rome, Allied forces launched the massive D-Day invasion on France's northern coast. Success on the Normandy beaches was hard won, and bitter fighting continued as the Allies advanced through northern France. Nevertheless, British and American forces captured Paris two months later, on August 25, 1944. Historians now believe that the D-Day invasion marked the turning point of the war and foreshadowed Hitler's eventual downfall.

The following excerpt from Martha Gellhorn's article "The First Hospital Ship" appears in her collection of correspondence, The Face of War. *This article tells of her experiences aboard the first hospital ship to arrive on the D-Day landing scene.*

The Face of War
The First Hospital Ship

Then we saw the coast of France and suddenly we were in the midst of the armada of the invasion. People will be writing about this sight for a hundred years and whoever saw it will never forget it. First it seemed incredible; there could not be so many ships in the world. Then it seemed incredible as a feat of planning; if there were so many ships, what genius it required to get them here, what amazing and unimaginable genius. After the first shock of wonder and admiration, one began to look around and see separate details. There were destroyers and battleships and transports, a floating city of huge vessels anchored before the green cliffs of Normandy. Occasionally you would see a gun flash or perhaps only hear a distant roar, as naval guns fired far over those hills. Small craft beetled around in a curiously jolly way. It looked like a lot of fun to race from shore to ships in snub-nosed boats beating up the spray. It was no fun at all, considering the mines and obstacles that remained in the water, the sunken tanks with only their radio antennae showing above water, the drowned bodies that still floated past. On an LCT [landing craft] near us washing was hung up on a line, and between the loud explosions of mines being detonated on the beach dance music could be heard coming from its radio. Barrage balloons, always looking like comic toy elephants, bounced in the high wind above the massed ships, and invisible planes droned behind the gray ceiling of cloud. Troops were unloading from big ships to heavy cement barges or to light craft, and on the shore, moving up four brown roads that scarred the hillside, our tanks clanked slowly and steadily forward....

When night came, the water ambulances were still churning in to the beach looking for wounded. Someone on an LCT had shouted out that there were maybe a hundred scattered along there somewhere. It was essential to try to get them aboard before the nightly air raid and before the dangerous dark cold could eat into their hurt bodies. Going in to shore, unable to see, and not knowing this tricky strip of water, was slow work.... [Gellhorn went on the water ambulance to search for wounded. She waded into shore, talked with American soldiers, and helped move wounded men into a beached British ship (called an LST) while they waited for the water ambulance.]

Suddenly our flak started going up at the far end of the beach and it was beautiful, twinkling as it burst in the sky, and the tracers were lovely as they always are—and no one took pleasure from the beauty of the scene. "We've had it now," said the stretcher-bearer. "There isn't any place we can put those wounded." I asked one of the

The icon of World War II women was "Rosie the Riveter," shown in this poster designed by J. Howard Miller. Rosie is depicted as a strong, competent, and determined patriot who works in factories to support the war effort. Altogether, about one-third of American women went to work outside the home during World War II.

Margaret Bourke-White

Margaret Bourke-White is one of the most celebrated photo-journalists of World War II. She began her career after graduating from Cornell University in 1927 by taking industrial photos in Cleveland, Ohio. In 1929, she became the first photographer for *Fortune* magazine. Hired by the newly formed *Life* magazine in 1935, Bourke-White was the first female photojournalist there, and one of her photos graced the cover of the first edition. During World War II, she captured searing images from Moscow, North Africa, Italy, and the liberation of Buchenwald concentration camp. Thereafter, Bourke-White photographed South Africa under apartheid and the Korean War. The photographs of this highly respected artist are now collected by museums across the country.

soldiers, just for interest's sake, what they did in case of air raids and he said, well, you could go to a foxhole if you had time, but on the other hand there wasn't really much to do. So we stood and watched and there was altogether too much flak for comfort. We could not hear the planes nor hear any bomb explosions but as everyone knows flak is a bad thing to have fall on your head.

The soldiers now drifted off on their own business and we boarded the LST to keep the wounded company. It seemed a specially grim note to be wounded in action and then to have to lie helpless under a strip of canvas while any amount of shell fragments, to say nothing of bombs, could drop on you and complete the job. The stretcher-bearer and I said to each other gloomily that as an air-raid shelter far better things than the hold of an LST had been devised, and we went inside, not liking any of it and feeling miserably worried about our wounded.

The wounded looked pretty bad and lay very still; and in the light of one bare bulb, which hung from a girder, we could not see them well. Then one of them began to moan and he said something. He was evidently conscious enough to notice this ghastly racket that was going on above us. The Oerlikons of our LST now opened fire and the noise inside the steel hold was as if your own eardrums were being drilled with a rivet. The wounded man called out again and I realized he was speaking German. We checked up then and found that we had an LST full of wounded Germans, and the stretcher-bearer said, "Well, that is just dandy, by golly, if this isn't the payoff." Then he said, "If anything hits this ship, dammit, they deserve it."

The ack-ack lifted a bit and the stretcher-bearer climbed to the upper deck, like Sister Anne on the tower, to see where in God's name those water ambulances were. I clambered like a very awkward monkey up a ladder to the galley to get some coffee and so missed the spectacle of two German planes falling like fiery comets from the sky. They hit the beach to the right and left of us and burned in huge bonfires which lighted up the shore. The beach, in this light looked empty of human life, cluttered with dark square shapes of tanks and trucks and jeeps and ammunition boxes and all the motley equipment of war. It looked like a vast uncanny black-and-red flaring salvage dump, whereas once upon a time people actually went swimming here for pleasure.

Our LST crew was delighted because they believed they had brought down one of the German planes and everyone felt cheerful about the success of the ack-ack. A soldier shouted from shore that we had shot down four planes in all and it was nice work, by God. The wounded were silent and those few who had their eyes open had very frightened eyes. They seemed to be listening with their eyes, and fearing what they would hear.

ELIE WIESEL (1928–)

Born in the town of Sighet, now part of Romania, Elie Wiesel was raised in an Orthodox Jewish family. World War II affected him in ways few Americans at the time could imagine. Germans rounded up all the Jews of his village and forced them to live in a ghetto. Soon thereafter, when he was 15 years old, Nazis sent him and his family to concentration camps in Poland, where his mother, father, and youngest sister died. Given the trauma and indescribable horror he suffered, he vowed that he would not speak of his death camp experiences. Wiesel broke his silence with the 1958 French publication of La Nuit, *which was translated into English and published as* Night *in 1960. Meanwhile, he had settled in the United States and had become an American citizen. A professor at Boston University, Wiesel has written more than forty books, many of them about Judaism, the Holocaust, and oppressed peoples. He has received many honors and awards, including the Nobel Peace Prize in 1986, for his tireless human rights efforts. Elie Wiesel is regarded as the primary spokesperson for Holocaust survivors in the United States.*

"Never shall I forget these things"

One of Adolf Hitler's stated objectives was creating a German "master race." His orders and the implementation of them resulted in the most diabolical genocide the world has ever recorded. From the mid-1930s to 1942, Nazis rounded up Jews, Gypsies, and other victims of racial, ethnic, and religious hatred and forced them to live in ghettos and concentration camps. Many physically or mentally disabled people were killed outright. As Hitler conquered more European territory, he forced increasing waves of European Jews into the camp system. Between 1942 and 1944, Nazis devised the "final solution" for what they perceived as the Jewish "problem." During those years, Hitler built many new concentration camps in an elaborate plan to annihilate Jews, Gypsies, other minorities, and political resistance fighters. Some concentration camps were run as forced labor camps. Life there was torturous, and starvation was an everyday occurrence. Those deemed unfit to work were sent to death camps designed for gassing masses of prisoners and incinerating their bodies. Largely in this manner, Nazis exterminated 6 million Jews and about 5 million Gypsies, Slavs, and other "undesirables." In April of 1945, British and American troops reached camps in Germany and Poland. They were horrified at the emaciated prisoners and corpses that the Nazis left in their hasty retreat.

The following excerpt from Night *tells of Elie Wiesel's arrival at Birkenau, the reception center for Auschwitz death camp. Separated from his mother and sister upon arrival, Wiesel had just undergone the trauma of "selection" with his father. Both had been chosen for work instead of death.*

Night

Never shall I forget that night, the first night in camp, which has turned my life into one long night, seven times cursed and seven times sealed. Never shall I forget that smoke. Never shall I forget the little faces of the children, whose bodies I saw turned into wreaths of smoke beneath a silent blue sky.

Never shall I forget those flames which consumed my faith forever.

Never shall I forget that nocturnal silence which deprived me, for all eternity, of the desire to live. Never shall I forget those moments which murdered my God and my soul and turned my dreams to dust. Never shall I forget these things, even if I am condemned to live as long as God himself. Never.

The barracks we had been made to go into was very long. In the roof were some blue-tinged skylights. The antechamber of Hell must look like this. So many crazed men, so many cries, so much bestial brutality!

There were dozens of prisoners to receive us, truncheons in their hands, striking out anywhere, at anyone, without reason. Orders:

"Strip! Fast! *Los!* Keep only your belts and shoes in your hands...."

We had to throw our clothes at one end of the barracks. There was already a great heap there. New suits and old, torn coats, rags. For us, this was the true equality: nakedness. Shivering with the cold.

Some SS officers moved about in the room looking for strong men. If they were so keen on strength, perhaps one should try and pass oneself off as sturdy? My father thought the reverse. It was better not to draw attention to oneself. Our fate would then be the same as the others. (Later, we were to learn that he was right. Those who were selected that day were enlisted in the *Sonder-Kommando,* the unit which worked in the crematories. Bela Katz—son of a big tradesman from our town—had arrived at Birkenau with the first transport, a week before us. When he heard of our arrival, he managed to get word to us that, having been chosen for strength, he had himself put his father's body into the crematory oven.)

In April 1945, American troops liberated the concentration camp in Dachau, Germany, to the joy and relief of cheering survivors.

Blows continued to rain down.

"To the barber!"

Belt and shoes in hand, I let myself be dragged off to the barbers. They took our hair off with clippers, and shaved off all the hair on our bodies. The same thought buzzed all the time in my head—not to be separated from my father.

Freed from the hands of the barbers, we began to wander in the crowd, meeting friends and acquaintances. These meetings filled us with joy—yes, joy—"Thank God! You're still alive!"

But others were crying. They used all their remaining strength in weeping. Why had they let themselves be brought here? Why couldn't they have died in their beds? Sobs choked their voices.

Suddenly someone threw his arms around my neck in an embrace: Yechiel, brother of the rabbi of Sighet. He was sobbing bitterly. I thought he was weeping with joy at being alive.

"Don't cry Yechiel," I said. "Don't waste your tears...."

"Not cry? We're on the threshold of death.... Soon we shall have crossed over.... Don't you understand? How could I not cry?"

Through the blue-tinged skylights I could see the darkness gradually fading. I had ceased to feel fear. And then I was overcome by an inhuman weariness.

Those absent no longer touched even the surface of our memories. We still spoke of them—"Who knows what may have become of them?"—but we had little concern for their fate. We were incapable of thinking of anything at all. Our senses were blunted; everything was blurred as in a fog. It was no longer possible to grasp anything. The instincts of self-preservation, of self-defense, of pride, had all deserted us. In one ultimate moment of lucidity it seemed to me that we were damned souls wandering in the half-world, souls condemned to wander through space till the generations of man came to an end, seeking their redemption, seeking oblivion—without hope of finding it.

Toward five o'clock in the morning, we were driven out of the barracks. The Kapos beat us once more, but I had ceased to feel any pain from their blows. An icy wind enveloped us. We were naked, our shoes and belts in our hands. The command: "Run!" And we ran. After a few minutes of racing, a new barracks.

A barrel of petrol at the entrance. Disinfection. Everyone was soaked in it. Then a hot shower. At high speed. As we came out from the water, we were driven outside. More running. Another barracks, the store. Very long tables. Mountains of prison clothes. On we ran. As we passed, trousers, tunic, shirt, and socks were thrown to us.

Within a few seconds we had ceased to be men. If the situation had not been tragic, we should have roared with laughter. Such outfits! Meir Katz, a giant, had a child's trousers, and Stern, a thin little chap, a tunic which completely swamped him. We immediately began the necessary exchanges.

I glanced at my father. How he had changed! His eyes had grown dim. I would have liked to speak to him, but I did not know what to say.

The night was gone. The morning star was shining in the sky. I too had become a completely different person. The student of the Talmud, the child that I was, had been consumed in the flames. There remained only a shape that looked like me. A dark flame had entered into my soul and devoured it.

So much had happened within such a few hours that I had lost all sense of time. When had we left our houses? And the ghetto? And the train? Was it only a week? One night—*one single night?*

How long had we been standing like this in the icy wind? An hour? Simply an hour? Sixty minutes?

Surely it was a dream.

JOHN HERSEY (1914–1993)

John Hersey spent the first eleven years of his life in China until his family returned to the United States. He later earned his degree from Yale and went on to work as a World War II correspondent for Time *magazine. His first novel,* A Bell for Adano, *was published in 1944 and earned him a Pulitzer Prize. In 1946, Hersey published his novel* Hiroshima, *which weaves the true stories of six people in that Japanese city when the atom bomb exploded.* Hiroshima *was widely acclaimed by U.S. audiences who believed that Hersey had made the incomprehensible ordeal of nuclear warfare potently real. The book also broke new ground in literary style and form, and some critics believe that it was the first "nonfiction novel."*

Throughout World War II, the U.S. government—operating on information that the Germans were developing atomic bombs—funded research labs to produce such weapons as quickly as possible. In July 1945, American physicists successfully detonated the first U.S. atomic weapon in the desert of New Mexico. President Harry Truman was faced with the task of deciding whether or not to use this gruesome bomb, with the power of 20,000 tons of TNT, to bring a quick end to the war in the Pacific. While his decision has since been questioned, Truman rationalized that thousands of American lives would be lost if U.S. forces had to invade the Japanese mainland. Consequently, at 8:15 a.m. on August 6, 1945, U.S. bombers dropped the first atomic weapon on Hiroshima, exacting an awful toll. About 78,000 residents were killed, and another 100,000 were injured in the blast. Three days later, a second bomb was dropped on Nagasaki. On August 15, Japan surrendered.

This selection from Hiroshima *details the observations of a Japanese cleric, Reverend Kiyoshi Tanimoto, in the immediate aftermath of the explosion.*

"skin hung from their faces and hands"

Hiroshima
Chapter 2, The Fire

From the mound, Mr. Tanimoto saw an astonishing panorama. Not just a patch of Koi, as he had expected, but as much of Hiroshima as he could see through the clouded air was giving off a thick, dreadful miasma. Clumps of smoke, near and far, had begun to push up through

More than 90 percent of the buildings were destroyed or damaged in the atomic blast in Hiroshima, Japan.

the general dust. He wondered how such extensive damage could have been dealt out of a silent sky; even a few planes, far up, would have been audible. Houses nearby were burning, and when huge drops of water the size of marbles began to fall, he half thought that they must be coming from the hoses of firemen fighting the blazes. (They were actually drops of condensed moisture falling from the turbulent tower of dust, heat, and fission fragments that had already risen miles into the sky above Hiroshima.)...

He had thought of his wife and baby, his church, his home, his parishioners, all of them down in that awful murk. Once more he began to run in fear—toward the city....

Mr. Tanimoto, fearful for his family and church, at first ran toward them by the shortest route, along Koi highway. He was the only person making his way into the city; he met hundreds and hundreds who were fleeing, and every one of them seemed to be hurt in some way. The eyebrows of some were burned off and skin hung from their faces and hands. Others, because of pain, held their arms up as if carrying something in both hands. Some were vomiting as they walked. Many were naked or in shreds of clothing. On some undressed bodies, the burns had made patterns—of undershirt straps and suspenders and, on the skin of some women (since white repelled the heat from the bomb and dark clothes absorbed it and conducted it to the skin), the shapes of flowers they had had on their kimonos. Many, although injured themselves, supported relatives who were worse off. Almost all had their heads bowed, looked straight ahead, were silent, and showed no expression whatever.

After crossing Koi Bridge and Kannon Bridge, having run the whole way, Mr. Tanimoto saw, as he approached the center, that all the houses had been crushed and many were afire. Here the trees were bare and their trunks were charred. He tried at several points to penetrate the ruins, but the flames always stopped him. Under many houses people screamed for help, but no one helped; in general, survivors that day assisted only their relatives or immediate neighbors, for they could not comprehend or tolerate a wider circle of misery. As a Christian he was filled with compassion for those who were trapped, and as a Japanese he was overwhelmed by the shame of being unhurt, and he prayed as he ran, "God help them and take them out of the fire."

He thought he would skirt the fire, to the left. He ran back to Kannon Bridge and followed for a distance one of the rivers. He tried several cross streets, but all were blocked.... So impressed was he by this time by the extent of the damage that he ran north two miles to Gion, a suburb in the foothills. All the way, he overtook dreadfully burned and lacerated people, and in his guilt he turned to right and left as he hurried and said to some of them, "Excuse me for having no burden like yours." ... At Gion, he bore toward the right bank of the main river, the Ota, and ran down it until he reached fire again. There was no fire on the other side of the river, so he threw off his shirt and shoes and plunged into it. In mid-stream, where the current was fairly strong, exhaustion and fear finally caught up with him—he had run nearly seven miles—and he became limp and drifted in the water. He prayed, "Please, God, help me to cross. It would be nonsense for me to be drowned when I am the only unin-jured one." He managed a few more strokes and fetched up on a spit downstream.

Mr. Tanimoto climbed up the bank and ran along it until, near a large Shinto shrine, he came to more fire, and as he turned left to get around it, he met, by incredible luck, his wife. She was carrying their infant daughter. Mr. Tanimoto was now so emotionally worn out that nothing could surprise him. He did not embrace his wife; he simply said, "Oh, you are safe." She told him that she had got home from her night in Ushida just in time for the explosion; she had been buried under the parsonage with the baby in her arms. She told how the wreckage had pressed down on her, how the baby had cried. She saw a chink of light, and by reaching up with a hand, she worked the hole bigger, bit by bit. After about half an hour, she heard the cracking noise of wood burning. At last the opening was big enough for her to push the baby out, and afterward she crawled out herself. She said she was now going out to Ushida again. Mr. Tanimoto said he wanted to see his church and take care of the people of his Neighborhood Association. They parted as casually—as bewildered—as they had met.

UNIT 5 • THE CHALLENGES OF POWER

1945-1975

The defining moment of the twentieth century—for the United States and for the world—came near its halfway point. On August 6, 1945, a U.S. military plane called the *Enola Gay* dropped an atomic bomb on the Japanese city of Hiroshima. That blast—immortalized by an ominous, mushroom-shaped cloud rising into a blue sky—and the one in Nagasaki that followed days later brought a final Allied victory to the Pacific front of the Second World War. This devastating nuclear technology was initially the property of the United States alone, but by 1950 the Soviet Union had also exploded a nuclear bomb. Possession of such a weapon of mass destruction was both empowering and sobering. Now that the world had the means to destroy itself entirely, how were its thinkers, artists, poets, and political leaders supposed to proceed?

For many in the United States, the response was a mixture of fear and ignorance. The 1950s were years of prosperity for much of the nation, a time when many people moved into the middle class. Most mainstream literature of these years focused inward. Some writers used their craft to criticize American conformity and complacency; others celebrated it.

A major racial crisis was brewing in the southern states. Through a series of well-chosen and deftly argued Supreme Court cases, the NAACP and other civil rights groups had brought about the demise of legalized segregation of the races. Now it was left to the people to take up the fight to make equality happen. Black Americans marched, protested, boycotted, and otherwise demanded their civil and constitutional rights. The eloquent words of leaders such as Martin Luther King Jr. and Malcolm X outlined the goals and dreams of the movement. Other minority groups, including women, were also organizing for equal opportunities and an end to discrimination. New versions of the American experience emerged from previously unheard female, Latino, and Native American voices. More than any other time in American history, the types and styles of artistic works being produced were as varied as their creators.

1947
Developer William Levitt announces plans to build a large housing community for young families on Long Island, thirty miles from downtown Manhattan.

1949
China adopts a communist government under Mao Zedong.

1950
Television enters mainstream American life.

1954
Senator Joseph McCarthy alleges communist involvement in the U.S. military.

The United States Supreme Court rules in *Brown v. Board of Education of Topeka, Kansas,* that school segregation is unconstitutional.

1955
Montgomery, Alabama, bus boycott begins.

The United States begins giving economic aid to South Vietnam.

1957
Soviet scientists launch *Sputnik* into space.

1962
The United States and the Soviet Union engage in the Cuban Missile Crisis.

American John Glenn orbits the earth.

But the emergence of new voices and new modes often produced tension and division in society. Throughout the 1960s, a polarizing rift developed between American generations, a rift worsened by the nation's deepening involvement in the Vietnam War. Much of the journalistic reporting out of Vietnam rose to the rank of literature, its authors relying on metaphor and poetic device to convey war's tragedy and triumph.

Ultimately, the events of Vietnam, social strife and assassinations at home, and the scandalous downfall of an American president would force the country through a painful coming-of-age. The nation's artists, poets, and writers helped guide and give voice to that process.

1963
President John F. Kennedy is assassinated.

1964
The United States Congress passes a far-reaching Civil Rights Act.

1965
The first U.S combat troops arrive in South Vietnam.

1966
Race riots erupt in major U.S. cities.

The United Farm Workers Organizing Committee is formed.

The National Organization for Women (NOW) is formed.

1968
Martin Luther King Jr. and Robert Kennedy are assassinated.

1969
U.S. astronauts walk on the moon.

1970
Ohio National Guardsmen kill four students at Kent State University.

1972
Watergate break-in occurs in Washington, D.C.

1973
The United States signs a cease-fire agreement with North Vietnam and the Vietcong.

1974
President Richard Nixon resigns.

1975
Saigon falls to communists; South Vietnam surrenders.

Prosperity and Anxiety

The 1950s were a time of prosperity and affluence unlike any ever seen in the United States. Veterans returned from years of war in Europe and the Pacific, eager to go to work and start families. Aided by the GI Bill of Rights, more than 6 million veterans enrolled at colleges and schools of trade and agriculture. Record numbers of babies were born, giving rise to that generation's nickname, "the Baby Boomers." Spurred by sales of automobiles and other consumer products, the economy thrived.

The physical landscape of the country changed too, as growing families left the cities to purchase homes in the newly created suburbs. The greater availability and affordability of automobiles enabled this shift, as did the rapidly increasing number of single-family dwellings sprouting up around the country. In 1950 alone, 1.4 million new homes were built.

However, not all Americans shared in the wealth. African Americans did not fare nearly as well economically as did their white counterparts. The continued segregation of the southern states, and the polarized world it produced, heightened racial tensions. Throughout southern cities, conflicts erupted between African Americans seeking to exercise their civil rights and segregationists eager to preserve a particular way of life.

As the country grew accustomed to its new superpower status, events overseas fueled Cold War tensions and seemed to substantiate fears of worldwide communist plots. In 1949, communist forces defeated U.S.-backed nationalists in China; later that year, the Russians exploded an atomic bomb, furthering fears of nuclear annihilation. In 1950, communist North Korean forces invaded South Korea, sending American troops back overseas. Fearing the communist threat could also lurk at home, Americans began to search among their own. Senator Joseph McCarthy led a congressional hunt for communists, determined to seek out every subversive in the country.

Knowledge of the possibility for total nuclear destruction affected the work of the nation's poets and authors. A sense that individuals were less and less able to understand or affect global events forced authors like John Updike and Phillip Roth to turn inward, producing works that dealt with familial relationships and interior lives. Popular novelists like Grace Metalious, author of the highly successful *Peyton Place,* set out to expose hidden hypocrisies and wrong-doings in American communities. Other writers, such as Arthur Miller, Sloan Wilson, and Jack Kerouac, responded artistically to the social and political events of the day, penning works of fiction and drama that addressed their concerns with American society.

Featured Authors

Annie Dillard
Sloan Wilson
Jack Kerouac
Anne Moody
Arthur Miller
Tom Wolfe

ANNIE DILLARD (1945–)

Annie Dillard came of age in one of the most affluent eras in the nation's history. In her memoir An American Childhood, *published in 1987, Dillard recalls the pleasures of growing up in Pittsburgh, Pennsylvania, in the 1950s. As Dillard describes, the optimistic mood of the country reflected its great prosperity. Many Americans who had suffered through the Great Depression of the 1930s and the war shortages and rations of the 1940s were eager to spend money on consumer goods. Companies competed to sell products ranging from the new frozen TV dinners to television sets and hi-fi stereos—all designed to make life easier and more pleasurable for the average American.*

New advancements in science and medicine were improving the quality of American life as well. The growing field of microelectronics was aided by the invention of a miniature transistor. In 1953, a heart-and-lung machine kept a patient alive during surgery. And in 1954, Dr. Jonas Salk of the University of Pittsburgh developed a vaccine for the deadly poliomyelitis disease, or polio, that had affected the lives of hundreds of thousands of Americans.

Polio is an infectious, viral disease of the nervous system. Victims suffer from paralysis, severe breathing difficulty, and permanent disability. It was not uncommon in the early 1950s to see children with crutches or wheelchairs, or to know of children who languished in "iron lungs," machines meant to aid labored breathing. Fearful parents worried about their children's health during the highly contagious summer months. In 1952 alone, almost 60,000 Americans, mostly children, contracted the infection.

In the following excerpt from An American Childhood, *Dillard recalls Salk's discovery of the polio vaccine in her hometown of Pittsburgh—an achievement that illustrated the growing belief that there was nothing Americans could not do, no problem they could not solve.*

"Hard work bore fruit. This is what we learned"

An American Childhood

Problems still yielded to effort. Only a few years ago, to the wide-eyed attention of the world, we had seen the epidemic of poliomyelitis crushed in a twinkling, right here in Pittsburgh.

Norman Rockwell's GI Homecoming represents the optimistic excitement that war-weary Americans felt in the years immediately following World War II. Secure in the Allied victory and eager to begin new lives, Americans were about to experience the greatest prosperity the nation had ever known.

We had all been caught up in the polio epidemic: the early neighbor boy who wore one tall shoe, to which his despairing father added another two soles every year; the girl in the iron lung reading her schoolbook in an elaborate series of mirrors while a volunteer waited to turn the page; my friend who limped, my friend who rolled everywhere in a wheelchair, my friend whose arm hung down, Mother's friend who walked with crutches. My beloved dressed-up aunt, Mother's sister, had come to visit one day and, while she was saying hello, flung herself on the couch in tears; her son had it. Just a touch, they said, but who could believe it?

When Amy and I had asked, Why do we have to go to bed so early? Why do we have to wash our hands again? we knew Mother would kneel to look us in the eyes and answer in a low, urgent voice, So you do not get polio. We heard polio discussed once or twice a day for several years.

And we had all been caught up in its prevention, in the wild ferment of the early days of the Salk vaccine, the vaccine about which Pittsburgh talked so much, and so joyously, you could probably have heard the crowd noise on the moon.

In 1953, Jonas Salk's Virus Research Laboratory at the University of Pittsburgh had produced a controversial vaccine for polio. The small stories in the Pittsburgh *Press* and the *Post-Gazette* were coming out in *Life* and *Time*. It was too quick, said medical colleagues nationwide: Salk had gone public without first publishing everything in the journals. He rushed out a killed-virus serum without waiting for a safe live-virus one, which would probably be better. Doctors walked out of professional meetings; some quit the foundation that funded the testing. Salk was after personal glory, they said. Salk was after money, they said. Salk was after big prizes.

Salk tested the serum on five thousand Pittsburgh schoolchildren, of whom I was three, because I kept changing elementary schools. Our parents, like ninety-five percent of all Pittsburgh parents, signed the consent forms. Did the other mothers then bend over the desk in relief and sob? I don't know. But I don't suppose any of them gave much of a damn what Salk had been after.

When Pasteur died, near a place wonderfully called Saint-Cloud, he murmured to the devoted assistants who surrounded his bed, *"Il faut travailler"* [One must work.]

Il faut indeed *travailler*—no one who grew up in Pittsburgh could doubt it. And no one who grew up in Pittsburgh could doubt that the great work was ongoing. We breathed in optimism—not coal dust—with every breath. What couldn't be done with good hard *travail?*

The air in Pittsburgh had been dirty; now we could see it was clean. An enormous, pioneering urban renewal was under way; the newspapers pictured fantastic plans, airy artists' watercolors, which we soon saw laid out and built up in steel and glass downtown. The Republican Richard King Mellon had approached Pittsburgh's Democratic, Catholic mayor, David L. Lawrence, and together with a dozen business leaders they were razing the old grim city and building a sparkling new one; they were washing the very air. The Russians had shot *Sputnik* into outer space. In Shippingport, just a few miles down the Ohio River, people were building a generating plant that used atomic energy—an idea that seemed completely dreamy, but there it was. A physicist from Bell Laboratories spoke to us at school about lasers; he was about as wrought up a man as I had ever seen. You could not reasonably believe a word he said, but you could see that he believed it.

We knew that "Doctor Salk" had spent many years and many dollars to produce the vaccine. He commonly worked sixteen-hour days, six days a week. Of course. In other laboratories around the world, other researchers were working just as hard, as hard as Salk and Pasteur. Hard work bore fruit. This is what we learned growing up in Pittsburgh, growing up in the United States.

SLOAN WILSON (1920–)

In the aftermath of World War II, Sloan Wilson returned home along with hundreds of thousands of other American GIs. These young men were eager to return to safety and security, and to pursue the "American dream." By the 1950s, this dream meant marriage, several children, home ownership in one of the burgeoning suburban developments that dotted the country, and money to spend on the many new consumer items that became available each day.

In the years following the war, Wilson began a career in journalism at various New England newspapers. It was during this period that he grew uncomfortable with the world around him. The nature of work and business in America was changing. For the first time in U.S. history, more Americans worked at white-collar jobs than did not. Large conglomerate

"like a half million other guys in gray flannel suits, I'll always pretend to agree"

corporations like Xerox and General Electric were taking the place of smaller, individually owned businesses. Companies wanted employees who would fit the mold, who were complacent rather than creative, who could adapt easily to become "company men."

However, Wilson and other critics saw this conformity and loss of individuality as stifling and phony. In 1955, he published his semi-autobiographical novel, The Man in the Gray Flannel Suit, *about a young businessman who struggles to balance his own morals and ethics with the societal pressures of the 1950s to conform, achieve, and obtain. The book enjoyed great popular success, resonating with many Americans.*

In the novel, protagonist Tom Rath is a war veteran himself, married and raising three young children in a Connecticut suburb. Trying desper-ately to afford the things he and his wife feel they need in order to "keep up," Tom takes a job with a large television network. The man he works for, Hopkins, has been phenomenally successful, but his achievements have come at the price of family and personal life. Over the course of the novel, Tom realizes that he does not want to pursue unfulfilling work just to support a particular lifestyle.

In the following excerpt, Tom has been asked to review a speech for his boss, a man with the potential to make Tom a very successful "com-pany man." Having helped in the initial writing of the speech about the creation of a philanthropic mental health committee, Tom finds he is uncomfortable with the level of commercialization contained in its final draft. Unsure about whether to tell Hopkins the truth, Tom reflects upon the meaning of work and the sacrifices one makes to "get ahead."

The Man in the Gray Flannel Suit
Chapter 26

The first thing Tom did when he got back to his office the next day was to call Hopkins on the interoffice communication box.

"Glad you're back!" Hopkins said cheerily, as though Tom had just returned from a voyage around the world. "Have a good trip?"

"Fine," Tom said. "Did you want to see me?"

"Yes," Hopkins replied. "I'll send a girl down with the latest draft of my speech for Atlantic City. Let's have lunch tomorrow, and you can tell me what you think of it. Would one o'clock be all right?"

So that's all he wanted, Tom thought. He said, "Fine! I'll meet you in your office tomorrow at one."

An hour later an exceptionally pretty office girl arrived and with a dazzling smile handed Tom a large manila envelope from Hopkins. Tom opened it and extracted the speech, which had grown and changed since he had worked on it. "It's a real pleasure to be here this evening," he read. "I tremendously appreciate this opportunity to discuss with this distinguished gathering what I believe to be the most crucial problem facing the world today." Having made this point, the speech went on—in fact, it went on and on and on and on for thirty pages, saying over and over again in different ways that mental health is important. The last ten pages were devoted to the thought that mental-health problems affect the economy of the nation. "Our wealth depends on mental health," this section concluded. "Yes, our wealth depends on mental health!"

Tom put the speech down, feeling slightly ill. Good Lord, he thought, they're going to sell mental health the way they sell cigarettes! He left the speech on his desk, walked over to the window, and stared out over the city. Standing there, he shrugged his shoulders in an oddly hopeless way.

For author Sloan Wilson, such a picture of young American businessmen, clad in gray flannel suits, carrying briefcases, and crowded onto suburban commuter train platforms, epitomized the new American "Everyman," lost in the vast homogeneity and impersonality of corporate culture.

"Let's have lunch tomorrow, and you can tell me what you think of it," Hopkins had said.

"Well, of course I'm just talking off the top of my head, but I think this draft has some fine things in it, and, on the other hand, I have some reservations," Tom imagined himself saying. That was the way it was done—always feel the boss out to find what he thinks before committing yourself. Tell the man what he wants to hear.

"I'm sorry, but I think this speech is absurd. It's an endless repetition of the obvious fact that mental health is important. You've said that over and over again and finally turned it into a cheap advertising slogan. If you want to form a mental-health committee, why don't you find out what needs to be done and offer to help do it?"

A few years ago I would have said that, Tom thought. Be honest, be yourself. If the man asks you what you think of his speech, tell him. Don't be afraid. Give him your frank opinion.

That sounds so easy when you're young, Tom thought. It sounds so easy before you learn that your frank opinion often leads directly to the street. What if Hopkins really likes this speech?

Tom shrugged again. The thing to remember is this, he thought: Hopkins would want me to be honest. But when you come right down to it, why does he hire me? To help him do what he wants to do—obviously that's why any man hires another. And if he finds that I disagree with everything he wants to do, what good am I to him? I should quit if I don't like what he does, but I want to eat, and so, like a half million other guys in gray flannel suits, I'll always pretend to agree, until I get big enough to be honest without being hurt. That's not being crooked, it's just being smart.

But it doesn't make you feel very good, Tom thought. It makes you feel lousy. For the third time, he shrugged. How strangely it all works out, he thought. The pretty girl smiles as she hands me the innocuous manila envelope with the speech. I'll go with my boss for luncheon to a nice restaurant somewhere, with music playing in the background, perhaps, and people laughing all around, and the waiters will bow, and my boss will be polite, and I'll be tactful, and there in such delicate surroundings, I'll not be rude enough to say a stupid speech is stupid. How smoothly one becomes, not a cheat, exactly, not really a liar, just a man who'll say anything for pay.

"Then came spring, the great time of traveling"

JACK KEROUAC (1922–1969)

Jack Kerouac was born in Lowell, Massachusetts, a mill town north of Boston. A Columbia University football scholarship brought him to New York City in 1939. It was here that he and a small group of writers, known as "the Beats," began one of the major American literary movements of the century.

The prose styles of Beat authors like Jack Kerouac, Allen Ginsberg (Howl), *and Lawrence Ferhlingetti* (A Coney Island of the Mind) *were strongly influenced by jazz, bebop music, and African-American life, and they often borrowed terms from those cultures. The Beats abhorred the conformity and complacency of American middle-class priorities and pretensions. They rejected the consumer culture and the accumulation of wealth. Both the content matter and style of their writing was a shift away from traditional literary modes.*

On The Road, *Jack Kerouac's most famous novel, is a loosely auto-biographical account of his early travels. While at Columbia, Kerouac was introduced to the poet Allen Ginsberg as well as to a wild young man from Colorado named Neal Cassady, an aspiring writer who spent more time in and out of police stations than at the typewriter. Cassady became the model for* On The Road's *Dean Moriarity, a fast driving, high living soul-searcher who befriends the young novelist Sal Paradise (Kerouac himself) and encourages him to take to the road.*

Throughout the course of the novel, the two crisscross the country numerous times, hitchhiking, stealing cars, and begging for food and money from the people they encounter along the way. Kerouac himself had taken several such trips in the 1940s, and he worked on On The Road *for many years, rewriting and revising differrent versions until it was finally published in 1957. Its popularity has been continual, inspiring people involved in the counter-culture movement of the late 1960s and 1970s and encouraging many American youth to take to the road in search of authentic experiences.*

The novel is a travelogue of American people and places, and Kerouac's rambling, exuberant prose reveals a frantic desire to set all of his experience down for the record. Kerouac was critical of the "sparse and halting" composition of authors like Ernest Hemingway, and he called his own nonstop, free-association style "spontaneous prose." In the following scene, narrator Sal Paradise catalogues the antics of Dean Moriarity and describes his own call to the road. The passage is characteristic of many of the novel's vignettes, evidence of the author's fascination and admiration with the larger-than-life Neal Cassady and written with the stream-of-consciousness, jazz-inspired style that is Kerouac's hallmark.

Edward Hopper's painting People in the Sun, *completed in 1955, illustrates the isolation some Americans felt in an increasingly modernized world.*

On the Road
Part One, 1

Then came spring, the great time of traveling, and everybody in the scattered gang was getting ready to take one trip or another. I was busily at work on my novel and when I came to the halfway mark, after a trip down South with my aunt to visit my brother Rocco, I got ready to travel West for the very first time.

Dean had already left. Carlo and I saw him off at the 34th Street Greyhound station. Upstairs they had a place where you could make pictures for a quarter. Carlo took off his glasses and looked sinister. Dean made a profile shot and looked coyly around. I took a straight picture that made me look like a thirty-year-old Italian who'd kill anybody who said anything against his mother. This picture Carlo and Dean neatly cut down the middle with a razor and saved a half each in their wallets. Dean was wearing a real Western business suit for his big trip back to Denver; he'd finished his first fling in New York. I say fling, but he only worked like a dog in parking lots. The most fantastic parking-lot attendant in the world, he can back a car forty miles an hour into a tight squeeze and stop at the wall, jump out, race among fenders, leap into another car, circle it fifty miles an hour in a narrow space, back swiftly

Teenage Rebellion
'I'd just be the catcher in the rye'

The 1950s marked the emergence of American teenage culture. For the first time in history, most American families could afford to keep their teenaged children out of the workforce and in school. The number of U.S. high school enrollments almost doubled between 1950 and 1960. Businesses clamored for teenage dollars, selling everything from record albums to tubes of lipstick. The new rock and roll music, created from a blend of blues and country-western, captivated the nation's carefree youth. Though American teenagers often mimicked their parents' consumerism and social conformity, popular culture—particularly rock and roll—offered American teens exciting new heroes.

American literature provided its own adolescent rebels. One of the most popular novels of the decade, J.D. Salinger's *Catcher in the Rye,* told the story of Holden Caufield, an American teenager disillusioned with the phoniness and hypocrisy of the adult world and determined to remain genuine. Recently expelled from his wealthy prep school and afraid to go home, he spends several soul-searching days in New York City. Holden's bitter but humorous cynicism, coupled with a naiveté about the realities of the world, has endeared him to generations of readers.

Here, Holden responds to his younger sister's question about what he wants to be when he grows up, referring to the poem from which the book's title is taken:

"I thought it [a line from the poem] was 'If a body catch a body,'" I said. "Anyway, I keep picturing all these little kids playing some game in this big field of rye and all. Thousands of little kids, and nobody's around—nobody big, I mean—except me. And I'm standing on the edge of some crazy cliff. What I have to do, I have to catch everybody if they start to go over the cliff—I mean if they're running and they don't look where they're going I have to come out from somewhere and catch them. That's all I'd do all day. I'd just be the catcher in the rye and all. I know it's crazy, but that's the only thing I'd really like to be. I know it's crazy."

into tight spot, *hump,* snap the car with the emergency so that you see it bounce as he flies out; then clear to the ticket shack, sprinting like a track star, hand a ticket, leap into a newly arrived car before the owner's half out, leap literally under him as he steps out, start the car with the door flapping, and roar off to the next available spot, arc, pop in, brake, out, run; working like that without pause eight hours a night, evening rush hours and after-theater rush hours, in greasy wino pants with a frayed fur-lined jacket and beat shoes that flap. Now he'd bought a new suit to go back in; blue with pencil stripes, vest and all—eleven dollars on Third Avenue, with a watch and watch chain, and a portable typewriter with which he was going to start writing in a Denver rooming house as soon as he got a job there. We had a farewell meal of franks and beans in a

Seventh Avenue Riker's, and then Dean got on the bus that said Chicago and roared off into the night. There went our wrangler. I promised myself to go the same way when spring really bloomed and opened up the land.

And this was really the way that my whole road experience began, and the things that were to come are too fantastic not to tell.

ANNE MOODY (1940–)

Contrary to popular images and contemporary television portrayals, not all Americans were reaping the benefits of postwar prosperity and affluence. In fact, many groups, particularly minorities, suffered discrimination, racism, and poverty. Though many African-American soldiers had fought bravely against fascism and racism in Europe during World War II, they returned home to face discriminatory labor and living conditions in their own country.

Anne Moody was born into a poor black family in rural Wilkinson County, Mississippi. She and her family struggled to feed, clothe, and house themselves, while at the same time battling the entrenched racism and segregation that ruled the South. Moody's autobiography, Coming of Age in Mississippi, *published in 1968, chronicles her childhood and early adulthood.*

In the American South in the 1950s, two separate worlds existed: one white, one black. African Americans were forced to use separate water fountains, sit in separate seats while using public transportation, and attend separate schools. Not surprisingly, those facilities provided for blacks were considerably less well-equipped than those for whites. African Americans could not eat at many restaurants or sit in certain sections of public areas such as movie theaters. In addition, marriages between the races were illegal in many places. Nationally, African Americans were particularly affected by the population shift from urban to suburban areas because they often could not afford to live, or were unwelcome, in the new suburban developments. Thus, predominantly black and poor urban centers arose.

In the following selection from Coming of Age in Mississippi, *the young Moody (called Essie Mae) describes the event which triggered her understanding that her skin color was considered inferior, that being white meant privilege and access and being black meant hardship and struggle. This realization, and the anger that accompanied it, led Moody to her involvement in the civil rights movement of the 1950s and 1960s.*

"*their whiteness made them better than me*"

Coming of Age in Mississippi
Chapter 3

Every Saturday evening Mama would take us to the movies. The Negroes sat upstairs in the balcony and the whites sat downstairs. One Saturday we arrived at the movies at the same time as the white children. When we saw each other, we ran and met. Katie walked straight into the downstairs lobby and Adline, Junior, and I followed. Mama was talking to one of the white women and didn't notice that we had walked into the white lobby. I think she thought we were at the side entrance we had always used which led to the balcony. We were standing in the white lobby with our friends, when Mama came in and saw us. "C'mon! C'mon!" she yelled, pushing Adline face on into the door. "Essie Mae, um gonna try my best to kill you when I get you home. I told you 'bout running up in these stores and things like you own 'em!" she shouted, dragging me through the door. When we got outside, we stood there crying, and we could hear the white children crying inside the white lobby. After that, Mama didn't even let us stay at the movies. She carried us right home.

All the way back to our house, Mama kept telling us that we couldn't sit downstairs, we couldn't do this or that with white children. Up until that time I had never really thought about it. After all, we were playing together. I knew that we were going to separate schools and all, but I never knew why.

After the movie incident, the white children stopped playing in front of our house. For about two weeks we didn't see them at all. Then one day they were there again and we started playing. But things were not the same. I had never really thought of them as white before. Now all of a sudden they were white, and their whiteness made them better than me. I now realized that not only were they better than me because they were white, but everything they owned and everything connected with them was better than what was available to me. I hadn't realized before that downstairs in the movies was any better than upstairs. But now I saw that it was. Their whiteness provided them with a pass to downstairs in that nice section and my blackness sent me to the balcony.

Now that I was thinking about it, their schools, homes, and streets were better than mine. They had a large red brick school with nice sidewalks connecting the buildings. Their homes were large and beautiful with indoor toilets and every other convenience that I knew of at the time. Every house I had ever lived in was a one- or two-room shack with an outdoor toilet. It really bothered me that they had all these nice things and we had nothing. "There is a secret to it besides being white," I thought. Then my mind got all wrapped up in trying to uncover that secret.

ARTHUR MILLER (1915–)

Arthur Miller was born in Manhattan and moved to Brooklyn after his father lost his business in the stock market crash of 1929. While at the University of Michigan, Miller studied journalism and began writing. In 1953, Miller's observations of the American political scene led him to write The Crucible, *a historical allegory that compares the Puritan witch trials of 1692 to the hunt for American communists in the 1940s and 1950s. Today, Miller is considered one of the most influential American playwrights of the twentieth century.*

"you must give us all their names"

As the Russian and U.S. alliance of World War II disintegrated over ideological differences, fears of a Soviet plot to take over the world grew. Americans began to suspect that the communist enemy might also be lurking at home. The United States Congress led the investigations of allegations and suspicions of subversive activity. The House Un-American Activities Committee (HUAC), established in 1938, forced a number of Americans to answer questions about their involvement with communist organizations. Senator Joseph McCarthy of Wisconsin made headlines in 1950 when he charged that the U.S. State Department was filled with communist sympathizers. Although many considered McCarthy a ruthless political opportunist, his investigations led to accusations of communist affiliations against many Americans.

This photograph captures the virulent anticommunism that pervaded the country during the early years of the Cold War. To prove their patriotism and keep their jobs, many federal government workers and teachers were forced to take loyalty oaths and denounce communism.

Those called to testify before investigators were often asked to give the names of suspected communists in order to obtain their own freedom. Some refused to incriminate others, arguing that it violated their constitutional rights. American intellectuals began to voice their criticism of McCarthy's tactics; eventually, the public followed suit. In 1954, McCarthy lost his credibility and was censured by Congress, after a series of televised hearings on communism in the U.S. Army prompted widespread disgust. The investigations did not end there, though. Arthur Miller himself was called to testify before HUAC in 1956 and charged with "contempt of Congress" for his unwillingness to provide names.

In The Crucible, *Miller likens the search for communists at home during the 1950s to the hunt for*

witches 250 years earlier. The play is based on a series of events that transpired in 1692 in Salem, Massachusetts. In this deeply religious Puritan community, church and state were inextricably linked. When young girls began taking ill and "no natural causes" could be found, people began to accuse villagers of witchcraft. What resulted, and what Miller recounts, was a tragic miscarriage of justice. Hysteria and paranoia replaced the rule of law and forced innocent people to confess to crimes they did not commit or be hanged. A state of perpetual suspicion developed in which everyone was a possible criminal. A simple accusation carried the weight of a conviction.

In the following scene, Reverend Hale, a minister with a reputation for ferreting out witches, has come to Salem to determine whether or not several young girls are possessed. Abigail Williams, 17, had been caught dancing in the woods along with the servant Tituba and a number of other young women. In Puritan times, such actions would not have been seen as childish fun, but as the work of the devil or evil spirits. The questioning takes place in the home of Reverend Parris at the bedside of his "sick" daughter Betty. The frightened young women seize upon the idea of blaming others to divert attention from themselves. As the hysteria grows, innocent people are accused of witchcraft.

The Crucible
Act One

TITUBA: I don't compact with no Devil!

PARRIS: You will confess yourself or I will take you out and whip you to your death, Tituba!

PUTNAM: This woman must be hanged! She must be taken and hanged!

TITUBA, *terrified, falls to her knees:* No, no, don't hang Tituba! I tell him I don't desire to work for him, sir.

PARRIS: The Devil?

HALE: Then you saw him! *Tituba weeps.* Now Tituba, I know that when we bind ourselves to Hell it is very hard to break with it. We are going to help you tear yourself free—

TITUBA, *frightened by the coming process:* Mister Reverend, I do believe somebody else be witchin' these children.

HALE: Who?

TITUBA: I don't know, sir, but the Devil got him numerous witches.

HALE: Does he! *It is a clue.* Tituba, look into my eyes. Come, look into me. *She raises her eyes to his fearfully.* You would be a good Christian woman, would you not, Tituba?

TITUBA: Aye, sir, a good Christian woman.

HALE: And you love these little children?

TITUBA: Oh, yes, sir, I don't desire to hurt little children.

HALE: And you love God, Tituba?

TITUBA: I love God with all my bein'.

HALE: Now, in God's holy name—

TITUBA: Bless Him. Bless Him. *She is rocking on her knees, sobbing in terror.*

HALE: And to His glory—

TITUBA: Eternal glory. Bless Him—bless God . . .

HALE: Open yourself, Tituba—open yourself and let God's holy light shine on you.

TITUBA: Oh, bless the Lord.

HALE: When the Devil comes to you does he ever come—with another person? *She stares up into his face.* Perhaps another person in the village? Someone you know.

PARRIS: Who came with him?

PUTNAM: Sarah Good? Did you ever see Sarah Good with him? Or Osburn?

PARRIS: Was it man or woman came with him?

TITUBA: Man or woman. Was—was woman.

PARRIS: What woman? A woman, you said. What woman?

TITUBA: It was black dark, and I—

PARRIS: You could see him, why could you not see her?

TITUBA: Well, they was always talking; they was always runnin' round and carryin' on—

PARRIS: You mean out of Salem? Salem witches?

TITUBA: I believe so, yes, sir.

Now Hale takes her hand. She is surprised.

HALE: Tituba. You must have no fear to tell us who they are, do you understand? We will protect you. The Devil can never overcome a minister. You know that, do you not?

TITUBA, *kisses Hale's hand:* Aye, sir, oh, I do.

HALE: You have confessed yourself to witchcraft, and that speaks a wish to come to Heaven's side. And we will bless you, Tituba.

TITUBA, *deeply relieved:* Oh, God bless you, Mr. Hale!

HALE, *with rising exaltation:* You are God's instrument put in our hands to discover the Devil's agents among us. You are selected, Tituba, you are chosen to help us cleanse our village. So speak utterly, Tituba, turn your back on him and face God—face God, Tituba, and God will protect you.

TITUBA, *joining with him:* Oh, God, protect Tituba!

HALE, *kindly:* Who came to you with the Devil? Two? Three? Four? How many?

Tituba pants, and begins rocking back and forth again, staring ahead.

TITUBA: There was four. There was four.

PARRIS, *pressing in on her:* Who? Who? Their names, their names!

TITUBA, *suddenly bursting out:* Oh, how many times he bid me kill you, Mr. Parris!

PARRIS: Kill me!

TITUBA, *in a fury:* He say Mr. Parris must be kill! Mr. Paris no goodly man, Mr. Parris mean man and no gentle man, and he bid me rise out of my bed and cut your throat! *They gasp.* But I tell him "No! I don't hate that man. I don't want kill that man." But he say, "You work for me, Tituba, and I make you free! I give you pretty dress to wear, and put you way high up in the air, and you gone fly back to Barbados!" And I say, "You lie, Devil, you lie!" And then he come one stormy night to me, and he say, "Look! I have *white* people belong to me." And I look—and there was Goody Good.

PARRIS: Sarah Good!

TITUBA, *rocking and weeping:* Aye, sir, and Goody Osburn.

MRS. PUTNAM: I knew it! Goody Osburn were midwife to me three times. I begged you, Thomas, did I not? I begged him not to call Osburn because I feared her. My babies always shriveled in her hands!

HALE: Take courage, you must give us all their names. How can you bear to see this child suffering? Look at her, Tituba. *He is indicating Betty on the bed.* Look at her God-given innocence; her soul is so tender; we must protect her, Tituba; the Devil is out and preying on her like a beast upon the flesh of the pure lamb. God will bless you for your help.

Abigail rises, staring as though inspired, and cries out.

ABIGAIL: I want to open myself! *They turn to her, startled. She is enraptured, as though in a pearly light.* I want the light of God, I want the sweet love of Jesus! I danced for the Devil; I saw him; I wrote in his book; I go back to Jesus; I kiss His hand. I saw Sarah Good with the Devil! I saw Goody Osburn with the Devil! I saw Bridget Bishop with the Devil!

As she is speaking, Betty is rising from the bed, a fever in her eyes, and picks up the chant.

BETTY, *staring too:* I saw George Jacobs with the Devil! I saw Goody Howe with the Devil!

PARRIS: She speaks! *He rushes to embrace Betty.* She speaks!

HALE: Glory to God! It is broken, they are free!

BETTY, *calling out hysterically and with great relief:* I saw Martha Bellows with the Devil!

ABIGAIL: I saw Goody Sibber with the Devil! *It is rising to a great glee.*

PUTNAM: The marshal, I'll call the marshal!
Parris is shouting a prayer of thanksgiving.
BETTY: I saw Alice Barrow with the Devil!
The curtain begins to fall.
HALE, *as Putnam goes out:* Let the marshal bring irons!
ABIGAIL: I saw Goody Hawkins with the Devil!
BETTY: I saw Goody Bibber with the Devil!
ABIGAIL: I saw Goody Booth with the Devil!
On their ecstatic cries

THE CURTAIN FALLS

TOM WOLFE (1930–)

Tom Wolfe, born in Richmond, Virginia, is recognized as one of the original practitioners of "New Journalism." Such work merges fiction and nonfiction, reporting and imaginative writing. New Journalists use real events as the basis for creative prose. For much of the history of American literature, nonfiction was considered a lesser literary form, with the novel, poem, or drama taking precedence. In the 1960s, Tom Wolfe and other writers such as Truman Capote and Norman Mailer began to use the fictional techniques of characterization, varying points of view, and figurative language to bring actual events to life. Creative nonfiction, as it is also known, can take the form of personal essays, commentaries, feature-length articles, or even "nonfiction novels."

Such is the case with The Right Stuff, *Wolfe's recounting of the beginnings of the American space program. Published in 1979,* The Right Stuff *chronicles the personalities, events, and competition with the Russians that drove the race to send a man into space. In the tense, early years of the Cold War, the nation's space program and its defense plans were intimately connected. Every front was another opportunity to win the battle against communism. Space would prove no exception.*

Much to the surprise of U.S. scientists, the Russians had launched the unmanned satellite Sputnik *into orbit in 1957, furthering the public's fears of the Soviets' military power. In response, Congress appropriated money in 1958 for the creation of the National Aeronautic and Space Administration (NASA). They also passed the National Defense Education Act,*

"A blazing aura was upon them all."

which allocated more federal funding for science and foreign language education.

The following excerpt recounts the first American astronauts' introduction to the U.S. press in 1959. The seven men had been selected from the ranks of the military's best fliers and endured rigorous physical and mental evaluations. But even they were unprepared for the tremendous response of a worried country, hungry for reassurance and success.

The Right Stuff
Chapter 5

They bubble, they boil, they steam and scream, they rumble, and then they boil some more in the most excited way. The sound of boiling voices was exactly like the sound an actor hears backstage before the curtain goes up on a play that everyone—*tout le monde*—must attend. Once there, everyone starts chattering away, out of the sheer excitement of being there at all, of being *where things are happening,* until everybody's beaming face is boiling away with words and grins and laughs that burst out whether or not anything the least bit funny has been said.

As he was not much of an actor, however, this was the sort of sound that terrified Gus Grissom. He was only moments away from the part he was likely to be worst at, and these people were all waiting on the other side of the curtain. At 2 p.m. the curtain was pulled back, and he had to walk onto the stage.

A sheet of light hit Gus and the others, and the boiling voices dropped down to a rumble, or a buzz, and then you could make them out. There appeared to be hundreds of them, packed in shank to flank, sitting, standing, squatting. Some of them were up on a ladder that was propped against the wall under one of the huge lights. Some of them had cameras with the most protuberant lenses, and they had a way of squatting and crawling at the same time, like the hunkered-down beggars you saw all over the Far East. The lights were on for television crews. This building was the Dolly Madison House, at the northeast corner of Lafayette Square, just a few hundred yards from the White House. It had been converted into NASA's Washington headquarters, and this room was the ballroom, which they used for all press conferences, and it was not nearly big enough for all these people. The little beggar figures were crawling all over it.

The surprising launch of the Soviet satellite Sputnik in 1957 provoked widespread criticism of America's schools, challenging that science and math education were not rigorous enough. Some feared the Russians would now be able to launch a missile attack from the sky.

The NASA people steered Gus and the other six to seats at a long table on the stage. The table had a felt cloth over it. They put Gus in a seat at the middle of the table, and sticking up over the felt right in front of him was the needle nose of a miniature escape tower on top of a model of the Mercury capsule mounted on an Atlas rocket. The model was evidently propped up against the other side of the table so that the press could see it. A man from NASA named Walter Bonney got up, a man with a jolly-sounding voice, and he said: "Ladies and gentlemen, may I have your attention, please. The rules of this briefing are very simple. In about sixty seconds we will give you the announcement that you have all been waiting for: the names of the seven volunteers who will become the Mercury astronaut team. Following the distribution of the kit—and this will be done as speedily as possible—those of you who have p.m. deadline problems had better dash for your phones. We will have about a ten- or twelve-minute break during which the gentlemen will be available for picture taking."

Some men from over on the sides appeared and began handing out folders, and people were rushing up and grabbing these kits and bolting from the room. Bonney pointed to the seven of them sitting there at the table and said: "Gentlemen, these are the astronaut volunteers. Take your pictures as you will, gentlemen."

And now began a very odd business. Without another word, all these grim little crawling beggar figures began advancing toward them, elbowing and hipping one another out of the way, growling and muttering, but never looking at each other, since they had their cameras screwed into their eye sockets and remained concentrated on Gus and the six other pilots at the table in the most obsessive way, like a swarm of root weevils which, no matter how much energy they might expend in all directions trying to muscle one another out of the way, keep their craving beaks homed in on the juicy stuff that the whole swarm had sensed—until they were all over them, within inches of their faces in some cases, poking their mechanical beaks into everything but their belly buttons. Yet this by itself was not what made the moment so strange. It was something else on top of it. There was such a frantic excitement—and their names had not even been mentioned! Yet it didn't matter in the slightest! They didn't care whether he was Gus Grissom or Joe Blow! They were ravenous for his picture all the same! They were crawling all over him and the other six as if they were creatures of tremendous value and excitement, real prizes....

By the next morning the seven Mercury astronauts were national heroes. It happened just like that. Even though so far they had done nothing more than show up for a press conference, they were known as the seven bravest men in America. They woke up to find astonishing acclaim all over the press. There it was, in the more sophisticated

Selling the American Housewife

The reading material of American women in the 1950s was just as likely to have been a magazine as a novel. *Ladies Home Journal, McCall's,* and *Good Housekeeping* enjoyed tremendous popularity among women of the growing middle class. These magazines served many purposes. They offered friendly advice on cooking, cleaning, parenting, and relationship management for young wives, many who were living away from extended family for the first time. They helped encourage women to leave or stay out of the labor force, thereby ensuring more jobs for returning veterans. Generally, they helped reinforce the revered status of the devoted housewife that Americans were seeing on television shows such as *Ozzie and Harriet, Father Knows Best,* and *Leave It to Beaver. Time* magazine called American homemakers "the keeper[s] of the suburban dream."

Few alternatives to this female ideal existed in the popular mass media. Ironically, the postwar years saw a reversal of trends in women's higher education and professional involvement for the first time in the twentieth century. Though women continued to go to college, fewer took employment outside the home that utilized their degrees. The idea that women who desired to work suffered from sexual dysfunction gained popularity in psychological circles. The effects of this pervasive message—that a woman should receive complete intellectual and emotional fulfillment from her role as wife and mother—would become evident in the women's movement of the 1960s and 1970s.

Women looked to magazines like Good Housekeeping *and* Ladies Home Journal *for advice on homemaking. Magazine advertisers competed for consumer dollars for goods such as household appliances and convenience foods.*

columns as well as in the tabloids and on television. Even James Reston of *The New York Times* had been so profoundly moved by the press conference and the sight of the seven brave men that his heart, he confessed, now beat a little faster. "What made them so exciting," he wrote, "was not that they said anything new but that they said all the old things with such fierce convictions ... They spoke of 'duty' and 'faith' and 'country' like Walt Whitman's pioneers ... This is a pretty cynical town, but nobody went away from these young men scoffing at their courage and idealism." Manly courage, the right stuff—the Halo Effect, with Deacon

Glenn leading the hallelujah chorus, had practically wiped the man out. If Gus and some of the others had been worried that they weren't being regarded as hot pilots, their worries were over when they saw the press coverage. Without exception, the newspapers and wire services picked out the highlights of their careers and carefully massed them to create a single blaze of glory. This took true journalistic skill. It meant citing a great deal from John Glenn's career, his combat flying in two wars, his five Distinguished Flying Crosses with eighteen clusters, and his recent speed record, plus the combat that Gus and Wally Schirra had seen in Korea and the medals they had won, one DFC apiece, and the bombing missions Slayton had flown in the Second World War and a bit about the jet fighters he had helped test at Edwards and the ones that Shepard had tested at Pax River—and going easy on the subject of Scott Carpenter and Gordon Cooper, who had not flown in combat (Shepard had not, either) or done any extraordinary testing. John Glenn came out of it as tops among seven very fair-haired boys. He had the hottest record as a pilot, he was the most quotable, the most photogenic, and the lone Marine. But all seven, collectively, emerged in a golden haze as the seven finest pilots and bravest men in the United States. A blazing aura was upon them all.

*R**ights and Revolutions***

The years between 1950 and 1975 were tumultuous times for American society. Under the cloud of the Cold War, Americans began a struggle for full civil rights for all citizens. Led by African Americans, the battles for equal opportunity and the complete rights of citizenship crossed color and gender lines and touched the lives of everyone in the United States. African Americans, women, Latinos, and Native Americans organized themselves to protest, resist, agitate, demonstrate, and demand equal treatment.

In the South, black church leaders and college students led the civil rights movement. Working-class African Americans, tired of racism and the repeated denial of their constitutional rights, largely carried it out. Martin Luther King Jr.'s call for nonviolent, passive resistance and direct action was taken up in segregated cities across the South. Later, a more militant but equally passionate Black Power movement arose.

Across the country, American women began to assert their collective frustration at being defined solely by their roles as wives and mothers, and not by their own professional or intellectual accomplishments. Most women were economically dependent on their husbands' incomes. Opportunities and encouragement in the professional world were scarce. Women who did work faced limited job choices and unequal pay. Consequently, feminist activists began to challenge the status quo, often in dramatic ways.

Such civil rights movements inspired other minority groups to organize and protest. Mexican migrant workers in California struck for better working conditions. Representatives from different Indian nations banded together to force the federal government to confront years of broken treaties and unfulfilled promises.

Unlike much of the mainstream literature of the 1950s, the "activist" writings of the civil rights years were passionate, provocative, and empowering. Martin Luther King Jr.'s "Letter from Birmingham Jail" is considered a classic piece of protest literature. Betty Friedan's descriptions of the stifling roles American women were forced into gave the country the phrase "the feminine mystique." In addition, multicultural voices emerged to offer different versions of the American story. The song lyrics of folk singer Bob Dylan became anthems for the protest movements of the 1960s, as American society painfully but rightfully reinvented itself into a more inclusive, fair, and just democracy.

Featured Authors

Martin Luther King Jr.
Malcolm X
Judy Brady
Sandra Cisneros
Mary Crow Dog
Bob Dylan

MARTIN LUTHER KING JR.
(1929–1968)

In 1955, the year Dr. Martin Luther King Jr. came to prominence on the national stage, segregated facilities were common in most southern cities. Armed with the Supreme Court's 1896 decision in Plessy v. Ferguson, *which ruled that separate but equal facilities did not violate the Fourteenth Amendment, many states had established a system of legal separation of the races. But the facilities provided for blacks—including schools, streetcars, restrooms, and elevators—were always inferior to those for whites. Black Americans regularly endured humiliation in their daily lives. Confronted constantly by signs reading "Whites Only," they were consigned to separate waiting rooms and seats at the back of the bus. Though less obvious than in the South, racism and segregation existed in the North as well.*

On December 1, 1955, in Montgomery, Alabama, a seamstress named Rosa Parks violated a local law by refusing to vacate her seat on a city bus for a white man. Her arrest triggered a citywide boycott of the public transportation system by African Americans. The successful protest was led by 26-year-old Baptist preacher Martin Luther King Jr. Schooled in the biblical teachings of Jesus to "love thy enemy," the civil disobedience methods of Henry David Thoreau, and the peaceful resistance philosophy of Mohandas Gandhi, King became the acknowledged leader of the South's civil rights movement.

Dr. King believed that, to effect change, people must peacefully refuse to obey unjust laws, even if that means enduring pain and violence. "We will . . . wear you down by our capacity to suffer," King said, and that is what thousands of African Americans did for years thereafter. Activists used boycotts, sit-ins, marches, freedom rides, and voter registration drives to agitate for equal rights. Responses from city and state leaders were often violent and at times deadly.

Gradually, national public opinion began to sway, influenced by television coverage of peaceful protesters in the South being attacked and beaten by white citizens and police officers. The federal government responded by passing the Civil Rights Act of 1964 and the Voting Rights Act of 1965. In 1964, Dr. King was awarded the Nobel Prize for Peace. On April 4, 1968, King was assassinated as he stood on a Memphis, Tennessee, hotel balcony. The death of a man who had emphatically opposed violence triggered the worst urban rioting in American history. More than 125 cities burned in anger and grief.

"freedom is never voluntarily given by the oppressor; it must be demanded by the oppressed"

"Letter from Birmingham Jail" is one of Martin Luther King's most famous writings. Composed while he was jailed in Alabama for leading a protest march, the letter is in response to an open announcement that had appeared in a city newspaper. In it, a group of local white clergymen had accused the civil rights leader of being a troublemaker and challenged his demonstrations as "untimely."

Letter from Birmingham Jail

April 16, 1963
Birmingham, Alabama
My Dear Fellow Clergymen:

While confined here in the Birmingham city jail, I came across your recent statement calling my present activities "unwise and untimely." Seldom do I pause to answer criticism of my work and ideas....But since I feel that you are men of genuine good will and that your criticisms are sincerely set forth, I want to try to answer your statement in what I hope will be patient and reasonable terms....

You deplore the demonstrations taking place in Birmingham. But your statement, I am sorry to say, fails to express a similar concern for the conditions that brought about the demonstrations. I am sure that none of you would want to rest content with the superficial kind of social analysis that deals merely with effects and does not grapple with underlying causes. It is unfortunate that demonstrations are taking place in Birmingham, but it is even more unfortunate that the city's white power structure left the Negro community with no alternative....

You may well ask, "Why direct action? Why sit-ins, marches, and so forth? Isn't negotiation a better path?" You are quite right in calling for negotiation. Indeed, this is the very purpose of direct action. Nonviolent direct action seeks to create such a crisis and foster such a tension that a community which has constantly refused to negotiate is forced to confront the issue. It seeks so to dramatize the issue that it can no longer be ignored. My citing the creation of tension as part of the work of the nonviolent-resister may sound rather shocking. But I must confess that I am not afraid of the word "tension." I have earnestly opposed violent tension, but there is a type of constructive, nonviolent tension which is necessary for growth. Just as Socrates felt that it was necessary to create a tension in the mind so that individuals could rise from the bondage of myths and half-truths to the unfettered realm of creative analysis and objective appraisal, so must we see the need for nonviolent gadflies to create the kind of tension in society

Elizabeth Eckford was one of nine African-American students who integrated Little Rock, Arkansas's, Central High School in 1957. Here, angry white students harass her on her first day of school.

that will help men rise from the dark depths of prejudice and racism to the majestic heights of understanding and brotherhood.

The purpose of our direct-action program is to create a situation so crisis-packed that it will inevitably open the door to negotiation. I therefore concur with you in your call for negotiation. Too long has our beloved Southland been bogged down in a tragic effort to monologue rather than dialogue....

My friends, I must say to you that we have not made a single gain in civil rights without determined legal and nonviolent pressure. Lamentably, it is an historical fact that privileged groups seldom give up their privileges voluntarily. Individuals may see the moral light and voluntarily give up their unjust posture; but, as Reinhold Neibhur has reminded us, groups tend to be more immoral than individuals.

We know through painful experience that freedom is never voluntarily given by the oppressor; it must be demanded by the oppressed. Frankly, I have yet to engage in a direct-action campaign that was "well-timed" in view of those who have not yet suffered unduly from the disease of segregation. For years now I have heard the word "Wait!" It rings in the ear of every Negro with piercing familiarity. This "Wait" has almost always meant "Never." We must come to see, with one of our distinguished jurists, that "justice too long delayed is justice denied."

We have waited for more than 340 years for our constitutional and God-given rights. The nations of Asia and Africa are moving with jetlike speed toward gaining political independence, but we still creep at horse-and-buggy pace toward gaining a cup of coffee at a lunch counter. Perhaps it is easy for those who have never felt the stinging darts of segregation to say, "Wait." But when you have seen vicious mobs lynch your mothers and fathers at will and drown your sisters and brothers at whim; when you have seen hate-filled policemen curse, kick, and even kill your black brothers and sisters; when you see the vast majority of your twenty million Negro brothers smothering in an airtight cage of poverty in the midst of an affluent society; when you suddenly find your tongue twisted and your speech stammering as you seek to explain to your six-year-old daughter why she can't go to the public amusement park that has just been advertised on television, and see tears welling up in her eyes when she is told that Funtown is closed to colored children, and see ominous clouds of inferiority beginning to form in her little mental sky, and see her beginning to distort her personality by developing an unconscious bitterness toward white people; when you have to concoct an answer for

On August 28, 1963, Dr. Martin Luther King Jr. led more than 200,000 civil rights protesters, black and white, in a March on Washington, culminating in a dramatic and emotional climax on the Mall in front of the Lincoln Memorial. It was here that King delivered his historic "I Have a Dream" speech.

a five-year old who is asking, "Daddy, why do white people treat colored people so mean?"; when you take a cross-country drive and find it necessary to sleep night after night in the uncomfortable corners of your automobile because no motel will accept you; when you are humiliated day in and day out by nagging signs reading "white" and "colored;" when your first name becomes "nigger," your middle name becomes "boy" (however old you are) and your last name becomes "John," and your wife and mother are never given the respected title "Mrs."; when you are harried by day and haunted by night by the fact that you are a Negro, living constantly at tiptoe stance, never quite knowing what to expect next, and are plagued with inner fears and outer resentments; when you are forever fighting a degenerating sense of "nobodiness"—then you will understand why we find it difficult to wait. There comes a time when the cup of endurance runs over, and men are no longer willing to be plunged into the abyss of despair. I hope, sirs, you can understand our legitimate and unavoidable impatience.

"We have a common enemy."

MALCOLM X (1925–1965)

Not all civil rights leaders believed, as did Martin Luther King Jr., that nonviolent protest was the best course of action in winning equal rights for African Americans. Northern racism had become a focal point of civil rights activists in the 1960s and some believed that the de facto segregation of the North would be harder to overcome than the Jim Crow laws of the South, since it necessitated convincing white America not just to overturn segregation laws but to share economic and social power with black America. In the mid-1960s, urban racial tensions flared and rioting broke out in more than 100 U.S. cities. Some African Americans called for a more militant style of protest than the nonviolent civil disobedience that King was preaching.

One such leader was Malcolm X. Born Malcolm Little in 1925, he survived a tragic childhood in which he witnessed numerous acts of violent racism and discrimination. He turned to crime and spent eight years in prison. While there, he undertook ambitious self-education and studied the teachings of the Nation of Islam, sometimes called Black Muslims. After his release, he became a minister for the group.

Malcolm X preached that African Americans need to reclaim their heritage, culture, and communities for themselves by separating from the white race. (He had dropped his own last name because he considered it to be a slave name.) In contrast to the teachings of Dr. King, Malcolm X called upon African Americans to fight back in self-defense against their white oppressors. Malcolm X's radical statements frightened many whites and moderate blacks, and attracted major media attention.

In 1964, Malcolm X broke with the Black Muslims and went on a religious pilgrimage to Mecca, where his experiences worshipping with ethnically diverse Muslims helped to change his views on relationships between the races. After his return to the United States, he took up a new campaign, which emphasized the power of the ballot in achieving racial justice. Shortly thereafter, on February 21, 1965, Malcolm X was shot and killed while delivering an address in a Harlem ballroom.

This excerpt is taken from a speech he delivered in November 1963 while still a member of the Black Muslims. In it, he criticizes protesters who, like Martin Luther King Jr., believed in a "bloodless revolution."

Message to the Grass Roots

We want to have just an off-the-cuff chat between you and me, us. We want to talk right down to earth in a language that everybody here can easily understand. We all agree tonight, all of the speakers have agreed, that America has a very serious problem. Not only does America have a very serious problem, but our people have a very serious problem. The only reason she [America] has a problem is she doesn't want us here. And every time you look at yourself, be you black, brown, red or yellow, a so-called Negro, you represent a person who poses such a serious problem for America because you're not wanted. Once you face this as a fact, then you can start plotting a course that will make you appear more intelligent, instead of unintelligent.

What you and I need to do is learn to forget our differences. When we come together, we don't come together as Baptists or Methodists. You don't catch hell because you're a Baptist, and you don't catch hell because you're a Methodist. You don't catch hell because you're a Methodist or Baptist, you don't catch hell because you're a Democrat or Republican, you don't catch hell because you're a Mason or an Elk, and you sure don't catch hell because you're an American; because if you were an American, you wouldn't catch hell. You catch hell because you're a black man. You catch hell, all of us catch hell, for the same reason.

So we're all black people, so-called Negroes, second-class citizens, ex-slaves. You're nothing but an ex-slave. You don't like to be told that. But what else are you? You are ex-slaves. You didn't come here on the "Mayflower." You came here on a slave ship. In chains, like a horse, or a cow, or a chicken. And you were brought here by the people who came

At the 1968 Olympics in Mexico City, American medalist sprinters Tommie Smith and John Carlos chose to protest the treatment of black people in the United States. While the "Star-Spangled Banner" played at their medal ceremony, the two defiantly refused to look at the flag and raised their dark-gloved fists, a well-known symbol of Black Power.

here on the "Mayflower," you were brought here by the so-called Pilgrims, or Founding Fathers. They were the ones who brought you here.

We have a common enemy. We have this in common: We have a common oppressor, a common exploiter, and a common discriminator. But once we all realize that we have a common enemy, then we unite—on the basis of what we have in common. And what we have foremost in common is that enemy—the white man. He's an enemy to all of us. I know some of you all think that some of them aren't enemies. Time will tell....

I would like to make a few comments concerning the difference between the black revolution and the Negro revolution. Are they both the same? And if they're not, what is the difference? What is the difference between a black revolution and a Negro revolution? First, what is a revolution? Sometimes, I'm inclined to believe that many of our people are using this word "revolution" loosely, without taking careful consideration of what this word actually means, and what its historic characteristics are. When you study the historic nature of revolutions, the motive of a revolution, the objective of a revolution, the result of a revolution, and the methods used in a revolution, you may change words. You may devise another program, you may change your goal and you may change your mind.

Look at the American Revolution in 1776. That revolution was for what? For land. Why did they want land? Independence. How was it carried out? Bloodshed. Number one, it was based on land, the basis of independence. And the only way they could get it was bloodshed. The French Revolution—what was it based on? The landless against the landlord. What was it for? Land. How did they get it? Bloodshed. Was no love lost, was no compromise, was no negotiation. I'm telling you—you don't know what a revolution is. Because when you find out what it is, you'll get back in the alley, you'll get out of the way....

So I cite these various revolutions, brothers and sisters, to show you that you don't have a peaceful revolution. You don't have a turn-the-other-cheek revolution. There's no such thing as a nonviolent revolution. The only kind of revolution that is nonviolent is the Negro revolution. The only revolution in which the goal is loving your enemy is the Negro revolution. It's the only revolution in which the goal is a desegregated lunch counter, a desegregated theater, a desegregated park, and a deseg-regated public toilet: you can sit down next to white folks—on the toilet.

That's no revolution. Revolution is based on land. Land is the basis of all independence. And land is the basis of freedom, justice, and equality. . . .

Revolution is bloody, revolution is hostile, revolution knows no compromise, revolution overturns and destroys everything that gets in its way. And you, sitting around here like a knot on the wall, saying, "I'm going to love these folks no matter how much they hate me." No, you need a revolution. Whoever heard of a revolution where they lock arms . . . singing "We Shall Overcome"? You don't do that in a revolution. You don't do any singing, you're too busy swinging. It's based on land. A revolutionary wants land so he can set up his own nation, an independent nation. These Negroes aren't asking for any nation—they're trying to crawl back on the plantation.

JUDY BRADY (1937–)

Political activist and author Judy Brady was born in San Francisco in 1937. She married, had two children, and awoke to the emerging women's liberation movement in the late 1960s. She became a passionate feminist and social justice activist. In the 1990s, after a bout with breast cancer, Brady became a cancer research advocate, emphasizing the link between health and environmental issues.

After winning the right to vote in 1920, the women's movement in the United States slowed dramatically. By the 1950s, many women's rights activists believed that progress had stopped altogether. Eighteen million women worked outside the home in 1950, making up less than one-third of the total labor force. Many of these women worked out of economic necessity or to "add a little" to their husband's income; fewer women worked to fulfill intellectual or professional aspirations. Many jobs were closed to women, and newspaper employment advertisements specifying "men only" were common. The professional fields that welcomed women—social work, nursing, education—generally paid very little.

A variety of events triggered the modern women's rights movement. The 1963 publication of Betty Friedan's book The Feminine Mystique *brought sighs of understanding from women across the country. Involvement in both the civil rights and anti–Vietnam War movements inspired some women to voice their anger at the sexism and gender discrimination that pervaded much of American society.*

"I, too, would like to have a wife"

Throughout the 1960s and 1970s, the women's movement made great strides. The 1964 Civil Rights Act added gender to federal anti-discrimination policies. In 1966, Betty Friedan formed the National Organization for Women (NOW) to advocate for women's rights and issues, lobbying for changes such as more childcare facilities and higher education opportunities for women.

Differences over policy divided American feminists. Some believed in radical changes; others supported more moderate means and ideas. In 1972, Congress passed an Equal Rights Amendment to the Constitution, guaranteeing equality under the law regardless of gender. Though the amendment failed to be ratified by the required three-fourths of states, the women's movement had succeeded in highlighting the unfairness of women's second-class status in American society, and in opening up new educational, economic, and political opportunities for women.

In 1972, journalist Gloria Steinem founded Ms. *magazine, a feminist alternative to the mainstream media. The following tongue-in-cheek essay appeared in the magazine's April 1972 issue. In it, Judy Brady uses humor and sarcasm to make the point that men benefited unfairly from women's supporting role.*

Why I Want a Wife

I belong to that classification of people known as wives. I am A Wife. And, not altogether incidentally, I am a mother.

Not too long ago a male friend of mine appeared on the scene fresh from a recent divorce. He had one child, who is, of course, with his ex-wife. He is obviously looking for another wife. As I thought about him while I was ironing one evening, it suddenly occurred to me that I, too, would like to have a wife. Why do I want a wife?

I would like to go back to school so that I can become economically independent, support myself, and, if need be, support those dependent upon me. I want a wife who will work and send me to school. And while I am going to school I want a wife to take care of my children. I want a wife to keep track of the children's doctor and dentist appointments. And to keep track of mine, too. I want a wife to make sure my children eat properly and are kept clean. I want a wife who will wash the children's clothes and keep them mended. I want a wife who is a good nurturant, attendant to my children, who arranges for their schooling, makes sure that they have an adequate social life with their peers, takes them to the park, the zoo, etc. I want a wife who takes care of the children when they are sick, a wife who arranges to be around when the children need special care, because, of course, I cannot miss classes at school. My wife must arrange to lose time at work, and not lose the job. It may mean a small cut in my wife's income from time to time, but I guess I can tolerate that. Needless to say, my wife will arrange and pay for the care of the children while my wife is working.

I want a wife who will take care of *my* physical needs. I want a wife who will keep my house clean. A wife who will pick up after me. I want a wife who will keep my clothes clean, ironed, mended, replaced when need be, and who will see to it that my personal things are kept in their proper place so that I can find what I need the minute I need it. I want a wife who cooks the meals, a wife who is a *good* cook. I want a wife who will plan the menus, do the necessary grocery shopping, prepare the meals, serve them pleasantly, and then do the cleaning up while I do my studying. I want a wife who will care for me when I am sick and sympathize with my pain and loss of time from school. I want a wife to go along when our family takes a vacation so that someone can continue to care for me when I need a rest and change of scene.

I want a wife who will not bother me with rambling complaints about a wife's duties. But I want a wife who will listen to me when I feel the need to explain a rather difficult point I have come across in my course of studies. And I want a wife who will type my papers for me when I have written them.

I want a wife who will take care of the details of my social life. When my wife and I are invited out by my friends, I want a wife who will take care of the babysitting arrangements. When I meet people at school that I like and want to entertain, I want a wife who will have the house clean, will prepare a special meal, serve it to me and my friends, and not interrupt when I talk about things that interest me and my friends. I want a wife who will have arranged that the children are fed and ready for bed before my guests arrive so that the children do not bother us.

And I want a wife who knows that sometimes I need a night out by myself....

If, by chance, I find another person more suitable as a wife than the wife I already have, I want the liberty to replace my present wife with another one. Naturally, I will expect a fresh, new life; my wife will take the children and be solely responsible for them so that I am left free.

When I am through with school and have a job, I want my wife to quit working and remain at home so that my wife can more fully and completely take care of a wife's duties.

My God, who *wouldn't* want a wife?

Three thousand marchers paraded down Washington, D.C.'s, Pennsylvania Avenue on August 26, 1977, to mark the 57th anniversary of the passage of the Nineteenth Amendment. The Equal Rights Amendment, written on the large banner these women carry, was passed by Congress but never ratified by the states.

"We are home.
This is home."

SANDRA CISNEROS (1954–)

*Sandra Cisneros grew up in Chicago in the 1950s
and 1960s, the only daughter of a Mexican-
American mother and a Mexican father. She is a
poet, short story writer, novelist, and teacher of creative writing. Her Mexican roots are always evident in her writing, as is her struggle to locate her
own identity between two cultures.*

*Mexican Americans were at the forefront of the rise in ethnic con-
sciousness in the 1960s and 1970s. At this time, people of Mexican
descent made up the largest percentage of the U.S. Latino population,
followed by Puerto Ricans and Cubans.*

*The geography of Mexican America is a complex one. Some
Mexicans became Americans when the southwestern territories they
were living on were absorbed by the United States in the mid-1800s.
Others arrived legally as part of government attempts, from the early
1940s through the mid-1960s, to import temporary farm workers
(known as* braceros) *to help develop the agricultural economy of
California and the Southwest. Many other Mexicans arrived illegally,
escaping their native country's weak economy.*

*Mexican Americans had not traditionally been active in the political
process and thus had little voice in advocating for their economic well-
being. Many were migrant farm workers who often spoke little English
and could not vote because of their illegal-resident status. On average,
Mexican-American families made one-third less than did the general
population, yet their labor contributed greatly to the tremendous growth
of the agricultural industry of the West.*

*After World War II, some Mexican Americans, many of them veter-
ans, began to form political associations and move into the middle
class. In 1968, they helped win passage of the federal Bilingual
Education Act. Some activists adopted more militant political stands
in the 1960s, uniting under the slogan "brown power" and advocating
increased public services and better education for Latinos. Throughout
the 1960s, labor leader Cesar Chavez organized numerous migrant farm
workers into a union, the National Farm Workers Association, which borrowed many of the nonviolent tactics of the black civil rights movement
to agitate for a living wage for agricultural laborers.*

*Though Sandra Cisneros grew up far from the fields of migrant
pickers, she endured much of the cultural alienation common among
recently immigrated groups. The following tale is from her novel*
The House on Mango Street, *a collection of coming-of-age stories about*

a young girl growing up in a Latino section of Chicago. Throughout the book, Cisneros uses slice-of-life vignettes about growing up between two cultures to make larger points about the universal themes of identity and community.

The House on Mango Street
No Speak English

Mamacita is the big mama of the man across the street, third-floor front. Rachel says her name ought to be *Mamasota,* but I think that's mean.

The man saved his money to bring her here. He saved and saved because she was alone with the baby boy in that country. He worked two jobs. He came home late and left early. Every day.

Then one day *Mamacita* and the baby boy arrived in a yellow taxi. The taxi door opened like a waiter's arm. Out stepped a tiny pink shoe, a foot soft as a rabbit's ear, then the thick ankle, a flutter of hips, fuschia roses and green perfume. The man had to pull her, the taxicab driver had to push. Push, pull. Push, pull. Poof!

All at once she bloomed. Huge, enormous, beautiful to look at, from the salmon-pink feather on the tip of her hat down to the little rosebuds of her toes. I couldn't take my eyes off her tiny shoes.

Up, up, up the stairs she went with the baby boy in a blue blanket, the man carrying her suitcases, her lavender hatboxes, a dozen boxes of satin high heels. Then we didn't see her.

Somebody said because she's too fat, somebody because of the three flights of stairs, but I believe she doesn't come out because she is afraid to speak English, and maybe this is so since she only knows eight words. She knows to say: *He not here* for when the landlord comes, *No speak English* if anybody else comes, and *Holy smokes.* I don't know where she learned this, but I heard her say it one time and it surprised me.

My father says when he came to this country he ate hamandeggs for three months. Breakfast, lunch and dinner. Hamandeggs. That was the only word he knew. He doesn't eat hamandeggs anymore.

Whatever her reasons, whether she is fat, or can't climb the stairs, or is afraid of English, she won't come down. She sits all day by the window

Broadsides and posters such as this one encouraged people to join labor organizer Cesar Chavez and his "la causa": demanding better pay and working conditions for the many Mexican Americans who worked as migrant pickers and farmers in the growing fields of California.

Betty Friedan and *The Feminine Mystique*

The 1963 publication of a book about women's status in American society contributed a new phrase to the English language. *The Feminine Mystique,* the title of feminist writer Betty Friedan's study of middle-class American women at mid-century, has become synonymous with the constraints of "domestic captivity."

Friedan, a freelance writer who had contributed articles to women's magazines, began researching the book after attending her fifteenth college reunion. There, she wrote, all the women seemed to have everything that society told them should make them happy and fulfilled: loving husbands, healthy children, and pretty homes in the suburbs. But most of the women that Friedan encountered in her years of research seemed deeply unhappy, searching for something else beyond their roles as wives and mothers. Freidan's book sparked a major nationwide dialogue and led to a renewed drive by feminist activists for full intellectual and economic opportunities for all Americans, regardless of gender.

The problem lay buried, unspoken, for many years in the minds of American women. It was a strange stirring, a sense of dissatisfaction, a yearning that women suffered in the middle of the twentieth century in the United States. Each suburban wife struggled with it alone. As she made the beds, shopped for groceries, matched slipcover material, ate peanut butter sandwiches with her children, chauffeured Cub Scouts and Brownies, lay beside her husband at night—she was afraid to even ask of herself the silent question—"Is this all?"

and plays the Spanish radio show and sings all the homesick songs about her country in a voice that sounds like a seagull.

Home. Home. Home is a house in a photograph, a pink house, pink as hollyhocks with lots of startled light. The man paints the walls of the apartment pink, but it's not the same you know. She still sighs for her pink house, and then I think she cries. I would.

Sometimes the man gets disgusted. He starts screaming and you can hear it all the way down the street.

Ay, she says, she is sad.

Oh, he says. Not again.

¿Cuando, cuando, cuando? she asks.

¡Ay, caray! We *are* home. This *is* home. Here I am and here I stay. Speak English. Speak English. Christ!

¡Ay! Mamacita, who does not belong, every once in a while lets out a cry, hysterical, high, as if he had torn the only skinny thread that kept her alive, the only road out to that country.

And then to break her heart forever, the baby boy, who has begun to talk, starts to sing the Pepsi commercial he heard on T.V.

No speak English, she says to the child who is singing in the language that sounds like tin. No speak English, no speak English, and bubbles into tears. No, no, no, as if she can't believe her ears.

MARY CROW DOG (1953–)

Mary Brave Bird, a Lakota Sioux Indian, was born into deep poverty on a South Dakota reservation, raised in a one-room cabin with no running water or electricity, and sent to a missionary boarding school meant to rid her of her Indian ways. Instead, she joined the American Indian Movement (AIM), becoming, in the 1970s, an Indian rights activist. She suffered through years of harassment by government officials, the deaths of several activist friends, and the imprisonment of her husband, medicine man Leonard Crow Dog. Her autobiography Lakota Woman, *published in 1990, was a national bestseller and is considered to be a classic work of modern American Indian literature.*

More than a century of broken promises and flip-flopping federal policy had left Native Americans isolated, poor, and ravaged by unemployment and alcoholism. By the 1960s, close to 40 percent of American Indians lived below the poverty line, many on reservations with few job opportunities. Though Presidents Kennedy and Johnson had encouraged business development on Indian land as well as greater congressional funding for Indian welfare, it was the rise of a "red power" movement in the late 1960s and early 1970s that brought hope to many.

Borrowing from the more militant leaders of the African-American civil rights movement, the American Indian Movement was formed in 1968. Over the next few years, AIM members, and other groups, were involved in a series of dramatic events meant to publicize Indians' plight. In 1969, Indian activists took over Alcatraz Island in San Francisco Bay, the former site of a federal prison. The stand-off lasted over a year and a half. In 1972, several thousand American Indians

"a new spring for the Sioux Nation"

traveled in a caravan to the Bureau of Indian Affairs (BIA) headquarters in Washington, D.C., on what was called "The Trail of Broken Treaties" to demand that the federal government address Indian concerns.

The most violent confrontation came in 1973 when AIM members occupied the South Dakota village of Wounded Knee—the historic site of a terrible massacre of Indians by federal troops eighty-two years earlier. Here, protesters took hostages and barricaded themselves inside the compound, while federal troops surrounded the occupied buildings. The siege lasted ten weeks. One of the protesters was killed in a gunfight between Indians and federal officials. Mary Crow Dog gave birth to her first child during the siege at Wounded Knee. Leonard Crow Dog, who would later become Mary's husband, was the group's spiritual leader.

The following passage from Crow Dog's autobiography describes how Leonard brought back the sacred Ghost Dance ritual as a way to inspire his fellow protesters. During battles in the late 1800s between plains Indians and federal troops, the Teton Sioux of South Dakota had revived the Ghost Dances, which they believed would rid the land of the white people and return the buffalo to the Indians. In 1890, fearing the dancers at Wounded Knee, federal troops intervened to stop the ritual. More than 200 Indian men, women, and children were slaughtered in the snow.

Here, Crow Dog describes the haunting memory of the massacre and the importance of the site in Sioux history.

Lakota Woman

The most memorable thing Leonard did was to bring back the Ghost Dance. I think he did this not only for us, the living, but also for the spirits of those lying in the mass grave. As I mentioned before, the Ghost Dance tradition has always been strong in our family. Leonard's great-grandfather, the first of the Crow Dogs, was not only one of the earliest Ghost Dancers among the Sioux, but also one of their foremost leaders....

On the evening before the dance, Leonard addressed the people. We got it down on tape. This is what he said: "Tomorrow we'll ghost-dance. You're not goin' to say 'I got to rest.' There'll be no rest, no intermission, no coffee break. We're not going to drink water. So that'll take place whether it snows or rains. We're goin' to unite together, no matter what tribe we are. We won't say, 'I'm a different tribe,' or, 'He's a black man, he's a white man.' We're not goin' to have this white man's attitude.

"If one of us gets into the power, the spiritual power, we'll hold hands. If he falls down, let him. If he goes into convulsions, don't be scared. We won't call a medic. The spirit's goin' to be the doctor.

"There's a song I'll sing, a song from the spirit. Mother Earth is the drum and the clouds will be the visions. The visions will go into your mind. In your mind you might see your brothers, your relations that have been killed by the white man.

"We'll elevate ourselves from this world to another world where you can see. It's here that we're goin' to find out. The Ghost Dance spirit will be in us. The peace pipe is goin' to be there. The fire is goin' to be there; tobacco is goin' to be there. We'll start physically and go on spiritually and then you'll get into the power. We're goin' to start right here, at Wounded Knee, in 1973.

American Indians protesting the U.S. government's indifference toward Indian peoples' grievances seized the South Dakota hamlet of Wounded Knee in 1973. Here, Indians stand guard outside Wounded Knee's Sacred Heart Catholic Church.

"Everybody's heard about the Ghost Dance but nobody'd ever seen it. The United States prohibited it. There was to be no Ghost Dance, no Sun Dance, no Indian religion.

"But the hoop has not been broken. So decide tonight—for the whole unborn generations. If you want to dance with me tomorrow, you be ready!"

For the dance, Leonard had selected a hollow between hills where the feds could neither see the dancers nor shoot at them. And he had made this place *wakan*—sacred. And so the Sioux were ghost-dancing again, for the first time in over eighty years. They danced for four days starting at five o'clock in the morning, dancing from darkness into the night. And that dance took place around the first day of spring, a new spring for the Sioux Nation. Like the Ghost Dancers of old, many men danced barefoot in the snow around a cedar tree. Leonard had about thirty or forty dancers. Not everybody who wanted to was able to dance. Nurses and medics had to remain at their stations. Life had to be sustained and the defenses maintained.

On the first day, one of the women fell down in the snow and was helped back to what used to be the museum. They smoked the pipe and Leonard cedared her, fanning her with his eagle wing. Slowly she came to. The woman said she could not verbalize what had happened to her, but that she was in the power and had received a vision. It took her a long time to say that much because she was in a trance with only the whites of her eyes showing. On one of the four days a snowstorm inter-rupted the dancing, but it could not stop it....

The Oglala holy man Black Elk, who died some fifty years ago, in his book said this about [the 1890 massacre at] Wounded Knee: "I can still see the butchered women and children lying heaped and scattered all along the crooked gulch as plain as when I saw them with eyes still young. And I can see something else died there in the bloody mud, and was buried in the blizzard. A people's dream died there. It was a beautiful dream.

"And I, to whom so great a vision was given in my youth–you see me now a pitiful old man who has done nothing, for the nation's hoop is broken and scattered. There is no center any longer, and the sacred tree is dead."

In that ravine, at Cankpe Opi, we gathered up the broken pieces of the sacred hoop and put them together again. All who were at Wounded Knee ... we mended the nation's hoop. The sacred tree *is not dead!*

"The answer is blowin' in the wind."

BOB DYLAN (1941–)

Singer and songwriter Bob Dylan has been called the poet of his generation, speaking to and for those Americans who came of age in the heady, tumultuous years of the 1960s. Born Robert Zimmerman in Hibbing, Minnesota, Dylan's folk music helped spark a nation's social conscience. Whether sung by folk artists like Joan Baez or Peter, Paul, and Mary or delivered in his own inimitable voice, Dylan's music is internationally synonymous with the turbulent student movement, counterculture, and social protests of the 1960s.

"We are the people of this generation, bred in at least modest comfort, housed now in universities, looking uncomfortably to the world we inherit," began the manifesto of the Students for a Democratic Society (SDS)—a radical association of American university students formed in Port Huron, Michigan, in 1962. SDS members and others like them, many of whom had participated in the civil rights movement in the South and had seen the racial and socio-economic injustices there, believed in "grassroots democracy" for social change. They advocated the elimination of the bureaucracy and the ending of the Cold War and the arms race, and they encouraged individual participation in politics. They also resented what they saw as the impersonalization of universities and corporations, and they abhorred the persistence of racism and poverty and the concept of "affluence" as the organizing principle of American society. After 1965, such protesters would become the core of the anti–Vietnam War movement in America.

Throughout the 1960s, Bob Dylan's protest songs inspired activists of all stripes, challenging the status quo and appealing to the idealism of the baby boom generation now beginning to come of age. Ironically, many of the loudest protesters were young, upper-middle-class whites—those who had benefitted the most from the system they were revolting against. Regardless, the music of Dylan gave voice to the beliefs of hundreds of thousands—that the violence, poverty, and inequality present in society needed to be eliminated.

Dylan considered "Blowin' in the Wind" a song in the tradition of the spiritual. The litany of rhetorical questions, left unanswered throughout the verses, touched upon the deepest, most troubling aspects of American society. Throughout the 1960s, the answers to these questions seemed to Dylan, and to many others, to be just out of reach.

Blowin' in the Wind

How many roads must a man walk down
Before you call him a man?
Yes, and how many seas must a white dove sail
Before she sleeps in the sand?
Yes, and how many times must the cannon balls fly
Before they're forever banned?
The answer, my friend, is blowin' in the wind,
The answer is blowin' in the wind.

How many times must a man look up
Before he can see the sky?
Yes, and how many ears must one man have
Before he can hear people cry?
Yes, and how many deaths will it take till he knows
That too many people have died?
The answer, my friend, is blowin' in the wind,
The answer is blowin' in the wind.

How many years can a mountain exist
Before it's washed to the sea?
Yes, and how many years can some people exist
Before they're allowed to be free?
Yes, and how many times can a man turn his head,
Pretending he just doesn't see?
The answer, my friend, is blowin' in the wind,
The answer is blowin' in the wind.

The Vietnam Years

Since the late 1800s, France had controlled the area of Southeast Asia called Indochina—Vietnam, Laos, and Cambodia—and had profited from the region's rice and rubber plantations. In 1940, Japan took control of Vietnam. A year later, Ho Chi Minh, a Vietnamese communist exiled by the French, returned and consolidated communists and other nationalists to form a pro-independence movement called the Vietminh.

After the Allied victory over Japan in 1945, the French returned to reclaim Vietnam, and succeeded in driving the Vietminh from the southern half of the country. For the next eight years, as the Cold War intensified around the globe, French troops fought communist guerrillas in Vietnam. By 1950, the United States, fearful that all of Southeast Asia might fall to the communists, had begun sending economic aid to the French. However, in 1954, the Vietminh decisively defeated the French. At peace talks in Geneva, Vietnam was divided in half at the seventeenth parallel, leaving the North under Ho Chi Minh's control and the South under a government of anticommunist nationalists. Countrywide elections were scheduled for 1956.

Those elections never occurred. By 1957, a communist opposition group in the South, known as the Vietcong, was attacking South Vietnamese forces. In 1959, Ho's North Vietnamese Army began supplying the Vietcong with weapons and munitions. U.S. military advisers—notably the famous Green Berets—had been training the South Vietnamese in counterinsurgency tactics; U.S. president John Kennedy increased their numbers. Just weeks before Kennedy's assassination in 1963, a U.S.-supported South Vietnamese coup overthrew the corrupt and ineffective leader Ngo Dinh Diem. When Lyndon Johnson abruptly became president, he inherited a decades-old conflict and a South Vietnamese government in chaos. His decision to escalate U.S. involvement in Vietnam by sending ground troops to fight there began the longest war in American history—and the only one it ever lost.

During the Vietnam War years, American society endured a painful and bitter coming-of-age as growing antiwar protests bred divisiveness and violence. As the years went on, official reports of U.S. successes in Vietnam seemed irreconcilable alongside the growing number of dead American soldiers. A "credibility gap" developed between the nation's people and its leaders.

Tales of life in combat began to emerge even as the war was still under way. Some young writers, such as novelist Tim O'Brien, came home from war so changed by what they had seen and undergone that the Vietnam War and its aftermath became the central and recurring subject of their writing. Poetry by both veterans and antiwar protesters served as social commentary and tribute.

Featured Authors

David Halberstam
Tim O'Brien
Denise Levertov
Philip Roth
Robert Olen Butler

DAVID HALBERSTAM (1934–)

David Halberstam has chronicled American life in fiction and nonfiction for more than three decades. He spent several years in Vietnam, reporting on the undeclared war there and the experience of American troops in combat. In 1967, he published one very hot day, *his novel about Vietnam.*

> *"war was not a game"*

Combat in Vietnam was different from that in previous wars. In addition to massive aerial bombing, U.S. military leaders pursued a strategy of "attrition"—attempting to wear down the enemy by killing as many of them as possible. The guerrilla warfare style used by the North Vietnamese Army (NVA) and the Vietcong (VC) meant they were often hidden in the jungles, attacking with little warning. Rather than set-piece battles for control of certain territory, much of the Vietnam War was fought on "patrol." Platoons of U.S. and South Vietnamese soldiers were sent out to search the countryside, seeking out enemy soldiers. Avoiding landmines and booby traps, which could kill or maim instantaneously, required intense and constant concentration. The oppressive heat, sun, and moisture often resulted in illness and infection. Long periods of fear, tedium, and boredom, punctuated by brief, terrifying encounters with the enemy, marked many a soldier's experience in Vietnam.

In the following excerpt from one very hot day, a U.S. Army lieutenant, supported by South Vietnamese soldiers, encounters the enemy while on patrol in the Vietnamese jungle. He is frustrated and frightened because he cannot see who he is fighting. In addition to their guerrilla tactics, the NVA and VC had constructed elaborate underground tunnel systems and often fought from hidden positions, making them a wily and demanding foe.

one very hot day
Chapter 4

At eleven thirty they were moving haphazardly along the canal, one of those peaceful moments when earlier fears were forgotten, and when it was almost as if they were in some sort of trance from the heat and the monotony, when they were fired on. Three quick shots came from the left, from the other side of the canal. They appeared to hit short, and they landed near the center of the column, close to where Lieutenant Anderson was. He wheeled toward the bullets, spoke quickly in

Vietnamese, taking three men with him and sending a fourth back to tell Thuong what he was doing—not to send anyone unless it was clearly a real fight, and he could hear automatic weapon fire; they were taking no automatic weapons, Anderson said.

He sensed that it was not an ambush; you trip an ambush with a full volley of automatic weapons fire—to get the maximum surprise firepower and effect, you don't trip it with a few shots from an M-1 rifle; the fact that the sniper had fired so quickly, Anderson thought, meant that there was probably one man alone who wanted to seem like more than one man. But damn it, he thought, you never really know here, you tried to think like them and you were bound to get in trouble: you thought of the unique and they did the obvious; you thought of the obvious and they did the unique. He brought his squad to the canal bank, and two more bullets snapped near them. *Ping, snap. Ping, snap....*

Anderson waited for a third burst of fire, and when it came, closer this time, he moved quickly to the canal bank and into the water, sinking more than waist high immediately. As he moved he kept looking for the sniper's hiding place; so far he could not tell where the bullets were coming from. He sensed the general direction of the sniper, but couldn't judge exactly where the sniper was. He was all alone in the water, moving slowly, his legs struggling with the weight of the water and the suck of the filth below him. He knew he was a good target, and he was frightened; he moved slowly, as in a slow-motion dream; he remembered one of the things they had said of the VC in their last briefings. ("The VC infantryman is tenacious and will die in position and believes fanatically in the ideology because he has been brainwashed all his life since infancy, but he is a bad shot, yes gentlemen, he is not a good shot, and the snipers are generally weak, because you see, men, they need glasses. The enemy doesn't get to have glasses. The Communists can't afford 'em, and our medical people have checked them out and have come up with studies which show that because of their diet, because their diet doesn't have as much meat and protein, their eyes are weak, and they don't get glasses, so they are below us as snipers. Brave, gentlemen, but nearsighted, remember that.") He remembered it and hoped it was true.

Ahead of him all he could see was brush and trees. Remember, he thought, he may be up in the trees: it was another one of the briefings: "Vietcong often take up positions in the tops of trees, just like the Japanese did, and you must smell them out. Remember what I'm telling you, it may save you your life. You will be walking along in the jungle, hot and dirty. And you hear a sniper, and because your big fat feet are on the ground, you think that the sniper's feet are on the ground too. But you're wrong, he's sitting up there in the third story, measuring the size of your head, counting your squad, and ready to ruin your headgear. They like the jungle, and what's in the jungle? Trees. Lots of 'em. Remember it, gentlemen, smell them in the trees."

Anderson had left the briefing thinking all Vietcong were in the trees; even now as he walked, he kept his eyes on the trees more than on the ground....

He moved past the canal and into the dense brush, found what looked like a good position, and fired off a clip to the left, right in front of him, most of the clip to his right, and finally, for the benefit of his instructors, for Fort Benning, the last one into a tree nest. Nothing happened and he reloaded and moved forward. Then there were two little pings, still in front of him, though sounding, perhaps it was his imagination, further away. But the enemy was there, and so, encouraged, he began to move forward again, his senses telling him that the sniper was slightly to his right. He was alone, he had kept the others back at the canal bank; they would be no help here, for they would surely follow right behind him and he would be in more trouble for the noise they would make and for being accidentally shot from behind, that great danger of single-file patrolling; yet going like this, he sensed how terribly alone he was—he was in *their* jungle, they could see him, know of him, they could see things he couldn't see, there might be more of them. He moved forward a few yards, going slowly both by choice and necessity in the heavy brush.... Suddenly there was a ping, landing near him, the sound closer, but coming from the left, from about eleven o'clock. The shot sounded closer, and more excited and frightened now, he moved quickly in that direction, feeling the brush scratch his arms and his face (he couldn't use his hands to protect his face, they were on his weapon); now he squeezed off another clip, two quick ones, three quick ones, the last three spaced out, a musical scale really.

There was no answer and he pressed forward, the jungle still around both of them. Then he was answered again, the mating call, two little pings, the VC's weapon had a lower pitch than his, and the sound—and this made him angry—was coming from the right, near one o'clock, where he had just been. He cursed under his breath, and moved quickly to his right, realizing even as he pushed ahead that he was doing a foolish thing, that he was violating all the rules he had been taught, that he was offering an American officer to a trap that he might be taken prisoner; at Benning they had warned against that, don't be captured, there was too much psychological advantage the VC could take, showing him around in the villages.

Soldiers on patrol in the dense jungle foliage of South Vietnam.

Still he pressed on, angry, frustrated. He thought the VC was mocking him, playing a game with him; you didn't do that in a war, war was not a game, you didn't screw around, play jokes with rifles. He fired off another clip toward one o'clock and moved there. He continued to plunge forward. But there was nothing there. Then there was a ping from the left, back at ten o'clock. He moved a little to his left, but he didn't fire. A few minutes passed while the Vietcong finally grasped his message, that Anderson for the time being was not going to fire. Finally there was a ping, from eight o'clock this time; the sniper was behind him. But he couldn't fire in that direction or he might hit one of his own men. He waited and waited and then charged toward six o'clock, ready to fire at point-blank range. But nothing happened.

Suddenly, there was a ping ping from eleven o'clock. He turned and fired angrily, shouting: "Come out, you sonofabitch, come on, come on out. Fight. Come on, I'm waiting. I'm here."

He waited but nothing happened. Did he hear a giggle? He made the same challenge in Vietnamese, but it sounded foolish to him. No giggle this time. There were no more shots. He checked his watch. He had been gone ten minutes. He waited two minutes more, and nothing happened. Still angry, he went back to the canal bank, and collected the other Viets.

"Sometimes," said one of them, "Vietcong are like the pederasts. Don't feel so badly. It is their game."

Anderson nodded grimly, and they crossed the canal in single file; Anderson much taller than the Viets, his head barely above water, was amazed; just as much of them showed above water as of him.

"The war is good for the leeches in the canal," said one of the Viets, "that is all. A full meal for them today."

He nodded, and then moved back to the main path. At least they would be able to move quickly, while catching up with the rest of the unit.

"He just didn't know if the war was right or wrong."

TIM O'BRIEN (1946–)

As a political science student at Macalester College in Minnesota in the 1960s, Tim O'Brien protested the war in Vietnam. He planned to join the U.S. State Department, help stop the bombings, and advocate policies of diplomacy with the Vietnamese. Instead, he was drafted in 1968. Even though O'Brien opposed the war, he feared the disapproval of his family (his father was a World War II veteran) and the anger of his country and reluctantly reported for duty with the U.S.

Army. During his tour as an infantry foot soldier in Vietnam, O'Brien sent home personal accounts of the war that were published in Minnesota newspapers. When he returned to the United States, he expanded those reports into a book, If I Die in a Combat Zone, Box Me Up and Ship Me Home, *published in 1973. In 1978, Tim O'Brien won the National Book Award for* Going after Cacciato, *a novel about a soldier who decides to put down his gun and walk to Paris for the 1968 peace talks.*

Initially, most Americans had supported President Lyndon Johnson's decision to escalate U.S. involvement in Vietnam to contain communism. But by 1966, draft calls had increased from less than 10,000 to more than 30,000 a month. Disproportionate numbers of African Americans and poor whites were being drafted, often because they were unable to obtain the student deferments that middle- and upper-middle-class white men received. One popular Vietnam War–era song chorused "It ain't me, it ain't me—I ain't no senator's son. It ain't me, it ain't me—I ain't no fortunate one," a thinly veiled reference to the fact that the American boys being sent to do the fighting were predominantly from the working class.

Many of those serving had mixed feelings about the United States' decision to involve itself in another country's civil war. Some believed that their country had a moral imperative, as well as a grave national security interest, in making sure that South Vietnam did not fall to communism. Others felt from the start, or began to believe more and more as the war dragged on, that the Vietnamese themselves needed to decide their own fate and fight their own war. In-fighting and corruption among the South Vietnamese only served to deepen feelings of anger and resentment among American troops.

In the following excerpt, Lieutenant Paul Berlin, sent to find and retrieve an American soldier (Cacciato) gone AWOL, describes his ambivalence about the conflict and his sense that most American soldiers probably had a great deal in common with the Vietnamese people, whose lands and homes were being destroyed by the war. Wrestling with his conscience, Berlin speculates about what it might be like to return after the war is over.

Going after Cacciato
Chapter 39, The Things They Didn't Know

Not knowing the language, they [the U.S. soldiers] did not know the people [the Vietnamese]. They did not know what the people loved or respected or feared or hated. They did not recognize hostility unless it was patent, unless it came in a form other than language; the complexities of tone and tongue were beyond them. Dinkese, Stink Harris called it: monkey chatter, bird talk. Not knowing the language, the men did not know whom to trust. Trust was lethal. They did not know false smiles from true smiles, or if in Quang Ngai a smile had the same meaning it had in the States. "Maybe the dinks got things mixed up," Eddie once said, after the time a friendly-looking farmer bowed and smiled and pointed them into a minefield. "Know what I mean? Maybe ... well, maybe the gooks cry when they're happy and smile when they're sad. Who the hell knows? Maybe when you smile over here it means you're ready to cut the other guy's throat. I mean, hey ... didn't they tell us way back in AIT that this here's a different culture?" Not knowing the people, they did not know friends from enemies. They did not know if it was a popular war, or, if popular, in what sense. They did not know if the people of Quang Ngai viewed the war stoically, as it sometimes seemed, or with grief, as it seemed other times, or with bewilderment or greed or partisan fury. It was impossible to know. They did not know religions or philosophies or theories of justice. More than that, they did not know how emotions worked in Quang Ngai. Twenty years of war had rotted away the ordinary reactions to death and disfigurement. Astonishment, the first response, was never there in the faces of Quang Ngai. Disguised, maybe. But who knew? Who ever knew? Emotions and beliefs and attitudes, motives and aims, hopes—these were unknown to the men in Alpha Company, and Quang Ngai told nothing. "Fuckin' beasties," Stink would croak, mimicking the frenzied village speech. "No shit, I seen hamsters with more feelings."

But for Paul Berlin it was always a nagging question: Who were these skinny, blank-eyed people? What did they want? The kids especially—watching them, learning their names and faces, Paul Berlin couldn't help wondering. It was a ridiculous, impossible puzzle, but even so he wondered. Did the kids like him? A little girl with gold hoops in her ears and ugly scabs on her brow—did she feel, as he did, goodness and warmth and poignancy when he helped Doc dab iodine on her sores? Beyond that, though, did the girl like him? Lord knows, he had no villainy in his heart, no motive but kindness. He wanted health for her, and happiness. Did she know this? Did she sense his compassion? When she smiled, was it more than a token? And ... and what did she want? Any of them, what did they long for? Did they have secret hopes? His hopes? Could this little girl—her eyes squinting as Doc brushed the scabs with iodine, her lips sucked in, her nose puckering at the smell—could she somehow separate him from the war? Even for an instant? Could she see

Two young Vietnamese siblings flee the town of Bien Hoa, South Vietnam, after communist forces attacked the area in February 1969.

him as just a scared-silly boy from Iowa? Could she feel sympathy? In it together, trapped, you and me, all of us: Did she feel that? Could she understand his own fear, matching it with hers? ...He simply did not know. He wanted to be liked. He wanted them to understand, all of them, that he felt no hate. It was all a sad accident, he would have told them—chance, high-level politics, confusion. He had no stake in the war beyond simple survival; he was there, in Quang Ngai, for the same reasons they were: the luck of the draw, bad fortune, forces beyond reckoning. His intentions were benign. By God, yes! He was snared in a web as powerful and tangled as any that victimized the people of My Khe or Pinkville. Sure, they were trapped. Sure, they suffered, sure. But, by God, he was just as trapped, just as injured. He would have told them that. He was no tyrant, no pig, no Yankee killer. He was innocent. Yes, he was. He was innocent. He would have told them that, the villagers, if he'd known the language, if there had been time to talk. He would have told them he wanted to harm no one. Not even the enemy....

After the war, perhaps, he might return to Quang Ngai. Years and years afterward. Return to track down the girl with gold hoops through her ears. Bring along an interpreter. And then, with the war ended, history decided, he would explain to her why he had let himself go to war. Not because of strong convictions, but because he didn't know. He didn't know who was right, or what was right; he didn't know if it was a war of self-determination or self-destruction, outright aggression or national liberation; he didn't know which speeches to believe, which books, which politicians; he didn't know if nations would topple like dominoes or stand separate like trees; he didn't know who really started the war, or why, or when, or with what motives; he didn't know if it mattered; he saw sense in both sides of the debate, but he did not know where truth lay; he didn't know if Communist tyranny would prove worse in the long run than the tyrannies of Ky or Thieu or Khanh—he simply didn't know. And who did? Who really did? He couldn't make up his mind. Oh, he had read the newspapers and magazines. He wasn't stupid. He wasn't uninformed. He just didn't know if the war was right or wrong. And who did? Who really knew? So he went to the war for reasons beyond knowledge. Because he believed in law, and law told him to go. Because it was a democracy, after all, and because LBJ and the others had rightful claim to their offices. He went to the war because it was expected. Because not to go was to risk censure, and to bring embarrassment on his father and his town. Because, not knowing, he saw no reason to distrust those with more experience. Because he loved his country and more, more than that, because he trusted it. Yes, he did. Oh, he would rather have fought with his father in France, knowing certain things certainly, but he couldn't choose his war, nobody could. Was this so banal? Was this so unprofound and stupid? He would look the little girl with gold earrings straight in the eye. He would tell her these things. He would ask her to see the matter his way. What would she have done? What would anyone have done, not knowing? And then he would ask the girl questions. What did she want? How did she see the war? What were her aims— peace, any peace, peace with dignity? Did she refuse to run for the same reasons he refused—obligation, family, the land, friends, home? And now? Now, war ended, what did she want? Peace and quiet? Peace and pride? Peace with mashed potatoes and Swiss steak and vegetables, a full-tabled peace, indoor plumbing, a peace with Oldsmobiles and Hondas and skyscrapers climbing from the fields, a peace of order and harmony and murals on public buildings? Were her dreams the dreams of ordinary men and women? Quality-of-life dreams? Material dreams? Did she want a long life? Did she want medicine when she was sick, food on the table and reserves in the pantry? Religious dreams? What?

The Vietnam Veterans Memorial

In 1982, just nine years after the last American combat troops left South Vietnam ending the United States' involvement in its longest-running war, the Vietnam Veterans Memorial was dedicated on the Mall in Washington, D.C. Just as the war itself provoked painful public controversy, so did the design of the monument meant to honor those who sacrificed their lives for their country. When 21-year-old Maya Lin's design was unanimously selected from over 1,400 submitted entries, many veterans responded negatively to its simple design. Lin's vision included two black granite walls situated in a large "V" shape, inscribed with the more than 58,000 names of the dead and missing. In order that the veterans memorial not become as divisive as the war itself had been, a bronze statue of three servicemen was added nearby. Ten years later, still more veterans were recognized with the construction of the Vietnam Women's Memorial, a statue honoring the American women who served.

Since its construction, the memorial has become the most visited National Park site in the nation's capital. Numerous veterans and veterans' families journey to "the wall" to find comfort or pay tribute. The National Park Service has collected hundreds of thousands of mementos, including letters, photographs, and medals left at the wall and the accompanying statues. The following words, inscribed where the two walls meet, greet visitors:

In honor of the men and women of the Armed Forces of the United States who served in the Vietnam War. The names of those who gave their lives and those who remain missing are inscribed on the wall in the order they were taken from us.

What did she aim for? If a wish were to be granted by the war's winning army—any wish—what would she choose? Yes! If LBJ and Ho were to rub their magic lanterns at war's end, saying, "Here is what it was good for, here is the fruit," what would Quang Ngai demand? Justice? What sort? Reparations? What kind? Answers? What were the questions: What did Quang Ngai want to know?

DENISE LEVERTOV (1923–1997)

The poet Denise Levertov was born and raised in England where she published her first book of poetry at the age of 23. In 1947, she married American writer Mitchell Goodman, and emigrated to the United States; in 1955, she became a U.S. citizen. During the early 1960s, Levertov was the poetry editor for the liberal journal The Nation. *She and her husband became well-known antiwar activists. Her opposition to the Vietnam War was the focus of much of her poetry in the late 1960s and early 1970s.*

By 1967, antiwar protest in the United States had become common, and the nation found itself increasingly divided over its role in the Vietnam conflict. As President Lyndon Johnson continued to increase troop strength and draft deferments became harder to obtain, protest marches in New York City and Washington, D.C., attracted hundreds of thousands of Americans to rally against the war. Young men chanting "Hell no, we won't go!" burned their draft cards in protest. More than 10,000 fled to Canada to escape the draft, some from a moral objection to war, others simply from fear. With the continued stalemate and the rising number of American casualties, protests became more angry and violent. Families and friendships were torn apart over conflicting loyalties and beliefs. On January 30, 1968, the North Vietnamese Army and Vietcong forces launched a devastating surprise attack—known as the Tet offensive—which significantly swayed public opinion against President Johnson and his policymakers. Many Americans now believed that political and military leaders were being untruthful about progress in Vietnam. Later that year, President Johnson, who had already announced that he would not seek reelection, began to look for a way to negotiate his country's path out of Vietnam. But it would be another five years before President Richard Nixon could manage to get all U.S. troops out of Southeast Asia.

"The same war continues."

A man protesting the Vietnam War places flowers in the barrels of U.S. military officers' rifles. In October 1967, antiwar protesters had marched on the Pentagon, where they were met by armed troops.

In the following poem, Levertov challenges the very idea of war, using the Vietnam conflict as her central example. Through a series of carefully crafted images and statements, Levertov wonders aloud at how humankind, capable of such beauty and creativity, "whose eyes are flowers that perceive the stars," can so easily become numb to the horrors and "disasters" of war. In the poem's final stanza, Levertov concludes that "living at peace" can be the only intelligent decision.

Life at War

The disasters numb within us
caught in the chest, rolling
in the brain like pebbles. The feeling
resembles lumps of raw dough

weighing down a child's stomach on baking day.
Or Rilke said it, 'My heart . . .
Could I say of it, it overflows
with bitterness . . . but no, as though

its contents were simply balled into
formless lumps, thus
do I carry it about.'
The same war

continues.
We have breathed the grits of it in, all our lives,
our lungs are pocked with it,
the mucous membrane of our dreams
coated with it, the imagination
filmed over with the gray filth of it:

the knowledge that humankind,

delicate Man, whose flesh
responds to a caress, whose eyes
are flowers that perceive the stars,

whose music excels the music of birds,
whose laughter matches the laughter of dogs,
whose understanding manifests designs
fairer than the spider's most intricate web,

still turns without surprise, with mere regret
to the scheduled breaking open of breasts whose milk
runs out over the entrails of still-alive babies,
transformation of witnessing eyes to pulp-fragments,
implosion of skinned penises into carcass-gulleys.

We are the humans, men who can make;
whose language imagines *mercy,*
lovingkindness; we have believed one another
mirrored forms of a God we felt as good—

who do these acts, who convince ourselves
it is necessary; these acts are done
to our own flesh; burned human flesh
is smelling in Viet Nam as I write.

Yes, this is the knowledge that jostles for space
in our bodies along with all we
go on knowing of joy, of love;

our nerve filaments twitch with its presence
day and night,
nothing we say has not the husky phlegm of it in the saying,
nothing we do has the quickness, the sureness,
the deep intelligence living at peace would have.

PHILIP ROTH (1933–)

*Philip Roth was born in Newark, New Jersey, in
1933 and was educated at Bucknell University
and the University of Chicago. He has published more than twenty books, many of
which deal with the life of the modern Jewish
community in America. Roth is noted for his
witty, insightful, often biting commentary on*

*"he lived in
America the
way he lived
inside his
own skin"*

the status of Jews in the post-Holocaust world. His 1997 novel American Pastoral, *which chronicles the devastating effects of the Vietnam War on a successful American businessman and his family, won the Pulitzer Prize.*

Violence from the Vietnam War spilled into the daily lives of Americans in many ways. Television brought home graphic, bloody images of life at war. Countless families and communities mourned the losses of their sons, brothers, fathers, and husbands, killed or missing in action. In total, more than 58,000 Americans died there between 1954 and 1973; another 153,000 were wounded.

In addition, antiwar sentiment sometimes provoked deadly violence at home. In 1970, after President Richard Nixon announced that U.S. troops had invaded Cambodia to eliminate NVA and VC supply centers, American colleges erupted in huge student demonstrations. In May, tragedy struck at Ohio's Kent State University where four people were killed and nine injured when National Guardsmen opened fire on a crowd of student protesters. Less than two weeks later, two more students were killed in a similar incident at Jackson State University in Mississippi.

Still, not all Americans believed the United States was wrong to be at war in South Vietnam. Many were disgusted with what they perceived to be a lack of loyalty and patriotism on the part of protesting American youth, and they staged their own rallies in support of their country's troops and foreign policy efforts. Most Americans abhorred the violent tactics used by some radical antiwar protesters.

Philip Roth's novel American Pastoral *examines the life of Seymour "Swede" Levov who comes of age in the heady, prosperous years after World War II. The Swede—a gifted high school athlete, and hard-working, loyal, and successful businessman—is caught unaware and almost destroyed by the impact of the Vietnam War when it is suddenly brought home to his doorstep. His only child and beloved teenage daughter, Merry, is the prime suspect in an antiwar protest bombing at their small town post office. Levov is distraught over the involvement of his own child in such an ugly and cowardly act of violence, which unintentionally kills a young doctor, and he cannot understand how two generations could feel so differently about the same country. As Levov describes in the following excerpt, his America was a land of freedom, wealth, and opportunity, symbolized by the emotional victory celebrations he recalls after the Allied triumphs in Europe and the Pacific in 1945. But for Merry, and for many other young people of the 1960s and 1970s who were disillusioned by their country's involvement in the Vietnam War, America was an unjust oppressor, corrupt and vicious.*

American Pastoral
Part II, Chapter 5

…Who was she [Merry] to sneer at all this, to reject all this, to hate all this and set out to destroy it? The war [World War II], winning the war—did she hate that too? The neighbors, out in the street, crying and hugging on V-J Day, blowing car horns and marching up and down front lawns loudly banging kitchen pots. He was still at Parris Island then, but his mother had described it to him in a three-page letter. The celebration party at the playground back of the school that night, everyone they knew, family friends, school friends,

Four persons were killed and eleven others wounded when National Guardsmen fired into a crowd of Kent State University students in May 1970. Here, bystanders administer first aid to a wounded student.

the neighborhood butcher, the grocer, the pharmacist, the tailor, even the bookie from the candy store, all in ecstasy, long lines of staid middle-aged people madly mimicking Carmen Miranda and dancing the conga, one-two-three *kick*, one-two-three *kick*, until after two a.m. The war. Winning that war. Victory, victory, victory had come! No more death and war!

…Hate America? Why, he lived in America the way he lived inside his own skin. All the pleasures of his younger years were American pleasures, all that success and happiness had been American, and he need no longer keep his mouth shut about it just to refuse her ignorant hatred. The loneliness he would feel as a man without all his American feelings. The longing he would feel if he had to live in another country. Yes, everything that gave meaning to his accomplishments had been American. Everything he loved was here.

For her, being an American was loathing America, but loving America was something he could not let go of any more than he could have let go of loving his father and his mother, any more than he could have let go of his decency. How could she "hate" this country when she had no *conception* of this country? How could a child of his be so blind as to revile the "rotten system" that had given her own family every opportunity to succeed? To revile her "capitalist" parents as though their wealth were the product of anything other than the unstinting industry of three generations. The men of three generations, including even himself, slogging through the slime and stink of a tannery. The family that started out in a tannery, at one with, side by side with, the lowest of the low—now to her "capitalist dogs." There wasn't much difference, *and she knew it,* between hating America and hating them. He loved the America she hated and blamed for everything that was imperfect in life and wanted violently to overturn, he loved the "bourgeois values" she hated and ridiculed and wanted to subvert, he loved the mother she hated and had all but murdered by doing what she did.

"I was a child of dust."

ROBERT OLEN BUTLER (1945–)

Robert Olen Butler, a short story writer and novelist, won the 1993 Pulitzer Prize for his collection of stories, A Good Scent from a Strange Mountain, *about the Vietnamese community in south Louisiana. (After the war, many Southeast Asian refugees fled to the United States, establishing themselves in various parts of the country.)*

On April 30, 1975, Saigon, the capital of South Vietnam, fell to communist forces from the North. Frightening photographs of helicopters evacuating the last American personnel and terrified Vietnamese refugees trying desperately to escape their war-ravaged country haunted news broadcasts in the United States. The almost decade-long conflict had cost America dearly: 58,000 killed; several thousand more considered prisoners of war (POWs) or missing in action (MIA); and countless others wounded. Veterans struggled with debilitating physical injuries and the psychological aftermath of war—depression, social alienation, and post-traumatic-stress syndrome.

The country these veterans returned home to was scarred in many ways, too. Frustration and grief over the war's bloodshed, which many believed to have been in vain, provoked bitter, often misdirected, anger toward those who had served. Many veterans reported being spit upon or heckled by ungrateful Americans. Unlike the celebrations that had filled the U.S. streets after victory in World War II, this "lost" war was one Americans wanted to forget. Attitudes about the United States and its role in the world had shifted too; for the first time since World War II, Americans sensed that there were limits to what their country should attempt in its foreign policy—and limits to what it could accomplish.

Another painful legacy of the Vietnam War forms the basis for Robert Olen Butler's story, Letters from My Father. *A number of American men serving in Vietnam had befriended and, in some instances, fallen in love with Vietnamese women. Some of these relationships produced children. In the years following the fighting, many former soldiers tried to reconnect with their Vietnamese lovers and the children those women had born.*

The narrator in the following story is a young, Vietnamese-American woman who, after seventeen years of separation, has finally been rejoined with her American GI father in the United States. She describes the great difficulty in establishing a relationship with a parent whom she has never met, and the mixture of pride and disappointment that being a "child of dust" brought with it.

Letters from My Father

I look through the letters my father sent to me in Saigon and I find this: "Dear Fran. How are you? I wish you and your mother were here with me. The weather here is pretty cold this time of year. I bet you would like the cold weather." At the time, I wondered how he would know such a thing. Cold weather sounded very bad. It was freezing, he said, so I touched the tip of my finger to a piece of ice and I held it there for as long as I could. It hurt very bad and that was after only about a minute. I thought, How could you spend hours and days in weather like that?

It makes no difference that I had misunderstood the cold weather. By the time he finally got my mother and me out of Vietnam, he had moved to a place where it almost never got very cold. The point is that in his letters to me he often said this and that about the weather. It is cold today. It is hot today. Today there are clouds in the sky. Today there are no clouds. What did that have to do with me?

He said "Dear Fran" because my name is Fran. That's short for Francine and the sound of Fran is something like a Vietnamese name, but it isn't, really. So I told my friends in Saigon that my name was Trán, which was short for Hôn Trán, which means "a kiss on the forehead." My American father lived in America but my Vietnamese mother and me lived in Saigon, so I was still a Saigon girl. My mother called me Francine, too. She was happy for me to have this name. She said it was not just American, it was also French. But I wanted a name for Saigon and Trán was it.

A Vietnamese refugee, his belongings held in his mouth, boards a U.S. combat store ship in July 1979.

I was a child of dust. When the American fathers all went home, including my father, and the communists took over, that's what we were called, those of us who had faces like those drawings you see in some of the bookstalls on Nguyễn Huệ Street. You look once and you see a beautiful woman sitting at her mirror, but then you look again and you see the skull of a dead person, no skin on the face, just the wide eyes of the skull and the bared teeth. We were like that, the children of dust in Saigon. At one look we were Vietnamese and at another look we were American and after that you couldn't get your eyes to stay still when they turned to us, they kept seeing first one thing, then another.

Last night I found a package of letters in a footlocker that belongs to my father. It is in the storage shack at the back of our house here in America. I am living now in Lake Charles, Louisiana, and I found this package of letters outside—many packages, hundreds of letters—and I opened one, and these are all copies he kept of letters he sent trying to get us out of Vietnam. I look through these letters my father wrote and I find this: "What is this crap that you're trying to give me now? It has been nine years, seven months, and fifteen days since I last saw my daughter, my own flesh-and-blood daughter."

This is an angry voice, a voice with feeling. I have been in this place now for a year. I am seventeen and it took even longer than nine years, seven months, fifteen days to get me out of Vietnam. I wish I could say something about that, because I know anyone who listens to my story would expect me right now to say how I felt. My mother and me were left behind in Saigon. My father went on ahead to America and he thought he could get some paperwork done and prepare a place for us, then my mother and me would be leaving for America very soon. But things happened. A different footlocker was lost and some important papers with it, like their marriage license and my birth certificate. Then the country of South Vietnam fell to the communists, and even those who thought it might happen thought it happened pretty fast, really. Who knew? My father didn't.

I look at a letter he sent me in Saigon after it fell and the letter says: "You can imagine how I feel. The whole world is let down by what happened." But I could not imagine that, if you want to know the truth, how my father felt. And I knew nothing of the world except Saigon, and even that wasn't the way the world was, because when I was very little they gave it a different name, calling it Hồ Chí Minh City. Now, those words are a man's name, you know, but the same words have several other meanings, too, and I took the name like everyone took the face of a child of dust: I looked at it one way and it meant one thing and then I looked at it a different way and it meant something else. Hồ Chí Minh also can mean "very intelligent starch-paste" and that's what we thought of the new name, me and some friends of mine who also had American fathers. We would meet at the French cemetery on Phan Thanh Giản Street and talk about our city—Hồ, for short; starch-paste. We would talk about our lives in Starch-Paste City and we had this game where we'd hide in the cemetery, each in a separate place, and then we'd keep low and move slowly and see how many of our friends we would find. If you saw the other person first, you would get a point. And if nobody ever saw you, if it was like you were invisible, you'd win.

Watergate

On August 8, 1974, President Richard Nixon, the thirty-seventh president of the United States, resigned from office, leaving in his wake a scandal so searing that its nickname has become synonymous with corruption and fraudulent abuse of power. In 1968, after a narrow victory, President Nixon came to office pledging to lead America out of the unpopular Vietnam quagmire and to establish "peace with honor." However, Nixon's personal shortcomings brought about a humiliating defeat six years later, when he was forced to either resign his office or be impeached by Congress for obstruction of justice and abuse of power.

The events that precipitated Richard Nixon's downfall had begun innocuously enough two years before. In early 1972, as President Nixon campaigned for reelection, two reporters from the *Washington Post* began to pursue a story about a break-in at the Democratic National Party offices housed at the Watergate apartment complex in Washington, D.C. The burglars, who were caught and arrested, were affiliated with a Nixon organization called the Committee to Reelect the President. They had planned on bugging office phones and stealing Democratic Party election strategies. Immediately after the incident, the Nixon White House vehemently denied knowledge of the robbery, but secretly began a massive cover-up involving the president.

Over the next two years, the "Watergate scandal" evolved into a constitutional crisis unlike any seen since Andrew Johnson's impeachment 100 years before. It would ultimately leave Americans' trust in their government at an all-time low; a 1974 poll showed that close to half of all Americans had "hardly any" faith left in the executive branch of their government.

Hunter S. Thompson, a writer and practitioner of "Gonzo" style journalism—in which the author takes a very subjective view of his material—had repeatedly excoriated Richard Nixon in print since his presidential campaign. When Nixon finally resigned in 1974, Thompson's farewell to the fallen leader was cynical and bitter, a telling sign of the nation's mood. Here, he describes watching Nixon's last moments as the disgraced former president prepared to board his final helicopter from the White House lawn:

His [Nixon's] face was a greasy death mask. I stepped back out of his way and nodded hello but he didn't seem to recognize me. I lit a cigarette and watched him climb the steps to the door of the helicopter. . . .Then he spun around very suddenly and threw his arms straight up in the famous twin-victory signal; his eyes were still glazed, but he seemed to be looking over the heads of the crowd at the White House. . . .

I was still very close to the helicopter, watching the tires. As the beast began rising, the tires became suddenly fat; there was no more weight on them. . . .The helicopter went straight up and hovered for a moment, then swooped down toward the Washington Monument and then angled up into the fog. Richard Nixon was gone.

Credits

UNIT 1 • A "NEW WORLD," A NEW NATION

Illustrations
17: U.S. Capitol Historical Society **19:** Library of Congress **21:** Library of Congress **22:** National Portrait Gallery **24:** Library of Virginia **25:** Library of Congress **28:** National Gallery of Art **29:** Library of Congress **32 (top):** Loaned by the Department of Parks and Recreation, Historical Burying Ground Initiative, City of Boston Courtesy Museum of Fine Arts, Boston **32 (bottom):** Library of Congress **33:** Photograph Courtesy of the New York State Museum **35:** The Society for the Preservation of New England Antiquities **39:** Library of Congress **40:** Collection of The New-York Historical Society **41:** Library of Congress **43:** Library of Congress **44:** Courtesy the Quaker Collection Haverford College **46:** Library of Congress **47:** Library of Congress **49:** The Field Museum A938651 **51:** National Gallery of Canada, Ottawa **52:** Library of Congress **53:** Library of Congress **54:** Library of Congress **55:** Library of Congress **57 (top):** Library of Congress **57 (bottom):** Library of Congress **58:** Library of Congress **59:** Library of Congress **63:** Library of Congress **65:** Collection of The New-York Historical Society **66:** Bequest of Winslow Warren. Courtesy, Museum of Fine Arts, Boston **67:** Library of Congress **68:** Library of Congress **69 (top):** Independence National Historical Park **69 (bottom):** Independence National Historical Park **71 (top):** Library of Congress **71 (bottom):** Missouri Historical Society Archives, Clark Family Papers **72:** Library of Congress **74:** Library of Congress **75:** Woolaroc Museum, Bartlesville, Oklahoma **76:** John Dos Passos Papers, #5950 Special Collections Department, University of Virginia Library **77:** The Peale Museum, Baltimore

Readings
76: From SHACKLES OF POWER by John Dos Passos, copyright © 1966 by John Dos Passos. Used by permission of Doubleday, a division of Random House, Inc.

UNIT 2 • NATIONALISM AND SECTIONALISM

Illustrations
79: Metropolitan Museum of Art, Gift of Mrs. Frank B. Porter **81:** Library of Congress **82:** Library of Congress **83:** Library of Congress **85:** Library of Congress **86:** Library of Congress **87:** Smithsonian Institution, National

Museum of American History **88:** Corbis **91:** Library of Congress
92: Library of Congress **93:** Library of Congress **94:** Library of Congress
95: Center for American History, University of Texas at Austin **97:** Library
of Congress **99:** Library of Congress **101:** Library of Congress
105: Brooklyn Museum of Art, Gift of Miss Gwendolyn O.L. Conkling
106: Library of Congress **107:** Office of Special Collections, New York
Public Library **108:** Library of Congress **110 (top):** Corbis **110 (bottom):** Library of Congress **111:** Library of Congress **113:** Library of
Congress **114:** Library of Congress **117:** Library of Congress **118 (top):**
Library of Congress **118 (bottom):** Library of Congress **120:** Library
of Congress **121:** Library of Congress **122:** Library of Congress
124: American Red Cross **125:** Library of Congress **126:** Library of
Virginia **127:** Library of Congress **129:** "Soldiers of the 54th
Massachusetts Regiment at the Robert Gould Shaw Memorial May 30, 1897,"
Robert A Bell Post Memorial Handbook. Collection, Massachusetts Grand
Army of the Republic Memorial Room, Massachusetts State House, Courtesy
Commonwealth of Massachusetts. **130:** Library of Congress **131 (top):**
National Portrait Gallery, Smithsonian Institution **131 (bottom):** Library of
Congress **133:** Library of Congress **135:** Library of Congress

UNIT 3 • INDUSTRIALIZING AMERICA

Illustrations
137: Fine Arts Museum of San Francisco, Gift of Mr. and Mrs. John D.
Rockefeller 3rd **139:** Nebraska State Historical Society **141 (top):** Kansas
State Historical Society, Topeka, Kansas **141 (bottom):** Library of Congress
142: Library of Congress **144:** Corbis/Bettmann **146:** Courtesy of the
California History Room, California State Library, Sacramento, California
147: Library of Congress **149:** Library of Congress **152 (top):** Courtesy
of the Burton Historical Collection, Detroit Public Library **152 (bottom):**
Joseph E. Brown **155:** Smithsonian Institution **157:** Library of Congress
158: National Archives **162:** Collection of the American Academy of Arts
and Letters, New York, N.Y. **163:** National Museum of American Art,
Smithsonian Institution **164:** Walker Evans Archive, 1994, Metropolitan
Museum of Art **166:** Library of Congress **167:** American Jewish Archives,
Cincinnati, Ohio **168:** Library of Congress **170:** Library of Congress
171: Library of Congress **173:** Avery Architectural and Fine Arts Library,
Columbia University in the City of New York **175:** Library of Congress
176: Courtesy George Eastman House **177:** Library of Congress
179 (top): Library of Congress **179 (bottom):** Library of Congress/E.W.
Gustin **180:** University of Virginia Library **183:** Jane Adams Collection,
Swarthmore College Peace Collection **184:** Library of Congress
186: Special Collections Department, University of Virginia Library

Readings

music by Woody Guthrie TRO -©- copyright 1961 (Renewed) 1963 (Renewed) Ludlow Music, Inc., New York, N.Y. Used by Permission. **256:** Genevieve Taggard Papers (Box 27), Manuscripts and Archives Division, The New York Public Library, Astor, Lenox and Tilden Foundations. **259:** Excerpt from "Freedom" from *One Man's Meat*, text copyright © 1940 by E. B. White. Reprinted by permission of Tilbury House, Publishers, Gardiner, Maine. **262:** From BATTLE CRY by Leon M. Uris, copyright 1953 by Leon M. Uris. Copyright Renewed © 1981 by Leon M. Uris. Used by permission of G. P. Putnam's Sons, a division of Penguin Putnam Inc. **266:** Excerpts from FAREWELL TO MANZANAR by James D. Houston and Jeanne Wakatsuki Houston. Copyright © 1972 by James D. Houston. Reprinted by permission of Houghton Mifflin Co. All rights reserved. **269:** Reprinted by permission of GRM ASSOCIATES, INC., Agents for the Estate of Ida M. Cullen. From the magazine *Phylon*, 4th quarter 1942. Copyright © 1942 by Countee Cullen; copyright renewed 1970 by Ida M. Cullen. **272:** From FACE OF WAR Used by permission of Grove/Atlantic, Inc. © 1988 by Martha Gellhorn. **275:** Excerpt from NIGHT by Elie Wiesel, translated by Stella Rodway. Copyright © 1960 by MacGibbon & Kee. Copyright renewed © 1988 by The Collins Publishing Group. Reprinted by permission of Hill and Wang, a division of Farrar, Straus and Giroux, LLC. **279:** From HIROSHIMA by John Hersey. Copyright 1946 and renewed 1974 by John Hersey. Reprinted by permission of Alfred A. Knopf, a Division of Random House Inc.

UNIT 5 • THE CHALLENGES OF POWER

Illustrations

283: National Archives **285:** Bill Burkhart/Alfred A. Knopf **286:** Norman Rockwell Museum at Stockbridge **287:** Corbis/Bettmann-UPI **289:** Photo by Dan Weiner, Courtesy Sandra Weiner **290:** CORBIS/Bettmann **291:** National Museum of American Art/Art Resource, N.Y. **293:** Jack Schrier **295 (top):** Lynn Goldsmith/Corbis **295 (bottom):** Magnum Photos Inc., Elliott Erwitt **299:** Lynn Goldsmith/Corbis **300:** © 1957 by the New York Times Co., Reprinted by Permission **302:** Lever Brothers Company **305:** Library of Congress **306:** Corbis-Bettmann **307:** Flip Schulke/CORBIS **308:** Library of Congress **310:** Associated Press **311:** Courtesy Judy Brady **313:** Corbis-Bettmann **314:** Diane Solis **315:** Walter P. Reuther Library, Wayne State University **316:** National Portrait Gallery, Smithsonian Institution **317:** Richard Erdoes **319:** Corbis-Bettmann **320:** Library of Congress **323:** Associated Press **325:** National Archives **326:** AP/Wide World Photos **328:** Corbis/Bettmann/Kent Potter **330:** Close Up Foundation/Renée Bouchard **331:** Chris Felver/Courtesy of New Directions **332:** Bernie Boston **333:** AP/Wide World Photos

Also available from Close Up Publishing

Ordinary Americans:
U.S. History Through the Eyes of Everyday People

Ordinary Americans: The Civil Rights Movement (video)

Ordinary Americans: Vietnam (video)

Ordinary Americans: The Red Scare (video)

The Breakup of the Soviet Union:
U.S.-Russian Relations Ten Years Later

Current Issues: Critical Policy Choices
Facing the Nation and the World

The Bill of Rights: A User's Guide

Profiles of Freedom: A Living Bill of Rights (video)

Democracy and Rights: One Citizen's Challenge (video)

The First Amendment: America's Blueprint for Tolerance